D0217406

WOMEN IN RUSSIAN HISTORY

The New Russian History

Series Editor: Donald J. Raleigh,
University of North Carolina, Chapel Hill

This series makes examples of the finest work of the most eminent historians in Russia today available to English-language readers. Each volume has been specially prepared with an international audience in mind, and each is introduced by an outstanding Western scholar in the same field.

THE REFORMS OF PETER THE GREAT
Progress Through Coercion in Russia
Evgenii V. Anisimov
Translated with an introduction by John T. Alexander

IN STALIN'S SHADOW
The Career of "Sergo" Ordzhonikidze
Oleg V. Khlevniuk
Translated by David Nordlander
Edited with an introduction by Donald J. Raleigh,
with the assistance of Kathy S. Transchel

THE EMPERORS AND EMPRESSES OF RUSSIA
Rediscovering the Romanovs
Edited by Donald J. Raleigh
Compiled by Akhmed A. Iskenderov

WOMEN IN RUSSIAN HISTORY
From the Tenth to the Twentieth Century
Natalia Pushkareva
Translated and edited by Eve Levin

WOMEN IN RUSSIAN HISTORY

FROM THE TENTH TO THE TWENTIETH CENTURY

Natalia Pushkareva

Translated and edited by
Eve Levin

M.E. Sharpe
Armonk, New York
London, England

Copyright © 1997 by M. E. Sharpe, Inc.

All rights reserved. No part of this book may be reproduced in any form
without written permission from the publisher, M. E. Sharpe, Inc.,
80 Business Park Drive, Armonk, New York 10504.

Library of Congress Cataloging-in-Publication Data

Pushkareva, N. L. (Natal´ia L´vovna)
Women in Russian history : from the tenth to the twentieth century /
by Natalia Pushkareva : translated and edited by Eve Levin.
p.   cm.—(The New Russian history)
Includes bibliographical references and index.
ISBN 1-56324-797-6 (c : alk. paper).—ISBN 1-56324-798-4 (p : alk. paper)
1. Women—Russia (Federation)—History.
2. Women—Soviet Union—History.
3. Women—Russia—History.
I. Levin, Eve, 1954–   .
II. Title.
III. Series.
HQ1665.15.P87   1997
305.4´0947—dc20
96-30667
CIP

Printed in the United States of America

The paper used in this publication meets the minimum requirements of the
American National Standard for Information Sciences—
Permanence of Paper for Printed Library Materials,
ANSI Z 39.48-1984.

∞

BM (c)   10   9   8   7   6   5   4   3   2   1
BM (p)   10   9   8   7   6   5   4   3   2   1

For Tjoma, my son,
with the hope of the happiest of futures

Contents

List of Illustrations ix

Author's and Translator's Preface xiii

Introduction 3

Chapter 1. **Warriors, Regents, and Scholars:**
The Tenth to Fifteenth Centuries 7
  Princesses in Their Own Right 7
  Before and After the Wedding 28
  "If Anyone Has a Daughter" 44
  A Woman's Calling Card 53

Chapter 2. **The *Terem* and Beyond:**
Women in Muscovy 61
  From Ruler to Regent 61
  Who Shall Find a Virtuous Woman? 88
  A Woman's Honor 105
  "Painted Beauties" 113

Chapter 3. **Empresses and Diarists:**
Women in the Enlightenment 121
  Out of the *Terem*, Onto the Throne 121
  Marriage for Love, or Money 154
  The Lesser Share 171
  Fashion and Tradition 178

Chapter 4. **The New Women of the New Epoch:**
        Nineteenth and Early Twentieth Centuries   187
            The Many Roles of Women   187
                The Empress as Angel of Mercy   188
                Hostesses of Distinction   194
                Revolutionary Women   201
                Women in the Academy   209
                Writers and Poets   212
                The World of the Arts   215
            Lives of Toil and Leisure   220
            The "Woman Question"   233
            Crinolines and Sarafans   241

Epilogue. **Women in the Soviet Union and After:**
        1917 to the 1990s   255

Notes   267

Selected Bibliography   293

Index   305

List of Illustrations

Grand Princess Olga visits with the Byzantine Emperor in
Constantinople. Miniature from the Radziwill Chronicle,
fifteenth century.   11

Childbirth. Women attendants see to the welfare of the
woman in labor, bathe the newborn baby, and prepare the
celebratory feast. From a fresco in the Church of the Prophet
Elijah (Ilia) in Iaroslavl, 1680–1681.   40

The Dormition of the Virgin. The soul of the Mother of God
is depicted as a swaddled infant in Christ's arms. Icon by
Feofan Grek, early fifteenth century.   41

Formal headdress of a wealthy married woman of the
twelfth–thirteenth centuries, as reconstructed by P.P. Tolochko.   57

Sofia, daughter of Tsar Aleksei and half-sister of Peter the
Great, during her imprisonment in the Novodevichii
Convent. Painting by the nineteenth-century artist Ilia Repin.   87

Procession of the tsaritsa and women of the imperial court.
Sketch from the album of the Austrian diplomat, Baron
Meyerberg, seventeenth century.   96

Scene from the "Tale of Peter and Fevronia." Fevronia
blesses the curative ointment she is sending to her intended
husband, Prince Peter. Miniature from a manuscript book of
the seventeenth century.   101

Tsaritsa Natalia, mother of Peter the Great. By an unknown
artist of the early eighteenth century.   124

Empress Catherine I, second wife of Peter the Great, née Marta Skavronskaia. Reigned 1725–1727. Contemporary engraving. 129

Empress Elizabeth. Reigned 1741–1761. Contemporary engraving. 140

Catherine the Great. Reigned 1762–1796. Portrait by an unknown artist. 143

Catherine Dashkova, dressed in the decorations of the president of the Academy of Sciences. Portrait by D. Levitskii. 149

Praskovia Kovaleva-Zhemchugova, "the Pearl," serf opera singer, upon her marriage to Count Sheremetev. Portrait by the serf artist N. Argunov. 152

Matchmaking among Russian peasants of the eighteenth century. The matchmaker ceremoniously presents the bride to the groom. "Celebration of the marriage contract," painting by the serf artist G.A. Potemkin, 1777. 160

Gentry of the late eighteenth century at leisure: "The Stroll," painting by V.B. Sukhodolskii. 163

Woodcut, "Please give me the bucket!" Second half of the eighteenth century. The wife, dressed in European clothes, passes the yoke with the water pails to her traditionally clad husband, lest she ruin her fashionable outfit. 186

Empress Maria Fedorovna, the second wife of Emperor Paul I, and patroness of girls' educational institutions. Contemporary engraving. 189

Wealthy patrons gather at a banquet to celebrate the founding of the Orphans' Institute, St. Petersburg, late nineteenth century. 193

Empress Alexandra, wife of Nicholas II, dressed as a nurse during World War I. Portrait by P.I. Volkov. 194

Russian peasants of the early nineteenth century in everyday clothing and headdresses. From the painting, "The Threshing Floor," by A.G. Venetsianov, 1822–1823. 221

Religious education class at the Smolnyi Institute school for noble girls in St. Petersburg, late nineteenth century. 227

Peasant woman from Olonetsk province in holiday dress.
Drawing by I.A. Bilibin, from the series "Peoples of the
Russian North."   241

Woman's costume of the mid-nineteenth century, with an
Eliseev shawl. From the collection of the State Historical
Museum, Moscow.   243

M.F. Soboleva, a woman of the merchant class in traditional
dress. Portrait by N.D. Mylnikov, 1834.   246

Author's and Translator's Preface

This survey of the history of women in Russia, the first of its type since the past century, reflects the development of the field of Russian women's studies. In the last twenty years, many books and articles have appeared, and these have covered a huge range of topics in Russian women's history, vastly increasing our knowledge of this once-ignored subject. Until now, however, there has been no survey of Russian women's history to serve as an introduction to the topic and as a framework for these more specific works. We hope that this book will serve both these purposes.

The momentous changes that Russia has experienced in the past decade make a historical perspective on the status of women that much more timely. With the collapse of communism, Russians have begun to look, even more than before, to their own roots in order to understand their society and find direction for the future. But the myths about Russian women in the past are manifold and too often invoked for immediate political gain. A work such as this one that strives to be true to the sources and impartial in its examination of the topic, can provide a needed corrective. In this unstable and changing political climate, it is important that private citizens of all countries have knowledge of the Russian past.

The political, social, economic, and cultural changes in Russia that have made this book so necessary have also made it possible. Under the Communist government, a Soviet author could not write a book specifically for publication in the West, under the auspices of an American publisher. Yet this monograph was specifically commissioned by M.E. Sharpe, Inc., for distribution not only in the United States but worldwide. Furthermore, the type of close collaboration between the author and the translator that went into the production of this volume would have been almost impossible to arrange under the strictures of the pre-glasnost era. For in this case the "translation" consists not so much of rendering the author's words into English as conveying her ideas in a way that makes them readily accessible to an American audience. Frequently, that goal required a substantial rewording of sentences and reordering of paragraphs, as well as the addition of explanatory material and an English-language bibliography. These alterations in the manuscript were made in full consultation with the author during many hours of productive, and enjoyable, collaboration.

But this book is collaborative in another sense as well. It reflects more than fifteen years of scholarly association. We first met in the hostile years of Leonid Brezhnev and Ronald Reagan, when we were both graduate students: Natasha at Moscow University and Eve at Indiana University. Both of us had selected dissertation topics relating to women; Natasha's concerned women in medieval Russia from the tenth to the fifteenth centuries; Eve's focused on the women of Novgorod in the same period. At that time, the suspicions generated by the cold war inhibited contacts between Soviet citizens and foreigners, especially those from "capitalist" countries. But because we shared the same academic advisor, Academician Valentin Lavrentevich Ianin, we could become acquainted without concern about adverse political ramifications.

From our first meeting in Eve's dormitory room at Moscow University, we both realized that we had somehow reached the same conclusions concerning the status of women in medieval Russia. At Ianin's suggestion, we co-authored an article on the status of women in medieval Novgorod, which was published first in Russian in *Vestnik Moskovskogo universiteta* (1983) and later in English in *Soviet Studies in History* (1985). Such collaboration, which has since become so common, was practically unheard of then; our two scholarly communities expected us to embrace different, and incompatible, interpretations.

Despite the complications created by distance, we remained in close touch and advised each other about research and career choices. In due course, we both defended our dissertations and found employment: Natasha at the Institute of Ethnology and Anthropology of the Academy of Sciences, where she now holds the position of senior research fellow; and Eve at Ohio State University, where she is currently an associate professor. Both of us also eventually assumed editorial duties: Natasha on the journal *Rodina,* and Eve on the journal *Russian Review.* By mutual agreement, Natasha's first monograph, *Zhenshchiny drevnei Rusi* (Women of Medieval Russia) (1989) focused on women's legal, family, and social status; Eve's monograph, *Sex and Society in the World of the Orthodox Slavs, 900–1700* (1989), focused on a topic then forbidden in the Soviet Union. The changes in the intellectual climate in the late 1980s permitted us to publish a second collaborative article in 1990 on sex in medieval Russia. Over the years we have translated each other's work many times; even more important, we have contributed to each other's thinking in formative ways. Thus it would be difficult to delineate exactly what in this book came from which of us, although the basic text is Natasha's work.

Of course, both of us have benefited immensely from the knowledge and the intellectual support of our colleagues. We would first like to acknowledge in particular Donald J. Raleigh, the editor of the M.E. Sharpe series on the New Russian History, who had the perception to recognize how valuable a survey of Russian women's history would be to the profession. Of our intellectual forebears, first place must go to Valentin Lavrentevich Ianin, who recognized the validity of our topic and our collaborative work at a time when few senior scholars did. In addition, the late Vladimir Terentevich Pashuto provided special inspiration. Irina Mikhailovna Pushkareva and Lev Nikitich Pushkarev, both noted historians in their own right, gave us, their Russian and American daughters, immeasurable help of every sort. Saul and Ruth Levin similarly provided for us both. Of the many, many colleagues and friends who have guided us, we would like to recognize particularly Jean-Pierre Arrignon, Iurii Bessmertnyi, Michael Berndt, Robin Bisha, Nada Boshkovska, Angela Brintlinger, Carsten Goehrke, Mikhail Dmitriev, Semeon Ekshtut, Clemens Heller, Manfred Hildermeier, David Hoffmann, Christiane Klapisch-Zuber, Igor Kon, Alexandra Korros, Sandra Levy, Predrag Matejić, Carolyn Pouncy, Ninel Polishchuk, Ernst Schubert, Jutte Scherrer, Grigorii Tishkin, Valerii Tishkov, Isolde Thyret, Irina Vlasova, Wladimir Vodoff, and Allan Wildman. At M.E. Sharpe, Patricia Kolb, Ana Erlić, and Elizabeth Granda helped us with the many essentials of preparing the manuscript for publication.

No less important to us in the preparation of this book was the support received from institutions. Grant moneys from the International Research and Exchanges Board (IREX), the Fulbright-Hays program of the Department of Education, the Center for Slavic and East European Studies at Ohio State University, and the Center for Medieval and Renaissance Studies at Ohio State provided Eve with the financial means to travel to Russia. Natasha received research grants from the French government under the "Programme Diderot" to work at La Maison des Sciences de l'Homme in Paris, as well as Volkswagen and Humboldt grants to study in Germany at the Institut für Historische Landesforschung in Göttingen. The Institute of Ethnology and Anthropology in Moscow has been an institutional home for both of us, as have been the Resource Center for Medieval Slavic Studies/Hilandar Research Library and the Department of History at Ohio State University. Natasha gratefully acknowledges the assistance of the staff members at the Bibliothèque Nationale and the Bibliothèque d'Institute des Études Slaves in Paris, as well as the Staatsbibliothek in Göttingen. Eve made frequent and productive use of the facilities of the Summer Research Laboratory for Slavicists at the University of Illinois. We both benefited from the resources of several Russian archives: the Russian State Archive of Ancient Acts (RGADA) and the Manuscript Division of the Russian State Library (RGB) in Moscow; and the Manuscript Divisions of the Russian National Library (RO RNB) and the Russian Ethnographical Museum in St. Petersburg. We are grateful to Vladimir Dolmatov, editor-in-chief of *Rodina*, and to the editorial staffs of the publishing houses Izobrazitelnoe iskusstvo, Mysl, and Ladomir for permission to reproduce illustrations in this book.

Throughout the book, the Library of Congress system is used to transliterate Russian. For ease in reading, diacritical marks are omitted in the text. Russian personal names and common nouns that have become familiar in English with a spelling from a different transliteration system (e.g., Yeltsin) retain their familiar spelling. Dates in the text, except in the "Afterword," reflect the usage of the Old Calendar (Julian Calendar) that was used in Russia until 1917.

Moscow, January 1996

E.L.
N.P.

WOMEN IN
RUSSIAN HISTORY

Introduction

This book is about Russian women: how their intricate, multifaceted, dynamic history developed throughout a millennium. It concerns prominent Russian women, who are as renowned as male scholars and warriors for their role in public life; but also the hundreds of thousands of ordinary Russian women, wives and mothers, who made their own lives and their own history and who were the bearers and preservers of everyday customary life.

In thinking about the urgent issues concerning Russian women of today, many people seek answers in the events of the past. The topic of women has certainly occupied a place in the research of historians, jurists, ethnologists, sociologists, and economists. Nonetheless, even a quarter-century ago, women's studies as an independent scholarly discipline was unthinkable. Researchers were absorbed in building global models of society and conceptualizations of political history, and they were occupied with the study of class struggles and economic cataclysms. To them, it seemed that all events in world history were universal, part of a past that was common to everyone. They simply did not notice women.

But in the late 1960s and early 1970s, a revolution took place in the humanities—one that was not predicted, but was inescapable. It became clear that women had their own history and that the study of this history required special methods and understanding, and especially a broadening of historical vision. This impetus to examine the human past in a new way inspired dozens of researchers (and especially women researchers!) in the United States, England, France, Germany, Italy, and Scandinavia. Inquisitive readers soon had at their disposal a considerable number of interesting works that explored the history of women in Western Europe, America, Asia, and Africa

3

throughout diverse periods, from classical antiquity to the present.[1] A number of scholars of women's history joined in a collaborative effort, founding an International Federation and compiling a six-volume work, which has been translated into a number of languages.[2]

But Russian women found hardly any place in the pages of this prestigious multivolume publication. At the same time that specialists on Western European women were founding their own association, Russianists had barely begun their investigation of the history of Russian women. For a long time, the ideological hostility between the Soviet Union and the West kept scholars isolated. They were cut off from essential sources, archives, and libraries on the specious grounds that they were "bourgeois falsifiers." Thus the first attempts by Western European and American scholars to reconstruct a history of Russian women were far from impartial. When they compared the history of women in Russia with that of their sisters in Western Europe, they often could not manage to break with ideological stereotypes. Contrary to all logic, they strove to present only the negative side, contrasting the downtrodden, ignorant, and passive Russian woman with her contemporaries in England, France, Italy, and Germany.[3]

Meanwhile, the Russian colleagues of Western scholars tried to avoid the topic of women entirely. They were reluctant to take up subjects that the official ideology did not endorse. Women, who did not constitute a "class," were automatically deemed marginal to any scholarly problem. Those Soviet scholars who decided nonetheless to investigate the history of women were obliged to subscribe to Friedrich Engels's conception of the topic and make their conclusions conform accordingly. Engels had propounded a "universal historical subjugation of the female sex," coinciding with the appearance of private property, with the result that "all women were spiritually oppressed and disfigured."[4] The more difficult it became to provide for the daily needs of contemporary Russian women, the more important it became, apparently, to prove that in the past things were even worse.

But despite the obstacles, each year the number of scholars of Russian women's history, both Soviet and foreign, increased. Each newly discovered source; every new attempt at comparative analysis of the family, custom, and daily life; and every attempt to provide a human dimension to the panoramic political and economic interpretation of the Russian past brought Soviet and foreign scholars into contact. Gradually scholars of women's history freed themselves from the ideological bonds that impaired the development of an impartial picture of the history of Eastern Europe. In this new intellectual context, it was evident that women frequently played decisive roles in Russian history.[5]

This book is the result of many years of reflection about the status of women in Russia, and the first attempt to describe the full millennium of their history. In keeping with the traditional chronological categories, each of the four chapters of the book focuses on one era, describing the typical characteristics of women's place in that period. Each period reveals some continuation from the past, and also some departure from it.

The goal of this book is to present a comprehensive and multifaceted picture of the life of women in Kievan Rus, Muscovy, and Imperial Russia. But because Russia has always been an immense country, it is not possible, in the context of a survey, to provide equal treatment of all the regional variations. Thus the primary focus of the narrative is on the central core of Russia, with occasional attention to the variations found in the peripheries. Russia was also, from its inception, a multinational state, and each of these peoples had unique traditions concerning women's place in society. But coverage of these other peoples, so deserving of their own women's history, will have to await a different book. It is sufficient here to focus on Russian women and to counter the notorious assertion of the eternal subjugation of women in Russia that still afflicts much of the historiography.

This study rests upon a great variety of sources. Some of them have been published and are widely known, but they have not previously been examined from the point of view of women's history. Others, preserved in Russian archives, have been discovered only recently and are being discussed for the first time here. Among the most important historical sources are chronicles, travelers' accounts, hagiography, memoirs, and literary texts. Without them, it would be impossible to reconstruct the biographies of the prominent women who played roles in political and cultural life. Other sources must be used to reconstruct familial and quotidian life for women of different social strata: historical ethnography, archeological finds, descriptions of weddings, oral poetry, and normative and didactic literature produced by the church, in particular penitential manuals and prayer books. The legal status of women may be elucidated from the period of the formation of the first Russian state to the twentieth century through such law codes as *Russkaia Pravda* (of the eleventh century) and the complete codifications of the laws of the Russian Empire in the nineteenth and twentieth centuries. Numerous private legal documents dealing with property and lawsuits testify to women's empowerment in the judicial process. All these sources help to establish both the ideal and the reality, the norms and the actuality of life. Finally, iconography and portraiture yield information on how the shadowy women from the past looked and what image they conveyed through their choices of costume.

The history of women is a rewarding topic, one that provides new insights into the past. It combines the narrative history of politics and diplomacy with the history of economics and law, culture, religion, demography, and social psychology. It allows an infinitely more profound understanding of the literary, artistic, and cultural heritage that has come down to us from past generations.

Chapter 1

Warriors, Regents, and Scholars: The Tenth to Fifteenth Centuries

Princesses in Their Own Right

Ten centuries ago, an enormous Slavic state, called Rus, arose in Eastern Europe. It stretched from the Black Sea to the Arctic Ocean, and from the Danube to the Volga and the Ural Mountains. Scholars debate the ethnic origin of these Rus or Ros; some believe they were Scandinavian, while others are convinced that they were Slavic. These Rus dwelt among an ethnically mixed population of Slavs, Balts, Finns, steppe nomads, Greeks, and Jews. Yet when the first Russian state emerged in the tenth century, it was unambiguously Slavic and quite distinct from the other nascent Slavic states emerging in Poland, Bulgaria, and Moravia.

The history of this Russian state, recorded in chronicles and folklore, in Scandinavian sagas and Polovtsian songs, in the writings of Byzantine annalists and Arab travelers, contains the names of many prominent figures, including a number of women.[1] But unlike the history of early medieval Western Europe, which is rich in detailed accounts of the lives of great queens and sage women rulers, medieval Russian history does not abound in analogous figures. Russian literary and folkloric sources usually refer to women as insignificant, secondary figures.

But were women in reality so insignificant, or were they simply ignored by the men who controlled the writing of history in that period, who stressed events in accordance with their own understanding of the world? However truthful and judicious the chroniclers were

7

in their treatment of their women contemporaries, they invariably relegated women, if not to oblivion, at least to last place. Did they secretly wish to consign them to the role of silent, barely visible nonentities?

Only by compiling testimony from a variety of narrative sources, both secular and ecclesiastical, contemporary and retrospective, is it possible to reconstruct an accurate picture of women's participation in the historical dramas of the Kievan period. Some women have left only a few traces in the record, while of others, primarily rich and aristocratic women, a much fuller portrait can be drawn. The latter include women rulers of the principalities of Rus, as well as the foreign brides of Russian princes and Russian princesses who contracted marriages abroad. The noted Russian historian N.M. Karamzin (1766–1826) assembled his original "Gallery of Famous Russian Women" from among them, "depicting each face with the lively coloration of love for the female sex and for the Fatherland."[2]

The most impressive figure in the history of early medieval Russia is Grand Princess Olga, who ruled the Russian state from 945 to 964. Because of her sagacity in uniting the Russian lands and her introduction of Christianity to Rus, her descendants called her a "wise woman," and she is numbered among the saints of the Russian Orthodox Church.

It is difficult to establish the circumstances of Olga's birth and childhood, even through a meticulous reading of the sources. One of the legends composed many centuries later describes her as a peasant maiden, whose beauty and sharp mind prompted Igor, the ruling prince of Kiev, to propose marriage. The chronicle account of Olga's origins and her accession to the throne has little in common with this artless folktale. It is much more likely that Olga came from an aristocratic family of Pskov and that she married Igor sometime between 903 and 927.

As a woman of the upper aristocracy, Olga possessed the political experience to take the reins of power after the death of her husband in 945. Olga ruled the country for twenty years as regent for her underage son Sviatoslav, her single, closely guarded child. She earned fame throughout the known world for her efforts to build and enrich the Russian land.

Olga undertook the first reform of financial administration in Russian history. She was motivated to do so because of a personal tragedy: in 945 her husband, Igor, was killed during an attempt to collect tribute a second time from the Drevlians, a tribe subject to

Kiev. Having wreaked vengeance on those guilty of Igor's murder, Olga was able to overcome her personal grief. Unlike previous Russian rulers, who collected revenues from subject peoples through seizure and pillage, Olga ordered the establishment of a fixed tribute. She arranged for an orderly collection of taxes at specified intervals. The author of the Grand Princess's vita, which was composed many years after her death, was astonished and delighted by the talent of the "builder of the Russian land" and her striving to grasp thoroughly every aspect of governmental affairs. In his words, "she herself traveled throughout the Russian land, establishing the amount of tribute; like the mistress of a great household, she answered for everyone and everything."[3]

By strengthening the financial bases for her princely power early in her reign—that is, in the 940s—Olga was able to fortify the administrative apparatus and broaden the areas under princely rule, defining their boundaries. And in founding her powerful state, Olga relied not upon force but rather upon her intelligence.

However, this new system of governance required a new ideology. Princess Olga understood that the transformation of her country could be achieved only through the conversion of Rus to Christianity. Having weighed her powers and evaluated the possibilities, the princess decided to accept baptism from Russia's neighbor, the Byzantine Empire. Her baptism in the Byzantine capital of Constantinople strengthened the princess's personal power and enhanced Russia's international prestige.

Olga's journey to Constantinople (which the early Russians called "Tsargrad," the "Emperor-City") in the 950s has been embellished by legend, like so many other events of her life. The Byzantine emperor Constantine Porphyrogenitus personally received the "hegemona and archonissa of the Rus," as Byzantine chronicles titled Olga.

The compiler of the Russian Primary Chronicle, parts of which date from the eleventh century, propagated a legend about the circumstances of Olga's baptism. Supposedly, the emperor hoped to wed the Russian princess, although she was "much past thirty" and he was already married. But Olga was proud and independent, and singleminded in her pursuit of her goals. She asked the emperor to stand as her godfather at her baptism, and then responded to his marriage proposal, "How can you desire to marry me, when you have just baptized me and called me your daughter?"—for Orthodox canons forbid marriages among spiritual relatives.

Thus the legend presents Olga's baptism as a clever device to escape from the emperor's proposition. In actuality, everything was much more straightforward. Olga undertook the journey to Constantinople for reasons of state. After receiving baptism, she hoped to arrange a marriage for her son to one of the princesses of the Byzantine imperial family, but did not succeed.

Even so, the journey to Byzantium was fruitful. After the administrative reform, this was Olga's second success as ruler of the Russian state. The princess discussed diplomatic and commercial issues in the Byzantine Empire and received generous gifts. She was elevated to the honorary rank of "daughter" to the Byzantine emperor, to whom she promised military aid in case of need. The sixteenth-century Radziwill Chronicle contains a miniature of the signing of the treaties, depicting Olga and Constantine Porphyrogenitus sitting together on the same level, emphasizing their equality.

Having blazed a trail for Russia's entry into the ranks of Christian states, Olga sent an embassy to Holy Roman Emperor Otto I in 959. She also gave her consent for German missionaries to preach among the Rus. Although these missionaries did not enjoy much success, Olga's initiative opened Russia's first "window on the West."

During the last years of her life, Olga once again assumed the functions of head of state while her son Sviatoslav went off to war. In 968 it fell to her to organize the defense of Kiev from a sudden attack by steppe nomads. The chronicle notes that Sviatoslav showed his mother exceptional respect and returned from his campaign in order to be with her in her final hours.[4]

Olga's fame and accomplishments survived her. No later chroniclers and historians doubted the significance of her reforms. At a time when war was the primary means of resolving international disputes, the first Russian princess demonstrated that prestige could and should be earned peacefully, through diplomatic means. However, while granting Olga her due, these same historians regarded her as atypical of Russia, where otherwise heroes were exclusively male.

But in fact Olga was not unique, as careful scrutiny of the sources attests. The chronicle account of the legendary founding of the Russian state in the eighth century names not only Kii, Shchek, and Khoriv as the first Russian princes, but also their sister, Lybed. A reference to her is preserved in the name of a small river near Kiev, and she also appears as a character in Russian and Armenian epic poetry. However, early Russian chroniclers suppressed accounts of Lybed's activities, considering them paltry in comparison with Olga's achievements.

Grand Princess Olga visits with the Byzantine Emperor in Constantinople. Miniature from the Radziwill Chronicle, fifteenth century.

Two decades after Olga's death—that is, in the late tenth century, another prominent woman appeared on the Russian throne. This was Princess Anna, the wife of Grand Prince Vladimir (980–1015), who baptized Russia. Anna was the granddaughter of the Byzantine emperor Constantine VII, and Vladimir was Olga's grandson; thus the marital alliance of the Byzantine and Kievan monarchies, for which Olga had striven in the 950s, was accomplished a quarter-century later. Not even Vladimir's great reputation—he is called the "Red Sun" in folk epics— could eclipse Anna's participation in governmental affairs.

As a Byzantine *porphyrogenita*—a princess "born to the purple," the daughter of a reigning emperor—Anna received an excellent education. Scholars of classical learning—historians, hagiographers, linguists, and jurists—filled the court of her father and grandfather. As the wife of the grand prince of Russia, she was competent to receive foreign embassies, for example, ambassadors from Germany who came to Kiev in 989–90. Acting at the behest of Byzantine clergy, Anna contributed to the promulgation of the "Charter of Prince Vladimir," which granted immunities to the Russian Orthodox Church.

It was common in the eleventh to fourteenth centuries for princesses to be involved in legislation and governance alongside their husbands. For example, the "Charter of Prince Vsevolod of Novgorod Concerning Church Courts" lists "Vsevolod's princess" among other influential city administrators in the preamble.[5] The number of women lawmakers, akin to Anna and Vsevolod's wife, grew substantially in the thirteenth and fourteenth centuries, when the Russian state dissolved into numerous autonomous principalities.

But earlier, in the first half of the eleventh century, the Russian state was united and at the height of its power under the rule of Olga's great-grandson, Iaroslav, called "the Wise." During his reign, Kiev became a major cultural center. The rulers of many Western European countries sought to ally themselves with Russia through marriage with one or another of Iaroslav's daughters: Anastasia, Anna, Elizabeth, and a fourth, whose name is not preserved in the sources. Iaroslav and his wife Ingegerd (baptismal name: Irina), the daughter of King Olav of Norway, raised their daughters in an atmosphere of learning, surrounded by books. They were educated at home, but very rigorously, learning writing, mathematics, astronomy, and Latin, then the lingua franca of Europe.

Three daughters of Iaroslav and Ingegerd married into the ruling houses of powerful European states, where they could put their knowledge to good use. Anastasia, the eldest daughter, became the bride of King Andrew I of Hungary, where she became a fervent advocate of Hungarian unity. In widowhood, she ruled Hungary as regent, founding a number of Orthodox monasteries. Her sister Elizabeth (Elisava) married the Norwegian prince Harald Hardrada. Scandinavian sagas report Harald's countless expeditions in Sicily, Africa, Asia Minor, and Salonika. Having gained much fame and fortune, Harald convinced Elizabeth to marry him, or as the Scandinavian chronicle *Hauksbók* put it, "the Russian maiden with the golden necklace stopped holding him in disdain." Neither Russian

nor Western chronicles report anything about the princess's life in
Norway. It is known only that she did not return to Russia after
Harald's death in 1066 but instead agreed to marry the ruler of Den-
mark.

The third daughter of Iaroslav the Wise left the greatest mark on
European history. Anna became the wife of King Henry I of France,
who, according to the chronicler, "was enchanted by tales of her
accomplishments." In May 1051 the bridal cortège arrived in Paris.
Anna was unimpressed with Paris, then a tiny city with muddy streets;
it could not compare with Kiev, which styled itself the rival of Constantinople. "What sort of barbaric country have you sent me to!"
Anna complained in a letter to her father. "The dwellings here are
dark, the churches misshapen, and the customs appalling!" Anna's
dark mood worsened when, despite the birth of her son Philip, her
husband became more and more distant; he preferred the company
of comely troubadours.

The more Henry withdrew from governmental affairs, the more
Anna threw herself into them, aided by her intelligence, energy, and
undisputed administrative ability. The most important state documents of the 1050s often bear her signature, "Anna Regina," written
in neat Cyrillic letters. Underneath are crosses inscribed by illiterate
French courtiers. Anna could express herself easily in Latin—a skill,
according to contemporaries, that disquieted some French aristocrats. It was in Latin that Pope Nicholas II wrote to Anna, praising her
for "fulfilling royal duties with enviable fervor and remarkable intelligence."

After the death of Henry I in 1060, Anna settled at Senlis, a small
castle north of Paris. From that point her life took on the character of
a courtly romance. While walking in the forest, a pastime, a French
chronicler observed, "for which she had great liking," she met Count
Raoul de Crépy de Valois, a descendant of Charlemagne. The count
fell head over heels in love with Anna, and in 1062 he abducted her
from the fortress of Senlis. The local priest of the church on the
count's estate wed them, but under duress, because Raoul was still
married to someone else at the time. Raoul's wife Alionor sent a
complaint to Pope Alexander II, and incensed at Raoul's bigamy, he
invalidated the marriage to Anna. But the lovers defied the pope's
command and continued to live together happily.

Anna's son Philip, who in the meantime had inherited the throne,
did not find anything scandalous in his mother's actions. His relationship with her remained friendly, and he harbored no resentment

against his "stepfather." Anna and Raoul accompanied Philip on his travels around the country, and Anna provided him with intelligent and farseeing advice on governmental matters. French documents of the second half of the eleventh century, such as charters to monasteries, land deals, and juridical acts, testify to Anna's continuing administrative role.

Raoul de Crépy died in 1074, and Anna immersed herself in governmental affairs. She returned to court and even, according to Western chroniclers, traveled to Kiev. But Russian sources make no mention of such a visit; doubtless she stayed only for a short time and then returned to France, where she had spent most of her tumultuous life.[6]

Anna's successful career in France is not exceptional against the background of the many politically active women of the Russian royal house in the eleventh to thirteenth centuries. Shortly before the marriage of Anna to the king of France, her aunt, Maria-Dobronega, became the wife of King Casimir of Poland. She ruled with her sons in the 1030s and 1040s. Two of Anna's nieces became rulers and successful diplomats: Evpraksia and another Anna—often called by her family nickname, Ianka—the daughters of Iaroslav's son Vsevolod.

Evpraksia married the Holy Roman emperor Henry IV in the 1090s, taking the German name Adelheid. Later German historians did not mince words in their insinuations about Evpraksia; they denounced her as "immoral" and "dissolute" ("*proprio marita prostituta est*"), because she refused to play the part of political puppet. At the crucial moment in the ongoing political battle between Henry IV and Pope Urban II over the appointment of German bishops, Evpraksia decided to side with her husband's opponents. In doing so, she served the interests of her native Russia, which had broken off relations with Henry at the behest of the Byzantine Empire. At the same time, Evpraksia filed a complaint against her husband with the church synod of Piancenza. Her revelations about their family life, in particular her husband's immoral conduct and secret orgies, were very damaging to him politically. She achieved her ends: Henry was condemned by an imperial court and was removed from the throne to die in ignominy. But Evpraksia committed political suicide through her revelations, because of her insubordination to her husband. Rumors of Evpraksia's performance at the synod reached Russia, where she not only received no support for her audacity but was also condemned by Orthodox clergy. Forced to flee Germany,

Evpraksia hurried to her aunt Anastasia in Hungary and from there to Kiev. There she tried to remain inconspicuous; she took vows as a nun and lived out her days in a convent under the religious name of Anna.

In 1089, when Evpraksia was being crowned empress in Germany, Anna-Ianka was leading an embassy to Byzantium, much like her ancestress Olga. The purpose of the trip was to arrange the selection of a new metropolitan of Russia. After her return from Constantinople, a center of culture and education, Ianka was inspired to found a monastery for women (named Ianchinii—"Ianka's" in her honor) and the first school for girls in medieval Russia. At the school, she decided the requirements, the preceptresses, and the teachers. Students studied "writing, needlework, and other useful crafts," including rhetoric and singing.[7]

The traditions of female education in Byzantium, which Russia adopted through its close contacts, bore fruit in the spread of literacy among Russian women. In the twelfth and thirteenth centuries, monastic schools for girls became common. Their founders were, as a rule, women from the Kievan aristocracy or abbesses. Hagiographical sources indicate that women of the clerical order, in particular, enjoyed a comparatively high level of literacy. Many princesses, having taken monastic vows, recopied ecclesiastical manuscripts and compiled texts for the *Prolog*, a collection of didactic readings for each day of the year. The daughter of Prince Sviatoslav of Polotsk, Predslava (d. 1173 and canonized as St. Evfrosinia of Polotsk), not only "wrote books with her own hands," she also taught her sisters Gorodislava and Zvenislava to do so at her monastery.

At home, the daughters of princes were educated the same way as their brothers, in grammar, mathematics, philosophy, the healing arts, astronomy, rhetoric, and foreign languages (particularly Greek and Latin). Instruction began at an early age and continued through the study of the classics in Greek. According to the vita of St. Evfrosinia of Suzdal, she studied the philosophical works of Aristotle and Plato, the medical manuals of Galen and Aesculapius, and the poetry of Vergil and Homer. Many wealthy women, and not only the very educated, possessed their own home libraries, consisting of several volumes. Before the introduction of printing into Russia in 1564, books were rare and represented a substantial investment.

The chronicles record the names of the most educated princesses, who impressed their contemporaries with their knowledge. These included Princess Olga Romanovna of Volynia, who "devoured book learning to the limit"; the wife of Prince Roman Rostislavich of Smolensk (whose given name is not provided); Evfrosinia (Predslava) of Polotsk; and Evfrosinia of Suzdal, among others.[8]

One of these erudite princesses, Dobrodeia-Evpraksia (baptismal name: Zoia), was born in Kiev at the beginning of the twelfth century. She was the daughter of Grand Prince Mstislav Vladimirovich and Christine of Sweden and the granddaughter of the powerful Grand Prince Vladimir Monomakh. "She was not born in Athens, but she learned all the wisdom of the Greeks," contemporaries said of Dobrodeia.

In 1122, Dobrodeia married the nephew of the Byzantine Emperor Alexius Comnenus. Immediately after the wedding feast, the young bride set out for Constantinople, where a whole circle of intellectual women awaited her: Princess Anna Comnena, the famous historian, and the noblewoman Irina, the patroness of scholars and astrologers. Anna Comnena and Irina encouraged Dobrodeia to develop her talents. Her particular area of interest became medicine, especially herbal treatments. The Byzantine writer Balsamon noted that the Russian princess "displayed a fascination with healing methods" from her first arrival in Constantinople, and that she formulated medicinal salves and described their efficacy. She knew the works of the ancient physician Galen well, and she subsequently translated some of his works into Russian. Dobrodeia summarized her knowledge and practical experience in a long treatise entitled "Ointments" (*Alimma*). This work of medicine, the first of its sort by a woman author, survives in fragments in the Medici Library in Florence.[9]

Dobrodeia's sisters—Malfrid, the wife of the king of Norway, Ingeborg, the wife of the king of Denmark, and Evfrosinia, the wife of the king of Hungary—also gained renown for their intellects. The first two are mentioned in the "History of the Kings of Denmark" (the *Knutlingasaga* of the thirteenth century) as active rulers who spoke fluent Latin and a variety of other European languages and who advised their husbands on political and cultural affairs. Evfrosinia, the ambitious wife of King Geza II of Hungary, devoted all her energies and talents to strengthening the ties between Hungary and her native Russia. In complicated internal and external conflicts, Evfrosinia often showed herself to be more sagacious and farsighted than her husband, who valued and respected her opinion. After the death of Geza, Evfrosinia became regent, resolving all matters of state independently. Defending her rights to the Hungarian throne, Evfrosinia emerged as an advocate of political unity in her adopted country.

But the adherents of Evfrosinia and her son, the young King Istvan III, proved weaker than their opponents, the pro-Byzantine faction, backed by the armies of Emperor Manuel. Recognizing that they could not defend their throne, Evfrosinia and her son fled to Austria. In the meantime, a revolt took place in Hungary, bringing Evfrosinia's second son, Bela III, to the throne. Bela recognized that his mother's ambitions could be extinguished only through confinement in a convent; he ordered her arrest. Evfrosinia was kept under close guard for a short time in the fortress of Branichev and was then shipped off to Byzantium, where she was forcibly shorn as a nun.[10]

While Evfrosinia was devoting all her efforts toward the preservation of Hungarian unity, her native Russia was being torn apart by internecine war. By the mid-twelfth century, the once-united medieval Russian state had dissolved into a multitude of petty principalities. Princesses and noblewomen participated in the political life of each of these states, and even to all intents and purposes ruled them.

The conditions in western Rus in the early twelfth century were particularly fortuitous for the development of women's rule. In 1129, all the men of the princely house of Polotsk were taken captive by the rival prince of Kiev, Mstislav, the father of Dobrodeia, Malfrid, Ingeborg, and Evfrosinia. Mstislav not only deprived the princes of Polotsk of their throne but also exiled them to Byzantium. The princesses of Polotsk filled the power vacuum left by their absent menfolk, and for almost twenty years the city was ruled by a "matriarchy." Archeological digs in Polotsk and the nearby vassal town of Kukeinos have yielded three seals belonging to women: Princess Sofia, the wife of Prince Sviatoslav-Georgii; her daughter Predslava; and a third, unidentified woman.[11] Predslava had taken monastic vows (under the name Evfrosinia, as discussed above) before the political crisis arose, but her status as a nun did not prevent her participation in governmental affairs.

The existence of seals, which represented administrative power in Russia, are the most irrefutable evidence of women's participation in governance. The seals, cast in lead or cut in stone, were usually inscribed only with the name of the owner, but sometimes also a pictorial design. They were used, like signatures, to validate official documents. Only prominent and respected individuals, high officials in city or princely administration, had the right to seals. It was not only princesses of Polotsk who possessed seals and their concomitant administrative functions, but many other Russian princesses as well.

Medieval Russian princesses and noblewomen not only served as caretakers of government but actively engaged in political struggles. For example, Ulita, the wife of Prince Andrei Bogoliubskii (mid-twelfth century), joined in his boyars' plot against him. In a miniature in the Radziwill Chronicle, she is depicted standing unflinchingly beside her dying husband, holding his severed hand. Ulita's participation in the conspiracy and the murder itself is not evidence of some pathological cruelty on her part, but rather of her determination to avenge an insult to the honor of her father's clan: Prince Andrei's brother, Iurii, had confiscated their patrimonial lands, located on the site of present-day Moscow.[12]

Thus it would be a mistake to think that women acted only as conciliators in political life; on the contrary, they often collaborated in intrigues and conspiracies. Princesses, noblewomen, and very often their retainers frequently sacrificed their own welfare and that of their own families for a chance of realizing their political aspirations. One such ambitious woman was Nastaska, the concubine of Prince Iaroslav *Osmomysl* ("the Eight-Sensed") of Galich, in the late twelfth century. The Galician boyars condemned her for witchcraft; her real crime was meddling in the internal political affairs of the principality. According to medieval Russian chroniclers, familial disputes and internecine wars—for example, the one between Chernigov and Smolensk in 1180—frequently resulted from the exhortations of such women.[13]

Most princesses and noblewomen used their energies to support the interests of their principalities. One such woman was Anna Romanovna, the wife of the prince of Galich, of the late twelfth and early thirteenth century. In widowhood, she enjoyed the support of only a small portion of the nobility in her efforts to develop Galich's growth, commerce, and international stature. In the short period of her ascendancy, she succeeded in negotiating treaties with Hungary, Lithuania, and Poland on an equal basis. When a coup d'état deprived her of her throne, she fled, according to one chronicle account, "through a gap in the city wall" to Poland. Anna's opponents believed that they had crushed her pretentions to rule, but in exile she planned her return with her former allies. She sent notice to her enemies in Galich that she "wanted to rule by herself" and was determined to do so.

It took Anna nearly forty years to achieve her goal. Finally she did, with the support of the neighboring states with which she had previously concluded treaties of mutual aid. King Andrew II of Hungary provided the most assistance. The chronicler, usually so laconic, noted Andrew's primary motivation, his affection for Anna: "not forgetting his first love, he showed up with his army."

Anna ordered the arrest of the boyars who had opposed her and the confiscation of their property. Once restored to power, Anna devoted herself to expanding the territory of her principality, annexing several small cities on the eastern frontier of Galicia: Tikhoml, Peremysl, and Vladimir-in-Volhynia. In 1214 she decided to transfer the throne to her sons, dictating terms to them in the same way she determined the distribution of her property.[14]

Princess Maria Mikhailovna of Rostov likewise worked throughout her life to elevate the stature of her principality. She might be titled the "Princess-Chronicler," for she directed the writing of chronicles and perhaps even dictated some of them herself. It is from these texts that many of the facts of the history of Rostov in the thirteenth century are known. Maria's reign occurred during the invasion by the Mongols (also known as Tatars) in 1237–40. With their unrivaled military prowess, these steppe nomads established an empire that stretched from China to Hungary. When faced with resistance, the Mongols ruthlessly subjugated cities, leaving "smoke, sand, and ashes" in their wake. In the course of the Mongol conquest, libraries were burned and monasteries pillaged, and these were the primary repositories of documents, books, and chronicles. Historical materials created in these years thus are particularly valuable.

Maria's husband, Prince Vasilko of Rostov, lost his life in battle against the Mongols at the battle on the River Sit in 1238. According to custom, a woman widowed in such circumstances might take monastic vows and retire from the world. But Maria was responsible for her young sons, and she took on the responsibilities of regent in the unstable political atmosphere of the times.

Misfortunes continued to plague Maria. In the late 1240s, the Mongol Khan Batu executed Maria's father, Prince Mikhail of Chernigov. Her son witnessed his grandfather's trial and torture and recounted to Maria what had happened. His accounts, through Maria as intermediary, found their way into the Rostov chronicles and into the hagiographical "Life of St. Mikhail of Chernigov." These texts are much more personal and emotional than the norm for Russian writings, depicting the suffering of the entire nation through the prism of the life and death of one person. These accounts describe in detail the characteristics of all the members of Prince Mikhail's family and the personal qualities of Prince Vasilko of Rostov: supremely capable, brave beyond measure, intelligent, and honorable. Maria's perspective is evident in the unusually poignant account of how Prince Vasilko did not succeed in engaging the Mongols in battle the first time and so remained unharmed. The account of Vasilko's death and its tragic aftermath is similarly moving, reflecting deep sadness. Princess Maria's chronicles and the vita of St. Mikhail of Chernigov, while colored by a female perspective, do not display a narrowly personal slant but rather are imbued with ideas of patriotism, a yearning for the liberation of the entire country, and the conviction that the external strength of conquerors may be overcome through spiritual power.[15]

The period of Tatar rule, which lasted from the mid-thirteenth century to the second half of the fifteenth century, caused incalculable suffering for the Russian people. The Tatars ruled Russia as absentees, leaving its political and legal system intact. But the Tatars appointed the Russian Grand Prince, bestowing on him the *iarlyk*—a patent from the Mongol khan to rule—and charging him with collecting and delivering the tribute and preventing rebellions against Mongol authority. The tribute itself represented a substantial and continuing financial drain, and the frequent Mongol onslaughts to punish attempts to regain Russian independence cost Russia a great deal both economically and in human terms. Women bore these costs no less than men.[16]

As a Mongol tributary, Russia focused its foreign relations on Asia and limited dynastic contacts with European countries. It was only with neighboring Poland that political intermarriages continued as before. The Russian-born Agafia Sviatoslavna became queen of Poland in the mid-thirteenth century; she so overshadowed her inconsequential son Boleslaw that he received the nickname "the Bashful"![17] Both she and Gremislava Ingvarovna, who ascended to the throne in the late thirteenth century, earned reputations as prudent diplomats, promoting a pro-Russian policy, and also as prudent property managers, who left their children a substantial inheritance.

The conditions of Mongol rule changed the political activities of women. It is not accidental that chronicles report many fewer politically active women. Instead, they more often present women as objects of kidnapping and rape. In a number of instances, contemporary accounts present women as the initiators of peace missions, attributing to women the farsightedness to protect their husbands from bloodshed, extinguish conflict, and promote self-restraint and tranquillity. The chronicles depict Oksinia (Ksenia), the wise and educated princess of Tver, in this manner, and also

Elena Olgerdovna, who worked to preserve domestic tranquillity in her husband's realm.

Despite the constraints of Mongol rule, certain princesses refused to abstain from the pursuit of their political ambitions. They intervened in conflicts between princes and influenced the outcome of their struggles to obtain the grand princely *iarlyk*. Princess Ksenia of Iaroslavl, for example, exhibited no trepidation in the face of Mongol power. The chronicles recount that in 1288, Prince Fedor Rostislavich, the husband of Ksenia's daughter Maria, set out for the Golden Horde to seek a *iarlyk* to rule Iaroslavl. According to this account, Fedor's physique piqued the interest of the khan's daughter. How long Fedor resisted her importunities (or whether he tried to resist at all) is unknown. Nor is it clear whether Ksenia and Maria knew about Fedor's peccadillo. But in any case, when Fedor deigned to return home, he found the gates locked; Ksenia and Maria had taken advantage of his long absence to incite the boyars to revolt. Fedor's underaged son, Mikhail, had been acclaimed prince, with Ksenia and Maria named regents for him.

Finding himself in an absurd position, Fedor returned to the Horde. There his vanity was assuaged through marriage to the khan's daughter, who received the baptismal name of Anna. But a homeless and penniless son-in-law did not suit the khan. Twice the khan sent ambassadors to Iaroslavl, threatening reprisals and demanding that Fedor be given a portion of his former possession. Ksenia, who had gained the support and affection of the Iaroslavl boyars and their retinues, ignored the threats. The dispute lasted for years. Only after the deaths of Ksenia, Maria, and the young prince Mikhail in the 1290s was Fedor able to reestablish his right to rule Iaroslavl.[18]

Ksenia of Iaroslavl's actions were the exception rather than the rule. Most women of the privileged orders of society conducted themselves as pious and unassuming daughters and wives who devoted themselves entirely to familial matters: the running of the household and the rearing of children. Typical of such women was Evdokia, the wife of Prince Dmitrii Donskoi, the victor over the Tatars at the Battle of Kulikovo in 1380.

Evdokia was the daughter of Prince Dmitrii of Suzdal. In 1366, she was given in marriage to the young prince Dmitrii, the heir of the grand prince of Moscow. The marriage apparently was a happy one; Evdokia invariably called her husband "my dear sunshine." She helped him in the management of his estates, and she asked after his many political and military projects, taking responsibility herself for financial matters. A woman of particular piety, Evdokia contributed considerable funds for the construction of churches and attended their dedications. She gave birth to children, all of them sons, almost every year, and she did not spare any expense in their upbringing. In 1383, when the Tatar khan summoned Dmitrii to the Horde, Evdokia dissuaded him from going; instead they sent their twelve-year-old son, Vasilii, who was held as a hostage to guarantee Moscow's loyalty.

When she was widowed in 1389, Evdokia remained loyal to her husband's memory. She continued to concern herself with the rearing of her sons but recognized her first-born, Vasilii, as the head of the family; he had returned from the Horde and ascended the grand princely throne. Evdokia expended much of the huge bequest she received from her husband in the building of monastic cloisters and churches throughout the Muscovite realm: the Church of the Nativity of the Virgin in the Kremlin, the Church of John the Baptist in Pereiaslavl, the Church of the Ascension in Moscow, and others. Having accomplished her purposes in the secular world, Evdokia bequeathed her property to her youngest son, Konstantin, and took vows as a nun under the name Evfrosinia. She died a few days later, in May 1407.[19]

Evdokia was in many ways typical of aristocratic women of the fourteenth and early fifteenth centuries. The momentous political changes in this period—the end of Mongol suzerainty and the rise of the Muscovite state—wrought changes too in the place of women. Evdokia's daughter-in-law, Sofia Vitovtovna, is representative. She was the complete opposite of her mother-in-law: ambitious, sure of her talents, decisive, and sometimes arrogant. In these traits she resembled her father, Grand Prince Vitovt of Lithuania, who was noted as a defender of Lithuanian independence and as an advocate of European culture. When Vitovt sent Sofia to wed Prince Vasilii of Moscow in December 1390, he intended the marriage to solidify the alliance between the two states, with Moscow the lesser partner. But once in Moscow, Sofia showed herself to be independent, not wishing to be merely the embodiment of her father's policy. Instead, she became a loyal advisor and assistant to her husband. When he died in 1425, he bequeathed to her extensive landed property. Relying upon her intelligence and energy, Vasilii trusted her not only to rear their children but also to defend their rights.

Having mourned her husband, Sofia gathered the boyars and called upon them to stand firmly behind Vasilii I's heir, his ten-year-old son, Vasilii II. Vasilii I's younger brother, Prince Iurii of Zveni-gorod, disputed the succession. Sofia turned to her father in Lithua-nia for help. Thanks to the intervention of Vitovt, Iurii was forced to recognize the seniority of his ten-year-old nephew. Meanwhile, Sofia continued her efforts to build up the power of the grand prince, promulgating a new law code in the late 1420s. The preamble reads, "and so Grand Princess Sofia decreed."

But in the early 1430s the political situation worsened. Sofia's fa-ther died, and his successor was Prince Svidrigailo, the brother-in-law of Prince Iurii of Zvenigorod. Taking advantage of this shift in the balance of power, Iurii broke off relations with his nephew and de-manded that the Tatar khan bestow the *iarlyk* on him. Sofia did not wait to see what would happen next. She sent her boyar Vsevolozhskii to the Horde, and he succeeded in bribing the khan's advisors. Sofia's son retained the patent as grand prince.

Prince Iurii, however, did not abandon his hopes of securing the grand princely throne. The opportunity to press his claims came in February 1433, at the wedding of the sixteen-year-old Vasilii II to Princess Maria of Serpukhov. Iurii's two sons, Dmitrii and Vasilii, attended the wedding feast. Iurii's son Vasilii came dressed in rich attire, including a golden belt that was part of the ancestral regalia of the princes of Moscow. Seeing the belt that rightfully belonged to her son, Sofia tore it off. The incident led to a huge scandal, and ulti-mately to war.

Sofia and her son underwent a great deal of suffering before they achieved the victory they sought over the Zvenigorod pretenders. During the civil war, Vasilii was blinded by his enemies in an effort to disqualify him from ruling (he thus gained the nickname "the Dark"); then he and his wife were exiled to Uglich. Sofia herself was imprisoned for ten years in the distant city of Chukhloma. But in the late 1440s, the fortunes of Sofia and her son improved. Vasilii II was able to gain the support of the boyars of Moscow, who gained release from prison for him and his mother and acclaimed him the lawful ruler of Muscovy.

After her return to Moscow, Sofia again took up her previous activ-ities. In the 1440s and 1450s, she managed the affairs of her estates and founded a number of churches and monasteries. In 1451, at the age of nearly eighty years, she once again faced a crisis. While Vasilii the Dark was on a campaign down the Volga, the Tatar pretender Mazovsha attacked Moscow with his detachment. But Sofia and her boyars organized the citizens to defend the city, which they did so forcefully that the Tatars fled, leaving behind the booty they had collected elsewhere.

Sofia deliberately shaped the character of her daughter-in-law, Princess Maria Iaroslavna of Serpukhov, the wife of Vasilii II. Soon after her marriage, the young princess was forced to share her husband's and mother-in-law's political degradation. But in the mid-fifteenth century, she also shared in their return to power, and she ruled a united Muscovite state beside them. Having experienced intrafamilial conflict herself, she strove to avert such conflict among her sons. Her aptitude for diplomacy was revealed in her reception of ambassadors and her negotiations with them. Even after the death of her husband in 1462, Maria continued to participate in governmental affairs. The chronicles report that she approved of the military campaign to annex Novgorod in 1471. She also gave her son, Ivan III, her blessing in his expedition against Khan Akhmat at the Ugra in 1480, when Russia terminated its subordination to Tatar rule.

In order to extend Moscow's influence over neighboring principalities, Maria arranged the marriage of her daughter Anna to Prince Vasilii Ivanovich of Riazan, who was, incidentally, brought up at the Muscovite court. Anna had been born in 1451, when her grandmother, Sofia Vitovtovna, was organizing the defense of Moscow against the Tatar Mazovsha. Reared by an assertive mother and grandmother, Anna felt liberated from familial guardianship when she left to become the mistress of her own princely household in Riazan. No documents survive from the twenty-odd years of her husband's reign in Riazan. However, once widowed, Anna proclaimed herself regent for her underaged son Ivan. As ruler of Riazan, she undertook a deliberate policy to expand its territory, annexing lands to the west of the principality, where Moscow also had interests. Seeing her determination, her brother, Ivan III of Moscow, concluded a treaty with her in 1496. Anna returned to Moscow to live with her brother and mother, and Maria Iaroslavna tried to temper her daughter's ambitions for Riazan. She was unsuccessful. To the end of her life, Anna continued to work to expand and strengthen Riazan. In her will she sternly instructed her daughter-in-law Agrafena, regent for Anna's young grandson and heir, to continue what she had started.[20]

Between the early twelfth century and the late fifteenth, Moscow grew from a minor outpost into the recognized center of the Russian state. The growth of the Muscovite state brought an end to the rivalry among Russian principalities that had begun in the pre-Mongol period and had been exacerbated by Tatar rule. Moscow assimilated the weaker territories of "Great Russia"—that is, those north and east of the original Kievan state—sometimes through diplomacy, and more often by military conquest.

The annexation of Novgorod was the last episode in the consolidation of Muscovite suzerainty over the Russian lands. Novgorod had been Russia's major port for Baltic trade since the tenth century. Since the twelfth century, Novgorod had enjoyed autonomy from the grand princes of Russia, and the local boyars governed the city on their own. The boyars of Novgorod invited outside princes to provide military defense, dismissing them when they failed to please. Union with Moscow would mean an end to this medieval "republican" form of government. In the last decades of independence, it was a woman of the boyar class, Marfa Boretskaia, who played the leading role in the politics of the city.

Marfa was born into the Loshinskii boyar clan of Novgorod. Her second husband, Isaak Boretskii, was the powerful mayor of the city, as well as the prince's representative. Because of his position, Marfa gained the nickname of "Marfa the Mayoress" (*Marfa Posadnitsa*). The Boretskii family owned vast estates in Novgorod's extensive territories, which stretched north to the White Sea. After Isaak's death, all these lands passed to Marfa. Year after year she expanded these holdings through additional purchases and by colonizing unsettled lands along the Onega River. As a result of these acquisitions, Marfa rapidly became the third largest landholder in Novgorod, after the archbishop and the monasteries. Her fur-bearing territories yielded many thousands of pelts—sable, marten, and others—each year. Because of her wealth, Marfa enjoyed considerable political weight.

Marfa Boretskaia was not the only Novgorodian woman who "took on male strength," as medieval sources describe forceful women. Novgorodian chronicles are full of the names of militant women, such as the "glorious, wealthy Nastasia" (boyarina Anastasia Grigorieva), who participated in the uprisings and conspiracies that shaped the city's political history. Thus, after the Muscovite annexation, not only the boyars but also "boyars' wives and widows" were bidden according to tradition to "kiss the cross," swearing loyalty to the grand prince of Moscow. Had Marfa still been alive in 1478, she would have been among them.

Folk legends describe Marfa as stern and imperious; supposedly, when she heard how two of her sons perished in Zaonezhie, she ordered villages there to be burned. Chronicles portray her as grasping and money-grubbing. Ecclesiastical sources brand her with dozens of uncomplimentary epithets, all characteristics of the "sly, evil woman" willing to do anything to advance her power. But the Russian historian Karamzin later praised her as "the supreme republican woman."

In the 1460s, Marfa led the boyar faction that openly opposed the centralizing policies of Moscow. Several other noblewomen similarly supported this position, including the aforementioned Anastasia Grigorieva and Evfimia Gorshkova, the widow of the mayor Esip Gorshkov. In order to save Novgorod from the Muscovite autocracy, Marfa formed an alliance with Poland–Lithuania. According to the hostile account in the chronicle, Marfa's proposed alliance was not only political, but personal: "She wished to bring him [the son of the king of Poland] to herself in Novgorod, and she wished to rule the entire Novgorodian land with him in the name of the Polish king." The alliance was advantageous to both sides. For Novgorod, Lithuania was the lesser of two evils, compared with growing Muscovite absolutism. For Lithuania, it meant the acquisition of an enormous territory.

Ivan III could not acquiesce to the loss of such a large territory, and one so important to Russia's international trade. He and his army launched an attack on Novgorod on June 20, 1471, with the blessing of his mother, Princess Maria Iaroslavna. However intelligent and capable Marfa was, she was not a military leader, and her lieutenants lost the battle on the Shelon River. The boyar faction she had led turned Marfa over to the grand prince of Moscow and swore loyalty to him. Marfa's son Dmitrii was executed, and Ivan III ordered that Marfa be exiled and her huge landholding confiscated for the state treasury. Marfa herself perished under ambiguous circumstances.[21]

At the same time that Marfa Boretskaia ruled Novgorod, another strong woman was making her impact in Moscow: the second wife of Grand Prince Ivan III, Sofia Paleologue. She receives as much credit as her husband for the transformation of Moscow into the center of Russia's political, religious, and cultural life.

Sofia, born Zoë, was the niece of the last emperor of Byzantium, Constantine XI Paleologus. After the fall of Constantinople in 1453, her father and uncle brought her to Rome. In 1469, the pope suggested her as a bride for Ivan III, hoping in this way to achieve the reunification of the Eastern Orthodox and Roman Catholic churches, which had split in 1054. When the Muscovite grand prince received a portrait of Zoë, "painted like an icon," he agreed to marry her. According to the standards of the day, she was not deemed beautiful, but contemporaries commented on her petite size, exceptionally fair

skin, and impressive eyes. Sofia Paleologue's bridal party was ceremoniously welcomed to Moscow. The marriage greatly enhanced the
international prestige of the Muscovite state. Since the fall of Constantinople, Moscow had characterized itself as Byzantium's successor, the center of Eastern Orthodoxy.

Sofia's appearance at the Kremlin led to the elaboration of a new
court etiquette and a new solemnity in ceremonies. Having been
reared in Italy during the height of the Renaissance, Sofia brought to
Russia a European sense of education and culture. She attracted
many European professionals to Moscow: physicians, philosophers,
and artists. The influence of Italian architects, commissioned by
Sofia, is visible in the Kremlin cathedrals and protective walls. Sofia
was also responsible for the importation to Russia of the Byzantine
imperial emblem, the double-headed eagle.

From the first Sofia involved herself in state affairs. She held audiences with foreigners and kept her own diplomatic retinue, which
included the famous Greeks, Iurii and Dmitrii Trakhanioty. Later
accounts attributed the development of Moscow's new anti-Tatar policy to Sofia, because according to legend she was the one who insisted
on terminating the payment of tribute to the Golden Horde.

In internal matters, Sofia's major achievement was guaranteeing
succession to the throne to her son, Vasilii. Ivan III had another heir,
his grandson Dmitrii, whose father was born from Ivan's first marriage. Muscovite inheritance practice was ambiguous concerning
which of the two, Vasilii or Dmitrii, had the stronger claim to the
throne. Sofia gathered a group of supporters for her son's claim,
even stooping to take money from the grand prince's treasury to
bribe potential followers. Ivan III, who had chosen Dmitrii as his heir,
regarded Sofia's machinations as a plot against him. Many of Sofia's
supporters were executed, and the grand princess and her son were sent
away in disgrace. After a year, Ivan III forgave them and once again
began to live with her, "vigilantly," as the chronicler says, "refusing to
decide his affairs in bed from then on." But nonetheless Sofia ultimately
succeeded in convincing her husband to take action against her political
enemies and even to execute his grandson Dmitrii. After her position
was thus secured, she started to style herself "Daughter of the Emperor
of Tsargrad, Grand Princess of Moscow." When she died in 1503, she left
five sons and had attained great honor and glory.[22]

These, then, were the most prominent women of the period from
the tenth to the fifteenth centuries: those who initiated reforms, established law codes, and initiated governmental projects. To the figures

just surveyed, at least fifty more women could be added—princesses, boyarinas, queens, and empresses. The basic facts of their biographies are known, and their activities may be documented through numerous sources. In most cases, women gained the wherewithal to engage in political and cultural activities from their own landholdings.

By and large all these aristocratic women shared certain characteristics. They were well educated for their time, and they felt free to involve themselves in politics, bringing matters before secular rulers, church councils, and even the pope himself. They could send their own envoys to foreign countries, on occasion forming and leading their own embassies. They undertook negotiations with foreign diplomats in order to advance the interests of their Russian homeland. For the most part they advocated peaceful, diplomatic, and restrained solutions to international tensions—and this in a period of constant warfare.

Despite their governmental duties and their own political ambitions, these women leaders remained devoted mothers. Often, as guardians and regents, Russian princesses directed all their efforts to help their sons ascend to the throne and to achieve their political goals. Sometimes, to advance these ends, these women deliberately downplayed their contribution to their menfolk's successes.

In such difficult and dangerous times, Russian aristocratic women had to battle to preserve their positions, and they did so energetically and decisively, although they did not take up weapons personally. In their own time, medieval Russian women had a reputation in Europe for their attractiveness and intelligence. Russian princesses who married abroad frequently rivaled their husbands in their level of education, knowledge of foreign languages, and understanding of philosophy, medicine, and astronomy. Many Russian aristocratic women studied not only needlework but also book learning; quite a few had their own personal libraries.

However, most women, even of the upper classes, did not participate in the political, diplomatic, and cultural life of medieval Russia on a par with their male counterparts. But it is these highly visible figures who demonstrate the range of possibilities open to the exceptional women of early Russia.

Before and After the Wedding

The family and household had greater significance in the ancient and medieval world than they do in the modern. The obligations and cares of everyday life took up the greater portion of people's lives, especially women's. From childhood, women were trained to become mistresses of their households. But a woman could head a household only after she married and founded her own nuclear family.

From the earliest times in Russia, marriage represented the most important point of transition for women, from a position of dependence and inequality to emancipation. In the eighth to the tenth centuries, a ritual of abduction was the usual means of concluding a marriage. The oldest chronicles report that young men would "carry off" their brides during "games." The Russian pagan god of marriage, Lado, sanctified these "games," which were organized near springs or rivers in late spring or summer. According to the chronicles, the "abduction" took place with the mutual consent of the bride and groom: "each man carried off a wife for himself, the one with whom he had come to an agreement." The common people retained this form of marriage in the countryside for centuries after the adoption of Christianity. Traces of marriage by "abduction" can still be found in folklore and in rituals that survive to the present day—for example, the custom of carrying the bride over the threshold.

More formal wedding ceremonies arose later.[23] In the tenth century, with the development of more complex social structures, a new contractual form of marriage appeared. The parents and relatives of the bride would bring her to the groom's house, and on the next day they would bring her dowry. This form of marriage gave greater weight to the family's choice of spouse than to the bride's, and it also emphasized the financial arrangements surrounding the marriage.

After the adoption of Christianity in 988, ecclesiastical rituals were added to the celebration of contractual marriages. A betrothal accompanied by a formal marital contract became an obligatory stage in the formation of a marriage. At a ceremony called *pomolvka* (from a root meaning "speak"), the parents of the bride stipulated the contents of her dowry, fixed the date of the wedding, and received the final consent of the groom and his family. The *pomolvka* and the marital contract were ratified by the bride and groom joining hands ("handfast") and feasting at the home of the bride's parents. The feast consisted of foods with ritual significance: pies, kasha (boiled grain), and cheese. The cutting of the cheese confirmed the *pomolvka*; if the groom broke off the betrothal after this ritual, he was fined for violating the terms of the contract and insulting the bride's honor. In medieval Russia, women had a high value because the continuity of the clan depended upon them; thus their honor, and particularly their reputation for sexual chastity, had to be preserved.

Although the parents made the arrangements for the marriage, their children's wishes were not entirely overlooked. Church canons made parents who gave their daughters (and sons) in marriage against their will subject to a fine. Parents could also be punished if "a girl wants to marry someone, but her father and mother do not arrange it." If a free man married a slave woman, he became a slave also. But in the reverse situation, if the groom were a slave and the bride free, the woman preserved her status and could even pass it on to her children, who were similarly considered to be free. Because slave women were vulnerable to sexual exploitation by their masters, this provision protected the chastity of free women.

From about the thirteenth century on, it became customary for the marital contract to be signed not only by the adult members of the clan but also by the bride and groom. Sometimes the bridal couple made all the arrangements themselves. Private correspondence, written on birchbark (which archeologists have uncovered in Novgorod and other Russian cities), testifies to this. One such letter, from a man to a woman and dating from the twelfth century, reads, "From Mikita to Ulianitsa. Marry me! I want you, and you want me. Ignat will be the witness. . . ." But it was more customary for the parents to make the arrangements for the wedding. The Russian tradition forbidding the groom to see the bride between the betrothal and the wedding day represents a survival of this custom. The etymology of the Russian word for "bride," *nevesta*, also reflects this tradition; it means, literally, "unknown woman."

Orthodox Christian canons set a number of conditions for the establishment of a valid marriage. The first of these concerned age; ecclesiastical law prohibited the marriage of girls under the age of twelve and boys under the age of fifteen. On average, girls married at the age of thirteen or fourteen, but chronicles report cases when parents arranged marriages for children eight or even five years of age. But such marriages took place only among the aristocracy and were concluded for political gain.

Young marriages offered several advantages. First, because of the short life expectancy (less than 50 years), early marriage maximized the reproductive period of the couple's life. In addition, a girl who was not yet grown up could be expected to be more tractable, more willing to obey her parents and her husband.

A second requirement of the church was for marriages to be concluded exclusively among believers. Marriages with persons of other faiths were deemed "unworthy." However, this rule did not prevent

Russian princes from continuing to make dynastic marriages with Catholic rulers after the schism of 1054. Russian churchmen rarely made an issue of such royal marriages before the wedding of Vasilii III and Sofia Paleologue. Sofia was required to affirm her adherence to Orthodoxy upon her arrival in Moscow.

Ecclesiastical teachings limited the number of times a person could marry. The church permitted no more than two marriages, regardless of the reason they were dissolved. An exception allowed a third marriage, if no children had been born of the first two. A church proverb dictated, "The first marriage is lawful; the second—a dispensation; the third—a transgression; the fourth—dishonor, for it is a swinish life."

The church also established extensive rules regarding incestuous marriages, prohibiting unions between "close relatives," defined as individuals related in the sixth degree (second cousins) or closer and spiritual relatives. It was not always possible to trace degrees of kinship more distant than that. The church not only issued rules on this subject but also enforced them strictly. As a result, marriages between cousins did not take place in Russia, even into the nineteenth century.

Although the Orthodox Church preached chastity, the failure to preserve virginity before marriage did not constitute an impediment. Canon law prescribed a fine for wives who had not safeguarded their "maidenly purity" and "entered into marriage unchaste." Churchmen did not want to prevent people from marrying; on the contrary, they wanted people to form official unions, established in accordance with ecclesiastical norms. As one religious service book directed priests, "You should see to it that [your parishioners] marry [in church] and live together lawfully!"

The actual wedding day had to be chosen very carefully. The bride and her parents had to choose a day that did not coincide with the numerous church holy days or fasts. Canon law forbade the celebration of marriages on the fast days of the week, Wednesdays and Fridays, throughout the year, and also during the penitential periods before Christmas and Easter. The traditional time for weddings was in the spring (the time of the "abduction games" in the pagan period) after Easter and then through the summer. Secondarily, weddings might be celebrated in the winter, when there was no work in the fields to interfere. The parents oversaw the preparations for the wedding, in consultation with the eldest members of the family, who knew the proper customs best.

On the eve of the appointed day, the bride's mother, girl friends, and female relatives arranged a ritual bath for her. After the bride had washed, the bath water was saved; it was supposed to have magical powers transferred from her body to excite love in her future husband. Although Orthodox clergy tried to stamp out the custom of collecting "wedding water," the custom continued into the seventeenth century, and later. Then came the bride's "farewell to maidenhood," when her hair was combed out of the maidenly single braid and was rearranged in the double-braid style of married women, crowned with a wreath. The hair combing was accompanied by traditional singing and sometimes lasted throughout the night.

On the wedding day itself, the bride awaited the bridegroom at her parents' home, symbolizing that she was "unknown" to him. The day before, her dowry and the marital bed had been brought to the groom's house, and the groom and his relatives had sent marital gifts to the bride's family in return. Usually the groom sent the bride a small chest that traditionally contained pins and needles, the symbols of domestic work and said to protect from the "evil eye." The chest also might contain a small whip. Pagan beliefs held that a ritual lashing of a woman with such a whip enhanced her fertility; later, the whip became a symbol of the husband's authority over his wife.

On the day of the wedding, the women of her family baked round loaves of bread decorated with figures of birds and then carried them to the bride, strewing the floor with coins. This ritual symbolized their wish that she would have a rich, satisfying life. After the bride was arrayed in her wedding garments, she was sprinkled with hops (to symbolize joy) and grain (to symbolize prosperity). Fur coats were brought into the house, to guarantee wealth and to scare away evil spirits. Straw mattresses or sheaves of straw were brought to promise the bride easy childbirths. Then the bride, accompanied by her relatives, rode in a wagon to the wedding ceremony. The groom and his relatives came separately. The more wealthy the family, the more elaborate the wedding procession. At the church, fur rugs were laid down at the bride's feet, and she walked over them to enter the sanctuary.

In Russia, the wedding service usually took place after mass. Only secular priests, not monks, had the right to perform marriages. The couple joined hands and exchanged rings. The priest placed "marital crowns" on their heads, blessed them with incense, and prayed for them to have a "peaceful, long life" and to have "children and grandchildren, filling your home with abundance and beauty."

The next stage of the wedding celebration took place in the home of the groom. The wedding procession traveled there from the church to the noise of shouts and whip cracking to frighten off evil powers. At the groom's house, the young couple was greeted with bread and salt to wish them prosperity and happiness. Fur rugs were spread out, and the bridal couple was showered from head to foot with coins, grain, and hops. The guests watched closely to see which of the two would be the first to step over the threshold, because that person would dominate in the family. (Of course, if the groom carried the bride over the threshold, then he became the master!) Another similar game followed, in which the bride took off her husband's boots. One boot contained money, and if she guessed correctly which one and removed it first, she would be the manager of the household budget. (Later interpreters regarded this custom as a symbol of the wife's subordination.) Yet another game representing the struggle for supremacy in the family involved the breaking of a wine goblet. "Whichever of the two [bride and groom] first steps on the glass, that one will forever rule," an anonymous English visitor wrote.

After games of this sort came the wedding feast, to which all relations and the entire village were invited. The menu traditionally included kasha, pies, cold meat, and a chicken, which the bride and groom were supposed to divide in half, spearing their own sections on a knife. During this ritual, it was customary for the guests to make suggestive comments about the wedding night, which the ritual represented. Consequently, clerics condemned this practice, labeling it "demonic."

On the first evening of the wedding celebration, only the groom and guests were permitted to drink strong intoxicants. During the feast, the young couple was ceremoniously escorted to the prepared marital bed. The bed was made up with straw mattresses, which were said to mitigate the pain the bride would suffer with the breaking of the hymen. In the fourteenth and fifteenth centuries, a new ritual appeared to determine the bride's virginity, apparently as a result of the Orthodox insistence on premarital chastity. After the wedding night, the groom appeared among the guests carrying a wine glass with a hole in the bottom. If he had found his bride a virgin, he plugged the hole with his finger and drank down the wine poured into the goblet. If not, he left the hole open and the wine drained out. This custom, described by foreign travelers, had not been part of earlier popular wedding rituals.[24]

The Orthodox Church altered many popular traditions and rituals,

adapting them to Christian norms of marriage. Clerics tried to inculcate in their spiritual children the conception of marriage as first
and foremost a religious act, concluded "in heaven." However, the
church was unable to convince people to forgo the traditional wedding ceremonies; in the popular conception, church nuptials alone
did not suffice to validate a marriage.

Because the making of a marriage was a legal act, a sort of civil
contract, it was also necessary to have a means of dissolving it.[25]
Divorce had existed in Russia as long as marriages had. Church authorities preferred to sanction divorce only as a concession to human
weakness; Orthodox teachings preached the divine origin of marriage and its consequent indissolubility. But even in the eleventh
century, the church recognized a whole range of justifications for
divorce, for both husbands and wives.

The first justifiable reason for divorce was adultery, which was
defined differently for the husband than for the wife. For the husband, adultery meant his keeping a concubine and fathering children by her. This "second woman," judging by chronicle accounts,
was usually a woman of lower social standing. The wife, however, was
guilty of adultery if she formed any sort of liaison with another man.

In medieval Russia, a wife was not entitled to divorce her adulterous husband; instead, he was punished by a fine payable to the
church. The husband of an adulterous wife had not only the right
but the obligation to divorce her, especially if he was a priest. (In the
Orthodox Church, parish priests are expected to be married.) A
husband who forgave his wife's betrayal and "gave her her will" (i.e.,
agreed to forget everything) was himself punished with a fine.

Under Orthodox canons, many lesser offenses by a wife were
equated with adultery. A husband was permitted to divorce his wife
"if [she] eats, drinks, or sleeps with outsiders"; if she voluntarily
made an attempt on his life; if she "thoughtlessly" brought thieves
into their home; or if she attended amusements against her husband's
wishes. Both husband and wife were permitted to seek a divorce in
the case of physical incapacity (impotence or infertility) or financial
impairment—the inability to support the family. In addition, spouses
could divorce in order to take monastic vows.

In the thirteenth and fourteenth centuries, women gained new
rights to dissolve a marriage. A wife could demand a divorce if her
husband sold himself into bondage without her knowledge or hid
that he was already a slave. A wife could also seek a divorce if her
husband "accused [her] without substantiation of sorcery, witchcraft,

murder, or any other evil conduct," including false insinuations against her chastity. In short, a husband's slander against his wife was considered to be a serious enough transgression to justify divorce. In these cases, the wife could claim compensation for the costs of the hearings in ecclesiastical court and receive a share of her husband's property "for her support."

Although legally all divorces were supposed to go through ecclesiastical courts, the divorce process involved an enormous amount of red tape, and some couples preferred simply to separate on their own. The church was unable to stop them from doing so. Churchmen forbade the remarriage of women who fled their legal husbands. If the first husband succeeded in recovering his runaway wife, clerics called upon him to punish her harshly. But frequently the women who attempted to remarry without previously obtaining divorces were "straw widows"—women whose husbands had gone off to war and never returned. In the fourteenth century, a law was introduced to require such women to wait for three years, and then the church would be willing to countenance their remarriage. The new husband was then required to make a small monetary payment to the church for the dispensation.

For the church, the issue in divorce was not only social and economic—divorce disrupted family units—but also moral. When a husband left his wife on his own, the church not only levied a fine for the violation of canon law, but also mandated a sizable payment to the divorced wife "for the shame"—that is, for the insult she suffered. The amount of the payment depended upon the status and wealth of the family, but it always represented a ruinous sum. Consequently, for all the many legal provisions to regulate divorce, few actual cases are recorded. Chronicles do report occasional cases where princes calculatingly shipped their wives off to convents and then remarried. Often the wife's "ill health" was the official excuse for her "decision" to take monastic vows. However, from the twelfth century on, canon law did not actually authorize divorce because of blindness, deafness, lameness, or chronic illness; husbands were forbidden to expel wives from their homes for these reasons.

Although the evidence from real couples is limited, normative sources survive in large numbers, and they recount how people were supposed to live. Orthodox canon law, hagiography, homilies, and penitential and didactic literature preach about how men should relate to women and what their place in the family should be.

The basic Orthodox conception of marriage in this period was that it was a necessary compromise with human sinfulness. Marriage was inferior in comparison with celibacy and perpetual virginity: "the unmarried person is higher than the married one," "marriage is a common evil." However, celibacy was realistic only for ascetic monastics, who voluntarily renounced sexual relations. For lay people, Orthodox churchmen cited the authority of Scripture to affirm that "an honorable marriage and undefiled bed" was indeed a holy state. Matrimony was essential to the organization of the secular community and for the continuity of the species.

The birth of children, which increased the number of workers in the family and also the number of pious Christians, depended directly upon women. Even so, the church did not exalt women's role in the family and society but instead consigned them to a secondary place properly under male domination. Scriptural passages were invoked to demonstrate the inferiority of the female sex. The story from Genesis about how Eve was created from Adam's rib showed how wives must subordinate themselves to their husbands: "you were taken from your husband so that he will rule over you." The hierarchy in the family matched the hierarchy in the state: "the man is the head of his wife; the prince is the head of the man; and God is the head of the prince." Didactic sermons, epigrams, and tales reinforced the ideological basis of the family hierarchy.[26] In reality, familial power did not necessarily conform to such dictates. As we have seen, male leaders frequently depended upon their wives to govern their lands, and these women were hardly "quiet" or "humble" in their decisive actions.

Ecclesiastical literature inculcated a concept of the ideal marriage, where the wife was "quiet," "humble," "silent," and "submissive to her husband's will." "Whoever is ruled by his wife, may he be the worst damned! Such men become soft, shameless, silly, unfree, inarticulate, and servile." The church warned that "to give a woman freedom" was like suicide for a man. "Men may rule cities," one didactic collection fulminated gloomily, "but they are like slaves to their wives." Disorder and destruction would be the inevitable results.

Orthodox sermons and tales counterpoised the image of the "good woman" with the figure of the "evil woman."[27] This contrasting pair is found widely in the literatures of the world, and in each case the characteristics of the protagonists are altered in conformity with local conceptions. In Old Russian literature of the tenth to fifteenth centuries, the "good woman" is bland and unrealistic, while the "evil woman" is painted in vivid tones. The ideal woman would

have to be not only silent and submissive but also God-fearing, asceti-
cally chaste, indifferent to her own welfare, and ready to fulfill any
task for her husband. As the authors of the treatises on the nature of
women pointed out, such "good" women were extremely rare. They
found "evil women" to be rife.

"Evil women" included those who tried to enhance their physical
beauty with cosmetics, because they thus provoked marital infidelity.
Ecclesiastical authors depicted the methods that repulsive, perfidious
temptresses used to ensnare the hearts of innocent and credulous
men. They somehow got their husbands to do their bidding, rather
than the other way around. They "laughed in church, fearing neither
God nor the priest"; they "had the impudence to speak," and even to
"reproach and condemn." Such outspoken women represented a real
threat to the authority of the clergy, who condemned them as a
"great injury" to Orthodox rules and norms. Clerical authors invoked
these images in order to condemn real women, such as Marfa
Boretskaia, who engaged in activities that challenged male authority,
particularly in the political sphere.

Although ecclesiastical writers disallowed female superiority or
even equality within the marital union, they still idealized a loving
relationship between husband and wife. The ideal of marital love,
however, did not include gratification of the flesh. The literary examples of such couples, where mutual affection was manifested through
pious virtue, abounded: Mikhail and Agafia of Chernigov, Fedor and
Evpraksia of Riazan, and, most notably, Peter and Fevronia of
Murom.[28] Invariably, didactic literature depicted the protagonists as
upper class. By depicting the aristocracy as the bearers of spirituality
and high morality in familial relations, the authors hoped to inculcate similar traits among the common people, as well as a sense of
veneration for their social betters.

Did family relations in medieval Russia coincide with the ecclesiastical model? The sources provide meager information about the reality of day-to-day life. Only inferences drawn from normative literature
and chance comments in narratives, judicial documents, and birchbark letters provide clues. One birchbark letter hardly reflects the
ecclesiastical dread of physical sensuality: "As my heart and my body
burn, and my soul from the vision of your body, so may your heart
burn, and your body, and your soul from the vision of my body, from
all of me." Through the institution of confession and penance,
churchmen tried, if not to eliminate such sexual feelings, at least to
bring them under control. When parishioners came for confession,

usually not more than twice a year, the priest asked about their sins, referring to penitential handbooks, which contained lists of questions and recommended penances on the basis of the severity of the sin. The focus of these penitential inquiries was sexual behavior. If parishioners deviated from the ecclesiastical norms of conduct, the priest imposed a penance that usually consisted of fasting, prayers, and sometimes public contrition.

From penitential handbooks, it is possible to reconstruct the conception of sexual morality in medieval Russia as formulated by the Orthodox Church. Engaging in sexual activity for pleasure rather than for procreation was considered a manifestation of spiritual weakness. Literature that churchmen produced for the secular audience might diverge from this teaching; for example, the "Letter of Kliment Smoliatich" stated that because the son of God was born of a woman, it was "no sin" for a man to have intercourse with his wife. Other ecclesiastical literature was categorical: any gratification of the flesh was sinful. Sexual relations on holy days or fast days were particularly reprehensible. Any sexual expression outside of marriage, the premarital loss of virginity, and homosexual contacts qualified as serious transgressions. Not only sexual actions but also sexual thoughts were categorized as sinful, in accordance with the Scriptural admonition: "Whoever has looked at a woman with desire has already committed adultery with her."

For women, the defilement of sexual sin could be justified only through the birth of children. Not only the church but also the society as a whole encouraged women to bear many children. In the Middle Ages, when families expected to support themselves on the basis of their own resources, bearing children was the obvious way to increase the family's productive force. Childless agricultural workers faced a grim old age of poverty and need. A woman's capacity to bear children defined her relationship with the family group: "A wife is given to a man for a single purpose, to bear children." Barrenness was viewed as a great misfortune: "It is a great evil, if no children are born"; "just as a field withers without rain, so does a childless woman wither, along with her family."

The church imposed severe penalties on women who committed infanticide, terminated pregnancies, or practiced birth control. The use of potions for these purposes was equated morally with murder. The penances for abortion varied by the stage of pregnancy. If the fetus had quickened, the penance was fifteen years of fasting; if it was just completely formed, the penance was seven years; if it was only an embryo, the penance was five years. If the child had been conceived out of wedlock, the abortion was regarded as doubly sinful.

The church particularly condemned women who consulted "wise women" or "sorcerers" for drugs to render them fertile or their husbands more potent. Despite the church's suspicion of folk medicine of this sort, connected as it was with pagan magic, it was highly developed in medieval Russia. Practitioners knew about the uses of all sorts of stimulants, spices, roots, and wild herbs. Certain substances, including honey, sweat, and breast milk, were thought to be efficacious in bewitching men. "Wise women" often served as midwives, cured infertility, and performed abortions ("wrested the fruit [of the womb] from women"). To promote fertility, women ingested material from the umbilical cord or placenta taken from women who had recently given birth. Although folk medicine was shrouded in superstition, modern medical science confirms the efficacy of certain traditional remedies.[29]

Folk belief in medieval Russia regarded pregnancy as a dangerous condition, and with good reason: a large percentage of women and newborn infants died from infection, disease, poor nutrition, and unhygienic surroundings. Women married young, and often became pregnant in their teenage years, increasing the likelihood of difficult deliveries. Pregnant women also performed heavy labor at home and in the fields. The church undertook to protect the health of pregnant women. It sternly punished men who raised a hand against their pregnant wives, and it forbade priests to insist that women who were "with child" make deep prostrations. Of course, pregnant women often had to bend down and lift heavy loads in the course of their everyday lives, and the ecclesiastical exemption could not relieve them of this work.

After the birth of a child, the new mother was considered "unclean" for forty days. She was forbidden from entering the church, and in general from going out in public. Sexual contact was also prohibited—a rule that worked to preserve the health of the woman and her baby. Purifying baths and ceremonies marked the end of the forty-day period.[30]

The birth of a son was greeted with great rejoicing in medieval Russian families. But daughters were also regarded as a gift, a "comfort" for their fathers. The church taught that the birth of a girl ought to be an occasion for joy, no less than the birth of a boy, because daughters were future mothers who would perpetuate the clan and bring honor to the family. Children were not only a source

Childbirth. Women attendants see to the welfare of the woman in labor, bathe the newborn baby, and prepare the celebratory feast. From a fresco in the Church of the Prophet Elijah (Ilia) in Iaroslavl, 1680–81.

of delight but also a justification for the existence of the family and the focus of women's lives. Many Orthodox sermons were directed toward mothers, instructing them on how to rear their children. "Do not punish your children in anger," one sermon read; "preserve your children, and correct their childish habits." Respect for mothers was pleasing to God, and disregarding one's "mother's labors" was condemned. Narrative and hagiographical literature stressed the importance of receiving one's mother's blessing before embarking on serious undertakings. Familial love was a matter not only of obligation but often of genuine emotion. Chronicles record affectionate nicknames given to wives and daughters: "dearest," "conciliatress," "little emerald."

The Dormition of the Virgin. The soul of the Mother of God is depicted as a swaddled infant in Christ's arms. Icon by Feofan Grek, early fifteenth century.

Orthodox teaching promoted the veneration of mothers in the family and severely condemned any manifestation of ingratitude toward them. Although only a few fragments of legal documents survive, they indicate that such teachings did not necessarily safeguard mothers from insult and mistreatment. A birchbark letter from the fourteenth century was written by an unhappy stepmother whose stepson had driven her from her home. She sent her protest to a judicial official, clearly expecting to receive justice. This letter demonstrates that women knew their rights and that laws to protect them were enforced.

Orthodox teaching devoted particular attention to the status of elderly women and widows in the family. Russian tradition mandated respect for the elderly, and the familial structure promoted it as well. Unlike Western Europe, Russia preserved the large, multigenerational family, consisting of elderly parents, their grown sons and their wives, grandchildren, and even great-grandchildren. This extended, multigenerational family coexisted on a par with small, nuclear families, consisting of parents and their children only. The need for a large number of agricultural laborers promoted the preservation of the multigenerational family, especially in the countryside. The head of this family was the father, but also the mother—the most senior woman and the manager of the entire household. She could be a domineering figure, dictating to the other relatives, children, servants, and dependents.

The life expectancy for women was, despite all hardships, somewhat longer than that of men. Many widows remarried, sometimes more than once; Marfa Boretskaia, for example, outlived two husbands. Young girls sometimes were given in marriage to men of mature years and were widowed within a decade. Sometimes husbands on their deathbeds commended their young wives to the guardianship of a monastery. Sometimes widows voluntarily took monastic vows. But usually widows became the chief managers of their deceased husbands' property and guardians for their children. "Respect and obey your mother," Prince Vladimir of Serpukhov instructed his grown children in his will. "Hold your mother in honor and contentment," Grand Prince Vasilii II instructed his children. He ordered that his wife be considered the head of the family, "in place of me, your father." These broad rights and marks of respect for widows are characteristic of Russian custom in the tenth to fifteenth centuries.

Thus patriarchal power was not absolute, and there were no obvious restrictions on women's private or public rights. The reality of the medieval Russian family was such that women's contribution to the family practically equaled that of men. The household could not function properly in the absence of a woman head to manage the activities of family members and apportion the budget. Therefore, it is not surprising that widowers hurried to remarry and bring a new housewife into the home.

The running of a medieval Russian household took an enormous amount of work. In lower-class families, the women got up before sunrise in order to fetch water, stoke the fire, grind flour, bake bread, and feed the family. During the day, a wife would help her husband in the fields or the workshop. Along with her husband, she looked after the cultivation and harvest of crops and saw to it that they were stored properly, so the flour would not spoil or the linseed oil go rancid (it was buried in the ground in wooden vessels). It was up to the mistress of the house to make sure that the family had not only flour but linen for clothing and leather for shoes.

Women of all social orders, including noblewomen and princesses, knew how to spin thread and make lace. Peasant women also learned from childhood how to weave cloth. The weaving of complex patterns can be accomplished on the most simple loom, but it demands a great deal of knowledge, patience, and attention. It was easier to embroider ornamentation onto finished cloth, and still easier to appliqué decorated panels on top; however, the holiday dress of aristocratic women was made of cloth with woven-in designs. Archeological evidence testifies to the high level of skill Russian women possessed in spinning, weaving, and embroidery. Iconographic representations of women sitting at looms depict them as happy, serene, and dignified.[31]

Spinning and weaving were the most common daily tasks in women's monasteries. These convents were huge households, where all labor was performed exclusively by women. The number of convents grew swiftly, and their land holdings even faster. The abbesses who headed large monasteries naturally became major organizers of domestic labor and caretakers of the monastery's prosperity. To do so, they had to engage in commerce and oversee the productivity of their lands. Nuns who retreated "from the world" did not necessarily give up their concerns with secular affairs.[32]

Not only nuns dealt with such matters. Birchbark documents in particular testify to women's familiarity with business. Their activities were hardly limited solely to housekeeping but rather included sophisticated monetary operations, including trade and money lending. Such activities, whether they occurred from the base of the family household or the monastery, brought women into direct contact with the outside world and allowed them to exceed the more limited role Orthodox teachings prescribed for them.[33]

For princesses and noblewomen, the obligations of overseeing all matters relating to their landholdings as well as the work of household servants made their everyday life as busy as that of women from the lower classes. The rights of women of the privileged orders to own property and direct its disposition were enshrined in the laws of many medieval Russian principalities. This right to property gave women a degree of economic and psychological independence in marriage.

"If Anyone Has a Daughter"

The legal system of medieval Russia paid exceptional attention to the status of women. Numerous statutes appear in its codes and charters to clarify the property rights of princesses and noblewomen as well as women among the small landholders, burgers, artisans, and slaves. Many of these provisions reflect earlier customary practices.

The earliest Russian legal document, the treaty between the Rus and Byzantium in 911, specifically mentions women's property. A wife had her "portion," distinct from that of her husband. According to the chronicles, this practice existed even before the state itself came into being. The earliest Russian law code, *Russkaia Pravda*, from the eleventh century, confirms this fundamental partition in familial property.

From where, exactly, did the woman's "portion" come? Private legal documents and birchbark letters indicate that women received this property in part from their dowries, but also from other sources. The term for "dowry," *pridanoe*, actually appears only much later, in the fifteenth century. Documents before that time instead speak of providing a woman with "whatever was dedicated to her" or "whatever was agreed to." If a woman's first husband died, she could bring with her into a second marriage "whatever her husband designated for her," referring to her portion of the property they had acquired in common. The size of a woman's portion depended upon whether she inherited under the provisions of a private will or, in its absence, under the provisions of the law. Of course, only married women or widows—that is, women legally of age—were empowered to determine the disposition of property. The laws regulating property prohibited the expulsion of a wife from her home without the wherewithal to survive, no matter what offenses she might have committed. The woman's "portion," which was mentioned explicitly in marital agreements, guaranteed her material sustenance in the case of divorce or widowhood.[34]

A woman's "portion" became part of the fund of familial property that both spouses worked to augment and were prohibited from squandering. Both spouses were supposed to know which pieces of the family's economic portfolio represented which person's contribution. Of course, husbands and wives could disagree; legal documents report conflicts, and normative sources warn about "arguments between husband and wife over property." In surviving cases, it was usually the husband who encroached upon the property of his wife. The law decisively enjoined husbands from attempting to "steal" from their wives, or from using spousal property as collateral for their own business ventures, or from paying creditors secretly out of their wives' dowry or other possessions. At the same time, some sources document cases where wives and daughters encroached on men's property.

One Novgorodian birchbark letter from the twelfth century illustrates the workings of women's property relations. In it, Anna told her brother Kliment how she and her daughter had loaned out money belonging to her husband Fedor while he was away. They had made a substantial profit (interest rates on loans were high in medieval Novgorod), and they had hoped to use the money they had earned for their own needs, without telling Fedor. The secret came out, however, and Fedor became enraged. He called his wife a "cow" and the daughter a "whore," and probably took the money away from them. Anna complained to her brother not so much about the failure of her enterprise but rather about the insult to her honor. Such situations apparently were quite common in the fourteenth and fifteenth centuries, because purchase agreements from this period carefully designate moneys, goods, and plots of land as belonging either to the wife or to the husband.[35]

Spouses did not necessarily come into conflict over property, but instead often resolved issues relating to the disposition of their property together. Private legal documents report numerous cases of a husband and wife purchasing land together. In a case from the fourteenth century, a husband filed a complaint with the judicial authorities to defend the property rights of his spouse. Neighbors had seized land belonging to his wife, and he wrote to demand justice because his wife had been "very insulted."

Because of the property rights Russian women enjoyed, widows did not consider themselves helpless and vulnerable. They could not legally be driven from their homes or left without sustenance. In Western Europe in this period, by comparison, widows often became the wards of their nearest male relatives. Russian women usually did not have guardians but rather were themselves named as custodians for underage children. Even *Russkaia Pravda* in the eleventh century confirms a widow's right to exercise independent guardianship of her children and to oversee the household as the head of the family. She lost these rights only if she entered into a second marriage.

Once the children were grown, the widowed mother still had the right to remain in her children's home. She could do so even over the objections of her son and kept control of her own "portion." In the feudal republics of Novgorod and Pskov, a son who refused to support his aged mother could be deprived of his inheritance from his father. When a dying husband commended his childless widow to the care of a monastery, he might transfer considerable resources to it for her support. Even so, the woman's "portion" was preserved explicitly for her, "so that she will not go hungry," the law directed.

Russian inheritance laws laid down specific provisions not only for a man's male relatives but also for his wife and daughters. Sons were obliged to arrange marriages for their sisters, providing them with the necessary dowry. The widow ranked among the deceased's primary heirs. Even adult sons could be made dependent upon her pleasure, if their father commended them to her in his will. The widow could refuse to give the sons their designated share of the property, "if they will squander it or fritter it away"; instead, she could bestow it upon her daughters, "whoever feeds her." However, the widow was not entitled to full control over all the deceased husband's property.

Although legally women were entitled only to their designated "portion," they strove to enhance their rights to the entire inheritance through their position as head of the household after their husband's death. Over time, the number of widows who gained the right to full control of the entire inheritance grew. By the end of the thirteenth century, it became the rule, rather than the exception, for women to inherit landed property. This practice, however, was not confirmed in law. It simply happened that testators bequeathed all the property that they acquired in their lifetimes to their wives, justifying their action solely by love. For example, Prince Vladimir Vasilkovich wrote in his will, "If after my death my princess wishes to enter a monastery, she may go; if she does not want to, she may do whatever she wishes. It is not up to me to decide what someone should do after my death."[36]

If the wife died first, her husband had the right to inherit from her. But under medieval Russian law, women had to draw up and sign their wills themselves, bequeathing their property. In this provision, Russian practice differed from the norms of Western Europe in this period. The widower did not automatically inherit his wife's "portion" under the provisions of Russian law; he had the right only to use it, preserving its substance for the deceased woman's children.

If he dissipated his children's inheritance from their mother, the law required that he make good the loss out of his own property.

After the death of their parents, the children inherited the property. In the first part of this period, the tenth to twelfth centuries, daughters did not have the right to receive shares; only sons and grandsons did. These heirs were supposed to "give their sisters in marriage, however they are able." Daughters inherited only in the absence of sons.

In the thirteenth century, this inequality was eliminated, and daughters could claim a share of the property "equal with their brothers." Even a man's mistress could claim a share of his property from his legally married widow, in order that she and her children would not "go hungry" or "suffer from poverty."[37]

Such were women's rights to property and inheritance under the law. But to what extent were the legal provisions fulfilled in everyday life? To what extent were women legally empowered and independent in the medieval Russian state?

Some women enjoyed virtually no rights, either under the law or in reality. A bondswoman (called *kholopka* or *roba*) did not receive any dowry or inheritance. Even her personal items and household possessions belonged to her owner. Women from the dependent peasantry (called *smerdy*) had the right both to an inheritance and to a dowry, just as among other social orders. The law did not make any distinction in this regard. Women of the privileged orders—princesses, noblewomen, and small landholders—enjoyed a wide variety of powers over property, which provided them with material independence. They possessed their dowries, which they could use with the "advice" of their husbands; as well as inheritances from relatives and property acquired during the marriage. Through the end of the twelfth century, women owned primarily movable property. But from then on, women more frequently received land. This trend continued until the beginning of the sixteenth century.

The movable property that women could control freely at first consisted only of household and personal items, which might nonetheless be very valuable. In the eleventh and twelfth centuries, wives or widows with children had significant monetary sums at their disposal. Birchbark documents record lengthy lists of revenues and debts attributed to women. Chronicles report many women who provided the funds to erect cathedrals: the wealthy Novgorodian burger "Poliuzhaia, the daughter of Zhiroshka"; the wife of Grand Prince Vsevolod, "the daughter of a Czech prince," who endowed the building of churches in Kiev and Vladimir in the mid- and late twelfth century. Amid praises for pious princesses and boyarinas, chroniclers record the specific funds they donated to churches and monasteries. Sometimes the amounts were so large that they were enough to pay for the construction of an entire cathedral—or more than one—or for the purchase of agricultural lands to benefit the church.[38]

The free control of landed property by women of the privileged orders of society (from single-homestead farmers to grand princesses) is the best indicator of women's substantial financial independence. Two twelfth-century sources demonstrate women's ownership of land at that time. One is the record of a lawsuit by two women claiming rights to inherit a piece of land. The second source is graffiti on the wall of the Cathedral of St. Sophia in Kiev, which talks about the purchase of "all of Boian's wife's land."

The running of complex and intricate business dealings required acumen. Documents from the thirteenth and the fourteenth centuries are filled with names of married women and widows who engaged in financial and legal pursuits without any restrictions. They bought and sold land, traded it, inherited it, received it as a gift or dowry, mortgaged it, divided it among heirs, and donated it to the church. Unlike in Western Europe, women concluded many of these property deals independently, without the participation of male kinsfolk—sons, husbands, brothers, or fathers.[39]

Most of the surviving documents concerning women's landed property are donation charters, recording gifts to the church. This is not because women did little else with their land besides grant it to ecclesiastical endowments, but rather because documents housed in monastic archives tended to escape the destruction that afflicted family homes and governmental institutions. But donations to the church, often of significant amounts of property, were a common means of expressing piety in the Middle Ages, for both men and women. Frequently, dying landholders would bequeath a portion of their inheritance "for the sake of my soul," so that the clergy of the beneficiary institution would remember them in their prayers. A husband who made arrangements of this kind generally left another portion of his estate to his wife, who in turn made a similar bequest to fulfill her husband's "instructions."

Of course, sometimes widows found their husbands' estates to be in such a ruinous state that they had to turn the inheritance over to creditors instead of the church. In such cases, widows did not shy away from negotiating with the monastic leaders, arguing that the

monastery should inherit the debts as well as the property. In fulfilling their husbands' "instructions" to donate property, widows might
retain the right "to feed themselves from it"—that is, to retain lifetime use of the income from the bequest.

The wealthiest women in medieval Russia were the wives of the
princes of Kiev, Rostov, Vladimir, Moscow, and other major principalities. They held huge tracts of "dowry lands," which were portions of
state territories. Princesses were expected to preserve these holdings
intact, "not dividing them," in order to bequeath them to the eldest
son, or, in the absence of sons, to a daughter. Princesses could be
much more venturesome in their use of lands they acquired themselves, after marriage. Their husbands had no rights to such lands,
except those their wives gave them. For example, Grand Prince
Dmitrii Donskoi wrote that his wife Evdokia was "free to give or sell to
whomever she wants" the property that she had purchased or had
obtained by some other means.

In the fourteenth century, it became common to designate certain
property that could be disposed of without restrictions. Fathers could
give daughters such property as a dowry or inheritance; so could
mothers and grandparents. As a concession to real practices, lawmakers in the thirteenth century permitted daughters to inherit equally
with their brothers; wives were already entitled to their "portion."

Documents of the thirteenth and fourteenth centuries reflect dozens of variants in the forms of women's inheritance. Women not only
owned land free and clear, but they might also be co-owners with
their husbands or other relatives, including female relations. They
might also receive property in usufruct, with a lifetime guarantee of
income. Or they could be the beneficiaries of conditional donations
to ecclesiastical institutions.

Male heirs did not always receive preferential treatment. A daughter, in the absence of sons, or even a daughter-in-law might receive
five-sixths of an inheritance, while a nephew got only the remainder. An
analysis of the documents from the Muscovite royal house demonstrates
that the percentage of property held by women in the family gradually
rose. Certain lands passed exclusively through the female line; in the
absence of daughters, daughters-in-law inherited, and after them, their
own daughters, granddaughters, or even mothers-in-law.

In this way, by the end of the fifteenth century, the majority of
married women and widows from well-to-do social ranks had the right
to own and dispose of both movable and immovable property almost
on a par with men. Nonnormative sources, including deeds, narrative

literature, and epigraphical inscriptions, demonstrate that the rights inscribed in law were indeed exercised in practice.

Women's independence in property holding mirrored their autonomy in the judicial sphere.[40] Medieval Russian courts did not distinguish between accuser and defendant; both parties were considered plaintiffs, who could make charges and face conviction. In the case of conflicting testimony, a judicial duel was fought, where God (it was believed) would grant victory to the person telling the truth. (Judicial duels were not fought to the death, but combatants battled with pikes or staves until one or another party conceded defeat.) In addition to eyewitnesses, the medieval Russian judicial process valued character witnesses, who confirmed the veracity of someone else's sworn testimony. Women were empowered to participate on their own in the legal process, according to the judicial charters issued by grand princes and local principalities in the twelfth and thirteenth centuries. They even received certain privileges. For example, a nobleman who was suing a widow not only had to swear that he was telling the truth, but he was required to defend his testimony in a judicial duel. The law mandated that women fulfill the same procedures as men, except they were allowed to make their depositions not at court but in their own homes. Women could refuse to fight personally in a judicial duel and could hire a substitute instead. But when both plaintiffs were women, the law dictated that they "fight in single combat, and there shall be no substitute for either woman." The idea of women taking to the field of battle argues against the image of the fragile Russian female.[41]

Private legal documents recounting the illegal seizure of property demonstrate women's active participation in the judicial process. Women appear not only as victims but also as energetic and decisive defenders of their own legal rights. Women also used the legal process to gain control of other people's lands, fabricating false documents to "prove" their claims. In 1499, Princesses Maria and Alexandra of Slutsk forged papers in order to seize a portion of the lands owned by Maria's brother.

Not only princesses and noblewomen availed themselves of the judicial process in medieval Russia. One provision of the law empowered women of the lower class, the wives of dependent peasants, to sue noble landholders over property rights. In such cases, the woman was required to bring to court someone to vouch for her, such as a man of the same social class.

The rights of women to serve as character witnesses were more ambiguous. Women and men from the lower social ranks—slaves, indentured servants, and *smerdy*—could not serve as witnesses in cases involving their lords. As the law stated, "the words of a man or woman slave against their lord shall not be believed." But within the same social order, there were no limitations on women's capacity to serve as witnesses before the end of the fifteenth century. The only restrictions—and these held for men and women both—were that the character witness had to be adult, in right mind, and not implicated in the case. Women's names appear among the lists of witnesses to legal documents concerning both civil and criminal matters.

As discussed above, princesses possessed their own seals, which were an essential item for validating documents in the judicial process. Women of lesser but still noble families also had seals, usually made of wax rather than lead, as princesses' were. Noble women used these seals themselves, and their husbands, sons, and sons-in-law borrowed them. The legal documents themselves report how the seals were used: "He sealed this document of his mother's with Maria's own seal"; "he sealed this purchase agreement with the seal of Ovdotia, his mother-in-law." Women's seals might contain not only the name of the owner but also a small picture, similar to the weights women used in spinning thread.[42]

Princesses frequently served as judges in the territories they ruled. They decided who won in judicial duels. For example, one judicial decision from the fifteenth century concludes, "the grand princess, having heard the case, ordered that Danilko be acquitted, the meadow be awarded to the metropolitanate, and that Sysoi be convicted."[43] The judge in this case was the Muscovite princess Maria Iaroslavna. On estates belonging to convents, the abbess would preside over the court.

Women's judicial role helps to explain why the older legal restrictions on women's activities were so quickly abolished in medieval Russia. A system where a husband is responsible for the transgressions of his wife cannot survive in a society where women can themselves preside over courts of justice, participate in judicial duels, and testify as witnesses. All women, except those in bondage or slavery, answered for themselves. Most offenses in medieval Russia, whether criminal, civil, or moral, were punished by fines, which differed according to the social rank of the victim, without regard to gender. Each article in the criminal codes merely added "the same for a woman," underlining that men and women had the same responsibilities before the law.

In the medieval Russian legal system, a whole range of offenses, most of them involving religious or familial life and moral conduct, fell under the jurisdiction of the church. The church could levy fines and impose penances on women as well as men for violations of its norms. Concern with sexual misconduct dominated ecclesiastical regulations, but there were other sorts of improprieties as well: a woman who beat her husband was fined three *grivny* (a bar of silver, used as money); a woman who beat another woman was fined twice as much. Specific provisions punished "fighting in the manner of women," by biting, scratching, and pinching. Statutes imposed fines on women who swore at their husbands or other men, or hit them or spit in their faces. When women attacked clerics in this manner, the fines were greater than for attacks against laymen. The church strongly discouraged women, who ought to be submissive, from engaging in such aggressive behavior and made no allowance even for self-defense.

Much of our information about the norms of women's conduct comes from penitential questions. It is difficult to know how often women answered their priests in the affirmative when asked about such improprieties, or whether they felt obliged to confess at all. The women described in such glowing terms in the chronicles seem to be utterly without imperfection. But perhaps this image reflects only their virtues, and whatever vices they may have had have been lost to history. And while it is easier to imagine a fishwife cursing and brawling than a princess, perhaps they, too, could be assertive and defiant, even if they were not portrayed that way in the sources.

As a rule, Russian law defended women's honor and value, from princesses to simple peasant women. But slave women did not enjoy this protection; the law stated, "If a master beats his slave woman and she dies from it, there is no offense in this." If some other persons, besides the master, killed a slave woman, they were subject to a considerable fine, more, even, than for the murder of a slave man. The import of the law was not defense of the woman's life but rather of her master's property, and slave women were valuable because they produced more slaves. Otherwise the wergeld—the legal value of a person's life—was set at the same level for men and women of the same social order: "for a male or female artisan, 12 *grivny*;" "for a [free] man or woman, 40 *grivny*." The statute about the wergeld for free women added a caveat: "if she is guilty, only 20 *grivny*." Did medieval Russian women so often involve themselves in scandalous conduct that such a provision had to be made for extenuating circumstances in their deaths?

Medieval Russian law gave equal weight to attacks on a person's honor as to attacks on the person physically. The fine for raping a woman was the same as the fine for murdering a woman of the same social order. One law even offered protection of slave women from rape by their masters, ordering that the victims of such attacks be freed. It is hard to say whether this provision was actually followed, because there is ample evidence that masters made sexual use of their bondswomen. Officially, however, masters had no right to the sexual favors of women subject to them.

The crime of insulting an "honorable" woman by attributing sexual misconduct to her was equated with the crime of rape. The amount of the fine depended upon her social rank. The fine for insult usually equaled that for rape, but sometimes it even equaled the amount levied for a woman's murder. Public insult with words was regarded in medieval Russia as even more damaging to a woman's honor than a physical attack. Early Russian law did not stipulate a specific punishment for a husband who attacked his own wife physically, but the wife was entitled to make a complaint against him in public and to her priest. But in the fourteenth century, a statute permitted a woman to demand a divorce from an abusive husband. But only if a woman suffered a miscarriage as a result of her husband's beatings did the law punish him for his violence, charging him with murder. The law severely punished children who attacked their mothers; no matter what the cause of familial conflict, a son who beat his mother could be forcibly shorn as a monk, if his mother agreed to it.[44]

Thus, in general, the status of women before the law did not differ greatly from the status of men. The differences sometimes worked to women's benefit and sometimes to their detriment. But particularly from the thirteenth century on, women of the privileged orders enjoyed substantial empowerment before the law, especially in the area of property rights. These rights allowed women to act independently both in the family and in the society as a whole.

A Woman's Calling Card

Women have generally been evaluated, especially on first acquaintance, not so much on their intelligence or character as on their appearance. For many women, dress was and is a mirror of identity. The variety of forms of clothing testify to the manners in which women are viewed in society. The ways in which dress confines women's bodies or leaves them free, and the ways of revealing and emphasizing the beauty of the female body, all reflect women's status.

But in all periods, women's dress reflected not only societal norms but also individual women's originality and conception of beauty. In the medieval period, a person's costume functioned as a "calling card," displaying that individual's rank in society, wealth, profession, family status, and locality.

From the earliest period, Russian women wore two layers of clothing, inner and outer, necessitated by the cool climate and the requirements of hygiene. Even the poorest women wore a loosely cut shift, usually made of bleached linen, as an undergarment. The sleeves were made long, even past the fingertips; they were fastened at the wrist with bracelets made of metal, wood, leather, birchbark, or glass. The shift was gathered at the waist with a belt, which in the pre-Christian period served as an amulet to block the path of evil spirits. It was believed that unclean forces could not penetrate through openings protected by lacy, embroidered belts. Archeologists have uncovered such bracelets and belts in their excavations, and they are depicted in manuscript miniatures from the fourteenth to the sixteenth centuries.[45]

Those portions of the shift that were visible from under the outer garment—the sleeves, hem, and collar—were often heavily ornamented. Peasant women used tiny beads, embroidery, or ribbons with lace or punchwork to decorate their shifts. City women preferred small freshwater pearls. Noblewomen adorned their shifts with sequins of light metal. In the fourteenth and fifteenth centuries, princesses and the wealthiest boyarinas wore shifts of silk for formal dress. Russian merchants imported this lustrous silk from Byzantium and Persia at staggering cost. Silk garments were considered a great luxury, and they were tended with care and worn rarely.[46]

The outerwear of Russian women of the tenth to the fifteenth centuries did not vary in cut among social orders, but differed in the working of the cloth. The outer garments displayed the wearer's degree of wealth or poverty. The garments of princesses and boyarinas incorporated many more elements of detailing than those of the lower classes.

One basic element of women's dress was a wrap-around skirt, which Russians adopted from the costume of steppe nomads. These wrapskirts could be made of linen or wool and could be single- or multicolored.[47] Urban women stopped wearing these skirts by the fourteenth century, but peasant women continued to dress in this style for several centuries more.[48]

Over the shift and the wrapskirt medieval Russian women wore garments of various lengths and styles, made from wool, cotton, or, for the rich, velvet. Frescoes and miniatures of princesses, noblewomen, and their entourages show that they preferred long, unbelted robes topped by an open cloak. Both the robe and the cloak were decorated with edging along the seams.[49] Capes brought by travelers from the East were very fashionable among the nobility. These were simple rectangular pieces of cloth that were thrown over the shoulders and were fastened with brooches or buckles. Cloth then fell to the ground in wide pleats, sometimes gathered in at the waist with a belt. These belts, like outer dress in general, were heavily decorated. The ornamentation included favorite motifs: crescent moons, interwoven strands, or heart-shaped figures under round arches.[50] Because such ornamentation was such painstaking and time-consuming work, usually it was done on panels of cloth, which could be removed from old garments and sewn on new ones. Thus the wills of princesses bequeathed decorated cloth panels to their daughters and daughters-in-law.[51]

Women's ceremonial dress featured large detached collars, made of silk, velvet, or brocade and embroidered with gold and silver thread and pearls. Leather or birchbark interfacings provided stiffness. These collars could be extremely valuable. In the fourteenth century, Princess Uliana of Volotsk bequeathed a collar embroidered "with 3,190 seed pearls" to her children.[52]

In the cold Russian winters, women, even in the poorest families, wore furs. Wealthy women sewed coats of valuable furs, such as ermine, sable, marten, lynx, and beaver, while poor women used cheaper furs. The most accessible and durable pelt was sheepskin. From the thirteenth century on, it became stylish for women to decorate their dresses and sleeves with borders of fur. These borders could reach half a yard in width, as foreign visitors noted with surprise. Unmarried maidens wore squirrel and rabbit furs; wealthy married women considered it embarrassing to wear such frivolous coats.

These fur coats were sewn with the pile inside, as a lining. Poor families might lack the funds to buy cloth for an outer layer, but this "bare leather" coat was considered crude. Most women aspired to own not just one but several outer layers, made from different sorts of bright-colored cloth, to wear over the fur lining. Russian princesses of the fifteenth century might own dozens of such overcoats: "crimson, red, dove gray, pastel blue, green," or "from the skins of squirrel bellies," or "two sable coats from natural [blue-gray] velvet with gold embroidery," or "an overcoat, covered with Venetian silk," which were listed in the fifteenth-century will of a princess of Kholm as an inheritance for her daughter.

Fresco depictions of aristocratic women indicate that they preferred multicolored clothing in bright, rich tones. The medieval Russian language records dozens of terms for different colors in the context of the description of cloth. Natural dyes were used to obtain these colors: blue from cornflowers and bilberries; yellow from blackthorn and birchbark; golden brown from onion skins, oak bark, and pears. But the favorite color was red: the words for "red" (*krasnyi*) and "beautiful" (*krasivyi*) have the same root, and red had magical powers of protection. Sources of red-brown dyes were quite common: buckwheat, St.-John's-wort, the cores of wild apples, alder, and buckthorn.[53]

The richness of aristocratic women's ceremonial clothing, with their multicolored cloth and gold and silver embroidery, demonstrated their wealth at such occasions as wedding feasts. Descriptions of fashionable young women's wedding trousseaux survive. For example, Anastasia, the daughter of Prince Mikhail of Veria and Beloozero, owned close to thirty dresses, some for summer and others for winter. They were made of different fabrics, from silk to brocade to velvet to chiffon, which was called "cloth of air" in medieval Russia, so thin and light was this fine cotton. Anastasia's coats, according to the compiler of the document, were particularly fine: white, gold and yellow, crimson and green, and red, lined with marten, sable, and squirrel. The red coat was made of fox fur, and a single fox pelt cost more than a silver ruble—a peasant's dues for an entire year. The prince of Beloozero certainly provided handsomely for his daughter![54]

Many types of women's outerwear were intended to be worn thrown over the shoulders or unfastened, so that the clothing underneath was visible. Under coats or cloaks, women wore jackets of different types—short and wide to the waist or long in front, with narrow, wrist-length sleeves. These jackets were often meant to be worn unfastened but were decorated with valuable buttons or fur.

Women's costume, whether for daily wear or for special occasions, was completed with a headdress. Headdresses served many purposes: they completed the look of the outfit, they exhibited the prosperity of the family, and they fulfilled the obligation of feminine modesty, because married women were not supposed to go out in public with their heads uncovered. This last tradition derived from the period of paganism, when women's hair was considered dangerous, and

Formal headdress of a wealthy married woman of the twelfth–thirteenth centuries, as reconstructed by P.P. Tolochko.

women covered their heads to protect themselves and their relatives from evil forces. The Christian tradition of women covering their heads in church arises from the same sources.[55]

The headdresses of married women fully hid their hair, but unmarried girls were not obliged to cover their heads so rigorously. They could wear their hair loose or braided into a single plait. The rebraiding of a bride's hair into two plaits, which were pinned in a crown around her head, was one of the central rituals of the wedding celebration. A maiden joined the ranks of mature women only after her wedding night, when she first donned the married woman's headdress.[56]

Maidens' headdresses resembled crowns and were derived from the model of floral wreaths. A narrow band of metal or leather, covered with fabric, circled her forehead and was secured at the back of the head. Sometimes girls wore simply a browband of brocade or linen. Frequently, strands of hair at the temples were plaited into little braids and strung with little bells made of bronze or glass. Ornaments for maidens' hair or headdresses were very popular in the tenth to thirteenth centuries; they took the form of hollow metal hemispheres, filled with bits of cloth soaked in aromatic resins.

The headdresses of married women resembled those of unmarried girls in that they were also tall and had a rigid base. But these also incorporated elements of the kerchief, which was one of the oldest forms of headcovering for women. The most important part of a married woman's headdress was the scarf that was placed over her braided hair. The ends of the scarf fell over her shoulders, back, and bosom. In winter, a fur or fur-edged hat covered the scarf. In summer, it was a tall wreath that covered the top of the head. Both types of headdresses were richly decorated, especially in the front, with whimsical designs composed of eyelets, embroidery, metal and glass beads, and fringes strung with tiny metal, glass, or pearl beads.[57]

Married women made greater use of ornamentation than unmarried girls. The jewelry Russian women wore on their heads, hands, necks, and waists not only displayed their wealth but also functioned as amulets to protect them from the "evil eye." For that reason, much of the jewelry from the early period was designed to make noise—to scare away evil spirits. Other amulets took the shape of sun-signs, birds or sirens (the symbol of domestic prosperity), and horses with long ears and curled tails (the symbol of goodness, fidelity, and friendship).

Earrings were not particularly common in Russia in the tenth to thirteenth centuries, but bracelets, rings, beads, and necklaces were. Some necklaces, called *grivny* (like the form of money), were twisted or flat chokers, made of bronze, alloys, or silver. Others consisted of complex plaited chains and pendants with little bells or religious medallions. The intricacy of some pieces defies modern replication. Much jewelry from this period was manufactured to the specifications of the persons who commissioned the pieces and reflects their artistic inspiration. Jewelry of gold and silver with precious and semi-precious stones was passed from mother to daughters to granddaughters in princely families over many generations. Every will from a princely family includes a detailed description of the testator's jewelry, scrupulously listing all defects, damage, missing stones, and repairs.

An important part of a woman's costume was a purse, worn attached to her belt. Purses were both decorative and functional, because garments in this period had no pockets. The purses, made of cloth or plaited from fine metal wire, were often decorated with embroidery, pendants, bells, and little locks, and themselves could be very valuable.[58]

Decorative buckles, clasps, pins, and fibulae were used to fasten blouses at the neck, attach pendants and amulets to dresses, and hold household implements such as keys, knives, flint, and scissors to belts. Many of the clasps and pins intended for formal occasions were made of gold, silver, bronze, or alloys and decorated with precious stones.[59]

Footwear completed the costume of a Russian woman. In villages women wore shoes woven from bast—thin strips of the inner bark of larch or birch trees. The strips of bark were soaked and weighted in a press for a long time and then woven. Sometimes the selvages from bolts of cloth were interwoven with the bast strips. In order to make one pair of bast shoes in a size for a small woman, it was necessary to chop down three or four saplings. Such bast shoes might last only a week. Shoes could also be woven out of strips of coarse leather, but these were much more expensive than bast.

Urban women were embarrassed to go around in bast shoes and instead wore leather footwear. The leather came from the skins of horses, bulls, or pigs, or, for the well-to-do, soft goatskin. In order to have good-looking boots or half-boots to wear in public or to feasts, aristocratic women would place their orders months in advance. The shoemaker would measure their feet. Then he would prepare the leather, curing the skins for weeks in *kvas* (a sort of beer brewed from bread). He would then tan it with roots from willow, alder, or oak trees. The next stages involved scraping, stretching, greasing, kneading, and dyeing the leather. A pattern for the boots was sketched out on birchbark. The tops of dress boots were decorated with embroidery, leather braid, cut-outs, or metal studs. The toes were made elaborate, so the boots would attract notice from under long skirts. And the heels were quite high—two to three inches. The heels were made sometimes of horizontal layers of leather or else of a solid core wrapped in a leather covering. For bridal dress, half-boots were decorated with pearls.

Ordinary urban women wore much plainer footwear which in form resembled modern-day infants' booties. The leather for these shoes was not tanned (a long and expensive process) but only kneaded and greased. These slippers had no seams: the leather was simply cut in an oval shape, and a drawstring was laced through slits to gather it. The soles were reinforced with several layers of birchbark. These shoes were very durable but not water-repellent. If they developed holes, they could be repaired with decorative leather patches. Even everyday shoes usually had some sort of ornamentation, with embroidery, cut-outs, or beads, according to the owner's individual taste.[60]

In the larger commercial cities such as Novgorod and Pskov, cheap, professionally made shoes replaced home-produced footwear by the thirteenth or fourteenth century. Large cobblers' workshops flooded the market with mass-produced footwear in a limited variety of styles. Medieval Russian urban women's desire to dress like everyone else in this case became an inevitability.

The images of medieval Russian women's outward appearance, as recorded in miniatures and frescoes, indicate that clothing reflects not only the variations of tastes from period to period, and not only the individual predilections of individual women. Costume also reflects the attitude toward women in a society, and the dress of women in medieval Russia emphasized their inner dignity and emotional restraint, without restricting their freedom of movement. Nothing in women's dress degraded them. The depictions of the contemporaries of Princess Olga, St. Evfrosinia of Polotsk, Grand Princess Evdokia of Moscow, and boyarina Marfa Boretskaia, dressed in the fashion of their time, show them to be stately and filled with inner tranquility and confidence.

Chapter 2

The Terem *and Beyond: Women in Muscovy*

From Ruler to Regent

The sixteenth and seventeenth centuries marked the final stage in the formation and unification of the Russian state. This was the period of the rapid rise of Russian national consciousness and the formation of a distinct Muscovite culture that differed from its early Russian roots and the developing Ukrainian and Belorussian cultures.

The history of Muscovy may be divided into three periods. The beginning of the sixteenth century saw the strengthening of Muscovy's economic position, the expansion of its territory, and the attainment of international recognition. In order to rule a diverse and expanding realm, the Muscovite grand princes developed new governmental forms, new laws, and new administrative procedures that centralized power in Moscow and in the person of the monarch. As the only free bastion of Eastern Orthodox Christianity—Constantinople having fallen to the Turks, along with Bulgaria, Serbia, and Romania—Muscovy felt impelled to enforce its dictates more strictly than before.

The second half of the sixteenth century and the beginning of the seventeenth were marked by great failures. Despite the long and devastating Livonian War, Russia failed to gain a port on the Baltic Sea. Tsar Ivan IV, called *groznyi* ("the Terrible" or "the Awesome"), introduced repressive methods of governance, including the formation of a private army, the *Oprichnina*, to track down supposed traitors. Political chaos resulted from his policies, exacerbated by a dynastic crisis: Ivan killed his older son and heir, and his second son was mentally retarded and childless. The ruinous taxation Ivan imposed caused unrest in the countryside, culminating in a peasant revolt led by Ivan Bolotnikov. At one point, Polish and Swedish armies occupied large sections of Russian territory and jeopardized the very existence of an independent Russian state. This "Time of Troubles" came to an end only when the Zemskii Sobor—the "Assembly of the Land," then dominated by the gentry cavalry and the merchantry—elected Michael Romanov as tsar in 1613.[1]

From the second third of the seventeenth century onward, Muscovy recovered economically and politically. Economic and political improvements came at a cost, however; most of the peasantry was reduced to the status of serfs in order to provide for the financial needs of the elite. Reforms to the political and legal system were introduced gradually, and diplomatic and commercial ties with foreign countries were expanded. The Russian Orthodox Church also responded to the influence of the West, through Ukrainian and Belorussian academies that had close ties with Greek and Jesuit intellectuals. This influence was not welcomed in all circles, and it triggered a schism in the church when traditionalists, usually called "Old Believers," resisted innovations. All these changes laid the groundwork for the reforms of Peter the Great and Russia's transformation into a world power in the early eighteenth century.

The sixteenth and seventeenth centuries witnessed a sharp transition in the status of women, not only in Russia but in Europe as a whole. In the West, the rapid development of a money economy, urban centers, and the middle class; population growth; and the technological revolution (from the introduction of gunpowder to the invention of the printing press) all laid the groundwork for the transformation of women's legal and social status. The changes in the demographic contours of Western society altered the perception of women's place in it. The nuclear family became the norm, and the character of women's work changed. The intellectual movements of the period—the development of Renaissance humanism and the Protestant Reformation—brought their own insights into the role of women in the family and society, which differed significantly from medieval attitudes of misogyny and courtly love.

All these processes in Western Europe affected women in Muscovy only to a limited degree. Only echoes of Renaissance humanism reached Muscovy, filtered through Poland and Lithuania, and its precepts had little influence on the popular mindset. Russia also experienced the growth of cities in this period, but urbanization remained slight and the middle class small compared to Western Europe. While West European countries developed representative institutions and concepts of the rule of law and of civil society, the Russian government strengthened its centralized power, particularly with the consolidation of serfdom. The internal changes in Muscovite society also altered the status of women, but in ways different from those in the West.

The participation of women, even those from the privileged orders of society, in Russian political and cultural life declined. The chronicles of the sixteenth and seventeenth centuries do not report any "matriarchates" of the sort found in the earlier period. Especially during the period of political disunity of the twelfth to fifteenth centuries, many princesses had had the opportunity to take commanding positions with powers equivalent to those of men, but when power became centralized in the hands of the autocrat, even the women of the tsar's family were removed from participation in governmental affairs. And when they did become involved in political intrigues, it was more often by accident than by intent.[2]

But women's roles in the first part of the sixteenth century more closely resembled those in the preceding period, as illustrated by two women named Elena—the wife and the sister of Grand Prince Vasilii III of Moscow. Elena the wife secured the throne for her son, Ivan IV. Elena the sister became the wife of Grand Prince Alexander of Lithuania in 1496.

Russia and Lithuania were political, military, and religious rivals in the fifteenth century; the marriage of Elena and Alexander was an attempt to resolve their differences. According to the marriage contract, Elena retained her adherence to the Orthodox faith, even though Roman Catholicism was the official religion of Lithuania. The agreement also mandated that several Russian noblewomen remain with Elena, but her husband soon had them exiled from Vilnius, fearing the spread of Eastern Orthodoxy at his court and the Russification of Lithuanian society. Elena was isolated among people who spoke a different language and had foreign customs, and assimilation would compromise her adherence to her Orthodox faith. Still, Elena had learned from her mother, Sofia Paleologue, how to respond to a foreign culture with tact and dignity.

Elena was not just a figurehead sent to solidify a shaky peace but rather a principal player in Muscovite foreign policy. From the first days of her residence in Lithuania, she carried on a regular correspondence with her father in Moscow. This correspondence was part personal and part diplomatic. In his letters, Ivan III reported to his daughter about matters of state and foreign policy and urged her to be more persistent and more consistent in her requests to her husband, especially in regard to the acquisition of new territories. Many of these territories were ethnically East Slavic and religiously Orthodox, and Elena took on the role of mediator between groups of Russian and Orthodox aristocrats and their Lithuanian and Catholic counterparts. As a result of these circumstances and her own activities, Elena became the focus for Orthodox aspirations in Lithuania; she called herself her father's "servant and helper." She persistently refused to convert to Catholicism, although both her husband and the Catholic clergy of his court urged her to do so.

The year 1501 was a turning point for Elena, when her husband succeeded to the throne of Poland. Elena thus became the queen of Poland, but this event coincided with a declaration of war between Russia and Lithuania. The Catholic clergy stepped up the pressure on the Orthodox queen, and even the pope himself threatened to dissolve her marriage if she refused to convert. But Elena refused to bend. At the same time she tried to reestablish friendly relations between Muscovy and Lithuania and urged her father to make the first steps toward the ending the bloodshed. "Everyone had hoped," she wrote to Ivan III, "that good things, an eternal peace, love rooted in kinship, and friendship would come to Lithuania through me, but they see how I have brought everything bad."

The peace Elena fought for was concluded in 1503. Under its terms, Muscovy received a large territory in the west: seventy districts with nineteen cities. The genealogical history of the Russian royal house, compiled in the sixteenth century, gave Elena special recognition for the acquisition of this territory, calling it an "act of piety."

With the reestablishment of peace, Elena's correspondence with her aging father became still more extensive. He sought the advice of his former "servitor" on a wide variety of familial issues. Elena's influence among the Polish and Lithuanian aristocracy grew, and that generated secret disaffection in the court. The unexpected death of Ivan III in 1505 and of Alexander in 1506 caused Elena to abandon many of her ambitious plans. She began negotiations with her relatives about returning to Moscow, but before she was able to do so, enemies killed her by mixing poison with her mead.[3]

Elena's death opened the way for the formation of an anti-Muscovite alliance comprising Poland, Lithuania, the Livonian knights, and the Crimean and Kazan Tatar hordes. But Elena's brother, Vasilii III, who had ascended to the throne of Moscow, counted on the help of the powerful Lithuanian magnate Prince M.L. Glinskii in opposing this alliance. Glinskii had made his pro-Russian sympathies apparent during Elena's lifetime and had helped Moscow to secure quick victories in its armed conflicts with Lithuania from 1507 to 1522. The most significant of these victories resulted in the Russian annexation of the principality of Smolensk.

Meanwhile, Vasilii III was embroiled in an unhappy familial situation. He had married for political gain, and his wife Solomonia, the daughter of the boyar Iurii Saburov, was barren. He resolved upon a step unprecedented in the history of the Russian ruling house: forcibly to divorce the grand princess and confine her in a convent. According to popular rumors, after taking monastic vows, Solomonia bore a child.

According to the chronicler, Vasilii chose his second wife for love: "because of the beauty of her face and her young age." However, his choice indicates that he had political motives, because he chose Prince Glinskii's niece, Elena, the daughter of Glinskii's younger brother Vasilii.

Vasilii III and the entire Russian court expected only one thing from Elena Glinskaia: that she give birth to an heir. However, the young wife immediately took charge of the grand princely household, making her husband fulfill her whims, to the great disaffection of his boyars. For example, to please his wife, Vasilii broke with ancient Russian tradition and shaved his beard.

The long-awaited heir to the throne, the future Ivan IV, was born four years after the wedding, in 1530. The four-year delay, and Solomonia's long barrenness, fed rumors that it was not Vasilii who fathered the child, but rather his favorite, Prince I.F. Telepnev-Obolenskii. But Vasilii ignored these rumors, and commissioned the building of the Church of the Ascension in the village of Kolomenskoe, near Moscow, to celebrate the birth of his son.

A little more than a year later, Elena bore a second son, Iurii. Soon afterward, Vasilii contracted an incurable illness. Recognizing his condition, he secretly drafted a will in which he bequeathed the throne to his son Ivan and "to my wife Elena with the boyar council." He directed Elena to "govern the state in the name of her son" until he came of age. Thus Vasilii did not fully empower his wife, but rather gave priority to the boyars. However, when Vasilii died in 1533, Elena sidestepped the council and took on the reins of power herself. She arranged matters so that the members of the boyar council had to refer all questions and requests to her.

The political situation in Muscovy after the death of Vasilii III was very unstable. Besides Elena, not only the boyar council but also Vasilii's brothers Iurii and Andrei had claims to power. The ruling boyars and the old aristocratic families despised the Glinskiis, who did not have generations of service to the princes of Moscow behind them. Thus Elena had to work energetically to consolidate her hold on the throne.

Seven days after Vasilii's death, Elena imprisoned his brother Prince Iurii in order to intimidate him. She also categorically refused to honor the claims of Prince Andrei to extend the lands under his authority, at the same time expelling him from the regency council. She also realized that her own uncle, Prince M.L. Glinskii, represented a danger to her rule, because he had allied himself with the powerful boyar group aligned against her. She condemned him and his associates, and he died in prison. Thus Elena held on to power.

Elena was cold, calculating, and suspicious, and her son, the future autocrat Ivan the Terrible, learned from her, as conspirators tried to involve him in their plots from an early age. Like most rulers of her day, Elena chose a "carrot and stick" approach to governance, providing her supporters, including foremost Prince I.F. Telepnev-Obolenskii, with lavish grants of land and tax exemptions.

From the first days of her regency, Elena Glinskaia continued the policy of centralization advanced by her deceased husband. She introduced measures to limit landholding by the great boyars and especially by monasteries, effectively eliminating their immunity from taxation. Her attempt to alter the system of local government anticipated her son's reforms.

Elena also took steps to improve Russia's defenses against foreign invasion. Like Grand Princess Olga centuries before, Elena Glinskaia ordered the immediate construction of settlements in the border region and the construction of fortifications in cities situated on prime invasion routes. The cities of Balakhna and Starodub were founded during the years of Elena's rule, and on the western frontier, new cantons were established that eventually became defensive centers. New kremlins (fortified city centers) were built in Iaroslavl, Vladimir, and Ustiug. A second defensive wall was built to surround the center of Moscow—the area now called Kitaigorod.

The most significant of Elena's activities in regard to internal governance was the monetary reform of 1535. Previously, each principality had its own system of coinage; Elena's measure promoted the standardization of currency conversion throughout the country and strove to eliminate counterfeiting.

Elena also enjoyed successes in foreign policy. In 1534, King Sigismund of Lithuania demanded the return of the cities that had been ceded to Muscovy under Vasilii III. He hoped to take advantage of the internal disorder and the weak government in Moscow. However, Elena's government rejected Sigismund's ultimatum. In the war that ensued, Elena's favorite, Prince I.F. Telepnev-Obolenskii, was so successful that in 1536 peace was concluded on Moscow's terms. After that war, almost three hundred Lithuanian noble families emigrated to Moscow to seek service there. At the same time, the Russian government engaged in a complicated diplomatic game with the Tatar khanates of Kazan and Crimea to the south and east. Elena herself led the negotiations with their envoys and made the decisions. In 1537, she succeeded in concluding a treaty with Sweden for free trade, in which King Gustav Vasa also promised not to intervene on behalf of Livonia or Lithuania against Russian interests.

Elena was young—barely thirty years old—and full of ambitious plans when she died suddenly on April 3, 1538. Contemporaries did not doubt that she had been poisoned, but there is no conclusive evidence of it.[4]

After Elena Glinskaia, no woman occupied the Russian throne, even as regent, for almost a century and a half. Few Russian princesses married abroad, and little is known about the ones who did. Women did not totally disappear from the pages of history, but their activities were overshadowed by the undertakings of their more prominent sons, brothers, and husbands.

However, women still could carry significant political weight in the Muscovite court of the first half of the sixteenth century. One example is Agrafena Cheliadnina, the sister of Elena Glinskaia's favorite, Telepnev-Obolenskii, and nanny to the infant Ivan IV. The chronicles report that Ivan was very attached to her. Vasilii and Elena valued her services and granted significant amounts of land to her. While in charge of the young autocrat, Agrafena did not neglect her own interests, issuing orders to benefit her landholdings in different regions of northeast Russia. She wielded enormous influence at court until Elena's death. When a group of boyars under the leadership of the Shuiskii family came to power in April 1538, Agrafena was arrested. In order to limit her meddling in the internal affairs of government, she was exiled to Kargopol and forcibly shorn as a nun.[5]

In the 1540s, Elena Glinskaia's mother, Anna, took her place in the internal political struggles surrounding the accession of Ivan IV to the throne. After Elena's death, the entire Glinskii clan was consigned to a secondary role in governmental affairs. But Anna Glinskaia chafed at her isolation from power, and when Ivan came of age, she and her son Mikhail (Ivan's uncle) arranged an elaborate coronation for him. They were rewarded for their loyal service with vast grants of land to rule as an autonomous principality. This show of favor did not satisfy Anna and Mikhail, however, and they insisted on the physical annihilation of all potential opponents of their family's power. In accordance with their advice, Ivan ordered an inquest into the activities of all the nobles the Glinskiis identified. Reprisals against them were carried out not in the name of the tsar but "on the orders of Prince Mikhail Glinskii and his mother Anna." Even Ivan's childhood companion, Fedor, the son of Prince I.F. Telepnev-Obolenskii, was not exempted. The elevation of the young tsar's nanny and her subsequent condemnation before the court fed the aristocracy's indignation. The common people of Moscow had long since come to resent Anna and to spread gossip about her. When a great fire destroyed half of Moscow in June 1547, but left the Glinskiis' home untouched, popular rumors blamed Anna and Mikhail, accusing them of sorcery as well as arson. The two had to flee Moscow to the nearby village of Vorobievo and hide there. The people of Moscow demanded that the "sorceress" be turned over to them, because she had "extracted the hearts from people, soaked them in water, and then, taking the form of a magpie, she had flown over the entire city and sprinkled it with the water," causing the fire. Other troubles, such as poor harvests and famines, were also attributed quite frequently in this period to the sorcery of prominent women.[6]

Only with great effort could Ivan IV save his grandmother and uncle. But even at the risk of their lives, they did not want to remove themselves from court politics. Their appearance at the wedding of Ivan's younger brother, Iurii, aroused indignation. Realizing their danger, Anna and Mikhail decided to flee Moscow. But it was already too late; they were apprehended en route and brought back to the capital. In response to the insistence of the court aristocracy, Ivan publicly confiscated the estates he had formerly given them and declared them in disgrace. Their ultimate fate is unknown, but it is likely that they finished out their lives as prisoners.[7]

Along with Agrafena Cheliadnina and Anna Glinskaia, a third active and militant woman, Evfrosinia Staritskaia, influenced events in the early years of the reign of Ivan IV. By birth Princess Khovanskaia, Evfrosinia married Ivan IV's cousin Andrei Staritskii in 1533. Prince Andrei was a quiet and weak man, but his young wife compensated for him. Evfrosinia's goal was not only to preserve the Staritskii clan's position at court but also to gain recognition for their claims to power during Ivan's minority. It was she who incited her husband to seek a grant of lands from Elena Glinskaia, and when it was refused, to organize a conspiracy with the goal of overthrowing her. The attempt cost the family dearly: Evfrosinia, Andrei, and their three-year-old son, Vladimir, were cast into prison, where Prince Andrei died. After a number of years, Evfrosinia and her son were freed, and they returned to court, joining the faction of the Belskii family of boyars.

The earlier setback did not weaken Evfrosinia's ambition. She continued to try to approach the tsar and remind him of his kinship with her and her son. In the early 1540s she succeed in gaining the return of the properties seized from her husband and also the right to maintain her own court and boyar servitors. In 1550, Evfrosinia arranged for her son to marry Princess Evdokia Nagaia. Her ultimate goal was to place Vladimir on the throne. When Ivan fell ill in 1553 and his life seemed in danger, Evfrosinia assembled a group of allies to promote Vladimir's claims to the succession. Evfrosinia spared no expense to strengthen her son's position, giving large gifts to possible supporters and recruiting junior boyars into her household. She also summoned an army from her principality of Staritsa. But Evfrosinia had miscalculated: the majority of the Boyar Duma, the council of boyars that advised the tsar, swore loyalty to Ivan, despite his illness. Not only Evfrosinia's supporters but even Vladimir himself ultimately pledged their oath to the tsar. For a long time after this incident, Evfrosinia refused to validate Vladimir's signature on documents with the family seal, which she retained in her control. When the boyars beseeched her to give it up, she responded, according to the chronicler, only with "abusive language."

When Ivan IV recovered, he did not retaliate against the Staritskii family, as might be expected. Perhaps he did not regard the dull and sickly young Vladimir Staritskii as a threat. Not Vladimir but his mother, Evfrosinia, had played the major role in the conspiracy of 1553. To protect himself against her disloyalty, Ivan demanded that Vladimir enter into the text of his oath of loyalty the promise "not to protect" Evfrosinia if she "planned harm" against the tsar or his family.

Such an oath should have put an end to Evfrosinia's machinations, but Evfrosinia had no intention of giving up. In 1560, she donated an altar cloth to the Trinity–St. Sergius Monastery, in which she had embroidered an unambiguous reference to her son as the direct descendant of Vasilii II and thus a legitimate claimant to the throne. Learning of this altar cloth, Ivan IV became wary of Vladimir and his indomitable mother.

Vladimir, however, proved to be unexpectedly successful in the early years of the Livonian War, and relations between him and Ivan improved. After Vladimir displayed exceptional courage in a battle near Polotsk in 1562, Ivan sent news of it to Evfrosinia. But when he came to Staritsa to celebrate the victory feast, the mood at Evfrosinia's court once again led him to suspect secret disloyalty. The tsar resolved to retaliate against Evfrosinia, officially on the grounds that, according to informers, she offered hospitality to religious freethinkers.

The church aligned itself against Evfrosinia, a woman devoid of proper Christian humility. One of the clerks of her court denounced her at the end of 1563, and all Evfrosinia's intrigues came to light. The tsar ordered the confiscation of the principality of Staritsa and the trial of his rebellious relatives. According to the legal practices of the time, these charges could be decided only by the upper clergy and the autocrat himself. Castigating Vladimir for his "stupidity" and weakness of will in the way he ran his household, the tsar all the same announced that he would "forgive" him and even return a portion of the property that had been confiscated.

Evfrosinia had to take the blame for everything. The tsar ordered that she be sent to the Voskresenskii Convent in Beloozero, which she had founded, where she was forced to take vows as a nun under the name Evdokia. He permitted her to retain her servants and even an entourage of noblewomen. But even the monastery could not contain her. Evfrosinia quickly gained permission to travel to nearby territories on pilgrimage, and she set up a school for artistic needlework at her own convent. She continued to take an interest in the political life of the capital and survived the great tumult of war, famine, epidemic, and the depredations of the *Oprichnina*. More and more often she received reports of the tsar's retributions against powerful boyars and landholders.

In 1569, it was Vladimir Staritskii's turn to fall under suspicion of treason. The tsar recalled Evfrosinia's old hatred of him, but in the absence of any evidence of her participation in a new plot against him, and wishing to avoid a personal confrontation with her, he ordered that she be secretly poisoned "with smoke." This order was carried out on a boat on the Sheksna River.[8]

All three of these Muscovite noblewomen had similar characters and experiences. They were all related to the clan of the grand prince. In order to avoid being victimized by the intrigues of the Muscovite court, they had to engage in their own conspiracies. Their participation in the political battles surrounding the establishment of the autocratic state required decisiveness, firmness, foresight, and an ability to compromise, not only to achieve their ends but also to save themselves and their children. It was, however, an unequal battle. These women were opposed not only by groups of men but by the autocrat and his associates. And it was the latter who commissioned the official sources that report on events of the time.

The authors of the official chronicles, histories, and tales depict the "autocrat of all Russia" as more visible and more powerful than the women who surrounded him. In part these authors were responding to the requirements of the Orthodox canon and in part to the demands of the patron who commissioned the works. But the virtual disappearance of women from the political life of Muscovy is not just historical fiction, it reflects reality. Women appeared on the political scene with increasing rarity and only in connection with events concerning the tsar's family that had state significance, such as weddings, the birth of heirs, and funerals.

The family of Ivan the Terrible illustrates the point.[9] Ivan married many times, but each time unhappily. The reason for this lay not only in his unhappy childhood, growing up without a father and with a powerful mother, but also in the complicated life of the Muscovite court, full of plots and betrayals. Ivan's cruel and suspicious personality essentially precluded the possibility of his choosing someone like his mother, Elena Glinskaia, or his cousin, Evfrosinia Staritskaia, as his bride.

Ivan's first wife was Anastasia, the daughter of the boyar Roman Zakharin. It is from her patronymic, Romanovna, that the later dynasty, the Romanovs, took their name. Anastasia was reared in a spirit of humility, submissiveness, and docility. Ivan's relatives chose her as the bride for the seventeen-year-old Ivan at a pageant of bridal candidates. Apparently she was a bit older than her husband. The chronicles describe her as "virtuous and courteous." Anastasia took no interest in governmental affairs, and she had little influence on her husband, who was inclined to overlook people who were quiet and submissive.

Despite his wife's angelic character—or maybe because of it—Ivan "became violent to Tsaritsa Anastasia and very adulterous." Even so, the marriage lasted thirteen years, from 1547 to 1560, and coincided with the period of Ivan's major reforms. Perhaps that is why later interpreters of Russian history were inclined to speak of Anastasia's "positive influence" on the tsar. But frequent births wore out Anastasia and weakened her health, and she died before the age of thirty. Only two of her children, Ivan and Fedor, survived her. The chronicle reports that at her funeral "everyone wept, especially the poor, for whom she had done much good." But the chief misfortune that followed Anastasia's death, according to contemporaries, was the change in Ivan. He became fierce, and from this time earned the nickname *groznyi*: "terrible" or "awe-inspiring."

Barely two weeks after the death of "his gracious and kindly girl," as Ivan referred to Anastasia, the tsar ordered a search to begin for a new wife, this time from among the Polish aristocracy. However, this plan could not be realized. Instead, his second wife, Maria, was a Tatar, the daughter of Prince Temir of Kabarda. Ivan saw her at his court, and, as the chronicle says, he immediately "fell in love" with her. The new tsaritsa, according to reports, was more lively and active than her predecessor. Rumors of her feasts, and of her intemperance, reached Ivan, but he paid them no mind. In this period Ivan began to see conspiracies everywhere and founded the *Oprichnina*, which spread terror throughout Russia. Rumor mongers blamed the new tsaritsa. The compiler of the Muscovite chronicle noted that Ivan started the *Oprichnina* "on the advice of evil people," but out of fear or ignorance did not say who these "people" were. Perhaps he did not dare to mention the tsaritsa specifically. However, Ivan, it was said, implicated her in the death of his rival, Vladimir Staritskii. In any case, Maria died in 1569, having lived with Ivan for ten years. The tsar suspected that she had been poisoned by boyar enemies but exhibited little grief at her death. Neither the chronicles nor later generations memorialized her.

In 1570, the tsar called for a new bridal pageant, and again young beauties were gathered at the Palace of Facets in the Kremlin. Upon the advice of his favorite, the *oprichnik* Maliuta Skuratov, Ivan chose out of the 1,500 maidens Marfa Sobakina, the daughter of a Novgorodian merchant and tsarist official. But after the betrothal in 1571, according to the chronicle account, Marfa began to "wither." Ivan must have been suspicious; unhealthy maidens were supposed to have been excluded from the competition. He nonetheless carried through with the wedding. A week later Marfa died, still a virgin. The tsar had it reported that she had been poisoned.

Orthodox canon law forbade a fourth marriage. However, the tsar was not an ordinary layperson, and he married again in 1572. The bride was the eighteen-year-old Anna Koltovskaia, another participant in the bridal pageant of 1570 and another of Skuratov's protégées. Her family was even less distinguished than the Sobakins, but she was desirable. For some time Anna influenced the tsar. The ravages of the *Oprichnina* diminished, and Ivan spent his time in the tsaritsa's chambers. But the Koltovskii family could not adapt to the ways of the court, and Anna herself, despite her beauty, did not continue to please the tsar. After a year, Ivan banished her to a convent, having secured her relatives' acquiescence.

For his fifth marriage, Ivan did not even ask the blessing of the bishops, so as not to put them in a difficult position. In November 1573, Ivan first selected Princess Maria Dolgorukaia, but he found out that she had had a premarital love affair. Because she had not preserved her virginity, he ordered that "Maria be given over to the will of God": specifically, that she be drowned under the ice of the river. His next choice for his fifth bride was the seventeen-year-old Princess Anna Vasilchikova. Instead of a church ceremony, the wedding took place amid a small circle of the bride's relatives, including the Kolychev boyar family. When they fell into disgrace, the tsar sent Anna off to a convent.

Even people at court could not keep track of the series of women who appeared and disappeared beside the tsar's throne. These women and their supporters and relatives rarely came to a happy end, because Ivan cared little for their thoughts and feelings. Only Vasilisa Melentieva, Ivan's sixth wife, received generous treatment. This sixth marriage was not contracted amid political intrigues. Vasilisa's first husband had been a clerk; her second husband, Nikita, the equerry of the tsar. By Ivan's order, Nikita was poisoned and his widow installed in the palace. Vasilisa was considerably older than Ivan's previous wives. But the chronicle reports that she was "beautifully built," and "such a beauty, that none of the maidens at the bridal pageant could match [her]." With Vasilisa, Ivan seems to have experienced some genuine happiness; but in any case, he enjoyed some successes in the late 1570s. The Livonian War seemed nearly won, after years of protracted effort. However, his luck did not last. Military reversals brought Russia to defeat in the Livonian War, and in 1579 Vasilisa died. Rumor asserted that Ivan had ordered her killed, on suspicion of adultery.

A year later, in 1580, Ivan married again. The tsar's new favorite, A.F. Nagoi, a kinsman of Ivan's former opponents, the Staritskiis, arranged a marriage with his niece Maria. In 1582, Maria bore Ivan a son, named Dmitrii. However, the presence of a wife and child did not prevent Ivan from formulating a plan to contract a dynastic marriage with his new ally, England. He proposed to Queen Elizabeth I that he marry her kinswoman, Mary Hastings, promising that he would "leave his wife" if she agreed to the union. Had the plan succeeded, Ivan doubtless would have shipped Maria Nagaia off to a convent without a qualm. It came to naught, however, and in March 1584, Ivan died.

Tsaritsa Maria and her son were forced to leave Moscow after Ivan's death and settle in the city of Uglich, which he had bequeathed to Dmitrii. In Ivan's will, Maria received no property apart from her son's, and she was placed under the guardianship of boyars. The Muscovite throne passed to Ivan's second son, Fedor, born of his marriage to Anastasia Romanovna (Zakharina). Ivan had killed his eldest son, also named Ivan, in a fit of rage some time before.

Because of Fedor's mental deficiency, a regency council was set up to rule in his name. This council, and in particular its leader, Boris Godunov, whose sister, Irina, was Tsar Fedor's wife, de facto ruled Muscovy. The regency council fixed a maintenance stipend for the widowed Maria in recognition of her rank. However, no amount of money could mitigate her humiliation: the widowed tsaritsa was escorted from the capital.

In May 1591, Dmitrii died in Uglich during an epileptic seizure. Rumors started that Dmitrii had been murdered on secret orders from Boris Godunov. Incited by Maria Nagaia and her brothers, the people of Uglich rioted, pillaging boyars' homes and demanding an inquest into Dmitrii's death. An investigatory commission was sent from Moscow. Maria and her relatives tried to coerce the commission into accepting their version of the story: it was a political murder at Boris's instigation. However, the commission, which was appointed by the tsar, ruled against the Nagois: Dmitrii had died in an unfortunate accident. The Nagoi family were summoned to Moscow and were subjected to an investigation themselves. The entire clan was placed in disgrace, and their property confiscated. Tsaritsa Maria was forced to take monastic vows and was banished to a hermitage in Beloozero (the same one to which Evfrosinia Staritskaia had been sent) to live as the nun Marfa.

Maria's political involvement did not end with consignment to a monastic cell. A decade later, the political situation had changed. Boris Godunov had come to the throne, and Russia was gripped by famine, social unrest, and foreign invasions. A defrocked monk named Grigorii Otrepiev claimed to be the Tsarevich Dmitrii, who had miraculously escaped death at the hands of Boris Godunov's henchmen. This "False Dmitrii" gained the backing of Polish aristocrats, who had designs on the Muscovite state. In 1604, Otrepiev and his army of Poles and disaffected Russians were advancing on Moscow. In a panic, Boris Godunov had "the nun Marfa" brought from Beloozero to question her about whether or not her son was alive. According to rumor, the False Dmitrii had visited Maria in Beloozero earlier and come to an agreement with her. Maybe so; in any case, Maria revealed nothing to Godunov, and he ordered her sent back to the convent.

A year later Godunov died, and the False Dmitrii took advantage of the tumult surrounding his death to occupy Moscow. He immediately ordered that his "mother" be brought from exile and arranged a ceremonial welcome for her. Legends state that he ordered that, if Maria refused to come, she be killed. "Nobody knows whether Maria recognized Grishka [a pejorative nickname for Grigorii] as her son, the Tsarevich Dmitrii, out of fear of death or on her own volition," a contemporary observed. Maria's recognition of her "son" cemented his claim to the throne.

The coalition between Maria and the Pretender did not last long. The False Dmitrii ordered that the body in the grave in Uglich be exhumed, hoping to prove that it was not the tsarevich but rather some other boy, a priest's son. This intention outraged and horrified Maria. With the support of loyal boyars, she denounced Otrepiev as an impostor.

Her defection from his cause contributed to his overthrow. The False Dmitrii had already made himself unpopular with the Moscow populace by allowing his Polish backers free rein in looting the city. Upon word of Maria's rejection of the new tsar's legitimacy, popular anger exploded into revolt. The False Dmitrii was killed and his body burned. Maria was allowed to remain in the city for the reburial of the remains of her real son in the Moscow Kremlin; then she returned to her convent. During the Polish and Swedish invasion that followed, the monastery where she lived was captured and pillaged. When she died in 1610, at the height of the struggle among boyar factions for power, she was already superfluous.

None of the wives of Ivan the Terrible approached the real locus of power in the Muscovite state. Ignored by the official chronicles and histories, they left their traces only as shadowy figures. Ivan was a tyrant not only to his subjects but also to the women of his family. His treatment of his daughters-in-law was no better than his treatment of his wives; he continually interfered in the family matters of his grown children. He ordered both the first and second wives of his eldest son, Ivan, shorn as nuns. During a family argument, he struck his son's third wife, Elena Sheremeteva, and caused her to miscarry. When his son intervened in her defense, Ivan struck him also, leading to his death.

But not all Muscovite women were as retiring as the wives and daughters-in-law of Ivan the Terrible. There were strong and capable women, too, but they had few opportunities to reveal their intelligence and talents. The women of the Godunov clan—Boris's sister, Irina, and his daughter, Ksenia—fell into this latter group.

The Godunov family was not distinguished in ancestry but had gained some importance through the *Oprichnina*. Hoping to improve the family's status through kinship with the tsar, Boris Godunov arranged for his sister, Irina, to marry Ivan's second son, Fedor.[10] His plan worked; Boris himself was raised to the rank of boyar, and he found a place in Ivan the Terrible's inner circle. His sister's marital happiness was not a matter of concern. Fedor suffered from mental retardation and poor physical health, and his marriage to Irina was childless. Her barrenness—in medieval Russia, it was assumed that the woman was at fault—provided grounds for a divorce, but after the tragic incident with his eldest son, Ivan did not insist upon it. Irina remained at court.[11]

Irina surpassed her husband in intelligence, education, and sophistication, and so had great influence over him. Living in the court of Ivan the Terrible, she witnessed at first hand the familial infighting and boyar intrigues that characterized Muscovite politics. She learned how to attain her goals indirectly and discreetly, without advertising her intentions. Her dissimulations were essential at first, but later she was able to participate openly in governmental affairs, frequently putting her name on Fedor's decrees. As the new tsaritsa, Irina soon became known abroad. She skillfully carried on a correspondence with Queen Elizabeth I of England and also with Patriarch Meletis Pigasos of Alexandria.

Irina's rise to power and her visibility abroad provoked secret disaffection among high church officials; her influence exceeded the proper limits for a Russian tsaritsa. Irina's position at court advanced the status of the entire Godunov clan, at the expense of other prominent and more noble boyars—the Shuiskiis, Vorotynskiis, and Golovins. These boyars wanted to convince Fedor of the necessity of divorcing his barren wife and developed a plan to do so in 1587. But they had not realized that Fedor had long since come to depend upon his wife and referred all matters to her. He not only rejected the idea of divorce but approved of the actions his wife and brother-in-law took to punish the conspirators. At Irina's instigation, Fedor ordered that the daughters of several of these boyars—Irina's potential replacements—be forcibly shorn as nuns.

Fedor recognized his wife's leadership in many matters and did not try to exalt himself at her expense. In order to strengthen Irina's authority in the court, he ordered that the new fortress under construction in the watershed between the Don and Volga Rivers be named in her honor: Tsaritsyn, literally "the tsaritsa's [city]," present-day Volgograd.

However, the lack of an heir remained a serious problem of state. Boris summoned the best physicians and healers to cure Irina's barrenness. The treatments succeeded, to a point: Irina became pregnant and bore a daughter, but she died in infancy.

Fedor's health began to fail, and he withdrew more and more from governmental duties. Not long before his death on January 3, 1598, he drafted a will in which he directed that Irina take vows as a nun after his death. He elicited from Irina her written consent to this provision. But the widowed tsaritsa did not rush to fulfill this obligation. Instead, she feigned that Fedor had bequeathed the throne to her. She stipulated that she had decided to "take power for a short time," "so as to protect the tsardom from tumult." However, Irina's first actions as autocrat generated disgruntlement in the country. Her well-intentioned amnesty of prisoners resulted in the release of traitors, thieves, and brigands.

Still, the Godunov clan prevailed upon Muscovite subjects to swear allegiance to Tsaritsa Irina. Even the patriarch of the Russian Orthodox Church was willing to accept Irina as autocrat. But Irina had not been crowned as co-ruler with Fedor, thus she could not legally hold power or convey it to someone else, such as her brother Boris. Although the Boyar Duma pledged loyalty to Irina after Fedor's death and recognized her as "Great Sovereign," the populace of Moscow was disaffected, calling Irina's accession "shameless."

Irina realized that, in trying to protect Muscovy from disorder by taking power, she had actually endangered it. On the ninth day after her husband's death, "in order to prevent a great revolt," the chronicle reports, Irina relinquished power formally to the Boyar Duma, and de facto to her brother Boris. Several days later, Irina entered the Novodevichii Convent in Moscow, taking monastic vows under the name Alexandra and emphasizing that she was thus fulfiling her husband's instructions. Even so, Irina continued to sign official decrees until the day in February 1598 when the Boyar Duma acclaimed Boris as tsar.

Recognizing the significance of Irina's abdication in his favor, Boris directed that her name always precede his in the prayers for the imperial family in church services. This command was fulfilled strictly until Irina's death in 1603. Under other circumstances, Irina Godunova might have been a talented ruler. Her life illustrates the kind of role women could play in the political realm. But like many of her predecessors, she saw her place as creating favorable conditions for a male relative to come to the throne. Like many aspiring women rulers before her, Irina voluntarily relinquished any thought of governing in her own name, even though she had the talent to do so.

Boris Godunov had in mind for his daughter, Ksenia, a different future from his sister's.[12] When Boris was elected tsar, Ksenia was sixteen years old. An impressionable, intelligent girl, she preferred the effort of study to the boredom of inactivity that characterized the lives of young women in her social circle. From childhood she became "skilled at the writing of books." She authored poetry and prose works and even tried her hand at composing music. Her beauty became legendary: she was of medium height, with fair skin, rosy cheeks, and long, dark braids. With all her gifts, she could have gone far, and Boris Godunov tried to find a suitable husband for her among the crowned heads of Europe.

However, one misfortune followed another for Ksenia. The first bridegroom selected for her, a Swedish prince, refused to convert to Orthodoxy. The second bridegroom, the son of a Danish prince, unexpectedly died of a fever before the wedding. Boris undertook negotiations with the courts of England, Austria, Georgia, and the German state of Schleswig, with a sense of urgency; the political situation in Russia was not stable.

In May 1605 Boris died; Ksenia was twenty-three years old. The False Dmitrii took the throne in June of that year. The young woman who had been educated to become the consort of a European ruler was forced to submit to the impostor. The False Dmitrii annihilated the entire Godunov family, including Ksenia's brother, Fedor, but spared Ksenia to become his concubine. His legal wife, however, was the Polish noblewoman Marina, daughter of the magnate Jerzy Mniszek, because this family had financed his seizure of the Russian throne.

Marina and all her relatives objected to Ksenia Godunova's presence at court, and they demanded that she be sent away from Moscow immediately. She was forced to take monastic vows, under the name Olga, at the Voskresenskii Monastery in Beloozero, where Ivan IV's cousin Evfrosinia had lived. In 1606, after the overthrow of the False Dmitrii, Ksenia-Olga was permitted to return to Moscow to attend the ceremony of the reburial of her father and relatives in the Trinity–St. Sergius Monastery. She decided to remain at that monastery, where she witnessed the Polish intervention of 1608–9, which she described in grief-laden letters to a relative. When the monastery was captured by Cossacks, she and the other nuns were subjected to violence. But Ksenia endured even these ordeals stoically, impressing contemporaries with her patience and equanimity.

The resignation with which Ksenia Godunova accepted her fate resonated with Russian popular culture. Several historical songs of the seventeenth century, which were recorded by foreign travelers, focus on Ksenia and her patience, morality, and worth. Even the common people recognized her innocent suffering, and they depicted her compassionately in laments. Ksenia's serene character is also visible in the gold-embroidered vestments she stitched, preserved at the Trinity–St. Sergius Monastery. These vestments reveal her artistic taste and the fineness of her work.

Ksenia's mother, Maria, did not fare so well in popular memory. Maria, the daughter of the ferocious *oprichnik* Skuratov and the wife of Boris Godunov, was tarnished by their reputations. Unlike her daughter, Maria, who was reputed to be greedy and cruel, received no pity.

The female characters, both factual and invented, in the folklore of the seventeenth century reflect the real experiences of women during the Time of Troubles. Without the legends and tales composed by anonymous authors, it would be almost impossible to recreate a portrait of women who did not belong to the upper aristocracy and whose names do not appear in official documents. While the Time of Troubles ended in 1613 with the election of Michael Romanov as tsar, upheavals in the cities and in the countryside recurred throughout the century.

The *Raskol,* or "schism," that split the Russian Orthodox Church from the 1640s through the 1660s became a primary vehicle for the expression of discontent with the state, the church, and society in

Muscovy. A group of reformers called the "Zealots of Piety," led by Patriarch Nikon, implemented changes in Russian Orthodox rituals and the texts of prayer books. These changes, although minor, reflected foreign—Greek and Ukrainian—approaches to Christian observance. Furthermore, they were enforced highhandedly, without regard for the appeal of traditional practices. Thus these reforms provided a focus for men and women who were dissatisfied with the official church and with the state authorities who supported it.

Women were prominent among the Old Believers, as those who resisted the church reforms were called. Two of the best known were the boyarina Feodosia Morozova (d. 1675) and her sister Evdokia Urusova.[13] Both came from the highest aristocracy of Muscovy, but willingly gave up their rank, wealth, and families in order to follow their consciences. Their letters express their spiritual world view and their determination to struggle for the preservation of the Old Belief. The anonymous "Tale of Boyarina Morozova" similarly reflects the character of the women who joined the Old Believer movement.

Feodosia was seventeen when she married the seventy-year-old Gleb Morozov in 1649. Feodosia's natal family, Sokovnin, was not particularly noble or wealthy, but Gleb was the brother of Boris Morozov, one of the richest men in Muscovy. Feodosia became a friend and companion to Tsaritsa Maria, the wife of Tsar Aleksei (1645–1676). In 1662 Boris Morozov died, leaving his fortune to his brother, Gleb, who survived him by only a few months. Feodosia thus found herself the manager of an enormous fortune, for the heir to the two brothers was Feodosia and Gleb's son, Ivan, who was then only twelve years old.

The thirty-year-old widow led a luxurious life. Her carriage was decorated with silver and furs, like the tsaritsa's; peacocks grazed on the grounds of her home; and on every outing, she was accompanied by a suite of two hundred servants. Contemporaries did not regard Feodosia as extravagant, however, because they knew that she preserved the substance of the inheritance for her son and wished him to live in the kind of splendor that befitted the head of a leading family.

Feodosia's chance acquaintance with Archpriest Avvakum of the Kazan Cathedral sharply altered her life. Avvakum was a talented polemicist who exposed the vices of the church leaders who had initiated the reforms in the services. Feodosia found herself attracted to his teachings. Avvakum became her spiritual mentor, and she became a staunch adherent of the Old Believers, who were willing to endure even death for the old faith and true piety. Feodosia regarded the efforts of the church reformers as nothing less than the work of Satan.

Feodosia chose an unusual form of protest for her time: she decided to live the life of a nun, but in the secular world. At "the direction of her heart," and in "right mind," she gave up all the trappings of wealth and voluntarily associated herself with the common people. She took the sick, insane, homeless, and poor into her luxurious house and took on the role of "mother intercessor" for them. Her home became a refuge for all those persecuted for their adherence to the Old Belief.

It would be easy to see Feodosia Morozova as an obsessed zealot, but she was not. In Muscovy at that time, heretics and religious dissenters were numerous, and preoccupation with religious righteousness was seen as a mark of virtue, not fanaticism. Avvakum described Feodosia as "a woman of cheerful disposition and loving." Feodosia's devotion to her faith was based not on blind emotionalism but rather on a full understanding of the religious principles at stake.

In 1664, Archpriest Avvakum and his wife came to reside at Feodosia Morozova's house in Moscow. At that time, he was already subject to ecclesiastical and government persecution. Under his influence, Feodosia became even more generous in distributing her wealth to prisoners and to monasteries. She exchanged the luxurious, brightcolored dress of a Muscovite noblewoman for the simple habit of coarse wool worn by nuns and the poor. Feodosia's sister Evdokia Urusova followed her lead, along with the gentry woman Maria Danilova and several other women from her social circle. At Avvakum's behest, Feodosia arranged for the publication of secret literature of the Old Believer movement from her home. She herself wrote a great deal, and well: "You can be satiated by the words from her mouth, as though with honey," Avvakum wrote.

Feodosia's dissidence attracted the attention of the upper clergy and the tsar's officials in the Chancellery of Secret Affairs, which was charged with the investigation and punishment of criminals. The tsar himself was disturbed by the conflict between the patriarch and a noblewoman of his court. He sent the tsaritsa's sister, Anna Miloslavskaia, to admonish Feodosia, hoping that she could convince her to return to the official church, but to no effect. The tsar confiscated part of Feodosia's property and then returned it, trying to get her to rethink her stance. He then took the issue of Feodosia's "apostasy" to the Boyar Duma, but the Duma refused to rule on it. The tsar and his court ran out of patience when, in 1670, Feodosia began to resettle in her home nuns who had been driven out of convents for their adherence to the Old Belief, and herself took monastic vows. From that point on, Feodosia stopped attending functions at the tsar's court and openly rejected all rites of the official church.

In November 1671, Feodosia Morozova and Evdokia Urusova were arrested at the tsar's command. They were placed in chains and sent off to the Chancellery of Secret Affairs. But even under torture they refused to betray their faith. Feodosia was threatened with reprisals against her son, but her religious convictions were stronger than her maternal feelings. (Incidentally, when Feodosia's son learned of his mother's arrest and torture, he went insane and died.) Fearing that a public execution would give the sisters an aura of martyrdom, the tsar ordered them exiled from Moscow to the city of Borovsk. There they were consigned to a dungeon to die of hunger. Their bodies were buried secretly in the jail. Despite the attempts by the government to stamp out their memory, they remained symbols of faith and firmness of conviction among the people.

Feodosia Morozova and her circle were not the only women to challenge the social order of Muscovite society. Women were among the peasant rebels who joined the Cossack Stepan Razin's revolt in 1670–71, as they had been in previous peasant uprisings as well. Usually the names of peasant women rebels are not recorded in the sources, but Alena Arzamasskaia (Temnikovskaia) is an exception.[14]

Alena was the daughter of an ordinary peasant living in a village in the Volga region. She was married at a young age and, while still little more than a girl, took vows as an nun at the Nikolaevskii Monastery on the Volga. However, she chafed at the rules of convent life, finding it to be as unjust and non-egalitarian as the secular world. In 1669, she ran away from the convent, hoping to join Stepan Razin's army of the poor. She cut her hair and dressed in men's clothing, posing as a Cossack leader. In that guise, she gathered a detachment of two hundred men, which rapidly grew to six thousand. Her followers did not know that she was a woman. Meanwhile, the rebellion had been spreading, taking over numerous cities in southern Russia.

Alena's detachment succeeded in conquering the fortified city of Temnikov. Alena took over the former residence of the Temnikov military governor and effectively ruled the city for more than two months. The local Cossack encampment chose her as their leader. Within her own detachment, Alena earned recognition as an excellent archer. She commanded great authority because of her intelligence and self-control, accurate marksmanship, and medical knowledge.

When the tsar's armies launched their campaign against the rebels on the Volga, Alena chose to stay and fight. She was taken captive in 1670 and was tortured in an attempt to get her to reveal the names of rebel leaders. She refused to do so. Alena was convicted of brigandage, specifically in the capture of Temnikov, and of dressing as a man—an even worse crime, in the eyes of the church, than unauthorized departure from the monastery. She was sentenced to be burned at the stake. According to an eyewitness to the execution, Alena "did not express any fear, or even make a sound, when she was entirely enveloped in flames." In addition to the judicial records of Alena's activities, folk songs recall her as a heroine who defended the interests of the poor.

While Alena Arzamasskaia and Feodosia Morozova came from different social ranks and led entirely different lives, they were both uncompromising in their resistance to governmental authorities. Guided by their own, very different senses of what was right and just, they took on roles usually reserved for men and transcended the limitations placed on women by the law and society.

Most women, however, found that their horizons were becoming narrower rather than broader. Women in the highest aristocratic circles, in particular the tsar's family, found their horizons literally constrained through seclusion in the *terem*, or women's quarters, of the house. Although the *terem* was a recent innovation, hardly predating the Time of Troubles, it was endowed with an aura of antiquity, tradition, and piety. Seclusion was a mark of honor—women of the lower classes could not afford the luxury of remaining out of public view—and behind *terem* walls, women were safe from attack and insult. Their visitors could also be monitored, to prevent women from associating with people who would besmirch their character. Aristocratic men and women moved in separate spheres.[15]

As an institution, however, the *terem* was not long-lived. The restrictions on women's movement gradually diminished, even in the tsar's family, where they had been most strongly developed. The changes were evident among the womenfolk of Tsar Aleksei in the last quarter of the seventeenth century. When Aleksei died in 1676, he left six daughters from his first marriage to Maria Miloslavskaia, as well as a twenty-five-year-old widow, Natalia Naryshkina. The oldest daughter, Marfa, soon took vows as a nun. The other sisters exercised their new-found freedom in their own ways. They gradually began to appear in public more and more often and started to dress in Western European fashion instead of the traditional costume of aristocratic Russian women.

Among the daughters of Tsar Aleksei, the most well spoken and educated was Sofia (1657–1704).[16] She was no beauty and did not strive to be one; she was stout and severe in expression and looked older than her years. From her youth she was interested in reading, and the best scholars of her day were recruited as her teachers: the poet and pedagogue Simeon Polotskii, who taught her Polish, the philosopher Karion Istomin, and the writer and historian Silvester Medvedev.

Sofia's heroine became the Byzantine princess Pulcheiria, who seized power from her weak brother and ruled in his stead. Sofia also figured out how to win her father's sympathy, with her incisive speech and facade of piety. Her brother Fedor, who succeeded to the throne after Aleksei's death, similarly favored her.

Fedor died in 1682, and the succession was problematical. Fedor and Sofia's next oldest brother, Ivan, was sixteen and thus just barely of age, and he was sickly. Their younger half-brother, Peter (the future Peter the Great), was a child of ten. The relatives of Ivan and Sofia's mother, the Miloslavskiis, literally battled the Naryshkins, the relatives of Peter and his mother Natalia. The *streltsy*, the infantry regiments based in the capital, threw their support behind Sofia. As a compromise, the two boys were named co-rulers, with Sofia as regent because she was in fact older than her stepmother. The politically inexperienced Tsaritsa Natalia found herself marginalized.

Sofia proved capable at ruling Russia's vast territories. Soon she had reorganized the government, bringing farsighted and powerful nobles into its ranks, including the diplomat and general F.L. Shaklovityi and the diplomat and intellectual V.V. Golitsyn. The latter became Sofia's favorite. Golitsyn was a man of Western tastes, who valued art and poetry and collected books, paintings, and porcelain. With his help, Sofia was able to draw upon the unofficial networks of power in Muscovy. By gaining greater security in her position as regent, Sofia felt able to free herself from the *streltsy*, who had supported her rise to power.

The *streltsy* became dissatisfied with Sofia because she had promised them much but delivered little. Their leader, the military governor Prince I.A. Khovanskii, led a revolt against Sofia. But the revolt was unsuccessful, and Sofia retaliated against the conspirators. Prince Khovanskii, his son, and thirty-seven of their associates were executed, along with many Old Believers, who were implicated in the plot.

Sofia valued the intellectualism of the Old Believers, however, and engaged them in discussion with her personally. In the course of this debate, Sofia accused the Old Believers of "impudent lies," but she recognized that it was better not to persecute dissenters. As further testimony to her religious tolerance, she granted political asylum to Protestants who were expelled from France under Louis XIV. These French Huguenots joined other foreigners in the "German" Quarter of Moscow. (The Huguenots were not grateful to Sofia, however, and they supported her brother Peter when he ousted her from power.)

Sofia's government, under Golitsyn's influence, undertook a number of progressive steps. The trade barriers between Russia and Ukraine, which was annexed in 1654, were abolished. This move created a single market throughout the country and strengthened the commercial ties between the center and the periphery. In the 1680s, the government made a number of concessions to the artisanal suburbs, which helped the development of towns. At the same time, the state lessened its prosecution of runaway serfs. Golitsyn even proposed a plan to Sofia to abolish serfdom altogether in favor of an annual poll tax. However, the gentry, who owned the serfs, did not concur with this proposal; they wished only for reforms that confirmed their property.

Sofia had had an interest in foreign affairs since childhood, so it is no wonder that her government paid close attention to them. Several treaties were concluded during Sofia's regency: one confirming peace with Sweden; another in 1687, concluding "eternal peace" with Poland; and in 1689, the Treaty of Nerchinsk with China, which established Russia's eastern border at the Amur River. In order to oppose the threat of Turkey and its client state, the Crimean Tatar khanate, to the south, Russia entered into an alliance with the Polish–Lithuanian Commonwealth, Venice, and Austria. However, when war came, Russia ended up fighting alone. Russia's erstwhile allies profited, because Turkish strength was diverted away from them. Sofia named Golitsyn as the commander of the Russian army in the 1687 and 1689 campaigns against the Crimean khanate. The campaigns ended unsuccessfully, and the danger on Russia's southern border remained.

Capitalizing on her early successes on the diplomatic front, Sofia increased her show of power at home. She began to style herself "autocrat" and ordered that coins be minted with her portrait. A new palace was built in which she received ambassadors. Many of the court nobility decried Sofia's "immodesty," but Sofia was too full of grandiose new plans to heed their dissatisfaction. However, the failure of the Crimean campaigns undermined her position within the

Russian government. She disagreed sharply with Peter, who was now full grown; Peter considered these campaigns premature.

The opposition between Sofia and Peter divided the boyars and the Muscovite court into two sides. Gradually, Peter's supporters won. In June 1689, Peter forbade his sister to participate in the annual procession to Kazan Cathedral, and in September, he deposed her government. He ordered Sofia sent to the Trinity–St. Sergius Monastery.

Yet Sofia was not required to live like a nun; she retained her servants and companions, and her sisters and brother Ivan were permitted to visit. Nor was she expected to undertake the harsh fasting of monks and nuns, but instead she continued to dine as though at court. She was also free to stroll around the grounds of the monastery, although she was forbidden to leave its precincts.

After ten years, in 1698, Sofia once again seized a political opportunity. Peter had left Russia for an unprecedented tour of Europe. The *streltsy* of Moscow, discontented with their low salaries, exhausting drill, and the campaigns, staged a coup to overthrow Peter. Boyars loyal to Sofia tried to promote her as the rightful ruler.

The uprising, however, failed. Peter immediately returned home and personally saw to the suppression of the revolt. The instigators of the revolt were executed, and Sofia was forced to take monastic vows under the name Susanna at the Novodevichii Convent in Moscow, where she died in 1704.

Sofia represents the culmination of the aspirations of and limitations on women of noble families in the Muscovite period. Several of them strove to express their energy and expand the scope of their activities, even to the point of seeking to govern independently. However, none of these could realize her aims to the fullest. Other aristocratic women internalized the expectations of the church and remained meek and quiet, fearing to transgress the established norms of behavior. The latter were more typical of the period.

The political life of the Muscovite court during the consolidation of the centralized state reflected the formation of a national consciousness, a new perception of Russia's place in the world, and new norms of conduct, including those regulating familial and personal relationships. Personal life was often subordinated to the ends of political intrigues and the struggle for the throne. Both men and women from prominent noble families participated in these struggles, directly or indirectly.

The clearest example of the quiet participation of women in political

Sofia, daughter of Tsar Aleksei and half-sister of Peter the Great, during her imprisonment in the Novodevichii Convent. Painting by the nineteenth-century artist Ilia Repin.

life comes from the families of the tsars. The official histories, written in the chronicles, always focus on the tsar, and they devote much less attention to the women around him, as compared with histories from the preceding period. With the centralization of government, and also of history writing, in the tsar's court in Moscow, there were fewer arenas in which others, including women, could play autonomous political roles. The parameters of women's participation in political activity may be broadened by including boyar and provincial gentry families. Many wives of courtiers in the seventeenth century came from gentry families; they were reared in different surroundings but were fully integrated into the court elite. They carried, however, little weight in Muscovite political life. The secluded *terem* woman remained much more typical of the Muscovite court, despite the notable exceptions. Chronicles and didactic literature reinforced this idealization of women's lives, portraying, in accordance with Orthodox teachings, women as humble, meek, and deferential to a patriarchal hierarchy: the husband in the family was like the tsar in the state. Historians of Russia have perpetuated this image of the Russian woman, as though it were typical of all social classes and periods in the past.

However, even the chroniclers themselves, in their praise of outstanding noble governmental officials in Muscovy, at times refer incidentally to ambitious and decisive women who acted independently. Rarely were these married women; patriarchal traditions overshadowed their ambitions. However, when widowed, these women succeeded as much as men did, often in a shorter time period. Thus Ivan the Terrible's mother, Elena Glinskaia, a widow, accomplished her reforms, and Sofia, a spinster, left her mark on the Muscovite state. They influenced their male kinsmen, defining their future orientations, and they worked with all their strength to make sure that the throne passed to their own relatives. These socially active women might earn great admiration, but they did not conform to the norms established by the church.

The early modern period of history saw the emergence of new types of individuals: people who would sacrifice everything for their convictions, whether religious or societal. Women such as Feodosia Morozova, Evdokia Urusova, and Alena Arzamasskaia foreshadowed the changes in social consciousness that came into full flower in the following period.

Who Shall Find a Virtuous Woman?

According to the *Domostroi*, a manual of household management from sixteenth-century Muscovy, women were supposed to devote all their strength to their family and their home.[17] What, then, was the "family" and the "home" like?

Most houses in sixteenth-century Muscovy were built of wood, because Russia was covered with forest.[18] Wood was also used to heat the houses. Consequently, the danger of fire was great, and frequent conflagrations—called "the red rooster" by Muscovites—have not left a single wooden house from the sixteenth century standing to the present day. Only miniatures in manuscripts and iconography reveal what houses looked like at that time. They were squat and dark, with tiny windows in order to keep in the heat. The wealthy filled the window frames with mica panes, and ordinary people used stretched animal membranes. The walls were built with thick logs, with dry moss to fill in the chinks. Light and air entered the house primarily through the doorway. The house was topped with a modest double-pitched roof with an opening cut out for smoke to escape; there was no chimney. Many houses also had a cellar to store foodstuffs. The door and porch were carved with intricate decorations, even on the poorest houses. Nearly every house had a yard and garden, to provide vegetables as well as a place for relaxation.

Stone buildings were a rarity in Muscovy. Stone was used more in buildings on the western frontiers of Russia, but in the central part of the country, even defensive towers were usually built of wood, and even noblemen rarely erected stone houses. Nobles' houses varied in size, although they were usually two or three stories tall, but the wealthier the owner, the higher the roof. Attractively decorated with ornate wood carvings, they were elaborate enough to impress foreign travelers to Muscovy. Inside, the layout consisted of suites of rooms. A covered passageway connected the upper floor of the men's quarters with the *terem*. The hallways, doors, moldings, gates, and roof were all colorfully decorated, perhaps to compensate for the grayness of the Russian winter. The furnishing of the houses—benches, tables, trunks, and beds—were similarly carved and painted.

In the late sixteenth century, boyars' houses began to have large glass windows in the *terem*, or women's quarters, which opened out onto the street. In this period, rooms began to be designated for specific purposes: dining room, bedroom, pantry, and so forth. Unlike Western European nobles, Muscovites strictly preserved the separate quarters for men and women. The women's half of the house was often built as a separate building, connected to the men's quarters only via an outside passageway. In the tsar's palace, the imperial women had their own dining room and separate apartments for their children, women companions, personal maids, nannies, wet nurses, and serving women. The tsar's bedchamber was also located in this section of the palace. The tsar's massive bed was made of carved wood, with embroidered silk sheets, feather pillows covered in velvet, and brocade or chiffon curtains for warmth.

The oldest woman in the family was not only a housewife but also the "sovereign lady of the home," as the *Domostroi* called her.[19] She managed all the food production in the home and organized the work of all family members and household servants. Everyone except the master of the house had to help the mistress, and all were entirely subordinate to her. Russian custom and Orthodox teachings reinforced this order in the household, and the overwhelming majority of families in Muscovy conformed to this model.

All children, and especially girls, were dependent upon their mothers and grandmothers. In wealthy families, the entire burden of caring for children did not fall upon mothers. Boyarinas and princesses were not expected to feed their infants themselves; instead they used wet nurses. Because breast milk was correctly considered to be healthy, some wealthy families kept nearly a dozen wet nurses. Babies often continued to nurse even after they reached their first birthday. The story is told about Peter the Great that his mother, Natalia Naryshkina, so loved him that she nursed him herself and continued with breast feeding until he was two years old. This legend attributes Peter's unusual height (well over six feet) to his diet in infancy. In princely families wet nurses and nannies almost entirely took the place of parents for very young children. The children consequently often developed a deep affection for their caregivers, as Ivan IV did for his wet nurse, the boyarina Agrafena Cheliadnina.[20]

The authors of guides to righteous living did not devote much attention to the early youth of girls. At that time, people did not recognize childhood as a special phase of life, but instead they regarded children as little adults. Thus the depictions of children in Russian iconography, and the secular paintings from late in this period, always show them in constrained poses with serious expressions. However, children in Muscovite Russia behaved like children in later times, and they had their fun. Typical entertainments for girls were swings and seesaws. The German traveler Adam Olearius described the latter game in this manner: "They lay down a board on a round block, and one of the girls stands on the end. A second girl takes a running start and leaps onto the other end, sending the first girl flying into the air."[21] In winter, girls played at sledding on the hills (most Russian cities have steep banks down to the river). In wealthier families, girls and young women could ride in sleighs covered with fur, usually bearskins. In summer they rode in carriages pulled by horses, whose manes and tails were braided with ribbons and flowers. In such outings, unmarried girls could show off: who was richer, whose equipage was better, who had friskier horses, prettier tackle, louder bells.

However, daily life for the unmarried daughters in the family did not consist only of pleasures and amusements. Orthodox teachings recommended that parents rear their children strictly and not indulge them. Girls' mothers, and their elders in general, had a great deal of power over them. The compilers of instructional materials insisted that girls not challenge their parents' authority. In order to inculcate respect toward elders, as well as "more assiduousness in needlework," ecclesiastical teachers recommended that parents resort to frequent beatings. Young boys and girls were forbidden, on pain of a public flogging, to complain about their parents' cruelty ("to air arguments outside the home").[22] Children who were insubordinate were threatened with exclusion from church sacraments and even, in the words of certain preachers, "a horrible death."

These stern recommendations concerning child rearing, however, conflicted with parental feelings. The numerous toys—clay rattles, wooden bears, whistles, dolls, hoops—that archeologists have discovered in their excavations testify to parents' concern for their children's happiness. Letters from this period are also filled with expressions of tenderness for children and concern about their health. the *Domostroi* condemned games and expressions of tenderness as contradicting the principle of rearing children in fear.

In lower-class families, women first of all had to know how to subordinate themselves and how to work, and the rearing of girls was necessarily oriented toward these goals. By the age of five, girls already helped with household work. They gradually learned how to plant and harvest, how to process the crops, and how to cook everyday meals. Mothers and older sisters taught young girls women's work: how to sew, spin, weave, and embroider. At the same time, older women shaped girls' characters, inculcating serenity and patience.

The rearing of daughters in well-to-do families took place in the private space of the women's *terem*. Aristocratic girls were trained only to become wives. They had to be virtuous and make a show of submission, first to their parents and later to their husbands. In accordance with Orthodox teachings concerning premarital virginity, young girls were carefully secluded in the women's quarters of the house. The seclusion of aristocratic maidens became a motif in folklore: "She [the tsar's daughter] sits behind three-times-nine locks; she sits behind three-times-nine keys; where the wind never blew, the sun never shone, and young heroes never saw her."[23]

Historians have proposed a variety of different theories about the origin of the *terem* in Russia. Nothing similar existed in Western Europe in the same period. One theory is that the *terem* was intended to protect women from attack by nomads. Another theory proposes that the *terem* was a Tatar institution that Russians borrowed. However, the Tatars never secluded women in this way, and the women's quarters provided no protection from Tatar raids. A third theory attributes the *terem* to the growth of misogyny as propounded by the Orthodox Church. This interpretation is probably closer to the truth, because Orthodox teachings indeed idealized virginity and the ascetic life. But more than that, young women in Muscovy were a sort of currency with which nobility and wealth could be obtained, and virginity was one of the criteria for determining a girl's value. The daughter of a prince or boyar who had not "despoiled her virginity" might be successfully betrothed to a noble bridegroom, or even to the tsar himself.

Sources concerning moral education from this period devote an exceptional amount of attention to the issue of incest.[24] Neither narrative sources nor folklore provide sufficient information to determine whether incestuous relations were widespread, and even references to specific incidents are exceedingly rare. However, penitential materials devoted a great deal of space to this topic. Numerous questions in confessional lists inquired about sexual relations between relatives by blood, marriage, and spiritual kinship (godparent/godchild). Yet, very few of these lists include a question about incest between father and daughter. Parents, particularly fathers, had absolute control over the fate of their children (and could legally sell them into slavery), and daughters were obliged to submit themselves entirely to their fathers, in accordance with ecclesiastical teachings. In this context of power relations, incestuous relations between fathers and daughters doubtless occurred in some instances, particularly in poorer families, where women did not have separate living quarters.

Ecclesiastical teachings, however, warned parents to protect their daughters against "defilement" by anybody. The *terem*, with its strict isolation of marriageable young women, was intended to keep them pure. In addition to guarding their virginity, the *terem* protected men from association with women when they were "unclean." The idea that menstruating women were ritually impure was quite widespread in premodern societies. In Muscovy, earlier superstitions were reinforced with ecclesiastical regulations forbidding women to enter church buildings or participate in religious rituals on "unclean days." Menstruation was regarded as vaguely sinful, and menstruating women were admonished to spend time alone in penitential prayer.

For some aristocratic young girls, isolation in the *terem* inculcated fearfulness and indecisiveness and a conviction that they were incapable and inferior. Other young women rejected family life and instead remained spinsters at home, living as though they were nuns. Still others rebelled and strove to marry as soon as they could in order to gain release from the strict confinement imposed on marriageable maidens.

In all social orders in Muscovy, the parents concluded marriages for their children, as they did in the earlier period. The wishes of the girls themselves were rarely taken into consideration. However, parents overlooked their daughters' feelings at their peril: there are known cases where the family of the bride had to pay a large sum in forfeit when a daughter refused to carry through with a planned marriage. The case of Princess Avdotia Mezentseva is an example. Avdotia's grandmother, Marfa, who reared her, sold two villages in order to buy off Avdotia's betrothed fiancé: "I, Marfa, paid him five hundred rubles because of her tears," Marfa wrote in the sales document.[25]

According to narrative literature and folklore, for young men and women of non-noble rank, the favorite place to meet acquaintances was the street, and particularly at wells. (Wells were an innovation in sixteenth-century Muscovy. Previously, they had been dug only in fortresses in times of siege; daily water supplies were carried from rivers or creeks.) Young people came to wells all dressed up in order to look each other over, and older relatives kept watch for prospective brides. Usually the mother of the groom served as the matchmaker. Young girls, carefully dressed and made up, were prepared to carry more water than their households needed, "and even perhaps to pour it out around the corner," in order to have an excuse to go out again.[26]

The minimum age for marriage—fifteen for boys and twelve for girls—was often not observed. Among the minor gentry in the provinces, children were often married as young as ten or eleven, because the purpose of these marriages was to preserve claims to *pomeste* property, which the tsar distributed to gentry servitors on condition of military service. In theory the *pomeste* (service-dependent landed estate) reverted to the tsar upon the death of the holder (with a small portion reserved for the support of his widow). However, if there was a grown son or son-in-law who could provide military service, the *pomeste* was usually granted to him automatically. Consequently, young marriage continued to be standard practice, even after the Law Code (*Ulozhenie*) of 1649 forbade the marriage of girls under the age of fifteen.[27]

In addition to restrictions on marriage by reason of age and kinship, there were restrictions in regard to social class. More and more often, marriages were concluded not only within a single social order but among peers in social status and wealth. In the sixteenth century, it became customary among the boyars for the parish priest to record wedding announcements, which gave the names, ages, and familial genealogy of the bride and groom. These announcements cost money, so not everyone used them. In addition to the basic information about age and family, these announcements noted whether it was a first or a subsequent marriage for the bride or groom. The church watched assiduously over remarriages, because the priest was entitled to collect additional payments for presiding at a second or third marriage. As for a fourth or, "God forbid, a fifth" marriage, these were sternly forbidden; the faithful were prohibited from drinking or eating with someone involved in such a union, "for he is a pagan."[28]

The tradition of civil marriage contracts continued in the sixteenth and seventeenth centuries. The essential elements were the agreement, the witnesses, the ceremony of hand-fasting, the betrothal feast, and the understanding concerning the dowry. The popular ritual (*veselie*) and the church rite or "crowning" (*venchanie*) both remained part of the usual wedding celebration. As in the past, the popular ritual was considered indispensable to making a marriage valid; the church ceremony was dispensable, especially among the lower classes.

From the sixteenth century on, weddings were carefully scripted. Instruction manuals dictated in detail who must do what, in what order, with what words, and how. Some new elements entered the premarital celebration. Thus, after the initial agreement was negotiated, the mother of the groom came to examine the bride physically, bringing gifts with her to compensate for the indignity. At the tsar's bridal pageant, the candidates were accompanied by their wet nurses.[29]

On the wedding day, the bride was dressed in a red *sarafan* (jumper), with a yellow wreath-like headdress. In wealthy families, the headdress might be made of cloth of gold. (The white dress and orange blossoms of European custom came to Russia only at the end of the nineteenth century.) The celebration included a program of songs, dances, games, and contests. Only in the tsar's household were such popular festivities omitted.[30] Instead, the "beneficent girls" who were the future brides of the tsar's family were brought to the palace three days before the wedding. They were given the honorary title of "tsar's daughter" (*tsarevna*) and were arrayed in a golden crown adorned with emeralds and rubies. On the day of the wedding, the bride was dressed in a robe of cloth of gold with embroidery on the shoulders, sleeves, skirts, and hems, and on her head she wore a headdress with a lightweight white veil decorated with pearls and gold sequins.[31]

For the bride, in both upper- and lower-class families, the celebration was not exciting but rather sad and upsetting. For a girl of twelve to fifteen years, the wedding marked a leap into the unknown, a farewell to childhood and parental protection. After marriage, the girl became a woman with all the attendant responsibilities.

For women of the nobility, marriage did not mean release from the *terem* but rather continued seclusion, and in an unfamiliar household. Sometimes, the situation of a young bride could be even more strict than what she had experienced in her parents' home. "A husband must instruct his wife, and admonish her with fear in private," the *Domostroi* taught. The foreign ambassador Sigismund von Herberstein, who visited Russia in the sixteenth century, recounted that Russians did not respect a woman "if she was not locked up in the *terem*," and that "she was rarely permitted to go to church and even less often into the society of her women friends." According to Herberstein, an aristocratic woman could go visiting only with her husband's permission, and in this company of friends, she was permitted "to talk only about needlework." Tsaritsas, princesses, and boyar women were forbidden to ride about the city in open carriages, because nobody was supposed to see their faces. Tsaritsas went out rarely, and when they did, it was in a magnificent equipage with twelve horses. But usually the women of the Kremlin celebrated all occasions only in their own quarters.[32]

A special Golden Palace was built to provide a setting for those ceremonies in which Kremlin women could participate. "One cannot find the words to describe the dazzling splendor of this chamber," a contemporary wrote. The walls were covered with gilded depictions of the Savior, the Mother of God, angels, and heroic women. The room was furnished with a table chased in silver, mirrors adorned with pearls, and curtains of gold brocade. Amid all this splendor boyarinas sat decorously, dressed in diamonds, emeralds, and rubies. The luxury of the costumes of the tsaritsa and her noblewomen enhanced the magnificence of their audiences. In this setting tsaritsas received official congratulations from the patriarch, metropolitans, wives of foreign ambassadors, and women friends on their birthdays or the veneration days of their patron saints. In addition to the

Procession of the tsaritsa and women of the imperial court. Sketch from the album of the Austrian diplomat, Baron Meyerberg, seventeenth century.

tsaritsa, the wives of the rulers of vassal Tatar khanates of Kazan, Siberia, and Kasimov used this chamber to receive foreign diplomats.

The women of the imperial family spent their days in their section of the palace. There was even an internal courtyard, with swings, slides, and other amusements, shut in on all sides. The life of the tsar's daughters resembled that of nuns; they spent almost all their time in prayer and needlework. The tsar's wife, in contrast to his daughters, spent her mornings hearing petitions. Most of them originated with relatives and servitors, and contained requests for permission to marry. A few concerned the management of the household or the tsaritsa's properties. A woman secretary read the petitions and recorded the tsaritsa's response. From the second half of the sixteenth century on, these matters were handled not by members of the tsar's family but rather by officials chosen by men to act in the tsaritsa's name.[33]

If the status of women among the nobility was formulated primarily in response to Orthodox conceptions of modesty and submission, among common people it was based on ideals of the female contribution to household labor. There was no *terem* in the homes of the

rural or urban lower classes. Instead, women lived with their menfolk and managed all household matters on a par with them. This organization provided women with considerable independence and respect in the family. Women of the provincial service gentry also enjoyed a large share of independence, especially when their husbands were away from home on government service, as they were frequently and for long periods of time. Members of the gentry valued managerial capability in their wives and corresponded with them during their absences.[34]

The pattern of daily life was similar in most Muscovite families. Most Muscovites got up before dawn. Even in the tsar's family, according to the English visitor Giles Fletcher, the day started at four in the morning.[35] Breakfast was not a regular meal; in lower-class families, a proverb reminded one that in the morning, "it is still necessary to earn one's daily bread." At the midday meal, the women did not sit at the table with the men; they ate afterward, contenting themselves with what the men left. Adam Olearius noted that "Russians are accustomed to relax and sleep after their midday meal"; so, he thought, "during the midday rest one must not talk with anyone." For men, this siesta might last for three hours; for women, if they slept at all, it was for a shorter period, because they had household chores to complete.

Contemporary observers reported that, in the tsar's household, the tsar and his retainers might meet in the bathhouse, which provided both bathing facilities and a sauna. However, it is unlikely that the women of the tsar's family, much less women of the lower classes, followed the same custom. Women did visit the bathhouse, but it was usually on holidays or on Saturday evenings. The tsaritsa and her daughters had their own section of the palace bathhouse. The Stoglav Church Council of 1551 prohibited "men and women, monks and nuns, from bathing together," condemning those who did so as "without shame." But, the common people did not observe this prohibition, and men and women bathed together. In the winter, they ran out of the bathhouse naked to roll in the snow in order to cool off, without regard for curious onlookers. It took more than a century before Russian bathhouses were divided into separate men's and women's sections.

The workday in most households ended at dusk. In pious households, the entire family went to bed after daily tasks were done, and only the night watchman remained awake. A similar pattern prevailed in villages. But in cities, people dressed up in the evening and went walking, as many foreign travelers described. People gathered in meadows on the outskirts of towns or large villages, especially on holidays, to dance. It was the women who danced, in circles with other women; the men only watched. The dances provided an occasion for women to become acquainted with each other and with prospective husbands. However, a Russian proverb warned, "Look for a wife in her yard, not at a dance!"

Foreign observers noted that many Russians spent their evenings not at dances but in taverns. There Muscovites challenged each other in games of chance, sang songs, and, of course, drank intoxicants. The first tavern in Moscow was built at the order of Ivan the Terrible for the men of his *Oprichnina.* By the seventeenth century, there were thousands of taverns throughout Russia.[36]

Both men and women patronized taverns—clear proof that not all women were confined to the *terem!* There they enjoyed not only the drinks but also wandering minstrels (*skomorokhi*) and what ecclesiastical writers termed "obscene songs" and "demonic dancing" performed by "sorceresses."[37] The profession these "sorceresses" followed becomes apparent from a sermon: "In taverns drunkards are never found without prostitutes; bachelors engage in fornication and married men in adultery." Despite strict Orthodox prohibitions on extramarital sex, prostitution was quite common in Muscovy. Men petitioned judicial authorities for help in recovering their "runaway wives," who "went out with drunkards" to taverns. Foreigners reported meeting up with streetwalkers who would readily provide sex for a small payment.[38]

Most women from the slave, serf, and lower urban classes could not permit themselves free time for recreation. They worked from morning to night, without any after-dinner break, caring for livestock and tending vegetable patches. They grew primarily cabbage but also carrots, beets, cucumbers, radishes, onions, and melons, even in the northern parts of the country, where these are no longer cultivated. In villages located along rivers, women engaged in fishing, casting the nets, pulling them in, and drying them. Women then processed the fish and caviar for storage.

The author of the *Domostroi*, doubtless having the model of his own mother in mind, strongly recommended that the Muscovite housewife keep a large store of food at home—enough for the entire family for a year.[39] In the homes of wealthy urban residents and landowners, the female head of the household worked to keep track of the tasks assigned to servants, enumerating tasks in the morning and checking on their completion in the evening. Every day had its project: salting or pickling mushrooms or vegetables; smoking or drying meat or fish; pressing oil; churning butter; curing cheeses or sour cream; preparing berry extracts; and brewing kvas, beer, mead, and vodka, which foreigners called "Russian wine." They also baked bread at least once or twice a week, to judge from the *Domostroi*. Between bakings, the bread was kept fresh in wooden boxes in the cold room. To eat stale bread was considered an act of asceticism.

In the sixteenth century, many Muscovite households prepared food stocks not only for home use but also for sale. The female head of the household visited the local markets and fairs to determine what goods produced in her home would be the most salable.

Even everyday cooking required skill and a willingness to experiment. Muscovite women developed a wide repertoire of culinary dishes, for both holiday and everyday meals. One foreign traveler described Russian cuisine as "the whimsy of Europe combined with the luxury of Asia." Of course, it was wealthy families who could afford lavish cuisine. But even the women of modest families, who had to limit their ingredients to the least expensive local produce, knew how to make dozens of types of kashas and soups—as the proverb says, "Cabbage soup and kasha are our food."

When guests came to call, a hostess was obliged to show off her culinary skill by serving a wide variety of dishes. Entertaining guests relieved the tedium of domestic life, and women invited them often, at least twice a month. One occasion for a party was the day in commemoration of the patron saint of a family member, but sometimes guests were invited just for company. The arrangements for guests were left entirely to the female head of the household. However, she did not herself attend to the reception of male visitors. One exception to this rule was a ritual of kissing. In the middle of the men's feast, the female head of the household, her married daughters, and her daughters-in-law came into the room. They drank a toast to the guests and allowed the men to kiss them on the mouth. Then the women left and dined among themselves. Only at wedding feasts did the men and women eat together. Women also made fun out of work, inviting female guests to bees for salting cabbage or skinning dried fish. Urban satirical literature of the seventeenth century parodied the feasts women held for each other.

For women of the non-noble classes, the most common gathering was an early evening get-together. During long autumn and winter evenings, girls and married women sat together, spinning or sewing by rushlight, and sang. The songs, which recounted the heavy lot of women, were transmitted orally from generation to generation.[40]

While all women did needlework, some of them worked at it professionally. Lower-class urban women sometimes managed all the operations of workshops concerned with cloth production, from spinning to weaving to lace making to embroidering. In the workshops belonging to great magnates, women specialized in certain areas: sewing undershifts, embroidering outerwear, spinning gold and silver thread, sewing on fresh-water pearls.

The dynamics of intrafamilial life are difficult to reconstruct. The *Domostroi* and ecclesiastical teachings stressed the patriarchal order, but it is unlikely that their strictures were fulfilled in their entirety. Most Muscovites had never read the *Domostroi* and had no reason to obey its cheerless directives. Custom also dictated that women submit to the authority of their husbands, whom they recognized as their protectors and providers. However, even in the *Domostroi*, this subordination was not expected to be complete and voiceless; female intelligence was valued. Among ordinary people, as folkloric materials testify, a woman was most honored for diligence, loyalty to her family, and love for her children. Literary texts of this period, such as the "Tale of Peter and Fevronia," depict women as models of common sense, serenity, patience, modesty, and devotion.

Scene from the "Tale of Peter and Fevronia." Fevronia blesses the curative ointment she is sending to her intended husband, Prince Peter. Miniature from a manuscript book of the seventeenth century.

Private correspondence by Russian women of the seventeenth century also testifies to the respectful and affectionate relationship between spouses. The letters between the clerk Arefa Malevinskii and Annitsa, the sister of a deacon, from seventeenth-century Totem, speak of love; even the constraints of the *terem* did not keep them apart. The letters between provincial gentry servitors express not only love and devotion for their wives but also recognition of the help they provide. Gentry women showed a great deal of initiative, using the ties of family and friends to aid their menfolk's careers, giving useful advice, and increasing the family's income.[41]

Even ecclesiastical authorities, such as Metropolitan Daniil and Artemii, an elder of the Trinity Monastery, for all their promotion of familial hierarchy and female subordination, did not advocate physical brutality toward women. A notorious passage in the *Domostroi* instructs husbands on how to beat their wives but urges that it be done only for great cause and with restraint. (Such advice is similar to that found in West European housekeeping guides in the same period.) However, Sigismund von Herberstein and certain other foreign visitors, who had no great familiarity with Russian private life, asserted that Muscovites all treated their wives with cruelty. Herberstein even wrote that "Russian women consider beating a sign of love."[42]

Neither folklore nor documentary evidence from this period confirms Herberstein's assertion. The infamous folk saying, "When a husband beats, it means love," recorded by later ethnographers, is not evidenced in sources from the Muscovite period. And there is certainly no indication that women themselves ever endorsed such a view. But in the hierarchical structures of Muscovite society, where the male head of the household was himself subject to physical punishment from his superior, domestic beatings were unexceptional. Thus men beat their wives—and occasionally, wives beat their husbands. When Grigorii Kotoshikhin, a Russian official who defected to Sweden in the late seventeenth century, described Muscovite custom, he noted that marital cruelty was grounds for a divorce. A man's brutality toward his wife would raise the indignation of her relatives, who would intervene in her defense. Church canons that stated, "It is a bad thing, if a husband cannot live with his wife, or a wife with her husband," provided a justification for divorce.

Ecclesiastical laws, however, admitted to a variety of interpretations. An analysis of judicial decisions from the sixteenth and seventeenth centuries indicates that women rarely sought divorces and even more rarely received them. Usually it was men who sued for divorce, accusing their wives of infidelity. In such cases, the erring wife was remanded to a monastery, and the cuckolded husband was free to remarry. In some cases, at least, the husbands invented the accusation in order to rid themselves of inconvenient wives.[43]

It is hard to say what happened to the children in case of divorce. Whether the father received custody or the mother, in either case the children were entirely under the parent's authority.

The sources give little information concerning women's remarriage after divorce. The *Kormchaia kniga*, a compendium of canon law, states, "If a woman is divorced, she ought to remain unmarried."[44] The *Kormchaia* contains no similar exhortation to men. Thus women were expected to repress their natural urges and not remarry, while men were left free to act on theirs.

A few fragmentary bits of information about divorced women suggest that those divorcees who did not enter convents soon remarried, especially if they had children. The primary consideration was not religious but material. The same was true of widows, who usually remarried, whether they had children or not. Even clerics considered the issue of reproduction more than the issue of morality in determining their attitude toward remarriage. The high death rate, particularly during civil wars and outbreaks of the Black Death, promoted a policy of flexibility. While perpetual widowhood remained the ecclesiastical ideal for women who had lost their husbands, the state had an interest in promoting childbearing. However, the state did not force widows into new marriages, and the laws of the sixteenth and seventeenth centuries granted widows considerably more rights than married women enjoyed. Widows from the gentry service class were entitled to a pension from their late husbands' *pomeste*, if they were willing to forgo the comforts of a second marriage.[45]

The life expectancy of women in Muscovite Russia, even amid the prosperity of the tsar's household, was short. Death at a young age occurred frequently. Among urban residents in the seventeenth century, only 7 percent were over twenty-five years of age.[46]

Funerals were a regular event in Muscovites' lives. The funerals of the tsar's family largely conformed to the prescriptions of the church, but funerals among the common people owed more to traditional custom than to Orthodox canons. Because of the fear that death could be infectious, cemeteries were always located away from settlements. In order to prevent death from ensnaring the living, it was customary to cover mirrors in houses where someone had died, to carry the body out facing forward, and to wash hands after visiting a cemetery. In the sixteenth and seventeenth centuries, the graves of men and women were practically identical. The deceased was laid out with the head facing east, where he or she could awaken to the dawn of a new life. Even before this period, inhumation had become the established form of disposal of the dead, replacing the earlier custom of cremation, which the Slavs had adopted from their Scandinavian neighbors. The adoption of burial was closely connected with Christianization and the belief in life after death, which was also evident in mourning rituals.[47]

The belief that the deceased was starting on a long road led Muscovites to shape graves in the form of boats. An unmarried woman was buried in her bridal *sarafan* and a married woman in her favorite outfit. The deceased's most precious possessions were placed in the grave. It was customary to place coins in the hands of the deceased, to pay for passage into the next world.[48]

Giles Fletcher described funeral rituals in sixteenth-century Muscovy, including the presence of professional mourners. These were women who kept the deceased company and stood "howling over the body."[49] Until the seventeenth century, women relatives of the deceased lamented, rather than professionals. The lament was a ritual exclusive to women. In the lament, widows speak about the fault of the family, which permitted a loved one to die. The church discouraged such laments and, beginning in 1551, banned them outright. However, the traditional lament continued to be observed, even in the tsar's family, centuries later.[50]

If Orthodox rituals were observed, the coffin with the deceased lay in state in the church for eight days, and the burial took place on the ninth. The final farewells were observed in the cemetery, where each participant in the funeral threw a handful of earth into the grave. Usually the grave was marked by the traditional mound, but stone slabs covered the tombs of the most notable individuals. Unlike in Western Europe, tombstones did not contain elaborate inscriptions, but only the deceased's name and date of death and occasionally the name of the woman's husband and his profession.[51]

The memorial feast after the burial was already a millennium-old custom in the Muscovite period. By tradition, the memorial meals were lavish. The first memorial feast took place on the ninth day, immediately after the burial. The second took place on the fortieth day, when, according to Christian teachings, the soul ascended into heaven. Relatives of the deceased prepared ritual foods for the feast: *kutia* (a sort of rice kasha with raisins), pancakes, pies, and *kisel* (a thickened fruit drink). Despite the remonstrations of the church, the community ritual of the memorial feast with the deceased's relatives at home remained more important than Orthodox burial and commemoratory prayers. The home observances in memory of the dead, no matter how insignificant their social standing, celebrated their individuality and marked their accomplishments.

For most Muscovite women, life was full of tribulation, especially after marriage and the birth of children. The requirements of Christian piety and virtue could easily become so constraining that they

were oppressive. Misogynistic teachings that reinforced men's authority over women also reinforced lords' authority over their subordi-
nates and serfs. Prejudices against the "weaker sex" coexisted with
popular traditions that extolled women as sensible.

The lives of women differed according to their social order. In
comparison with the earlier period, the status of Muscovite noblewomen had undergone a qualitative change. In the pre-Muscovite
era, aristocratic women had actively involved themselves in governmental affairs, had received ambassadors, led diplomatic missions,
disseminated learning, and worked as physicians. Within the more
formalized and bureaucratized Muscovite government, with its array
of chancelleries and functionaries, women found no place. Women
were forced to accept a more limited way of life. Aristocratic women's
status within the family changed also, and the system of *terem* seclusion
arose. These noblewomen, who spent their days in the *terem*, could see
that women of the lower classes did not have their comfortable surroundings—nor their restrictions on freedom of movement. But overall
the rhythm of life continued as before: women spent their days in ordinary labors, struggling to survive, give birth, and rear their children.

A Woman's Honor

It is difficult to develop a unified picture of the legal status of women
in sixteenth- and seventeenth-century Russia, because the volume of
source material is so great compared with the earlier period. These
sources include legal documents concerning land and household
property, records of judicial proceedings, law codes, and governmental decrees. The information they provide is often contradictory. The
reports of foreign travelers to Muscovy do not comport with the facts
derived from private legal documents, and the descriptions of
women's activities in narrative sources do not coincide with the provisions of law codes.[52] Consequently, scholars of the history of women
in Muscovy have arrived at divergent interpretations of women's
legal status in this period and how it changed from the preceding
era. Some scholars see the changes as positive, and others as negative, as judged by a standard of equality with men. For some scholars, the existence of the *terem* argues against any legal capability on
the part of women. For others, the *terem* does not indicate any
serious limitation on women's rights, which remained substantially
at the level seen in the fourteenth and fifteenth centuries. It is only
through a new, critical, and dispassionate examination of the sources

that these disagreements in interpretation may be resolved.

Ownership of real estate in Muscovy in the sixteenth and seventeenth centuries was based on the concept of "community property" among family members. This concept arose long before the sixteenth century. Regardless of the source of the property, whether from dowry, purchase, inheritance, gift, or seizure, the family as a whole was considered the owner. The goal of this system of community property was to provide materially for the children out of the wealth a husband and wife accumulated in the course of their married life. As before, the property that each spouse had possessed prior to the marriage became communal. But, unlike in the earlier period, neither the husband nor the wife in Muscovy held a significant "portion" of property independently.[53]

The dowry a young woman brought into marriage, either provided by her family or produced by her own hands, became part of the community property of the new nuclear family. Beginning in the early seventeenth century, the dowry was formally conveyed to the woman's husband. However, the husband did not have the right to dispose of it without limits, because the dowry had to be preserved as an inheritance for the children born of the marriage. But with his wife's consent, he could make free use of the dowry. Surviving documents do not indicate whether wives could actually refuse consent, or whether husbands forced them to agree to dispose of their dowries. Russian law codes made no provision for such a situation.

As in the pre-Muscovite period, a husband was not permitted to use his wife's property or dowry as a surety bond or to pay legal fines. If he was subject to confiscation of property as punishment for a crime, her property was exempt. In order to guarantee the wife a minimal income in case the family dissolved, Muscovite laws of the sixteenth century required the husband to deposit a third of his property as a bond. The wife had a claim to this property as a guarantee of her dowry. If the marriage ended, either through the death of the husband or through divorce, the wife could feel secure: she was assured of receiving either her dowry or the collateral her husband had designated, if his other heirs could not replace the dowry's value. If the woman's dowry had consisted of land, she was entitled to receive back a parcel of land with the same dimensions from her husband's estate.[54]

Of course, the upheavals of the sixteenth and seventeenth centuries created situations that the authors of law codes had not predicted. But because so many marriages ended with the death of a spouse, the lawmakers gave significant attention to widowhood. Although Muscovite law of the sixteenth century did not recognize a specific "widow's portion," the law did mandate ways of providing for women who had lost their husbands. By the seventeenth century, an array of laws defined that to which a widow was entitled.

The most basic issue was the origin of the various pieces of property, both movable and immovable. In pre-Muscovite Russia, all the lands owned by noblemen and noblewomen were *votchina*, ancestral land that might be held by an individual but belonged to the entire clan. It was often held undivided by a group of relatives, including distant cousins. Regardless of who in the family held the *votchina*, whether an individual or a group, it could not be alienated without the agreement of all members of the clan.

In the late fifteenth century, a second type of landholding arose, the *pomeste*. The *pomeste* was granted by the sovereign to a specific man from the gentry class in exchange for service, usually in the army. The sovereign could take the *pomeste* back at will, either out of political motivations or at the termination of the period of service. With this new type of landholding, a new problem arose: how to provide for the widows and orphans of gentry servitors. The laws that guaranteed women their dowries and claims to the inheritance of land had to take into account the various forms of property ownership in Muscovy.[55]

From the sixteenth century on, there were three types of *votchina* land. "Clan" (*rodovaia*) *votchina* belonged to the extended family and lineage, and no single member was entitled to dispose of it on his own. Women did not share these rights to the "clan" *votchina*. In the imperial family, the "clan" *votchina* was never included in dowries. Lands formerly used this way were restored to the tsar, and they were replaced by nonlanded property from the government treasury. "Compensatory" (*vysluzhennaia*) *votchina* was land granted by the tsar to servitors, but unconditionally. Unlike the "clan" *votchina*, the law permitted the "compensatory" *votchina* to be included in dowries, at least at first. However, in 1627, this permission was revoked. "Purchased" (*kuplennaia*) *votchina*, which men and women acquired on their own with their private income, could be disposed of freely, with the agreement of their spouses. The "purchased" *votchina* could be given out as a dowry without restriction.

As for the service-dependent *pomeste*, in the early sixteenth century, women were barred from holding it or disposing of it. Women did not provide governmental service and could not participate in the disposition of lands that were granted on condition of service. If a gentry servitor did not have sons who were ready to take on their father's obligation, the *pomeste* reverted to the state treasury. However, by the beginning of the seventeenth century, the widows of gentry servitors could demand monetary compensation for the *pomeste* they had relinquished. The law designated fifteen *chetverti* of land (a *chetvert* equaled about 4.1 acres) for the widow, and seven *chetverti* for each unmarried daughter as an addition to her dowry.

Widows and daughters, however, did not actually control the *pomeste*. A special chancellery of the Muscovite government kept track of the distribution of *pomeste* lands and paid these pensions to survivors of gentry servitors out of taxes from peasants. In the 1620s, a new law permitted daughters to receive the *pomeste* as a dowry and own it themselves, "If an unmarried daughter survives [the gentry servitor], then she shall own the *pomeste;* when she marries, she shall take the *pomeste* with her into the marriage." However, in such cases the bridegroom was supposed to request this *pomeste* as compensation for his government service immediately after the wedding—and sometimes even before it. If the bridegroom refused to fulfill this obligation, it reverted to the bride's male relatives, who could then appropriate the *pomeste* as their own.

But during the confusion of the Time of Troubles, some men married women who were dowered with a *pomeste* but did not provide any governmental service in return. Sometimes, these recalcitrant gentry servitors, with the consent or even collusion of their wives, arranged to exchange the *pomeste* for a similar tract of *votchina* land, which was then sold or mortgaged. In order to combat this practice, laws were promulgated to permit the bride's relatives (who were still liable for the service requirement) to demand compensation from her husband.[56]

Thus women's claims to a dowry did not actually decline in the Muscovite period, as compared to the earlier era. Although the new laws complicated the use of land as dowry and set many conditions, women of the privileged orders continued to receive immovable property as part of their dowries, along with other valuables, money, and slaves. As long as the woman's natal family kept careful track of how the dowry property was used, the possession of this property guaranteed the woman a certain measure of independence. A wife who provided her husband with a dowry of land, with its serf labor, carried much greater weight in his household than one who brought nothing into the marriage.

The Muscovite state, in an attempt to advance its own political and economic interests, also tried to alter women's rights to inherit landed property from their parents. The Muscovite government hoped to eliminate the nonservice *votchina*, and particularly the holdings of the descendants of the old provincial princely families. In the process of the expansion of the Muscovite state, many formerly autonomous principalities were annexed. Although their princes (and local nobles) usually found places in the Muscovite government, they often retained ownership of large *votchina* estates in their original home provinces. Because the Muscovite government feared that these holdings and local loyalties could serve as a basis for separatim, it strove to establish its control over the provincial *votchina* and to transform it into a service-dependent *pomeste*. One method of accomplishing this goal was to limit the rights of daughters, wives, and widows to inherit land, which effectively made them materially dependent upon their husbands.[57]

Thus in the sixteenth and seventeenth centuries, women were forbidden to inherit the "clan" *votchina* from deceased parents, just as they were forbidden to receive it as a dowry. Nor could a testator any longer bequeath his familial estates to his wife, entrusting her, among all the members of the family, with his entire property. Even the widow's lifetime usufruct of her husband's property, which had become customary in the fifteenth century, was abolished in the seventeenth. The Law Code of 1649 established that "[widows] have no interest in the *votchina*, except for purchased ones." The state also strove to limit widows' claims to a "compensatory" *votchina*—estates that their husbands acquired in the course of their governmental service as gifts or grants from the tsar. Until the 1620s, a "compensatory" *votchina* was still equated with a "purchased" *votchina*, but a decree in 1627 forbade men to bequeath such lands to their wives: "Widows shall not sell or mortgage a compensatory *votchina*, or donate it [to the church] for the repose of their souls, or use it in their dowries." Widows retained the right to use this property during their lifetimes, provided they did not remarry, but they had no right to dispose of it.[58]

There were fewer restrictions on women's management of a "purchased" *votchina* in the sixteenth and seventeenth centuries. A "purchased" *votchina*, which was acquired by spouses during their marriage, could constitute the largest portion of familial property. If the husband died, the wife inherited the purchased lands. But because these lands were bought with funds from the community property of the husband and wife, they belonged to the family as a whole.

For that reason, a widow might hold a "purchased" *votchina* until her death, but then this land passed to her children and grandchildren, and after them to more distant relatives. By the mid-sixteenth century, widows were not free to sell or mortgage their "purchased" *votchina*. And in order not to run afoul of tradition and law, male testators preferred to bequeath all their holdings to male heirs.

The legalities of ownership aside, women were still essential to the management of landed property. The functioning of the Muscovite economic system depended upon the presence of experienced, informed wives to look after the household's financial affairs and the familial land holdings while their husbands were away on government service. Furthermore, the private legal documents of the sixteenth and seventeenth centuries are filled with subterfuges to allow testators to transfer property to their womenfolk. Sometimes husbands named their wives as co-heirs or proxies; sometimes they appointed surrogates to cover for women heirs; sometimes they arranged to have the land sold, with the proceeds going to their widows.

Eventually, Russian law codes of the seventeenth century introduced a provision for a pension for the widows of state servitors. At first, a widow who was deprived of her husband's *pomeste* could petition the tsar for financial relief. As long as the widow did not remarry and did not take monastic vows, the tsar could grant her a land allotment, which she owned outright and could dispose of freely, even selling or mortgaging it. Both the tsar and the tsaritsa frequently consented to petitions to "show mercy" to widows and award a grant of land to provide them with a lifetime income. From the point of view of the centralizing Muscovite state, it was preferable to provide widows of great nobles with temporary *pomeste*-type holdings rather than have them inherit vast *votchina* estates. Noble women could not construe *pomeste* as their own property and could not mortgage it or grant it to a daughter as dowry.

The state and the tsar did not object to the idea of a widow's pension. The amount of land granted in a widow's *pomeste* varied considerably, depending upon the circumstances of her husband's death. If the husband had died while on active duty, on campaign, the pension was greater than if he had passed away at home. The largest widow's stipend consisted of only twenty *chetverti* (a little over eighty acres) of land, while the *votchina* that a prince's widow might once have inherited could be as large as three hundred or four hundred *chetverti* and a hundred *chetverti* was below average.

Only toward the end of the seventeenth century was the right of the widows of gentry servitors to a small allotment of land with which to provide for themselves and their children embodied in law. A decree issued in 1676 permitted women to use and dispose of their parcels of land without constraint, including the right to sell. Thus elite widows' economic situation became more secure by the end of the seventeenth century. Instead of having to depend upon the generosity of the tsar and the foresight of their husbands to assure them of financial support in widowhood, as in the sixteenth century, women in the seventeenth century were provided by law with guarantees of economic security in the form of land or its monetary equivalent.[59]

In addition, widows who were left with underage children retained the right to administer the entire estate left by deceased husbands, either for their lifetime or until remarriage. This was a remarkable change, given that just a few decades earlier, widows had been proscribed from participating in decisions regarding surviving relatives and the "compensatory" *votchina*. The Law Code of 1649, the major compilation of the seventeenth century, confirmed the broad rights of widows who were the guardians of children. The 1649 Code demanded that widow-guardians fulfill the obligation to pay any debts left by the deceased and to be solicitous trustees, taking full responsibility for all actions connected with the inheritance.

Despite the extensive provisions in law, there were relatively few instances of women guardians in Muscovite Russia. More typical were cases in which widows themselves came under the guardianship of others, on the grounds that their households were "in difficulties." The male relatives of the deceased justifiably or unjustifiably obtained trusteeship over "unlucky" widows, and coincidentally acquired additional wealth and lands. Male guardians could also gain control of a *pomeste* bequeathed to women and children by fulfilling the service obligation attached to it. Decrees issued in 1620 and 1622 reflect how widespread this practice was. The preamble to the decrees states, "women and unmarried girls give their *pomeste* over to their relatives, but after that these same widows petition, saying that their relatives do not feed them, do not arrange marriages for them, and drive them away from their *pomeste*." In order to protect such unfortunate widows, the law categorically forbade others to re-register a widow's *pomeste* to themselves unless they were close relatives and they acted with the widow's permission.

Most of the laws concerning the property rights of widows seem to assume that women were comparatively well-to-do, owning both movable and immovable property. A widow from a less prosperous family was also guaranteed a pension, but it was barely adequate, no matter what economies she practiced or what investments she made. Such women stood in real need of male support, and for them the easiest way to escape poverty was to enter into a second marriage.

The changes that took place in women's property rights in the sixteenth and seventeenth centuries constituted just one small part of the great transformation of the Muscovite legal system. One of the most important changes was the development of laws to enshrine the system of serfdom, which became the basis for the economy. At the same time, the new type of conditional landholding, the *pomeste*, was introduced, in competition with the traditional hereditary *votchina* land ownership. But by the end of the seventeenth century, the two types of landholding had become almost indistinguishable. It was these developments that lay behind the variations in women's legal status in this period. The law changed from complete independence for women in regard to property in the fifteenth century to a sharp limitation of women's rights to own, inherit, and fulfill the obligations related to land. Then the law once again gradually broadened women's legal autonomy in property matters.[60]

The laws of the Muscovite state, like those of most European nations of this time, intensified the inequality most women experienced in their lives, making them more dependent and more subordinate to their husbands and to other male relatives. This situation applied not only to property but to personal relationships as well.[61]

Women's status changed in criminal law also. In the sixteenth century, a new category of murder appeared in legal documents: the "state killer," a criminal who murdered someone of higher social status. The term "state killer" was applied not only to peasant serfs who murdered their lords but also to women who killed their husbands or certain other males. The courts did not take the killer's motives into consideration. Women who slew their husbands received the death penalty. Until 1689, the law mandated that such women be buried alive. Foreign travelers reported seeing these executions.

Meanwhile, the double standard continued to exist: men who murdered their wives were not punished in this manner. In fact, neither the Law Code of 1649 nor any other judicial decree promulgated any particular penalty for husbands who killed their wives. At least under the law, men's power over their wives was unlimited. However, in real life, men who slew their wives did not necessarily escape unscathed. Judicial records indicate that men convicted of murdering their spouses were punished with floggings, which could in themselves be fatal.

In cases of crimes against women's honor, the first consideration of the law was, as before, the material well-being of the family, and particularly the victim's father or husband. The Law Code of 1649 preserved the earlier provisions to punish those who dishonored a woman by either offensive language or by actions. As before, the moral damage to the victim was compensated with a fine paid to her relatives. If the female victim was married, the fine, payable to her husband, was set at double the husband's annual tax payment. If the victim was an unmarried girl, the fine, payable to her father, was quadrupled.[62]

The growing limitation on women's autonomy in the spheres of property and dishonor legislation is also apparent in their access to the judicial system. In the sixteenth and seventeenth centuries, women of all social orders found themselves increasingly marginalized. In Muscovy all judicial functions were fulfilled by designated professionals—judges, governors, and viceroys—and women were excluded from these offices. Women initiated relatively few judicial proceedings. Few regulations from this period confirm women's rights to present evidence independently or to serve as witnesses. The Law Code of 1649 includes a specific provision forbidding wives to testify against their husbands, suggesting that otherwise women were permitted to participate in the judicial process.

Women convicted of a crime received the same punishment as men. The only exception was a provision in a decree from 1637 to delay the execution of a pregnant convict temporarily, until after she had given birth, because the child "born of her is not guilty." The child would be given to the executed woman's relatives, or in the absence of family, to a hired wet nurse. Thus women still remained fully responsible before the law for their actions, even if they did not enjoy equality of rights or capacity.

"Painted Beauties"

Many foreigners who visited Muscovy in the sixteenth and seventeenth centuries agreed that Russian women were, in the words of the Swedish diplomat Petrus Petrejus, "extraordinarily beautiful and pale of face, very shapely, with small busts, large dark eyes, fine hands, and slender fingers."[63] The German Adam Olearius agreed: "Russian women are in general of middle height, shapely, slightly built, and beautiful,"[64] as did the Austrian diplomat Johann Georg Korb: "Russian women have shapely builds and pretty faces."[65] However, other foreign observers disagreed, especially on the question of "shapeliness." The Englishman Samuel Collins, who worked as a doctor at the court of Tsar Aleksei, compared portly Muscovite ladies with his lean countrywomen:

> The beauty of Women they place in their fatness ... Narrow feet and slender wasts [waists] are alike ugly in their sight ... A lean Woman they account unwholsom, therefore they who are inclined to leanness, give themselves over to all manner of Epicurism, on purpose to fatten themselves, and lye a bed all day long drinking Russian Brandy (which will fatten extremely) then they sleep, and afterwards drink again, liste [like] Swine design'd to make Bacon.[66]

It is not difficult to distinguish truth from fantasy here. It is very hard to get fat from drinking vodka, and only in wealthy boyar families could the women afford to stay in bed all day. The foreigners' impression of Russian women's portliness had more to do with the unfamiliar silhouette formed by women's traditional costume than with their actual figures. As in the previous period, Russian women's dress was multilayered and widely cut. Although the costume had a defined waist, Russian women did not wear corsets. For that reason, Korb suggested, "their figures are not so well-proportioned as other European women, and their bodies, which are not constrained by their attire, can spread however they might."

To judge from folkloric evidence, the ideal female beauty among all orders of Muscovite society was tall, stately, and serene and fluid in movement, able to walk "as though sailing," "like a swan." To be beautiful, a woman was supposed to hold her head up proudly but cast her eyes down modestly—except, of course, for tsaritsas and noblewomen. In the popular conception, beauty was associated with health. Thinness and pallor were considered signs of illness or mean behavior, bad habits, or depravity. Certain ecclesiastical texts taught that the word for paleness (*blednost*) and the word for harlotry (*bliadstvo*) originated in the same root.[67]

In order to avoid such disagreeable characterizations, Russian women hoped to have bright red cheeks ("like the color of poppies"), white skin ("like white snow"), clear, lustrous eyes ("like a falcon"), and black eyebrows ("like a sable's tail"). The ideal was a "painted beauty" that appeared to have been drawn by a master artist.

This description of the ideal makes more sense in light of Muscovite women's predilection for cosmetics. Foreigners noted Russian women's use of makeup and thought it "clumsy," "unskilled," and "crude." Russian women wanted to conform to the style, however, and that meant bright coloration and lavish makeup. The German traveler Georg Schlenssinger, who visited Russia at the end of seventeenth century, noted, "No matter how beautiful a woman is, still she must paint herself, because that is the custom of the country. The custom is so ingrained that, when a bridegroom sends his bride his first gift, it must necessarily contain a box of rouge and powder."[68] Olearius recounted the story of the boyar women who literally forced Princess Cherkasskaia, "a woman of wonderful appearance," to make herself up crudely, upbraiding her that "in her striving for naturalism, she showed disdain for the customs of the country and sought to embarrass others" who were not so well endowed by nature. The result, according to Olearius, was that "this wonderful woman had to become like a candle burning in the full light of the sun."[69]

Thus Muscovite fashion in the sixteenth and seventeenth centuries demanded that women literally hide their natural beauty beneath heavy powder, bright rouge (often derived from beets), eyebrows and lashes darkened with antimony, and eyelids shadowed in blue up to the temples, and even to put drops in the eyes to dilate the pupils and give them more depth and expressiveness. Some of the cosmetics fashionable women used were injurious to their health, not to mention damaging to their skin. The court physician Samuel Collins listed the harmful substances in Russian women's makeup, which included mercury compounds, ochre, bismuth, and soot, which was mixed with water and used to outline eyes and brows. Most horrifying to many Europeans was the Muscovite custom of coloring the teeth black. Collins interpreted this fashion as making a virtue out of necessity. Because of the lack of vitamins and calcium, Russians' teeth tended to be discolored, and Russian women tried to whiten them with powdered mercury compounds. This process eventually caused their teeth to decay, and also had a deleterious effect on their health in general. Then women would rub their teeth with a black substance, so that the decayed teeth could not be distinguished from the healthy ones. It is little wonder that Europeans were repulsed by Russian women's white faces, red cheeks, and black teeth and reproached Russians for the barbarity of esteeming such disfigurement as beauty.[70] Fortunately, the custom of black teeth and the use of mercury powder did not last long, only for half a century.

At the same time, folk healers, who were not acquainted with urban fashions, dispensed a huge array of ointments, creams, and treatments that were supposed to preserve youthfulness and freshen the complexion. Descriptions of their preparations are preserved in herbal manuals from the sixteenth and seventeenth centuries. Under the heading "How to transmute old age into youth," herbal manuals described simple methods for skin care, using washes and aromatics, as well as pastes made of oatmeal, honey, curds, oil, rosin, and herbs "to remove wrinkles from the face."[71]

Even peasant women tried to cover the signs of aging in their faces and enhance their beauty. When they went visiting or dressed for holidays, they applied powder (from flour), rouge (from beets), and eyeliner (from burned cork).

Colorful and imposing headdresses enhanced the appearance of women of all social classes.[72] The thin, light scarf was intended to set off women's fair complexions, especially when adorned with pearls and silver thread. The headdress itself—the tall structure for married women and the wreath or fillet for unmarried girls—was often red in color to harmonize with rouged cheeks. The headdresses were often decorated with real or imitation semi-precious stones. In winter women wore hats bordered with fur—in the case of boyarinas and princesses, of beaver or sable. The hats sat low on their foreheads, with the dark fur complementing their eyebrows and lashes. The Czech Catholic missionary Jiri David described the appearance of Muscovite ladies in the late seventeenth century. They "pluck their eyebrows in a surprising manner with some sort of powder, and then they draw them back on with black paint in a semi-circular shape," higher up than the natural brow, so that their hats "almost touch their eyebrows."[73] Women's tall and bright-colored headdresses remained an essential element in women's everyday and holiday dress in sixteenth- and seventeenth-century Muscovy. They did not remove their headdresses even at home.

In general women's costume in Muscovy was uniquely Russian and quite unlike styles in Western Europe or in the Orient in the same period. Women's underdress remained the straight shift, similar to that of the Kievan period. The exact cut of the shift is difficult to reconstruct, because medieval artists felt it inappropriate to depict women clad only in undergarments. The collar and sleeves of the shift were richly decorated, as in the earlier period. According to the English traveler Giles Fletcher, the embroidery and beadwork could be "three or four fingers broad."[74] Everyday shifts were made of coarse linen. Other types of cloth had to be imported and consequently were more expensive.

Wealthy women wore a second, dressier shift over the plain underdress. Giles Fletcher found the custom of wearing two shifts odd. But the dressier shift was also longer, and it was made of striped or patterned silk. This shift also had very long sleeves, up to five yards in length. The shift was worn belted, as a symbol of virtue and piety, not to emphasize the figure. It was considered indecent for a woman to go around without a belt, even at home. According to official accounts, Ivan the Terrible, while visiting the women's *terem*, was outraged to find his daughter-in-law bareheaded, "in only a plain shift," without a belt. He began to beat her, and when her husband intervened in her defense, Ivan struck and killed him.[75]

Peasant women continued to wear a wrap-skirt over their shifts. Elite women and urban women, however, did not wear them. Instead, their favorite dress for both daily and holiday wear was a loose jumper called a *sarafan*. The *sarafan* originated in men's costume, and women began to wear it only in the sixteenth century. The *sarafan* came in many types, some for indoor wear, and some for outdoor. The *sarafan* had shoulder straps, but no sleeves or waist. Women pulled them on over their heads and then fastened them in front with metal or wooden buttons. The fabric for everyday *sarafans* was homemade, while expensive imported cloth was used for holiday wear. Finished *sarafans* were decorated with lace, precious stones, and appliqués of gold thread. In both cases, the fabric was closely woven and bright colored.

The *sarafan* was worn unbelted. With the spread of Orthodox ascetic ideals and *terem* seclusion, women's costume changed to hide the contours of the figure and deemphasize waist and bosom. Belts were used only for undershifts; outer garments were not gathered in at all. On the contrary, *sarafans* and jackets in no way revealed the physique of the wearer. The waist-length garments of the earlier period were transformed in the sixteenth century into a sort of open sleeveless vest, cut with many little gathers that could disguise either a round belly or emaciation.

The most popular outer garment for women in Muscovy was a sort of widely cut and loosely fitted coat, which became the essential item of bridal dress. It was cut from a single rectangle of cloth, with an opening for the neck. The sides were then fastened under the arms, leaving the undershift with its rich embroidery visible. The lower section of this coat was often made of heavier brocade or velvet fabric in a textured pattern. The coat was worn over the *sarafan*, which remained visible beneath it. Winter coats were composed of multiple layers of cloth and were lined with fur for warmth. Both summer and winter coats were adorned with embroidered panels and collars, each a unique work of art reflecting the taste of the seamstress. These panels and collars were passed down from generation to generation.

As an alternative to these garments, a woman might wear a coat that was waist-length in front (to permit ease in walking) but long in back. This coat had extra-long sleeves, with hand slits halfway down. Another sort of coat, with similar sleeves, was long in front but open. Women also might wear a sort of short jacket cut widely at the hip-length hem. Each of these could give the wearer a straight or an A-line silhouette. Many of these outer wraps were decorated from top to bottom with tiny buttons. But these buttons were purely decorative; all of these garments were worn open, to allow the costume underneath to show. By leaving the coats open, women could demonstrate their wealth, revealed in multiple layers of expensive cloth. However, the figure of the woman herself could not be discerned.

On ceremonial occasions, noblewomen, princesses, and the tsaritsa herself wore a mantle with a long train over all these other layers, including the fur coat in winter. These mantles were made of silk, either red in color or white with gold and silver embroidery.[76]

As in the earlier period, a wide variety of furs were used in Muscovite winter dress. Foreigners were much impressed with Russian women's fur coats and their decorations of silver lace. The daughter of the merchant V.I. Bastanov, for example, had five such coats in her dowry. One was made of ermine—a fur reserved for royalty in Western Europe.[77] Of course, even in Russia such luxurious furs were not worn on a daily basis; instead, they were kept carefully in trunks and donned only on rare ceremonial occasions. Even coats of cheaper furs could be quite expensive—about twenty rubles, or the equivalent of the entire property of a serf family. Women who could not afford to make or buy fur coats instead wore warm clothing made from multiple layers of wool broadcloth. Comics made jokes about these coats of "fish fur."[78] In cold weather, fur coats were accessorized with fur mittens or muffs, but it was more usual for women simply to withdraw their hands into the oversized sleeve of their coats. Gloves with separate fingers were a rarity, even in the wardrobes of tsaritsas.[79]

As in the earlier period, women's footwear came in a variety of styles and materials. Peasant women continued to wear shoes, of woven bast, and city women wore leather slippers. Well-to-do urban women preferred their boots and shoes to be made of leather, sometimes with uppers made from rich fabrics, such as velvet or brocade. Tsaritsas wore shoes entirely made of velvet or brocade, richly embroidered with gold designs and ornamented with filigree and leather and metal appliqués. Such shoes were decorative rather than functional. For holiday wear, all Muscovite women chose high heels.

For much of the year, women went bare-legged. When freezing temperatures occurred, peasant women wrapped their feet in strips of cloth. In cities, some wealthy women wore stockings cut from soft cloth. These stockings did not come with garters or elastic, and so they had a habit of sliding down around women's ankles. Only the tsaritsa's wardrobe reportedly contained two pairs of knitted stockings made from "azure silk with silver," which had been imported from Germany at great cost. Even tsaritsas usually wrapped their feet in cloth strips.

The diversity of fashions for well-to-do Muscovite women is best seen in the varieties of accessories they used to complete their outfits: necklaces, chains, crosses, miniature icons, rings, buttons, dangling earrings, ornate bracelets set with precious stones brought from the Urals, and all sorts of studs and hooks.[80] Costume jewelry was popular not only among the noblewomen of the court but also with any women of the urban and rural lower clases who happened to have pocket money. They bought such jewelry for their daughters' dowries and as gifts for their granddaughters. Brides from well-to-do families brought enormous trunks of clothing into the marriage, including huge quantities of seed pearls—sometimes as much as forty pounds. These pearls were used to disguise mends and patches on clothing. The costume Natalia Naryshkina wore when she was chosen to become the tsar's bride was so heavily adorned with pearls and jewelry that her legs began to hurt from bearing the weight.[81]

Only a few examples of the jewelry of the sixteenth and seventeenth centuries survive to the present day. Although jewelers produced large numbers of pieces, which were carefully passed down from generation to generation, women in the early eighteenth century chose to have them recast into new, European styles. However, the old traditions of using types of jewelry to set wearers apart by gender, age, social position, and family status continued. Olearius, for example, pointed out that all little girls wore earrings, and that was all that distinguished them from little boys, because all children had the same dress and haircuts. The custom in the pre-Petrine period was to pierce girls' ears at the time they began to walk; this convention was not observed later.

Women and girls from the lower classes also wore jewelry, but of more modest sorts. Instead of gold and silver, their jewelry was made of bronze and other alloys. However, the workmanship was not necessarily inferior to that of elite women's jewelry, and the simplicity of ordinary pieces often made them aesthetically more pleasing. Women in the countryside continued to adorn their clothing with amulets and embroidery designs reflecting pre-Christian beliefs. Peasant women's clothing was likewise less elaborate and pretentious in both form and fabric. For women of the laboring classes, comfort and functionality were of greatest importance; clothes ought to be, according to the adage, "easily cut and tightly sewn." But the sensible, traditional approach to clothing of rural women could not dissuade elite women from following impractical urban styles, first of the Muscovite and later of the Petrine type.

Overall, women's dress in the sixteenth and seventeenth centuries represented a culmination of the trends in costume from the earlier period. It was this style that became the distinctive Russian national dress. Women's fashion in the Muscovite period illustrates the proverb "first impressions are important": from clothing alone, Muscovites could judge the social standing and financial status of the wearer and her family. The cut of the dress and the type of jewelry identified the wearer's age and position in the family. Furthermore, the changes in styles of dress reflected the changes in the perception of women's place in society that occurred in this period. The development of a style of costume that hid the contours of women's bodies under layers and folds of cloth; that emphasized the flashiness of accessories rather than the wearer's tastes; that dictated the use of cosmetics to make faces conform to an archetype rather than enhance the woman's own features—all this reflected a society in which women were increasingly desexed and subjugated to the despotic authority of family patriarchs and the Muscovite state. Women were objects to possess and mannequins to display family wealth and status. The society that bestowed lavish and expensive costumes upon women did not, in fact, value them so highly.

Chapter 3

Empresses and Diarists: Women in the Enlightenment

Out of the *Terem,* Onto the Throne

All the important events in the history of Russian women in the eighteenth century and all the changes in social, political, legal, and familial status are connected directly or indirectly to the metamorphosis in the Russian state initiated by Peter the Great. Peter "chopped open a window to Europe" (to quote Alexander Pushkin, Russia's greatest poet); he brought Russia into close contact with Western European states. During Peter's reign (1682–1725), the bases of Russian industry were laid, the old governmental system was transformed, financial reforms were undertaken, and a standing army and navy were created. With its victory in the Great Northern War, Russia became a great military power on land and on sea, recognized as a superpower throughout Europe. The social, political, and economic transformation of Russia also affected the daily lives of Russian women, who began to imitate Western lifestyles, tastes, and customs.[1]

But the winds of change could already be felt in the last quarter of the seventeenth century, before Peter initiated his reforms. During this period, the women who surrounded the future reformer-tsar—his mother, sister, and wife—laid the groundwork for societal acceptance of the Petrine reforms. These women revived the tradition of female participation in political life, which had withered during the Muscovite period, building a foundation for the epoch of women rulers in the eighteenth century. Thus the late seventeenth century was a period in which new patterns in Russia's political and cultural life began to emerge from within the framework of Muscovite traditional life.

Natalia Naryshkina (1653–1694) exercised enormous influence on her son, Peter the Great, during his formative years. She was a ward of the famous diplomat Artamon Matveev, who headed the Ukrainian and Foreign Affairs chancelleries of the Muscovite government. Matveev was not only a governmental associate of the tsar but also his personal friend. Thus it was not surprising that in 1671 Tsar Aleksei chose Matveev's foster-daughter as his second wife. Contemporaries noted that Natalia was exceptionally beautiful, "tall, with shallow-set dark eyes, a firm mouth and a high forehead; she was also graceful, laughing, educated, sharp-witted, lively, and outspoken." Peter inherited his optimistic mien and curiosity about everything new from his mother.

Natalia was twenty years old when she was acclaimed tsaritsa. Aleksei, at age forty-one, was already advanced in years by the standards of the time. His health had been undermined by an incurable illness. Thus contemporaries rumored that the large and robust child born a year later might not have been the offspring of the tsar but rather of the boyar Tikhon Streshnev, whom the young tsaritsa favored. However, there is no evidence to confirm this story.

Soon after Aleksei's death, Natalia found herself immersed in political intrigue. Her status as the tsar's widow made her an obstacle to the ambitions of the Miloslavskii clan, the family of Aleksei's first wife. Natalia and her three children—Peter, Natalia, and Iurii—as well as her numerous relatives, had to defend themselves. Several members of the Naryshkin clan were exiled, and others were executed. Natalia's foster-father, Artamon Matveev, was murdered by the *streltsy* during the uprising of 1682. In order to save her own life and the lives of her children, Natalia openly relinquished all claims to power, even though during her husband's lifetime she had frequently participated in the reception of ambassadors, corresponded with foreign heads of state, and kept abreast of governmental affairs. Instead she yielded the regency to her rival, Aleksei's daughter by his first marriage, Sofia.

Natalia had the opportunity to return to public affairs in 1689, when Peter decided to overthrow his half-sister. At his mother's request, Peter restored the Naryshkin clan to favor and recalled its members from exile. Many of them received boyar rank and important positions in government. One of Natalia's brothers, Lev, became the head of the Foreign Affairs Chancellery; another, Semen, became commander in chief of the army.

Natalia herself undertook to reorganize the court. In violation of tradition, she went out riding in the imperial carriage with the curtains raised, allowing the common people to see the face of a woman from the tsar's *terem.* Another of Natalia's unheard-of innovations was her participation in the tsar's hunting exercises, in the manner of European royalty, held near the Moscow suburb of Izmailovo. Natalia felt no unease among foreigners and exhibited a genuine interest in the customs of distant lands, especially those in Western Europe, and she reared her children in this atmosphere. When she returned to the palace after her years in disgrace, she immediately involved herself in governmental affairs by virtue of her status as a member of the tsar's family. It was Natalia who determined the choice of patriarch in 1690, arranging the appointment of her candidate, Adrian.

In 1692, Natalia traveled with Peter to Pereiaslavl to launch the first ship of the newly founded Russian navy. She tried to ease the burden of governmental duties for him by taking some on herself. When Peter was absent from the capital, she wrote to him regularly and received tender, devoted responses from him, signed "your unworthy little Petrushka." But Natalia did not live to see Peter's great accomplishments; she died in 1694.[2]

Natalia bequeathed her activist character to her daughter and namesake. The younger Natalia (1673–1716) joined her mother in founding the first court theater in Russia, based on models encountered in Western Europe in this period. This theater was the precursor to real professional theater, which developed in Russia half a century later. Just a year younger than her brother Peter, Natalia shared the same wet-nurse, Feodora Petrovna. Because the family was in disgrace during Sofia's regency, Natalia did not receive a sufficient education. But like her brother, she was interested in learning. While Peter gravitated toward the natural sciences, Natalia preferred the humanities—literature, history, and art.

Natalia devoted her life to the creation of the theater. Its first shows took place in her apartment. But between 1707 and 1711, she arranged to have a special setting built for theatrical performances in the village of Preobrazhenskoe near Moscow. In her view, the purpose of the plays to be performed there was to reflect contemporary themes and inculcate a sense of service to the "common good," namely, the Russian fatherland. These aims accorded well with the purposes of Peter's reforms. Peter issued a special order to provide

Tsaritsa Natalia, mother of Peter the Great. By an unknown artist of the early eighteenth century.

Natalia's theater with costumes for "comedies and dances," as well as scenery brought specially from Germany. The actors in these shows were amateurs, drawn from among Natalia's friends and servants. Their repertoire consisted of productions of the lives of the saints and translated novels, which Natalia herself scripted.

Peter willingly supported his sister's theatrical activities, seeing that she shared his penchant for reform. Unlike her older half-sister Sofia, Natalia never claimed a share in governmental affairs, but instead contented herself with participating in court ceremonies marking military victories and familial holidays. Court intrigues were not for her, for she shared her brother's aims entirely. She was particularly enthusiastic about moving the capital of the Russian state from Moscow to the new city of St. Petersburg, which was founded in 1703 at the mouth of the Neva River on the Gulf of Finland. Natalia personally supervised the development of plans for the cultural life of the new capital, including its architectural plan. Peter's favorite, Prince Alexander Menshikov, discussed the layout of the most important part of the city, Vasiliev Island, with her. Later, Natalia herself lived there. She also continued her literary activities, herself writing plays for the theater and editing translated texts.[3]

In 1716, not long before her death, Natalia founded Russia's first charity home in St. Petersburg. The home took in the sick and elderly, as well as abandoned children, whom the government undertook to educate.

Peter's sister-in-law Praskovia Saltykova (1664–1723), the wife of his half brother and co-tsar Ivan V, shared both Natalias' interests. Sofia had promoted this marriage, which took place in 1684, with the goal of perpetuating her own regency. As an early biographer of Peter observed: "when he [Ivan] had a son, it would not be difficult to arrange for Peter to be forced into monastic vows, while she, Sofia, would remain in that rank [i.e., regent] for Ivan's underage son."[4] Praskovia, however, gave birth only to daughters—five of them, including the future Empress Anna.

To judge from a portrait preserved in the Novospasskii Monastery in Moscow, Praskovia was a very attractive woman, tall, well-proportioned and full-figured, with long hair falling in curls around her shoulders and dimpled cheeks. She was an unequal match for her husband, who was mentally retarded and suffered from toothaches and migraines.

During Sofia's regency and the early years of Peter's reign, Praskovia continued to live in the traditional manner, secluded in the *terem* and surrounded by wet nurses, nannies, and small children. Unlike Sofia, Praskovia never plotted against Peter and always spoke of him respectfully. After she was widowed in 1696, Praskovia became still more devoted to Peter. As a widow, she enjoyed much greater independence, more freedom of action, and an enormous inheritance.

Praskovia considered herself young enough to adapt to the new styles Peter introduced. She was one of the first women at court to adopt European dress, with its low-cut bodices, and to participate in the new types of socializing—public assemblies and masquerades. In accordance with the spirit of Peter's era, she gave her daughters a modern, European education, quite unlike the traditional upbringing of *terem* girls, which focused on needlework. Two of the girls, Maria and Feodosia, died young, but the remaining three, Catherine, Anna, and Praskovia, received an excellent education from tutors in history, geography, art, deportment, and modern French and German. Praskovia herself had not received such an education and remained, like Peter himself, only semi-literate.

Even in the 1690s, Praskovia's home in the Moscow suburb of Izmailovo had welcomed official and unofficial foreign visitors, who brought exotic gifts. She arranged lavish receptions, where she and her daughters themselves provided the entertainment, staging theatricals in imitation of those of Peter's sister Natalia. Foreigners learned of Praskovia's influence with her brother-in-law and curried favor with her. Peter was indeed fond of Praskovia, even to the point of overlooking her liaison with the boyar Vasilii Iushkov. In Muscovite tradition, widows of the royal family had been expected to remain virtuously chaste, but Peter recognized Iushkov's position in Praskovia's household.

In 1708, Praskovia moved to the new capital of St. Petersburg, even though life there was much less comfortable than in Moscow. She had been accustomed to managing the property she inherited from her husband directly, but once in St. Petersburg she had to depend upon correspondence with the stewards who oversaw her lands. Praskovia also carried on an extensive correspondence with leaders of the clergy in Moscow and the Trinity–St. Sergius Monastery, as well as with members of the imperial family who remained in Moscow.

Praskovia further revealed her devotion to Peter in trusting him to arrange marriages for her daughters. Catherine was married to the German prince Karl Leopold of Mecklenburg-Schwering. The daughter born of this union, Anna, ruled Russia briefly in 1740–41. Another of Praskovia's daughters, Anna, was married to the duke of Courland, the nephew of King Frederick William of Prussia. She eventually returned to Russia to rule as empress from 1730 to 1740. Although these marriages did not accommodate the brides' own sensibilities, they marked a political success—Russia's acceptance into the Concert of Europe.

Although Praskovia was some twenty years older than Peter, she knew, when necessary, to flatter him and occasionally gave him candid and sensible advice. Peter for his part accorded her genuine respect, "esteeming her counsel" as one of the foreigners at court observed. Peter's second wife, Catherine, far from feeling jealous of Praskovia, encouraged her husband's liking for his sister-in-law. It is said that Peter refused only one of Praskovia's requests, when she tried to intercede on behalf of his mistress, Mary Hamilton. Mary had become pregnant and attempted a secret abortion. When the abortion failed, she resorted to infanticide. This crime was punishable by death, and the tsar refused to make an exception.

Praskovia spent her last years in declining health while rearing her granddaughters, particularly her favorite, her daughter Catherine's Anna. In one letter Praskovia wrote to the young Anna in Germany to invite her to visit St. Petersburg: "My dear little granddaughter, my friend, would you like to see me, your poor old grandma? I want to become friends with you; old people and young people live very amicably together." Praskovia wrote to Anna often and in detail about her life and about her youngest daughters.

Praskovia died in 1723. Peter arranged a ceremonious farewell for her in the style of a West European funeral.[5] Her life bridged the seventeenth and eighteenth centuries, spanning the period of transition from *terem* seclusion to modernity. The collision between the old and new ways of life are embodied in the two wives of Peter the Great: Evdokia Lopukhina and Marta Skavronskaia, who later ruled under the name Catherine I.

It was Peter's mother, Natalia Naryshkina, who chose Evdokia Lopukhina (1670–1731) to be his wife, when he had just reached the age of seventeen.[6] The bride was a bit older than her husband, quite pretty, but not very smart. Her deficiency in intellect would not have been a problem in the traditional Muscovite order, but Peter ultimately found her insufferable. From the first months of their marriage, Evdokia, who had been reared in the traditional manner in a boyar *terem*, irritated Peter horribly. Within two years after the wedding, Peter had found more interesting female company in the person of Anna Mons, the beautiful and intelligent daughter of a foreign wine-merchant of the German Quarter of Moscow. Under Tsar Aleksei, foreigners resident in Moscow had been ordered to live there, separate from Russians, to keep them from corrupting Muscovites with their evil Western ways. Peter, fascinated with the curiosities he could find in the German Quarter, spent many hours of his youth there. It was not entirely coincidental that at this time Peter asked his uncle, Lev Naryshkin, and the powerful boyar Tikhon Streshnev to obtain Evdokia's consent to a divorce. But Evdokia stubbornly refused. Upon his return from a military campaign in 1698, Peter decided upon the desperate measure of exiling his wife forcibly to a convent in Suzdal.

However, once she found herself in the convent, the quiet and God-fearing Evdokia showed unexpected decisiveness. Stung by her husband's rejection, she opposed him and his activities. Evdokia became the focal point for people from all over the country who were dissatisfied with Peter's spurning of the traditional structures of Russian life. Little by little, she was drawn into a conspiracy against him. Evdokia's son, Aleksei, and his associates made the overthrow of Peter and a return to the past their goal. Once Peter uncovered the plot in 1718, he executed all the conspirators, including his son Aleksei, sparing only Evdokia. She was exiled to the Novoladozhskii Monastery, not far from St. Petersburg, where she lived for ten years, until 1727, when her grandson, Peter II, released her.

Peter's second wife, Catherine I (1684–1727), was born Marta Skavronskaia, the daughter of Samuil Skavronskii, a simple Lithuanian peasant.[7] In 1700, Russia was at war with Sweden, fighting for control of the Baltic coast. During one of the campaigns, Marta was taken captive by the Russian army. Field Marshal B.P. Sheremetev hired her as his laundress. But then Prince Alexander Menshikov noticed her and took her as his mistress. In 1703, she became the favorite of the tsar himself, who arranged to have her converted to Orthodoxy, with the baptismal name of Catherine. Peter recognized that the nineteen-year-old peasant girl had a lively mind, common sense, and natural organizational abilities. By the standards of the time, she was also pretty.

As long as Peter remained in good health, Catherine had little perceptible effect on his actions. However, she did integrate herself into his world. She rapidly learned to speak Russian, and after some years, she began to correspond with Peter while he was on campaign and also with many other influential courtiers and their wives, including Princess M.F. Golitsyna. Unlike Evdokia, Catherine could understand and share Peter's ideas, and she joined the ranks of his closest associates, which included Alexander Menshikov, B.P. Sheremetev, P.A. Tolstoi, and A.V. Makarov. Catherine also accompanied Peter on two military campaigns, witnessing his victories and defeats.

However, Catherine officially became Peter's wife only in 1712, and she was crowned as his consort later still, in 1724, not long before his death. According to the manifesto issued by the Senate and the Holy Synod (the new institutions that replaced the Boyar Duma and the Patriarchate) at the time of her coronation, Catherine was worthy of the crown "because of her courageous labors for the Russian State." The new empress—the first in Russia's history—was

CATHARINA IMPERATRIX
RUSSORUM

ЕКАТЕРИНА I ИМПЕРАТРИЦА И САМОДЕРЖИЦА
ВСЕРОССІЙСКАЯ.

Empress Catherine I, second wife of Peter the Great, née Marta Skavronskaia.
Reigned 1725–1727. Contemporary engraving.

granted privileges and powers that tsaritsas had not enjoyed: to pre-
scribe duties, to confer noble titles, and to award medals. To emphasize his wife's prominence in state affairs, Peter named one of the
new medals of honor after her—the order of St. Catherine—and
established special Guards regiments that swore service directly to
her, following European models.

Nobles who had come to prominence at court in the first quarter
of the eighteenth century understood that Catherine had influence
over the tsar and tried to win her favor. It was these aristocrats, in
particular Alexander Menshikov, who raised Catherine to the throne
after Peter's sudden death in January 1725. Peter had not left a will,
and his most direct heir in the male line was his ten-year-old grandson, also named Peter, the son of the executed Aleksei. Catherine's
succession satisfied the interests of the Guards regiments, the aristocratic units Peter had set up as palace bodyguards and elite troops.
The leaders of the Guards had Catherine crowned with great pomp,
and, grateful for their support, she quickly appointed them to the
highest governmental rank, that of Senator. At the same time, Catherine took measures to counterbalance the Senate, which contained
many representatives of old noble families who opposed the "low-
born" empress. Thus Catherine created a new governmental institution, the Supreme Privy Council. Its members proclaimed themselves
to be perpetuating Peter's Western-oriented policies. Like Peter before them, they encouraged the development of private industry
through the abrogation of state monopolies, and they augmented
the strength of the army and navy, albeit slowly. Sofronii Likhud, one
of Catherine's contemporaries, praised her "gifts of the soul," noting
that "in ordering her imperial household, she inculcated great pru-
dence, and there was a true logic in her direction." In a notably
liberal initiative, Catherine reduced the size of Peter's apparatus for
police surveillance and abolished the Secret Chancellery for Investiga-
tive Affairs, which had been notorious for its inquisitorial methods.

The brief period of Catherine's reign was also notable for its successes in the realm of foreign affairs. Although Russia lost territories
along the Caspian Sea, it fought off the Swedish attempts to reverse
Peter's gains in the Baltic. Peter's widow well understood how significant Baltic ports were to Russia and how much it cost in Russian
blood to acquire them. Thus Poland did not succeed in detaching
Courland, where Peter's niece Anna ruled, from Russian territory.

Catherine reigned as empress for only two years. Thanks to her
intelligent and educated advisors, the former peasant girl initiated

policies that subsequently influenced not only political life but also intellectual life. In 1726, she authorized a scientific expedition, under the leadership of Vitus Bering, to explore the coast of Siberia; his voyage led to the discovery of the Bering Strait between Russia and Alaska. The same year, Catherine established the Russian Academy of Sciences, in fulfillment of Peter's vision. She also directed the court historian P.P. Shafirov to compile a "History of the Reign of Peter I." Finally, Catherine was also aware of the need to create a new, contemporary compilation of Russian law.

Catherine died in 1727, having survived her husband by just two years. She had managed to govern an enormous Russian state that little resembled the one she had come to as a Lithuanian war captive so many years earlier. The Russia of her last years had become part of Europe and had earned the recognition of European powers. Catherine bequeathed Peter's accomplishment intact to Peter II, his grandson from his first marriage, to Evdokia.[8]

Peter II had never experienced any particular affection or support from his step-grandmother. Consequently, he fell under the influence of Prince Alexander Menshikov and the Dolgorukii clan, which was prominent at court. The Dolgorukiis managed to position themselves to direct the young emperor's future: two years after he ascended to the throne, the fourteen-year-old Peter was betrothed to the seventeen-year-old Catherine Dolgorukaia.

Catherine's brother, Ivan, a favorite of Peter's and something of a reveler, decided to celebrate his own wedding at the same time. He kept an eye out for a suitable bride, and his choice fell upon the young Natalia Sheremeteva (1714–1771), the daughter of Peter's famous field marshal.[9] Natalia was pretty, and she had received a fine education, but her most important virtue, as one of her grandchildren later wrote, was "her excellent character; from her youth she was prepared for spiritual heroism." The young Countess Sheremeteva fell head over heels in love with Ivan Dolgorukii, and her betrothal to him promised her untroubled happiness and honor at court. "I did not know then that nothing in this world is lasting, and everything is temporary," she wrote later in her "Self-Written Notes." Thinking of her own experience, she remarked, "I kept my own youth captive to reason. I restrained my desires, reasoning that there would be time later to satisfy them." However, that time never came for Natalia.

In the days preparatory to the wedding of Peter II and Catherine Dolgorukaia and Ivan Dolgorukii and Natalia, disaster struck. The fifteen-year-old Peter contracted smallpox and died three days later.

In order to keep himself in power, Ivan took advantage of his access to the emperor and composed a deathbed will on his behalf. In this will, Peter bequeathed the throne to Catherine Dolgorukaia, who had been his fiancée but not his wife. The fabrication was uncovered. Peter I's niece Anna, the daughter of Ivan V and Tsaritsa Praskovia, angrily expressed her displeasure with the Dolgorukii clan and quickly ordered steps taken against them.

The Sheremetevs and other court nobles tried to dissuade Natalia from marrying Ivan, to whom she was only betrothed. But Natalia rejected all their advice, responding that she had "decided upon her intention, and having given her heart to one man, they would live and die together." This moral steadfastness and maturity, remarkable in a fifteen-year-old girl, compelled her to fulfill her vow and marry Ivan despite his impending fate. The wedding took place in Gorenka, near Moscow; the same day, Ivan was deprived of his position, titles, honors, and freedom. Three days later, he was exiled to Siberia. "I suffer with my husband; I have become a vagabond," Natalia noted in her diary. "It is because of pure love, and I am not ashamed of it either before God or before the entire world."

Their place of exile was wretched. "The winters here last for eight or ten months, the temperatures are unbearable, and nothing grows here, not grain or fruit, not even cabbage." In this place Natalia, the field marshal's daughter accustomed to luxury, lived for eight years, giving birth to her children and rearing them without servants or nursemaids. In 1738, Ivan was again arrested because of an incautious utterance about the empress and was sentenced to be drawn and quartered as a political dissident. At the age of twenty-four, Natalia was left a widow, and she was inconsolable in her grief.

In 1740, the new regent, Anna Leopoldovna, pardoned Natalia and permitted her to return to Moscow along with her two sons (her other children had died in Siberia). She might have been able to start again, but Natalia could not be untrue to herself and her deep-seated feelings of loyalty to her late husband. As before, she stood ready "to pay for love with her life and to endure unparalleled hardships" for it. Her relatives refused to forgive her recalcitrance and repudiated her. Her brother deprived her of her legal share of the inheritance from her father; her husband's relatives cut her out as well. But Natalia had no pretentions to lead the life of a high-ranking aristocrat. Instead, she lived modestly, rearing her children. After they were grown, she took vows as a nun in a convent in Kiev. It was there that she wrote her memoirs of her husband. The last thought in her "Self-Written Notes" was about him: "I consider myself lucky that I gave myself up for him, not under duress, but of my own free will." Natalia's heart-felt confession shook her contemporaries, who had no previous acquaintance with women's autobiographies. In an era of fleeting sexual involvements, scandalous court favorites, and jealous intrigues, Natalia's autobiography symbolized the value of moral ideals, which could enrich a person spiritually in a way that worldly wealth and luxury could not.[10]

Natalia's nemesis, Empress Anna (1693–1740), succeeded Peter II on the throne. Contemporaries described her having "a brutal nature"; as a ruler, she did much harm to many families, not only the Dolgorukiis. Prince M.M. Shcherbatov, a historian and publicist of her time, attributed her character to her circumstances: "The brutal usages of her nature were not allayed either by her upbringing or by the customs of the period. For she was born during the period of Russian brutality; she was reared then, and she lived under great stringencies. And the result of this was that she did not spare the blood of her subjects, and she signed orders for execution by torture without a shudder."

Natalia Dolgorukaia, who was exiled to the wilderness of Siberia with her family, had no reason to look beyond the externals of Anna's character: "Her appearance was most dreadful. She had a loathsome face. She was so big that, when she walked among her guards, she was a head taller. And she was extraordinarily fat."

According to Prince Shcherbatov, however, Anna was ugly, but sensible, from childhood: "Although she did not have a brilliant mind, she had the kind of healthy intellect that is preferable in a mind to futile brilliance."[11] She succeeded in learning foreign languages quickly. Two Germans, Baron Heinrich von Huyssen and Johann Ostermann, the noted diplomat and translator in Russian service, taught her their language, which came particularly easily to her. But Anna's obstinate character caused her mother, Tsaritsa Praskovia, great unease. Had it had not been for Peter's intervention, Praskovia would have kept her daughter unmarried.[12]

It was in the wake of Peter's brilliant victories in the Baltic in 1710 that Anna was betrothed to Friedrich Wilhelm, the duke of Courland. The marriage took place soon afterward. Friedrich Wilhelm had already reached old age, and the seventeen-year-old bride—dour or not—could hardly have expected any happiness from such a marriage. Fortunately, she was not married for long: her husband died in 1711. The young widow wanted to hasten home to her mother in St.

Petersburg, but Peter did not permit her to do so. Instead, Anna was forced to live in Mitau (Mitava), under the surveillance of Peter's proxy, whose task it was to keep Anna from marrying again. Peter feared that the ruler of a neighboring country would seek her hand in order to acquire Courland. Anna spent nearly twenty years in Mitau, adopting the customs and lifestyle of the Baltic Germans. She lived with nothing to occupy her and without sufficient material sustenance, almost as a beggar. She was completely dependent upon her uncle, forced to take on the pose of a representative of the Russian court. Even Peter's death did not alter Anna's circumstances.

But in 1730, Anna's fortunes changed. When Peter II died, he left no direct male heir to the throne. One of the most influential courtiers of the time, Prince D.M. Golitsyn, proposed Anna, Peter's thirty-four-year-old niece, as a claimant to the throne. Anna returned to Russia.

The Supreme Privy Council, which Catherine I had created to serve as the voice of the aristocracy, elected Anna empress. The council members did not consider either her administrative capabilities or her psychological makeup in their decision. Instead, they thought that Anna, as a lone widow little acquainted with the politics of the Russian court, could readily be persuaded to accept conditions of rule favorable to the nobility. There was no better candidate, and Anna presented herself as malleable. Prince Golitsyn and other councillors composed the text of the "Conditions," and Anna agreed to sign them without demur. According to this document, she did not have the right to decide governmental matters, especially those concerned with finances and foreign policy, on her own. She could neither declare war nor conclude peace, nor could she impose new taxes, make governmental appointments, marry, or designate an heir.

Anna signed the "Conditions" on January 25, 1730, and ascended the throne. But a month later she tore them up in front of the councillors and claimed the title of autocrat. She refused to forgive the insulting prescriptions her councillors had tried to impose, and she harbored resentment against declared and potential enemies. Even Prince Golitsyn, who had initiated the invitation to rule, ended his life in the dungeons of the Schlüsselburg Prison.

The new empress was not as unsophisticated or naive about court politics as the nobility expected. She disbanded the Supreme Privy Council but enhanced the role of the Senate—an action that satisfied the nobility. At the same time, she fulfilled other petitions of the gentry, shortening and easing their required military service and opening cadet academies for aristocratic youth. In addition, she enhanced the privileges associated with the highest military ranks, permitting these officers to bequeath property to all their sons and, if they wished, to keep one son out of state service to look after family interests. She recognized that the nobility cherished a hope of subordinating the autocrat to their will. Consequently, she was willing to allow them the appearance of power.

Because Anna had become accustomed to the company of foreigners during her years in Courland, she invited many of them to Russia. She drew upon their support in governmental affairs. The most famous and influential of these foreign advisors was Ernst Biron. Biron came from a poor and non-noble German family, but he became Anna's favorite as early as 1727. Anna granted him enormous land holdings in Courland and bestowed the title of duke on him. Biron was an intelligent and adept politician who knew how to indulge the capricious empress. His career, which was filled with unanticipated successes and crushing defeats, ultimately spanned the reigns of five Russian rulers. He died in 1772 at the age of eighty-two.

Anna received all the credit for the activities of her reign, so it is difficult to determine the extent to which Biron was actually the one responsible. But his influence was so great that the common people called the period of Anna's reign, from 1730 to 1740, the "Bironovshchina"—the "era of Biron." The 1730s witnessed the development of Russia's communications infrastructure and financial institutions, as well as the renovation of many provincial towns. "She did not thirst after glory," M.M. Shcherbatov wrote of Anna; "she did not conceive new legal statutes or institutions, but instead she tried to keep the old established ones in order." During Anna's reign, Peter the Great's law of single inheritance was abolished, and as a result nobles' estates became fragmented among many heirs. However, at the same time noblewomen benefited economically, because daughters and widows received the right to dispose of many forms of landed property. It was also during these years (1735–39) that Russia waged war against Turkey. Although fairly successful in military terms, the war demanded a disproportional share of Russia's reserves of manpower and supplies, and it drained the treasury.

Compared to military expenditures, little of Russia's wealth was devoted to culture. However, intellectual life was not entirely neglected. It was in this period that Mikhail V. Lomonosov began his encyclopedia, the mathematician Leonhard Euler was invited to Russia, and Vasilii N. Tatishchev wrote many of his distinguished histories. The empress was even persuaded to promulgate instructions concerning the establishment of schools for the children of workers in state enterprises—the first such schools in Russian history.

Even Peter the Great would doubtless have approved of many of his niece's initiatives. But he would have been horrified by the stupendous expenditures on the imperial court, with its unbridled luxury and splendor, and the plundering of the country by foreigners. Foreigners streamed to Russia in Biron's wake, and gradually they formed a tight circle surrounding the empress. They filled the court and forced Russians out of it. Anna arranged intricate celebrations and entertainment especially to make an impression abroad. For example, she presented King Frederick of Sweden with a huge fresh sterlet (a kind of sturgeon) every day. Other guests received furs. Patriotically minded contemporaries labeled the empress's extravagance "ill- advised"; they called her an "idiot," who "is not able to judge." While the treasury was being drained, the system of political terror, with its denunciations, torture, and executions, was strengthened.

Anna's reign entered the annals of Russian history as the archetype of bad female rule: an example of what can happen to a state when a woman ruler thinks only of her whims and yields power to her favorites. Many conspiracies were organized against Anna with the goal of removing her from power, but all of them were uncovered. The trust and loyalty that the Russian aristocracy had been prepared to show to their empress at the beginning of her reign disappeared entirely.[13]

Anna died unexpectedly in 1740. Biron knew enough to arrange beforehand for her to name her grand-nephew, Ivan VI, as heir. Ivan was the grandson of Anna's sister Catherine; Biron was set to be his regent. However, Ivan's mother, Anna Leopoldovna, Empress Anna's niece, had other ideas. After a furious struggle for the throne, she succeeded in ousting and exiling Biron and proclaimed herself regent.[14]

Anna Leopoldovna (1718–1746) had no special talent or experience to bring to governmental affairs, and indeed she did not try to involve herself in them. Contemporary observers, especially the Russian field marshal B. Münnich, later recalled that she tried to spend her days peacefully, "carelessly dressed, sloppy, and hair uncombed." Anna had been born in Germany and had spent most of her life there; she spoke Russian only with difficulty. Courtiers and high government officials took advantage of Anna's negligence, pillaging the treasury and battling political enemies at court.

The pro-German orientation of Anna's suite could not help but disquiet the most active Russian nobles. They began to speak about a palace coup, and toward this end they began to cultivate support among the lower ranks of the Guards regiments. They planned to bring to the throne Peter the Great's daughter Elizabeth (1709–1761), who had been excluded from Russian politics for a decade and a half.[15]

The thirty-two-year-old Elizabeth was accustomed to an undemanding life and was apparently without vanity. But on the night of November 25, 1741, she conquered her fears, donned a Guards uniform, and went out to lead a coup d'état. Accompanied by Prince Mikhail I. Vorontsov and the court physician Johann-Hermann Lestocq, she made her way through the quiet streets of the capital to the barracks of the Preobrazhenskii Regiment. "My friends!" she exclaimed to the Guards. "Just as you served my father, serve me with all your loyalty!" The entire company of three hundred men answered her appeal. They advanced with Elizabeth to the Winter Palace, where Anna Leopoldovna and her entire family were placed under arrest. Anna was quickly sent under guard to Riga; later she, along with her son, was imprisoned for life in Kholmogory.

Elizabeth, the winner in this contest, proclaimed herself empress. Nobody had regarded Elizabeth as a serious political player: she was flighty and happy-go-lucky—or in the words of her enemies, "garish and crude." She had previously lived unremarkably and had exhibited no ambition for power. However, she ended up governing comfortably and forcefully for twenty years (1741–61), restoring order to the highest echelons of power. Nobody had predicted that Elizabeth would turn out to be a strong advocate of Russian patriotism, because she had been immersed from childhood in foreign culture, raised by French, German, and Italian governesses and taught to respect European ways and despise Russian ones. But in the tradition of Peter the Great, Elizabeth placed the interests of the nation before the interests of the dynasty.

The first problem Elizabeth faced was to restore the political stability missing during her predecessors' reigns. Her first impulse was to return to the forms of government established by her father. However, conditions had changed in the quarter-century since Peter's death in ways he could not have foreseen; certain reforms were in order. All the same, Elizabeth restored the governmental structure Peter had set up, especially for the Senate and the colleges (as Peter the Great had termed the ministries in his government). She also ordered an examination of all decrees that had been issued since 1725, noting where they contradicted Peter's original intent. Elizabeth personally directed the fulfillment of her orders, showing the kind of personal initiative necessary for the making of nonroutine decisions.

Within the old structure, Elizabeth's government took on new characteristics. The Senate not only resumed its former functions, but it also became the coordinating body for the activities of local authorities and provincial governors. In her innovations, Elizabeth was ahead of her time. Her decrees of 1753–54 bolstered commercial activity by initiating land surveying, setting up lending institutions for nobles and merchants, and eliminating internal tariffs. Elizabeth's humanitarian inclination was evident in the abolition of the death penalty and in the building of hospitals and almshouses.[16] The sciences and arts flourished in Elizabeth's reign, testifying to the steady improvement of the economy through the efforts of Elizabeth and her statesmen.

The laws and directives of Elizabeth's government were intended to satisfy the interests of the ruling elite and the privileged social classes rather than the common people. As under Peter the Great, the flourishing of the government was accomplished at the expense of the peasants, who were ruined by new taxes, exactions, and requisitions. Serfdom remained the basis of the Russian economy, and new decrees intensified it by permitting nobles to sell peasants into military service, to exile them to Siberia without any judicial review, and to sell them individually, without land and separate from their families. Elizabeth judged these measures to be in the interests of a broad range of the nobility, both those resident at court and those in the provinces. She also favored the nobility by lightening their service obligations. Freed from obligatory service to the state, the nobility readily occupied themselves with literature and education. A considerable number of private schools sprang up in Moscow, St. Petersburg, Kazan, and other major cities. In 1755, Russia's first university was founded in Moscow, and two years later, the Academy of Arts in St. Petersburg. In 1756, Russia's first professional theater opened in St. Petersburg.

Elizabeth dreamed of demonstrating Russia's greatness and might to Europe. Infected with military ambition, Elizabeth did not spare the lives of thousands of recruits, who were sent to Russia's northwest frontier. Under the terms of the Treaty of Åbo, which concluded the Russo-Swedish War of 1741–43, Sweden ceded new territories in Finland to Russia. In 1755, Elizabeth decided to join in an anti-Prussian alliance of European states. Dozens of regiments of Russian soldiers were thrown into battle against the superbly trained and equipped armies of the Prussian King Frederick the Great. But year after year the Russian troops proved their mettle in battle. Seven years later, the Russian army entered Berlin, and the keys to the city were sent to the empress as proof that her goal had been accomplished.

"She was an intelligent and good but also disorganized and willful Russian lady," the great Russian historian Vasilii Kliuchevskii wrote of Elizabeth. Russia did not need to expand its borders to these new lands. What Russia needed was prestige and recognition of its power. Amid the glitter of court life, Elizabeth did not think about the cost of her foreign victories: the millions of rubles and thousands of lives. Her willingness to expend them cannot be attributed to female thoughtlessness; after all, she was surrounded by talented men who eagerly advanced these policies, believing, like Elizabeth, that they were in Russia's interest. These advisors, like Elizabeth herself, tried not to see that the splendid facade of empire hid poverty and disaffection among the peasants and soldiers. These social antagonisms festered for a long time and eventually led Russia to Emilian Pugachev's peasant revolt—a veritable civil war—during the reign of Catherine the Great.[17]

Elizabeth's reign ended in crisis. Her death in late December 1761 did not allow Russia to solidify its wonderful successes in the war with Prussia. Elizabeth's nephew and heir, Karl Peter Ulrich of Holstein-Gottorp (who ruled Russia under the name Peter III), personally admired Frederick the Great. To the latter's delight, Peter broke off the Russian military campaign and concluded "eternal peace" with Prussia.

Peter had grown up in Holstein, and he was brought to Russia at the age of fifteen to be his aunt's successor. At Elizabeth's insistence, he married Sophia Frederika Augusta, the daughter of an impoverished German princeling. Sophia had no Russian ancestry at all, but she was destined to become one of the most outstanding rulers of Russia, Catherine the Great (1729–1796).[18]

Sophia arrived in Russia at the age of fourteen, a lively, golden-haired girl. She converted to Orthodoxy, under the name Catherine, on the eve of her wedding to the Russian heir. Finding herself in a foreign country, Catherine strove to familiarize herself with its customs and to assimilate herself to them. German remained her native language, but she learned to speak good Russian as well as the French

ELISABETA   PRIMA ,
Imperatrix et   Autocratrix
Omnium   Rossiarum.

Empress Elizabeth. Reigned 1741–1761. Contemporary engraving.

often used at court. She observed the tastes and passions of those around her, and she studied the forces in court politics, trying to find supporters for herself. She was by nature rather emotional (a trait readily apparent in her writings), but she learned to control herself; she possessed a native intelligence, a good memory, keen powers of observation, caution and discretion, and a striking presence.

The first decade and a half Catherine spent at the Russian court were not easy. While Peter amused himself drilling soldiers, Catherine single-mindedly educated herself. According to Catherine's later recollections, her preferred reading in those days was the works of French Enlightenment authors, which were popular among educated Russians. Catherine realized that the Russian passion for things French—furnishings, dress, and entertainments—was nothing more than a fad. She astutely recognized the strength of Russian national affinities and their connection with Orthodoxy. Although Catherine was not particularly religious, she wanted to appear so, in order to win the sympathies of the higher clergy.

Peter took the opposite attitude toward things Russian. During the short period of his reign, he scorned Russian customs and rituals, and he showed disrespect for the Orthodox clergy. His foreign policy violated Russian national interests: he concluded not only peace but also an alliance with Prussia, and he returned to Frederick the territories purchased with Russian blood. Discontent grew. The nobleman A.N. Bolotov later recalled, "We feared that there would be an uprising or coup d'état, particularly from the Guards, who were pushed to the limit." By mid-1762, Guards officers were indeed hatching conspiracies with the aim of removing the hated Peter III and installing his wife as monarch. They had come to think of Catherine, a German woman, as the embodiment of Russian patriotic ideals. On the night of June 28, 1762, Peter III was at Oranienbaum, an estate outside St. Petersburg. In his absence, the conspirators, led by Catherine's favorite, Grigorii Orlov, carried out their coup. Catherine was proclaimed empress, and unit by unit the army swore allegiance to her. Within a week Peter had been murdered at Catherine's orders. It was announced that he had died of a sudden stroke.

The new empress's popularity grew rapidly. This was due in no small measure to Catherine's show of reverence for Elizabeth's memory, in order to cast herself as Elizabeth's successor. In the privacy of her diaries and then later in her memoirs, Catherine showed no sympathy for Elizabeth, with whom she lived for nearly sixteen years. "A battle-axe, nearly always drunk, jealous and envious, full of suspicion"—these were just a few of the uncomplimentary characteristics Catherine attributed to Elizabeth. Catherine considered her cruel and reproached her for failing to show feminine mercy to state criminals who had once been her close associates. All the same, Catherine acted much the same way herself in later years.

Catherine ruled in much the same pattern as Elizabeth, but more intelligently and more skillfully. She knew how to maneuver among the interests of the different social groups. She conducted a policy aimed at strengthening the autocracy but advantageous to the aristocracy, the Guards regiments, the urban commercial elite, and lesser landowners. Because her claim to the throne rested solely on the nobility's support, Catherine confirmed many of Elizabeth's decrees expanding noble privileges. In particular, she confirmed Peter III's decree of February 1762, known as "The Emancipation of the Nobility," which made state service voluntary for the aristocracy. In 1785, Catherine issued a decree removing any obligation for the nobility to render service to the state, in effect making them an entirely parasitical estate.

Catherine's interests in lawmaking found their expression in a decree issued in 1767 creating a Legislative Commission, which was given the task of preparing a new compilation of laws for the empire. At the same time, she directed a restructuring of the Senate, weakening its authority.

To a greater degree than any other Russian ruler, Catherine II was crafty and devious—traits traditionally attributed to women in power. By her own admission, she appropriated the ideas of West European Enlightenment thinkers and used them to serve her own ends. In Catherine's hands, Enlightenment principles supported not republican government and individual freedom but autocracy, serfdom, governmental bureaucracy, and aristocratic power. Although Catherine characterized herself as a "philosopher on the throne," her enlightened absolutism combined progressive and reactionary, rational and irrational, elements; liberal phrases justified harsh conservatism. At the same time as she was issuing laws that further enslaved the peasantry, she carried on a correspondence with the French philosophers Voltaire and Diderot. She supported them financially and invited them to come to Russia; in return, they titled her the "Semiramis of the North"—a reference to the mythical warrior-queen of antiquity. The great nineteenth-century Russian poet Alexander Pushkin noted Catherine's talent for self-advertising, calling her "Tartuffe in a skirt and on the throne"—a reference to the hypocritical title character in the French playwright Molière's opus.

Catherine the Great. Reigned 1762–1796. Portrait by an unknown artist.

Enlightenment thinkers emphasized the importance of public education, so Catherine duly ordered the establishment of the Smolnyi
Institute, the first secular school for girls in Russia. Founded in 1764,
it was a private school open only to daughters of the nobility. In 1765,
she founded the Free Economic Society, Russia's first scholarly organization, dedicated to producing and disseminating up-to-date information on agriculture and industry. Two decades later, in 1786,
Catherine issued a decree concerning the founding of public schools.
She encouraged a wide variety of initiatives in the areas of culture and
scholarship, providing for them out of her own financial resources. In
her writings on political philosophy—most notably her "Instructions"
to the Legislative Commission and her Manifesto of 1762—she set

forth her conceptions of government, society, and human nature. She also composed satirical sketches and comedies poking fun at human foibles, which she published in her own magazine, *All and Everything* (*Vsiakaia vsiachina*).

Catherine's ability to see the funny side of human deficiencies did not prevent her from demanding competence in governmental matters. Because she was confident of her own intelligence and capabilities, she was not afraid to appoint talented individuals to official positions. In this regard Catherine resembled Peter the Great. She surrounded herself with a circle of political leaders who shared her philosophy of government. Count Alexander Bezborodko, who served as chancellor of Russia, enjoyed particular success in foreign affairs. Count Aleksei Orlov, who was also Catherine's lover for a time, was a noted general who defeated the Turkish fleet. Field Marshal Alexander Suvorov was the most famous military leader of the eighteenth century; he rescued the Austrian army from certain defeat at Napoleon's hands. Prince Gregory Potemkin, another of Catherine's one-time lovers, was an extraordinary diplomat, who arranged the annexation of the Crimean Peninsula to Russia. Catherine's ambition was not to rule just one of many states but rather Europe's most powerful empire. During her reign, Russia did not lose a single one of its dozen wars. Its victories against Turkey in 1775 and 1791 resulted in the annexation of the shore of the Azov Sea and a segment of the Black Sea coast, as well as the Crimean Peninsula. These territories gave Russia access to the Mediterranean. The partitions of Poland in 1773, 1775, and 1792 gave Russia possession of lands to the west that it had long claimed. In order to integrate these new territories into Russia, Catherine ordered that Russians be moved in to settle there.

But Catherine's successes, like the prosperity and enlightenment she preached, formed a facade over a dark reality: the condition of the Russian people was worsening. It was the peasants who paid for the privileges and luxuries of the aristocracy. The continuous warfare required tens of thousands of military recruits, nearly all from among the peasantry. The annexation of new territories was accompanied by the introduction of serfdom into those areas; nearly a million small farmers lost their freedom. New imperial decrees in 1765 and 1767 intensified the conditions of serfdom nearly to the point of slavery by allowing landowners a completely free hand in deciding the fate of their serfs. It became a serious criminal offense for a serf to file a complaint against his master, an offense punishable by exile to Siberia. Such conditions led inevitably to insurrection, and in 1773 the Cossack Emilian Pugachev led a massive peasant revolt. Catherine's government succeeded in putting it down only in 1775 and with unparalleled cruelty.

After the Pugachev revolt, Catherine dropped all pretense of liberalism and enlightenment. The reform of provincial administration enacted in 1775 aimed to strengthen the authority of the central government and to extend its control over the minds of its subjects even in the most distant territories. Critics and satirists were silenced. The founders of progressive journals were imprisoned. The great Russian publisher N.I. Novikov, famous for propagating the "first rays of enlightenment," was incarcerated, and he died in prison. The writer Alexander Radishchev dared to depict Russia as a land of poverty and slavery in his *Journey from St. Petersburg to Moscow*. He was condemned to death, although his sentence was commuted to Siberian exile. "This disseminates the French infection," Catherine commented concerning Radishchev's book. "He is a worse insurgent than Pugachev!"

Few of Catherine's supporters from the memorable days of her coup d'état in 1762 could fathom how that smart, capable, and supremely intellectual woman had been transformed into a petty, vengeful, cruel, and power-hungry ruler; she had hidden her true goals and ambitions too well. To explain and justify her actions during the latter part of her reign, Catherine wrote her memoirs not long before her death. In this book, she tried to save face by presenting herself as a great enlightened ruler who managed to develop many—if not all—of her talents as politician and diplomat, teacher and benefactor of the arts, jurist and writer. Because these memoirs were written for circulation, especially to her son, Catherine may have been disingenuous; it is hard to know whether she indeed thought herself the success she described. But for all her shortcomings, Catherine deserved more than any other Russian ruler to build a monument, the famed Bronze Horseman, to honor Peter the Great. Its inscription reads "To Peter I from Catherine II"—a fitting tribute to Peter's vision from his worthy heir.[19]

It is not surprising that Catherine's circle of supporters included many notable women. One of them, Princess Ekaterina (Catherine) Vorontsova-Dashkova, became the first woman president of two official scholarly institutions: the Academy of Sciences, founded by Peter the Great, and the Academy for the Study of the Russian Language, which she herself established.[20]

Catherine Vorontsova (1743–1810) belonged to an old noble family that included governmental leaders, generals, and diplomats. Her family background and her upbringing formed her character: she was an independent nonconformist who consequently experienced disgrace and exile during her lifetime as well as success. She was born in St. Petersburg to Count Roman Vorontsov, the brother of the state chancellor Mikhail I. Vorontsov. Because of her uncle's stature, little Catherine's godparents were the future emperor Peter III and the future empress Catherine the Great.

Catherine grew up in her uncle's home. Mikhail Vorontsov was an educated man and the patron of the scholar and poet Mikhail Lomonosov. Despite her image in flattering portraits, Catherine was not particularly pretty or graceful, and she was aware of her deficiencies from childhood. Balls and casual acquaintances never attracted her. She spent most of her time reading, and by age fourteen she could speak and write fluently in four languages. The Vorontsov family was liberal and Anglophile, and young Catherine was steeped in this atmosphere. Her favorite authors in childhood were Montesquieu and Voltaire. Nobody forbade Catherine to read through her uncle's official papers, and from them she early gained an understanding of the issues and personages of Russian and European politics.

In 1758, the fifteen-year-old Catherine was betrothed and then married to Ivan Dashkov. He came from a Russian princely family and was an officer in the Preobrazhenskii Guards Regiment. Dashkov introduced his wife into the highest levels of society. There Catherine Dashkova became acquainted with the wife of the imperial heir, the future Catherine the Great. Dashkova was dazzled by the future empress's beauty, intelligence, and articulateness.

Catherine was flattered by the adoration of her young protegée, and despite a difference in age of nearly fourteen years, the two women became confidantes and friends. When Catherine began to plot her coup d'état, she entrusted Dashkova with her secret. On June 28, 1762, both Catherines donned military uniforms and rode together at the head of the Guards. Peter III, shaken and confused by contradictory advice, abdicated the throne. "It was a revolution without bloodshed," Dashkova remarked of this day, using the French terminology she had learned from Enlightenment authors.

But Dashkova was horrified and scandalized by the murder of Peter III, who was, after all, her godfather. "The glorious reform has been stained," she commented briefly. To make matters worse, Dashkova had become a burden to the newly enthroned empress.

The empress often cast aspersions on the merits and talents of her intellectual rival and downplayed her role in the coup d'état. The friendship between them cooled.

In 1765, Catherine Dashkova found herself widowed, with two children and hardly any resources. Her husband had liked parties and hunting; he had taken out huge loans and then squandered the money. She somehow managed to pay off his debts. Then she retired to her estate near Moscow to live quietly for five years. "If someone had told me," she recalled later, "that I, accustomed as I was to luxury and extravagance, would learn to do without everything and to wear modest attire, I would not have believed it." But somehow the young widow—she was still in her early twenties—managed. She reared her children and gave them an education. With her practical managerial abilities, she restored her estate to its former profitability. Once she had acquired sufficient savings to undertake a trip abroad, she went to the capital to ask the empress's permission to go. In 1769, her request was granted.

First Catherine went to Scotland to enroll her son at Edinburgh University. Then, to satisfy her own long-standing curiosity, she made the rounds to meet the authors of the books that had so influenced her ideas. She met authors and government leaders, musicians and artists, diplomats and scholars. These included Voltaire, Diderot, the French historian and philosopher Guillaume Raynal, and Adam Smith, with whom she discussed her most vital question, the proper structuring of society. To Dashkova, serfdom was good for the peasants; without the protection of good masters, they would perish from the actions of abusive bureaucrats. Her argument struck European scholars as "serious, but unconvincing."

Diderot, who left recollections of his discussions with Dashkova, described her external appearance in uncomplimentary terms: "stoop-shouldered," "far from seductive," "a twenty-seven-year-old who looks forty." But he could not help but be impressed with her intelligence, her command of foreign languages, and the accuracy of her judgments. Dashkova easily made the acquaintance of everyone whom she wished to see, from the pope to prominent financiers to world-famous scholars. They were all attracted to her because of her lively curiosity, wide knowledge, and rare virtue.

Word of Dashkova's reception in the West reached St. Petersburg. Ever conscious of her reputation abroad, the empress altered her relations with Dashkova. She gave Dashkova a large sum of money as a sign of respect and, when Dashkova returned to Russia, nominated her for the post of director of the Academy of Sciences. The honor came with great obligations: Dashkova's predecessor as director, Kirill Razumovskii, the brother of Catherine's lover, had reduced the Academy to a lamentable state; financial resources for scholarly projects were completely lacking.

Dashkova undertook her new responsibilities with enthusiasm. "Be assured," she told the members of the Academy in her keynote speech, "that I will always burn with unquenchable zeal for whatever is best for our fatherland, and I will strive to replace the insufficiency of my capabilities with indefatigable diligence." Scholarly activities flourished under Dashkova's direction. She fostered the development of neglected disciplines and saw to the publication of scholarly works. At the same time, she applied to the empress for permission to establish a special Academy for the Russian Language. It was under the auspices of this Academy that the first Russian dictionary was later compiled and many philological journals and collections were published. Dashkova was a writer and translator herself, and she spared no effort to ensure that the scholarly study of the Russian language, and its purification and enrichment, remained the core of this Academy's work. Dashkova excelled in other areas of intellectual life as well. She was an accomplished naturalist who amassed priceless botanical and mineral collections. She also studied medicine, and herself treated the peasants on her estate, even performing operations. It is not accidental that N.N. Novikov, the famous publicist, called Dashkova "a lover of free knowledge."

Having worked without a break for several years, Catherine Dashkova requested a leave of absence from the empress, in order to look after business on her estate, where she was delayed for some time. By the early 1790s, relations between Dashkova and the empress had become strained. The empress suspected Dashkova of freethinking: Dashkova had permitted the Academy of Sciences press to publish Ia.B. Kniazhnin's tragedy *Vadim of Novgorod*, which glorified the murder of tyrants. The book was removed from circulation, and Dashkova was dismissed from her positions as director of both academies, which she had headed for twelve years.

Empress Catherine II died in 1796. Her son, Paul I, had hated all his mother's associates, and he ordered Dashkova exiled to the village of Korotovo, in Novgorod Province. She had no option but to obey. For five years she lived there, in a peasant hut, along with her daughter. She spent her time painting rural landscapes, translating, and reflecting upon her life. It was there that she compiled her

Catherine Dashkova, dressed in the decorations of the president of the Academy of Sciences. Portrait by D. Levitskii.

autobiography, which she entitled *Mon histoire*, she also wrote a number of scholarly works.

After the murder of Paul I in 1801, the new emperor, Alexander I, showed favor to Catherine Dashkova and invited her to return to the capital. However, she refused to go. Instead, she settled on her estate, Trotskoe, in Kaluga Province and devoted her time to managing it. Her English friend Catherine Wilmot spent some time with her there in 1805 and reported to her friends back home:

> Her originality, her appearance, her manner of speaking, her doing every description of thing, (for she helps the masons to build walls, she assists with her own hands in making the roads, she feeds the cows, she

composes music, she sings & plays, she writes for the press, she shells the corn, she talks out loud in Church and corrects the Priest if he is not devout, she talks out loud in her little Theatre and puts in the Performers when they are out in their parts, she is a Doctor, an Apothecary, a Surgeon, a Farrier, a Carpenter, a Magistrate, a Lawyer . . . and yet appears as if she had her time a burthen on her hands) altogether gives me eternally the idea of her being a Fairy![21]

Dashkova died there in 1810, bequeathing her enormous personal library and minerological collections to Moscow University.[22]

Catherine Dashkova's devotion and self-sacrifice to her chosen work distinguished her from most of the educated ladies of her day. Her career was not only atypical but unique. Even so, numerous other women made their mark in the Russian intellectual elite of the eighteenth century. Among authors and poets we find Pelageia Veliasheva-Volyntseva, who wrote plays for the theater and translated works from French; she also published a women's magazine. Anna Volkova, a noted poet, described customary life in rural Russia. Ekaterina Kniazhnina wrote poetry about the attractions of love. Women such as Maria Razumovskaia, Anna Vorontsova, and Maria Naryshkina came from the most prominent noble families of Russia, but they found life in high society less appealing than intellectual endeavors in the arts, history, philosophy, and law. Women also became prominent in the performing arts: the dramatic actress Tatiana Troepolskaia, the ballerinas Anna Timofeeva and Anna Berilova, and most notably the incomparable Praskovia Kovaleva (1768–1803), whom her devotees called "the pearl of the Russian stage."[23]

Praskovia Kovaleva was the daughter of a serf blacksmith. At the age of eight she was assigned to work in the theater belonging to Count N.P. Sheremetev, the grandson of Peter the Great's field marshal and the nephew of Natalia Dolgorukaia. The entire staff of Sheremetev's theater—performers, set designers, make-up artists, costumers, and orchestra—were serfs. The count himself was not only the owner but also the producer, director, and musical maestro. He invested all the income from his vast landholding in this theater, and it became famous throughout Russia. Count Sheremetev himself carefully selected the most beautiful and talented serf children to attend the theatrical school he had established on his estate. There the children were taught reading, writing, rhetoric, foreign languages, music, and exercise.[24]

Praskovia attended that school. At age eleven she began to appear on stage, and her first performances attracted the attention of theater goers. Her ingenue passion and the depth of her dramatic perfor-mance earned her the applause of the audience, who forgot that she was only a child. Calling her the "pearl" of Sheremetev's theater, they inspired her choice of stage name, Praskovia Zhemchugova (*zhemchug* meaning "pearl").

Praskovia's fine, lyric soprano voice, expressive features, and ability to bring stage characters to life, as well as her personal charm, im-pressed connoisseurs of theater and opera. Praskovia received the lead roles in the most popular productions of the day, mostly foreign tragedies set in European aristocratic surroundings. Count Shereme-tev frequently took his troupe out on tour to other Russian cities, including St. Petersburg. There Praskovia earned wide recognition: Catherine the Great herself praised her acting abilities, and aristo-cratic salons discussed her roles. Praskovia based her portrayals on her own feelings rather than on knowledge of her characters' circum-stances, of which her rural Russian origins and narrow theatrical edu-cation gave her no experience. She was particularly successful at playing emotionally rich romantic and dramatic heroines. Her sweet, strong voice, according to contemporaries, was "charming, bewitching."

Count Sheremetev himself was fascinated by Praskovia's talent, beauty, youth, and modesty, and he fell in love with his "little pearl." "Her reason is adorned by virtue," he wrote later; "it has captivated me even more than her beauty. Together they have forced me to flout societal prejudices concerning noble ancestry and take her as my wife." Praskovia returned his sentiments, despite the great differ-ence in their ages: she was barely past twenty, and he almost fifty. In 1798 Sheremetev freed Praskovia from serfdom. Soon it became well known among the count's friends that Praskovia was his common-law wife. But propriety forbade him from appearing with her in public, so he built a luxurious home for her next door to the theater. The actors in Sheremetev's troupe, for their part, were none too happy about Praskovia's special relationship with their master, and they called her "Mistress Mistress" to her face.

The drama of her forbidden love affair with Sheremetev enhanced Praskovia's acting, bringing a new and genuine passion to her roles, to the delight of her theatrical audience. But she found the complexi-ties of her personal situation too difficult to bear, and she had a nervous breakdown. In Moscow in November 1801, Count Shere-metev married Praskovia in secret. He freed all her relatives from serfdom and hired an attorney to trace Praskovia's genealogy to the Kowalskis, a Polish noble family.

Praskovia Kovaleva-Zhemchugova, "the Pearl," serf opera singer, upon her marriage to Count Sheremetev. Portrait by the serf artist N. Argunov.

But none of this could alter Praskovia's frame of mind. To try to make her happy, the count moved them to St. Petersburg. He hoped that the change of scene and a gradual acceptance into society would help her recover. It did not. The unfamiliar surroundings only increased the stress of performing; further, Praskovia was distraught over the death of her mother and sister. She caught a chill standing in a cold and damp Petersburg church and collapsed.

At this time, Count Sheremetev commissioned a portrait of Praskovia, painted by the serf artist N.I. Argunov, whom she had known since childhood. Perhaps Argunov foresaw the end, for in his portrait, Praskovia wears a sad expression. In February 1803, twelve days after the birth of her son, Praskovia died of acute tuberculosis. St. Petersburg society, which had previously praised her talents, refused to attend the lavish funeral Sheremetev arranged at the Alexander Nevsky Monastery. Only he and a few close friends came to her graveside, those who had held her in great respect. Without Praskovia Zhemchugova, the Sheremetev troupe lost its prominence. "The magical theater has fallen apart," one contemporary wrote. But Praskovia's reputation endured for decades, not only in the world of theater but also in folklore and peasant songs, which depicted the tragedy of her love and the insurmountability of societal prejudices.

Praskovia Kovaleva's experiences were typical for talented serf women. The only thing that was atypical about her life was the count's particular generosity toward her. Dozens of other serf actresses could not hope to gain freedom and a legitimate marriage, but instead they had to be satisfied to remain as concubines to their masters. In another way, Praskovia's career embodies the changes Russian women experienced in the eighteenth century. It was only in that period that a woman born in a family of blacksmiths could rise to the heights of an artistic profession and gain recognition from the highest ranks of society.

It was in the eighteenth century that a specifically women's consciousness first appeared in Russia. Women expressed their experiences in letters, diaries, memoirs, and autobiographies. The authors of these works were not only the great ladies of Petersburg society but also lower-ranking gentry women who felt that descriptions of their lives might be equally of interest to their contemporaries and descendants. Women felt particularly obligated to express a feminine moral sensitivity in their works: not only to describe events and the emotions and thoughts they evoked, but also to convey the authors' understanding of their place in the world, to voice their conceptions of good and evil and their experiences of the arts.

The number of educated, creative, active, and energetic women in eighteenth-century Russia had grown remarkably in comparison with the seventeenth century. The change in women's place in Russian society can be illustrated no better than by the fact that five women ruled the empire in their own names for a total of seventy years. By the end of the reign of the last of these empresses, Catherine the Great, Russia had become powerful economically and militarily in relation to other European states. The borders of Russia had been expanded to the south and to the west; Russian military prowess had no equal. Culture had blossomed. European architectural and artistic styles—the baroque, rococo, and classic—had manifested themselves with particular vitality and inspiration in Russia and had enriched Russian national traditions. Female rule, and the fact that several of the empresses were not Russian, in no way inhibited the crystallization of a Russian national consciousness in this period.

Traditionally, historians tended to play down the significance of female governance in Russia, asserting that these women rulers themselves played only a nominal role in the successes and achievements of their reigns. Instead, all their accomplishments were attributed to the educated, energetic statesmen who surrounded them. But a comparison of the history of women in the eighteenth century with that in the earlier, pre-Muscovite period refutes this stereotype. In external image, the painted, coquettishly dressed Petrine woman little resembled the sedate medieval princess in her gold-embroidered headdress, but underneath they were indistinguishable. Change in the history of Russian women was more evolutionary than revolutionary. The political and social activities of women of the privileged orders in the eighteenth century reflected eight centuries of Russian tradition, albeit an interrupted one, rather than an innovation by Peter the Great under the influence of the West European Enlightenment. The prominent Russian women of the pre-Petrine and Petrine periods shared the same characteristics: energy and ambition, the ability to decide for themselves, and most of all flexibility, which enabled them to seek and find the compromises necessary to allow them to continue their political activities.

But the history of women in eighteenth-century Russia is not confined to empresses; there were also writers, scholars, actresses, and ballerinas. They brought to Russian culture their talents and their ability to describe sensitively what they had experienced, to express the insights of playwrights and composers. The contributions of most other Russian women are less conspicuous. Thousands of nameless gentry women managed their estates and reared the next generation; hundreds of thousands of women from the peasantry and urban lower classes shared their menfolk's cares and labors. Even when they were occupied with the traditional work of women, running the household and bearing children, they were contributing, no less than their husbands, fathers, and brothers, to the history of Russia.

Marriage for Love, or Money

The eighteenth century marked a new era in the history of women's political and social activities. The changes in Russian life, which

Peter the Great either initiated or continued, gradually but irrevocably altered familial relations and traditional Russian customs. New times required new people.

Foreigners such as Samuel Collins, Jacob Streits, and Jacob Reitenfels, who visited Eastern Europe on the eve of the Petrine reforms, described Russia as a country of domestic prisoners, a place where women and girls were entirely dependent upon their husbands and fathers and were forbidden to show themselves in public or fulfill their own wishes.[25] Foreign eyewitnesses to Peter's reforms record very different impressions in their diaries and travel accounts. When Peter the Great himself contrasted his native Russia with the European nations he had visited on his foreign tour, he undertook to "give the people some polish," as he put it—that is, to raise the general cultural level. Through his laws, Peter enacted new forms of social interaction that destroyed the system of *terem* seclusion for women and girls of the upper aristocracy. His decrees of 1696–1704 concerning public celebrations of secular holidays such as the New Year and Yuletide carnival (*sviatki*) represented the first steps in that direction. In 1718, he introduced a new form of socializing, the "assembly," described as "meetings not only for amusement but also for business, to which any person is free to come, either of the male or the female sex." In 1725, the first evening balls began, where, by special order of the tsar, women were commanded to remain until morning and to dance "indiscriminately" with men. Any man could invite any woman to dance, even the tsar's wife or daughters. Peter personally ordered that parties for mixed company be held in a special palace for noble gatherings, or simply in the streets and in the countryside outside the city. Peter directed explicitly that marriageable daughters be brought out in public, accompanied by their adult relatives.

While in the early eighteenth century women of the imperial family viewed theatrical performances at court from private balconies behind grilles, by the second half of the eighteenth century, virtually all well-to-do urban women—and not only from the nobility—regularly attended public theaters. As Prince M.M. Shcherbatov wrote of women's newfound freedom, "It now became acceptable for the female sex, who formerly were unfree in their homes, to make use of all the pleasures of society."[26]

This "free" type of life, imposed by the tsar and imported from Western Europe, at first seemed outlandish, almost a charade. But gradually, decade by decade, it became normal. The most obvious change occurred in the forms of acquaintance and socializing for young people from well-to-do families. Now young men and women frequently met each other not only at the traditional sorts of gatherings but also at street dances and public strolls on holiday evenings. Married women ceased to consider it dishonorable to go visiting and receive guests in mixed company with men.[27]

The German traveler Georg Schleussinger labeled previous visitors' reports that Russian girls "may in no way show themselves in public" as "simply a myth." In his description of a large market spread in front of the Kremlin walls, he noted that many of the merchants peddling their wares were women of various ages. His observation confirms that of the Czech Jesuit Jiri David, who visited Moscow in 1699 and noted "women come out in public, where there are a lot of people, and they come in large numbers, besides."[28]

Villages changed less than the capital city. Seclusion in the *terem* had never existed there. Women and girls of the peasantry led lives filled with strenuous labor. They participated in work in the fields and in the making of handicrafts. Consequently, they had many opportunities to become acquainted with potential husbands. As in the cities, the most common place in villages to make acquaintances was in church.

Just as before, a girl's parents had great influence over her choice of husband. The old ritual of keeping the bride "unknown" to the groom did not reflect the reality. As Schleussinger noted, "The bridegroom sees his bride every day and knows her well. And the wedding ceremony proceeds just as it does among other peoples, except that the bride on that day hides herself in a separate chamber or some other place." In this period, the parents strove more to take their daughter's wishes and personal inclinations into account in arranging marriages, especially because her consent was sometimes required in the text of the marriage contract.

Early in the eighteenth century, the age of marriage for girls remained low, about twelve years, when they were still dependent upon their parents not only for their consent but also for their knowledge of adult responsibilities. The requirement in the Law Code of 1649 that girls not marry before the age of fifteen was rarely observed. Judging from memoirs, most gentry men chose wives who were twelve or thirteen years old; Peter the Great himself announced that his daughter Elizabeth (the future empress) had attained her majority when she reached the age of twelve.[29] However, the custom of early marriage changed in the course of the eighteenth century; the age of marriage increased, especially in the cities among the well-to-do strata of society. By the end of the eighteenth century, brides in cities were usually fifteen to eighteen years old, and even in villages young marriages were becoming more and more rare. The impetus for the rising age of marriage for peasant women is found more in practicality than in concern for their emotional well-being: only full-grown women had the physical strength to undertake the heavy field work, livestock herding, and household crafts expected of peasant wives. Thus in the countryside in the eighteenth century, the age of marriage for girls became fourteen years and for boys, sixteen years.

Peter the Great valued the needs of the state above all else and he believed that healthy children could not result from unhappy marriages. Consequently, he issued decrees in 1700, 1702, and 1724 against forced marriages. These decrees required that a betrothal take place no less than six weeks before the wedding, "so that the groom and bride can recognize each other." If after this period "the groom does not want to take the bride, or the bride the groom, they are free to decide so." In 1702 the bride herself (and not only her parents) received the official right to dissolve the betrothal and reject the contracted marriage; in this case, neither the groom's nor the bride's family had the right to petition the state to protest the forfeiture.[30] In this manner, marriage for love became more possible under Peter's rule.

But Peter was experienced enough to know that his directions were not always observed in reality. To fortify his decrees on marriage, he introduced the custom that parents swear that they are not forcing their daughter into marriage against her will. In families of the laboring classes, this oath already existed in the form of the ritual of the parental blessing. Without this blessing, no marriage was considered "respectable."[31] In their instructions to their children, parents did not so much call upon them to submit to their parents' decision concerning a spouse as to show wisdom and discretion in making their own choice. Ivan Pososhkov, a prominent manufacturer and publicist of Peter's day, instructed his son at length on how to find a wife, concluding, "It is good and holy if the two of you join together in love and out of your own free will." Curiously enough, Peter even turned his attention to orphans, who had no relatives to help them to meet potential spouses or advise them about adult life. Peter issued a special decree for these orphans, directing that "they meet together and converse publicly in order to marry, and that on Sundays they dine together and converse."

In real life, of course, things did not go so smoothly. In the decree of 1722 that forbade forced marriages, Peter commanded all social orders to accept this law, condemning the nobles who ordered their serfs to marry against their wishes. The nobility had complete power over their peasants, and they set up marriages for them according to their own agendas. Thus nobles frequently arranged unequal unions: young boys with old widows, little girls with old men. "Bad things result from this," the scholar M.V. Lomonosov wrote in the mid-eighteenth century, "tearful occurrences and murders that are damaging to the human race."[32] By the end of the eighteenth century, peasants who lived on the same estate might be able to follow their personal inclinations in choosing spouses, but romantic involvements between a serf man and woman belonging to different masters usually ended tragically.

All the governmental decrees regulating serf marriages (such as those issued in 1758 and 1796) paid the least attention to the interests of the women entering the marriages. Instead, they focused on the state's interests. For example, a law issued in 1722 required landowners to marry off their serf girls, so "they do not remain single until they are twenty years old."[33] A fine was imposed on masters who refused. The state's motive in this directive was to increase the population and thus the number of soldiers, rather than to improve the personal lives of peasant girls. "[Serf couples] who hate each other induce their lord to use his power to punish them," A.N. Radishchev, the progressive writer, mourned. M.V. Lomonosov echoed his sentiments, "where there is no love, there is no hope of fruitfulness either."[34]

Peter's idea of requiring oaths to verify that the bride and groom consented freely to the marriage remained in force only for half a century. Landowners felt that it infringed on their rights by requiring them to give their consent to the marriages of their serfs. Parents felt burdened by the threat of fines if they pressured their children into marriages. In 1775, Peter's decree was rescinded.

In general, the qualifications for marriage in the eighteenth century were the same as before. Priests continued to demand that the couple consent to the marriage and that they be of age. They also insisted that the same degrees of kinship be observed to prevent incestuous unions and that fourth marriages could not be considered valid (only three marriages were permitted each individual). The rule forbidding a person to enter into a second marriage "away from a living spouse"—that is, abandoning one spouse to marry another—came to be observed more strictly. If one or the other spouse hid a previous, undissolved marriage, the new union was invalidated. The many documents reporting such cases testify to their frequent occurrence. Metropolitan Silvester of Siberia complained in 1752, "Men leave their legal wives, call themselves bachelors, and marry again; women flee their husbands, and, running away from them, they form unions with other men."[35]

According to a 1722 law, it was forbidden to marry women "to idiots, that is, to those men who are not fit for either professions or service." Thus noblemen were obliged to garner at least a little education before entering marriage: "Parents should not want children and at the same time not know what they ought to be taught," a 1714 law commanded. Similar considerations led Peter to declare marriages with foreigners to be "not only permitted but even praiseworthy," provided the foreign spouse would "yield to the good of the state." Clerics previously had insisted that both spouses confess the same faith, but according to a decree of 1721, if the spouses adhered to different confessions, the priests should demand only that the children born of the marriage be baptized into the Orthodox Church.

At the same time, the obligation to marry within the same social order was observed more strictly, despite the fact that the tsar himself had wed Catherine I, a woman still married to a Swedish soldier and of doubtful ancestry. Many of Peter's decrees from 1702 to 1723 served the purpose of binding subjects firmly to their social estates.[36] For women, this rule made their adaptation to married life a little easier, because it meant that their husbands usually belonged to the same estate as their parents and came from similar circumstances.

Peter's innovations concerning marriage to a great degree contradicted the ecclesiastical conception of marriage as a sacrament. By detailing so many additional demands to legitimate a marriage, such as education and property qualifications, Peter violated the godly purpose of the union of spouses. It is not accidental that the church protested many of Peter's decrees, and in the 1730s they were rescinded.

Popular wedding customs remained nearly unchanged in the eighteenth century, although a few new elements entered into folk celebrations. Every marriage began, as before, with matchmaking, but now not only parents made the arrangements, but also professional marriage brokers. These marriage brokers were usually women, because the ability to keep track of suitable maidens, to be informed about their dowries, and to bring (for a small fee) both sides to an agreement was thought to be particularly a female trait.[37] By custom, the parents of the bride were supposed to refuse the matchmaker's

Matchmaking among Russian peasants of the eighteenth century. The match-maker ceremoniously presents the bride to the groom. "Celebration of the marriage contract," painting by the serf artist G.A. Potemkin, 1777.

proposition at least once, making the excuse that "the bride is not old enough to marry," or "the dowry is not yet ready." The presence of the future bridegroom—who, after all, would one day be the head of the family—was essential at a successful matchmaking and the handfasting that followed.

As in the past, the Orthodox insistence on premarital chastity was not closely observed among the peasantry. Correspondents and observers for the Geographical Society, which was founded in the eighteenth century, reported that peasants did not condemn premarital cohabitation by fiancés. On the contrary, in rural villages, an unmarried woman who bore a child was considered dishonorable only if she did not marry subsequently.[38]

In cities, Petrine ordinances issued in 1708 and 1720 were observed; a woman who bore a child out of wedlock could not be forced into marriage with her baby's father. However, the ordinance of 1720 continued, "if both parties want it, they may be married." If the man who fathered the child refused to marry the mother, then he was obliged to provide a sum of money "for the maintenance of the mother and infant." The amount of money depended on the father's economic resources. A man who "promised marriage and then cast off" the mother of his child and also refused to make support payments was to be punished by flogging and prison.[39] In aristocratic families, concern about the "shamefulness" of women's premarital unchastity became even further entrenched, and illegitimate births occurred rarely.

The ecclesiastical portion of the wedding celebration became more important among all social orders. Although earlier there was a sharp distinction between the secular celebration and the church crowning, in the eighteenth century the crowning was integrated into the wedding rituals. Because the ecclesiastical ritual first took hold among the upper classes, in the popular ceremony, the names given to members of the wedding party were taken from ranks at the grand princely court. Thus the bridegroom was called the "prince," the bride the "princess," and others were titled "commander" and "adjutant." The combining of the popular and the ecclesiastical ceremonies did not mean, however, that irregular unions disappeared. Among the lower classes, especially in the distant Siberian provinces where serfdom was largely absent, common-law marriages, including unions between individuals already married to someone else, remained quite common.

Even so, in the eighteenth century, observance of all the ecclesiastical marital provisions was called "the good way" for parents to arrange their daughter's wedding. The parents notified the priest about the upcoming wedding, and he announced the banns at the Sunday service. Strict observance of the rules required three announcements of the banns on three consecutive Sundays. Canon law forbade clandestine marriages and instead required that the ceremony take place "before many people." One purpose of the banns was to reduce the likelihood that marriages would be contracted with women who were already married to someone else or who were closely related by blood to the bridegroom. The Holy Synod, created in 1722 as the highest ecclesiastical body in Russia, issued a special order forbidding girls to be married without a wedding license that contained all pertinent information. The state collected the fees for these wedding licenses and used them to pay for veterans' hospitals and foundling homes for illegitimate children. In 1765, Catherine the Great abolished the practice of marital fees, rightly recognizing that they complicated the procedure for entering into marriage. Instead of the lengthy questionnaires of the licenses, the church parish books (which had appeared earlier in the century) contained only notations of all marriages, baptisms, and deaths.[40]

The medieval Russian ecclesiastical marriage service had been very long: the marital couple and the guests became exhausted from standing in front of the altar. At the wedding of the boyar I.F. Golovin in 1703, Peter the Great, who was always in a hurry, ordered that the reading of the service be cut short; the tsar was impatient to get to the wedding feast. From then on, the secular festivities increased in length at the expense of the church service. In 1724, the Synod enacted regulations to shorten certain rituals and the text of some of the prayers.

In the eighteenth century, the Orthodox rituals became indispensable, although not central, to weddings among both the aristocracy and the common people. The gradual integration of ecclesiastical observances with popular traditions can be seen in the practice of blessing brides with icons and crosses and in rituals connected with the "blessed wax" from the candle the bride held during the wedding service. However, some of the more misogynistic customs did not become common. For example, Peter forbade the custom of displaying the bride's nightgown after her wedding night, labeling it "cruel"; he ordered that anyone who practiced this custom, "even from the nobility," be punished.[41]

The changes in lifestyle experienced by people of all social classes also altered the public perception of the characteristics of an ideal wife. Urban life diverged sharply from peasant custom, especially toward the end of the century, and the experiences of urban women, especially those from the nobility, became more and more unlike those of women in peasant families. Russian nobles described their family life in their diaries and memoirs and compared their relations with their spouses to those in "old-fashioned rural families." They observed that, "while they [traditional families] had so many excesses in the proportion of power between husbands and subject wives, we [modern families] have deficiencies in the same measure."[42] The supporters of Peter's Western orientation toward women were in fact much less numerous in eighteenth-century Russia than proponents of traditional custom. Russians of both the upper and the lower classes had assimilated the Orthodox perception of women as inferior by nature, and they regarded every step toward increasing women's freedom in the family and society as damaging to morality. This conception became even stronger in secular literature. "By abol-

Gentry of the late eighteenth century at leisure: "The Stroll," painting by V.B. Sukhodolskii.

ishing the wife's submission, peaceful and pleasant cohabitation is also eliminated," the Russian historian and nobleman I.N. Boltin wrote. "To want to make men and women equal—this is to fight order and nature; it is wild, inhuman, and deformed."[43]

Because noblemen feared women's growing power in the family and their striving for equal rights, noblewomen felt themselves more attracted to life outside the family. The new forms of leisure activities imported from the West offered them outlets that traditional Russian festivals did not. In addition, women, particularly from the privileged orders of society, undertook to get an education. Even in 1711, Peter the Great designed a project to send young noblewomen abroad for education; it did not come to fruition.[44] In 1714, F. Saltykov, an Anglophile and the author of the law on single inheritance, proposed the creation of girls' schools in every Russian province. These plans, however, remained largely on paper until the reign of Catherine the Great in the 1760s and 1770s.[45] She revitalized the cause of women's education, but only to a limited degree; her new schools, such as the Smolnyi Institute, had an impact only on a narrow circle of women residing in the capital. They did, however, succeed in influencing the attitudes toward women among the nobility.[46]

Authors and poets were more influential in shaping attitudes toward women in eighteenth-century Russia. In creative style, their works reflected the literary trends common in European literature of this period, especially in France. While Simeon Polotskii's romantic lyrics of the pre-Petrine era barely escaped condemnation, in the eighteenth century such poetry, although still not particularly artistic, became fully accepted. The reading habits of the Russian nobility had changed, and the new literature contained invocations of the strong and lofty emotions that a woman might awaken, erotic passions, and courtly love—sentiments that previously had not been found in Russian social consciousness. It was the poet M.N. Muraviev who first evoked the idea that women by nature were finer and more profound emotionally than men and that women's happiness might be different from that of men, who were "distracted by their rules and duties." Russian stories of the eighteenth century depict female characters for the first time not merely as secondary figures but as leads—as objects of veneration and rapture on the part of men, who knew, in V.K. Trediakovskii's words, "the bewitchment and sweet tyranny of love."[47]

The most educated nobleman, whose heart, according to A.T. Bolotov, "was born with the most delicate feelings," readily sacrificed love in favor of a sober consideration of the economic gains forthcoming from a future wife. Novels, both Russian and West European, might inculcate "delicate feelings," but not so deeply that men came to prefer love with a dowerless maiden to marriage with a rich widow. In order to justify his consideration of practicalities in his choice of a bride, the nobleman M.V. Danilov explained in his memoirs, "Beauties should be chosen only as lovers, but wives should be virtuous."[48] Nobles' diaries, letters, and memoirs fully described the ideal "virtuous" wife. She should be a woman of average beauty from a family of average means. According to Danilov, a woman who was too beautiful would become an object of attraction to other men, while one who was too ugly would repulse her husband and drive him to seek a prettier companion. Parents taught their children to find wives with whom they could "spend their lives cheerfully," and in order to find such women, they should look in "good families" who possessed "significant means."[49] Noblemen now hoped to find wives who could share their thoughts and interests. The famous memoirist Andrei Bolotov recalled, "My primary wish was to find through marriage a comrade with whom I could share all my deepest feelings, joys, delights, cares, and worries." In describing his own marriage, the writer G.P. Derzhavin emphasized that he chose "a girl who did not lack intelligence or cleverness, and nice to deal with" who appealed to his mind more than to his emotions.[50]

The analogous preferences of noblewomen are best represented in Natalia Dolgorukaia's "Self-Written Notes." She voiced an advocacy of love and self-sacrifice in the name of love. But other, less romantic, noblewomen, who were close to court circles and who helped their husbands' careers, endorsed different views. For example, Maria Kantemir, one of the best-educated women of her day and the sister of the poet Antiokh Kantemir, advised her younger brother Matvei to marry a woman who was "older and even poor," but one with connections, so he would "always have a protector."[51] Such pragmatic considerations reflected not only the influences of the "depraved West" but also the realities of life in the imperial court. The intrigues, betrayals, and unfettered romantic liaisons at court altered the perception of what was permissible and impermissible between spouses and between men and women in general. To judge from the memoirs of figures from the imperial court, all the ladies there were surrounded by a bevy of admirers, and it became fashionable for noblemen to keep mistresses.[52]

The provincial nobility remained more conservative. Religious traditions and old customs, which reinforced the dominating role of the man in the home, female modesty, and restraint in personal feelings, remained more influential in these families.[53]

The common people, of course, did not experience the Enlightenment, or read foreign novels, or leave letters and memoirs describing their thoughts and feelings. Although it is difficult to recapture the mental universe of the peasantry, it is likely that for them the image of the ideal woman did not change much from the preceding centuries. It was a genuine surprise to Russian nobles of the eighteenth century when the writer Alexander Radishchev attributed to peasants the same feelings as other people. In relating the story of a peasant woman and her passions, he concluded with surprise, "You already know how to love!"[54]

Parents in peasant families told their children that they would grow to love the spouse they married. But the depositions in court cases, which provide insight into the intimate lives of peasant families, sometimes suggest otherwise. Peasant women often recounted the private experiences that led them to violate the law and used them to justify their transgressions of the moral norms of their communities: "I fell in love," "I always thought about him," "I wanted to be happy," "I was with him in spirit."[55] Ideally, every wife was supposed to maintain "love, respect, and obedience" to her husband, to remain faithful to him, and to provide him with "every satisfaction and affection, as the mistress of the house." The husband, for his part, was obliged to "cause her no offense" and to "live decently" with her. In real life, things did not always happen that way. Despite the laws forbidding forced marriages, they were far from uncommon among the lower classes. Many marriages took place at parents' insistence, even when the bride begged them not to marry her to someone she hated and even tried to run away. And such events did not occur only when the parents were stubborn. "Wives suffocate themselves, drown themselves, and slit their wrists because of their husbands' cruelty," the archpriest D. Belikov of Tomsk wrote. "And incidentally, the women do not treat their husbands less fiercely."[56] Cases of suicide and spousal murder occurred with surprising frequency.[57]

Ordinarily in peasant villages, however, instances of cruelty to women aroused the indignation and condemnation of the entire village. A man found it shameful to have to admit to his neighbors and to the authorities that he could not make peace with his wife. Wives often filed complaints against their husbands and sometimes ran away from them to distant villages in order to enter into new marriages. Women were quite able to defend themselves physically, too, having built up strength and endurance from agricultural work. Peasant women were hardly raised to be defenseless shrinking violets. A proverb of the time stated, "If a wife beats her husband, she doesn't do him any harm."[58]

However, the cases described in judicial records could hardly have reflected the norms for relations between spouses. As a rule, the peasant conception of spousal relations coincided with the dictates of the law and religious teachings. The letters of educated peasants, usually from Siberia, provide a rare glimpse into the psychological milieu of their families. They reveal their relations to be fully affectionate rather than brutal; loving and agreeable, not argumentative. The wealthy Siberian peasant Ivan Khudiakov sent this letter to his wife in Semipalatinskii district in 1797: "Anna Vasilievna, my most belovedest and darlingest companion, preserver of our honor, protector of our health, satisfier of our common good, and most honorable ruler of our home, I send you homage and a tearful petition with pure-hearted respect for you."[59] Similar letters are preserved in which peasants describe being "unable to bear the uncommon anguish of separation" from their wives and how their hearts overflow with tenderness for them. "Heat up the bathhouse for me, my wife, and let me toast myself there on your lap, like a little child, or rather like a great big child."[60] The mutual affection that husbands and wives felt for each other helped them to survive the burdens of peasant life, which were becoming heavier all the time.

Peasant families preserved the earlier tradition of multigenerational households. Although historians and ethnographers of the nineteenth century attributed an atmosphere of hatred, violence, and intrafamilial scandal to peasant households, it is not likely that this was the norm. Peasants learned both practical knowledge and moral standards from the examples of their elders, whom they were taught to respect for their experience. Had peasant families been dysfunctional, they could not have conveyed this knowledge from generation to generation.

In villages, there was no firm boundary between men's and women's work. In the spring, women helped with planting, as well as looking after the livestock and garden; this was also the time that they usually wove and bleached linen. During the summer, women, laboring alongside men, pressed vegetable oil, stacked hay, cut and pounded flax and hemp, cast fishnets, ground grain, and tended calves and piglets. In the autumn, harvest season, it was also time to card wool and prepare barns for the winter. During the winter, peasant women devoted themselves to housework, making clothes for the entire family, knitting socks, knotting fishnets, plaiting belts and harnesses, and embroidering and making lace for holiday outfits. In addition to these seasonal tasks, women also performed daily and weekly cleaning, especially on Saturdays, when they mopped floors, wiped down shelves, and scraped the walls, ceiling, and stove.

Young girls learned all these tasks at home, by watching their mothers, sisters, sisters-in-law, and grandmothers (who themselves might be only thirty years old!).[61] Respect for female elders was a core value in peasant upbringing. "Respect the mother who bore you," peasant men instructed their children. "Be obedient to her and do not do anything without her blessing."[62]

Custom required that parents support and rear their children even after they reached adulthood. Even grown children could count on material support from older relatives, such as a widowed mother. Widowed mothers often became the heads of peasant families. In cities, one out of five families had a female head; in the countryside, even more did.[63] Despite the proverb, "A grown child is a separate entity," parents who refused to share their resources with adult children faced disapproval from the peasant community.

Many of the hardships of peasant life resulted from serfdom. Because of the heavy exactions and requisitions, peasant families were forced into a desperate economic position, where children counted as a resource to be spent as necessary. This situation created an impetus for peasant women to bear more children at an earlier age. However, the incidence of infant mortality remained very high, despite the rising birthrate. As one contemporary noted, among women "who gave birth before the age of ten or sixteen, not a single child remains alive."[64]

The startlingly high rate of infant mortality occurred not only among the peasantry but even in aristocratic families in the eighteenth century. Andrei Bolotov's wife was only fourteen years old when their first-born son died at the age of six months. She regarded his death as inevitable and hoped only that a new pregnancy would help her "forget this misfortune, if this can be called a misfortune."[65]

Child-rearing practices in aristocratic families differed considerably from the informal training in peasant households. The formal education of children came to demand a great deal of time in noble households in the eighteenth century, and primary instruction often depended upon women. By the end of the century, many aristocratic homes had libraries—some larger and some smaller. Noblewomen had more leisure time than their husbands, and it was they who became their children's first teachers, instilling in them a thirst for knowledge. The poet G.P. Derzhavin recalled that it was his mother who "made him keen on reading, encouraging [him] with rewards of toys and candies." The mother of the writer S.T. Aksakov inspired him to become an assiduous student through her "judicious convictions, accompanied by the most tender endearments and a fervent wish to make [him] into an educated person." The playwright D.I. Fonvizin later wrote that his mother stimulated his love of literature and talent for writing through her "fine mind and perceptive, far-seeing vision."[66]

Virtually all prominent Russian men and women of the eighteenth century spoke reverentially of their mothers in their memoirs, expressing gratitude for their tenderness, love, attentiveness, and goodness. A.T. Bolotov wrote that his mother "loved him to the limit" and "never ceased to indulge him in every way." M.V. Danilov similarly commented on his mother's boundless love for him and her self-sacrifice. N.M. Karamzin wrote of his mother, "In the years of my youth you drew me toward the good, and you were my conscience in my times of weakness; with an unseen hand you guided my uneventful childhood."

Of course, relationships between parents and children, and particularly between mothers and sons, can develop in many different ways. Not all memoirists recalled their childhoods and mothers in such favorable terms; there were instances of cruelty, inattention, and indifference. But the new approaches to child rearing were beginning to take hold, even if only in a small circle of aristocratic families, and from this base the pattern would spread.[67]

Societal expectations concerning relations between spouses also changed in this period. Previously, irreconcilable differences did not constitute grounds for divorce. In the eighteenth century, this began to change. Visitors from Catholic countries, where divorce was entirely forbidden, commented with surprise that in Russia, "divorce is very common and occurs for very unimportant reasons."[68] In actuality, urban couples who agreed not to live together any more did not seek a formal divorce decree from a priest but simply gave each other in front of witnesses a "letter" stating that they no longer had claims upon each other. Peasant communities demanded greater formality, but even there, when there was just cause, the *mir* (peasant commune) would authorize a divorce. Causes could be psychological as well as material: "I do not wish to live with my husband Ivan because I hate him."[69] In such cases the marriage was dissolved, and both spouses had the right to seek new partners. Among nobles divorce occurred rarely, and it was unthinkable to separate informally, without ecclesiastical permission and a formal divorce decree. The number of divorce suits from all social orders was quite considerable. However, narrative literature from the eighteenth century does not often mention divorce.

The grounds for divorce widened, but adultery was still the most acceptable reason.[70] The historian M.M. Shcherbatov wrote a scathing polemical essay, "On the Decline of Morals in Russia," in which he hastened to condemn allowing divorce on moral (or more accurately, immoral!) grounds, such as "when a wife falls in love with someone else." This was the reason given for divorce when the wife of Prince Buturlin fell in love with Prince S.F. Ushakov. Princess A.B. Apraksina (née Golitsyna) gave the same justification for divorcing her husband. After the divorce she returned to using her maiden name, and she received a portion of her former husband's land as her share of their

common property. In 1722, the Holy Synod legalized temporary sepa-
rations as an interim step between marriage and divorce. Such sepa-
rations did not bestow upon spouses the right to remarry, but they
made allowance for familial discord.[71]

Upon first reading, divorce papers from eighteenth-century Russia
appear to embody the desire of proponents of women's emancipation that wives should be freed from unhappy marriages. However, it
was not women who benefited. Most divorces were initiated by men
who wanted to be free of aging wives yet keep their dowries.[72]

Despite the continuities, the family status of women from all social
orders changed in ways that were obvious to contemporaries. These
changes were connected with Peter the Great, whose reforms overturned so many of the old structures of life. The years of female rule
after Peter's death in 1725 continued virtually without a break until
the end of the century. Women began to have the right to a voice in
Russian families. Whereas previously only parents could decide upon
a marriage for their daughters, now young women had to be allowed
to become acquainted with future spouses, and forcing them against
their will became an offense punishable under the law. The wedding
ceremony itself changed. Although the church service became the
most important, essential element in the wedding, the misogynistic
rituals that demeaned the bride gradually disappeared. The new
forms of socializing and the construction of leisure destroyed the
remnants of *terem* seclusion. In families of the educated aristocracy,
the ideal wife became a woman who shared her husband's ideas. This
new perception of women found its way into literature, especially in
the new genre of love poetry.

The transformation Russia experienced in the eighteenth century,
which resulted in new perceptions of the family and of women's
place in it, also affected the nonprivileged orders of Russian society.
The new norms of conduct, the new ways of life, and even the new
ways of dress and manners deepened the chasm between the rulers
and the people, between noblewomen and peasant women. Even so,
the cultural achievements of the Westernized elite inevitably affected
the countryside. The changes in the lives of women of the laboring
classes may be seen in the growing preference for marriage based on
personal affection, in the broadening grounds for divorce (especially
among free peasants), the replacement of Orthodox conceptions of
marriage with the idea of mutual responsibilities between spouses,
and challenges to the medieval patriarchal tradition of the husband
as master over the wife. These changes came to peasant families

somewhat later than among the nobility, but they were nonetheless evident by the end of the eighteenth century.

The Lesser Share

Peter the Great's reforms swept away much that was obsolete and anachronistic, and they set Russia on a new path. New ideas took hold in all areas of societal discourse, including that of law. However, in the early years of the century, the old laws of Tsar Aleksei, dating to the middle of the seventeenth century, continued in force.

At the beginning of Peter the Great's reign, in the last decade of the seventeenth century, family law upheld the old structures, including the male head of the family's governance over his wife, children, and household servants. In these "good old days," the family not only provided for the natural function of the continuation of the race but also fulfilled the purpose of accumulating property and transmitting it as an inheritance to the children. Husbands and wives filled unequal roles in this second purpose, because the property rights of Muscovite women in the second half of the seventeenth century were substantially more limited than their husbands'. Only women's dowries mitigated their inequality, especially as these related to the ownership of land.

At least officially, the husband could not sell or mortgage his wife's dowry without her consent. However, the wife also could not dispose of her dowry freely, at least until a ruling in 1680 made sales and mortgages of a "dowry *votchina*" legal upon the signatures of both spouses or of the wife alone.[73] But the significance of these rights should not be exaggerated, because few Muscovite women could take advantage of them; the "dowry *votchina*" constituted only a small percentage of privately owned land. Furthermore, private landholdings in general had been splintered by generations of subdividing. This state of affairs was undesirable from the point of view of the absolutist state, and Peter the Great decided to prohibit the use of land in dowries. The "Law of Single Inheritance," issued in 1714, decreed that "in the future no one shall have immovable property as a dowry." The law contained no provision concerning women who had received land as a dowry before 1714.[74] But one way or another, this law was a blow to women's property rights. Furthermore, the law clearly interfered in the private life of Russian citizens, because it infringed upon the right of parents to determine the composition of dowries. Because the law of single inheritance was "inconvenient" for most landowners, it was revoked during the reign of Empress Anna. A new law issued on March 17, 1731, restored the old practice: "[land] may be given as a dowry for daughters as before."[75]

Although the law of single inheritance forbade new dowries of land, it also established women's independent ownership of their dowries, which they could use and dispose of without the participation of their husbands. This provision constituted a step toward restoring the property rights women had enjoyed in the pre-Muscovite period, when families had both common property and property owned separately by the husband and the wife. In the second third of the eighteenth century, the content and dimensions of the dowry, which had previously been important only in the context of familial property overall, became a burning issue for marriageable women themselves. Fortunately for them, neither Peter nor his successors attempted to regulate the size of women's dowries; this was left entirely to their parents. Parents could give a favorite daughter a large share of familial property, or completely deprive a daughter of a dowry because of her recalcitrance or disobedience. Even after their parents died, daughters had no right to dispute the decision they had made concerning dowries.

A second issue in laws concerning dowries was preserving the position of the father as the head of the family. The law did not grant absolute power to husbands, but in practice, they frequently could force their wives to comply with their wishes. Court cases from the eighteenth century recount many instances in which husbands beat or tormented their wives to force them to agree to mortgage or sell their dowries or dissipated their wives' dowries without their knowledge.[76]

Until the time of Peter's innovation of 1714, only *votchina* lands could be used as women's dowries. *Pomeste* land could not be used that way, and many lesser landowners in early eighteenth-century Russia held only a *pomeste*. Peter's law of single inheritance abolished the distinction between *votchina* and *pomeste*, eliminating many of the former restrictions on the inheritance of a *pomeste*. Widows benefited from the new arrangement. A childless widow formerly might have received only a "pension *pomeste*," but now she could inherit her late husband's entire landed property. If she died or took monastic vows, her estate reverted to her husband's family, except her dowry, which only her own natal clan could legally claim. If the widow chose to remarry, all her first husband's land had to be returned to his next of kin.

Peter's decree allowing a widow full rights to control her late husband's *pomeste* was greeted with incredulity in the old capital of

Moscow and in the provinces. The limitation on the use of land in dowries, which merely repeated older regulations, was a minor point compared to the authorization of noblewomen to involve themselves in the purchase and sale of a *pomeste*. Government bureaus in Moscow refused to confirm and register *pomeste* transactions concluded by women. When the Senate received reports of such instances, it issued instructions (in November 1715) ordering bureaus to accept purchases and mortgages "from female persons" without obstacles.[77] In this way, noblewomen, who had never themselves belonged to the service estate and who had been prohibited from holding service-dependent land, gained the legal right to own and dispose of it. In June 1753, during the reign of Empress Elizabeth, the Senate confirmed this right. In particular, this decree specified that a "female individual" was not obliged to ask for permission or for power of attorney from her husband in order to dispose of a *pomeste* or other immovable property that belonged to her.[78]

Not all of Peter's innovations concerning the property rights of elite women were as favorable. Under Peter's law, a childless widow inherited her husband's entire property, and with time, this provision could have altered the entire structure of familial relations. But a decree of March 17, 1731, rescinded this law, permitting a widow to inherit only one-seventh of her deceased husband's immovable property and a daughter only one-fourteenth. The rest reverted to the husband's natal clan.[79] It took the intervention of the empress herself, in the 1740s, to confirm the claim of the widow of Captain Lavrov, who died in the Turkish campaign, to inherit his land. Although Lavrov had no children, the law accorded his widow only one-seventh of his property. In this case, however, Empress Elizabeth interceded to grant the widow the right to use her late husband's entire estate until her death.[80]

Widows in less well-to-do families that did not possess landed property were entitled in some cases to receive pensions. Under Peter the Great, the categories of persons who had a right to widows' entitlements were significantly broadened. The first category consisted of women whose husbands perished while "in state service," in battle on land or sea, or who were taken captive. Somewhat later, the understanding of "state service" expanded to include medicine and mining—the latter, apparently, because its burdens were comparable to those of military campaigns.[81] The pension was paid to the widow in cash for her lifetime or until her remarriage. The amount was set in relation to her husband's salary, usually at one-eighth.[82] The widows of noncommissioned officers could even expect to receive a small allotment of land as well as a small sum of money to pay for the first planting. Such allotments were usually located far from the capital and from central Russia, in newly conquered territories. The government hoped in this way to spur economic development in these regions.[83] In 1739, under Empress Anna, another manner of providing for these widows was introduced: they were permitted to take vows as nuns and enter convents without making the customary donation. This decree was supplemented in 1761 by Catherine the Great's establishment of "a house for the maintenance of the wives of service people in widowhood"—that is, a retirement home "with a considerable number of chambers and with a stone wall."[84]

Among the peasantry, widows customarily received support from their children, as a rule, from their sons. If the children refused to do this, the widows could complain to the authorities and force compliance that way.[85]

In the pre-Petrine period, marriages could be dissolved not only when one of the spouses died but also when one took monastic vows. Yet, in the eighteenth century, laws prohibited young married persons from leaving their spouses to enter monasteries. Even during Peter's reign, many abuses of this sort occurred when husbands placed their wives by force into convents.[86] However, the number of monasteries declined in the eighteenth century by imperial order, so there were fewer spaces in convents for inconvenient wives. The law also forbade husbands whose wives entered convents from contracting new marriages and limited their claims to receive their wives' property. These prohibitions removed some of the motivation for husbands to force wives into convents. If, despite the restrictions, a wife did take vows as a nun, her husband who remained in the secular world received only a "subsistence portion" from the common marital property. This "subsistence portion" was the same as a wife received if her husband entered a monastery.[87]

In this way, women of the privileged orders saw the equalization of their rights compared with those of their husbands in the course of the eighteenth century. Despite the efforts of reactionaries, the old Muscovite restrictions on women's movement, capabilities, and property rights could not be restored. With the highest authorities of the government under the control of female rulers, there could be no logical reason to restrict women's independence in the disposition of land or money. Testimonials of the day depict the noblewomen of the capital and the provinces not only as capable housewives who knew the details of home economics but also as informed and prudent businesswomen who personally oversaw income and expenditures and understood the real-estate market.[88]

Not only noblewomen but also peasant women gained fiscal experience in eighteenth-century Russia. Many of the latter came from the so-called "black peasantry"—the nonserf farmers who owned their homesteads, usually in the far north or in Siberia. As among serfs, property relations among family members were determined in accordance with custom rather than through official law. The daughters in peasant families, like those from other social orders, had to be provided with dowries; the amount depended upon the family's prosperity. The bride's dowry always remained separate from the other economic resources of the new family formed by the marriage. Although state decrees from 1716 and 1725 dictated that the husband was entitled to one-quarter of the dowry of his deceased wife, customary law required that the entire dowry and the wife's personal effects be returned to her relatives.[89]

The disparity between the official written law and traditional custom resulted in conflicts. Widowers tried to retain a portion of their wives' estate for themselves, while the deceased women's relatives claimed that the law entitled them to receive it. The women's relatives would then petition the *mir* and the local governmental authorities of the *uezd* (district) against the greedy widowers, who had not conformed to traditional practices. The outcome of these intrafamilial lawsuits varied: sometimes the woman's relatives won; sometimes the widowed husband received a fourth of the dowry; sometimes he was forced to return his wife's possessions to her family; and sometimes he got to keep something out of them. For example, a peasant woman, Agrafena Tolmacheva, petitioned against her son-in-law, the peasant Nikifor Pakhomov, demanding the return of "one tablecloth, a cotton shawl, two yards of ribbon, and ninety kopecks in cash belonging to his deceased wife Avdotia." Nikifor complied, but Agrafena complained that "of these items returned to me by my son-in-law after the death of my daughter, the cotton shawl is threadbare, the tablecloth too small, and the ribbons [were] not hers." So Agrafena accepted only the money and tried to obtain an additional compensation of thirty-three rubles, ninety kopecks.[90]

If the husband predeceased his wife in a peasant family, the size of her inheritance (in addition to her dowry and any other property belonging exclusively to her) depended entirely upon whether there were sons. The sons were considered to be the "natural heirs" (widows and daughters were called "lawful heirs"—in the sense that the law, not custom, named them such). Sons also inherited their deceased father's tax obligations, including the soul tax on all adult males enacted in 1724. Sometimes the widow and daughters took on the tax burden, and they worked the familial parcel of land themselves, or rented it out, and paid the taxes themselves. However, legal records recount cases of widows who inherited their husbands' land and "refused" to pay the soul tax, "disrespecting the community," and the "community" could not make them change their minds.[91] The *mir* preferred that the bulk of the inheritance go to male heirs, because the *mir* as a whole was responsible for the payment of taxes and assessments due from its members. If female heirs later claimed that they were too weak or inexperienced to work the land, the *mir* would still have to pay the taxes on their behalf. These conflicts between female heirs and the *mir* could not always be resolved peaceably.

Peasants did not usually write wills, counting instead on the *mir* to make a just distribution of the deceased's estate. Even oral wills were rare. Thus inheritance matters were usually decided according to custom. The *mir* functioned as the executor and determined who would inherit and what each heir would receive. The *mir* based its decision on two factors: the heirs' degree of kinship by blood, and the amount of work they had invested in the household economy.[92] If widows and daughters had contributed to the acquisition of familial property, they could claim the inheritance on these grounds. However, if the *mir* decided to give "everything of value" to some distant male relatives of the deceased, the widow often refused to reconcile herself to this state of affairs. Such disinherited widows felt themselves to be "most extremely offended," and they "committed obstinacy and opposition," sending petitions to the state authorities and demanding a review of the *mir* assembly's decision. The district courts could not prevail against these implacable women, and they often ruled in their favor, granting them the quarter-share accorded widows under the law.[93]

In serf families, a widow who had adult sons (who might even be married with families of their own) was fully empowered to head the household without dividing the property with her children. This practice was particularly understandable in families where the wife had made most financial decisions even during her husband's lifetime. It often occurred in cases when the household had originally belonged to the wife or to her parents and her husband had been adopted into her family.

When grown sons and daughters expressed a wish to leave their mother's home, she was free either to give her permission or to withhold it. If she gave her permission, the peasant mother determined how much property, and specifically which items, she wished to "award" to her son, and the commune confirmed her decision.[94] Daughters received a portion of familial property, just like sons, but in the form of a dowry. Daughters' shares could be as little as one-tenth of those of the "natural heirs," or they could equal the sons' shares. In the absence of a widow or sons, daughters could sometimes claim the entire familial property, taking on the responsibility for payment of their father's soul tax. If the *mir* agreed, it bestowed upon the daughters the entire estate of their deceased father, "as an inheritance as they pleased."[95] If the daughters were under age, they might be fostered in a relative's home, but they were free to leave and to demand possession of their share of the property. The division of familial property among the heirs in such situations usually proceeded peacefully, according to the customs "that were accepted among our grandfathers and forefathers."

The improvements in women's status in tax, inheritance, liability, and procedural law recall their rights in the medieval period. From the second half of the eighteenth century on, despite occasional opposition from the higher authorities, the law gradually expanded the mutual obligations between spouses; it affirmed the principle that spouses were not responsible for each other's debts (as in the thirteenth to the fifteenth centuries); it appointed women to function as guardians. All these measures strengthened women's legal status.[96] Women from all social estates, including serfs, could once again participate in judicial processes, initiating lawsuits and defending themselves against them.[97]

In Russian criminal law in the eighteenth century (according to a decree from 1765), girls older than seventeen were considered responsible for their actions and could be punished to the full extent of the law.[98] In Catherine the Great's opinion, laws were supposed to "rein in the impudence of both sexes," and consequently they were to show no distinction or moderation for women.[99] But the exceptionally savage punishments of women who committed certain types of crimes against family members were mitigated under this principle.[100] In particular, Peter the Great forbade the practice of burying alive women who killed their husbands. Eighteenth-century laws punished husbands and wives who murdered their spouses equally, with the death penalty. The cruelest form of execution, breaking on the wheel, was seldom used, but it remained on the books as the penalty for the murder of an immediate relative—father, mother, sister, or brother. All other murderers of relatives, Peter dictated, should be executed by the sword.[101] Russian criminal law considered abortion by any means a form of murder. Women who "poisoned the fruit of the womb" were punished by flogging, and if they survived, they were exiled to penal servitude. Women convicted of the premeditated murder of a legitimate infant were punished with penal servitude or confinement in a convent. According to Catherine the Great's "Instruction," the abandonment of a child was equated with murder. The government concerned itself with "throwaway children;" in the era of Peter the Great, his sister Natalia founded the first shelter for abandoned children. The number of foundling homes and charitable institutions grew in the course of the century. The law adjured women "not to repudiate their children" but to bring them to "hospitals" and slip them secretly through the window.[102]

The history of women's civil and personal rights in eighteenth-century Russia testifies to the progressive and dynamic improvement of women's legal status, to the transformation of social and legal attitudes, and to the growing equality of rights between men and women of the same social order, without regard to marital status. The laws of the sixteenth and seventeenth centuries, which strove to confine women behind the walls of the *terem*, became unworkable in the Europeanized Russia of the eighteenth century. But in this new order, there was much that drew upon deep roots, dating back to the period of the tenth to the fifteenth centuries.

Fashion and Tradition

In Moscow on January 4, 1700, a new decree by Peter the Great was read to the accompaniment of drums, outlawing the old-fashioned style of Russian costume. All inhabitants of the Russian Empire were instructed from that time forward how they should and should not dress. Thus, on December 1, 1700, men were ordered to replace their entire wardrobe with "Hungarian and German outfits," and on December 1, 1701, the same order was issued to their wives and daughters, so that "in dress they will be matched, not different" from the menfolk. For those who did not submit, the tsar's decree ordered that they "pay a fine in money, and the [old-fashioned] dress be cut and torn up."[103] The loosely cut traditional dress of princesses and boyars' wives provided, in the words of the Austrian diplomat J.G. Korb, "full freedom to give room for corpulence."[104] The new tailored German style of clothing mandated by law consisted of dresses with corsets and ankle-length skirts. The traditional wreathes and headdresses were replaced by elaborate hairdos and tiaras.

Peter hoped to eradicate Russian traditional costume with one stroke. However, the changeover to European clothing was a long and complicated process, not only in the conservative countryside but also in cities, because it signified the destruction of old customs, traditions, and tastes. The traditional Russian costume had developed over the centuries, and it was functional and comfortable for the climate and lifestyle of Russia. According to the nobleman Ivan Nepliuev, the Western styles of dress were greeted with "mockery and curses." The tightly laced "wasp" waistlines and uncovered heads contradicted the traditional Russian conception of what was beautiful and what was ugly, what was permitted and what was forbidden.

The women of Moscow, who were forced to obey the decree earlier than others, were stunned. But the tsar's word was law. Although a contemporary noted ironically that even in the capital the change was not accomplished for a number of years, nonetheless young aristocratic women began to copy the new fashions modeled by the ladies of the tsar's family and the court, and the ordinary women of Moscow and Petersburg followed suit.[105] In the provinces, the process dragged on for decades, and only at the end of the eighteenth century did elements of Western costume enter the dress of peasant women, which had remained entirely traditional.

The entire concept of "fashion" was unknown in Russia before Peter, and following its dictates caused women no small trouble. It was necessary to find and educate dressmakers, so that they would know how to sew outfits in the European manner. The dressmakers needed models of European clothing styles to copy, or at least drawings of them. But most important, there had to be women brave enough to defy convention and wear the new dresses. Aristocratic young women in the capital proved willing to do so, and they became walking advertisements for the new European style. These women valued the advantages of Western clothing and the allure of their luxury. Despite the corsets and hoops, the high heels, and the intricate hairdos, aristocratic Russian women felt themselves liberated, while their mothers privately cursed the new vogues. The older generation felt particularly uncomfortable at the new public gatherings, the balls and assemblies, which were hot and crowded. They did not know the new etiquette.

But the most farsighted mothers made a point of providing their children with whatever they needed to make their way in this new society. These women, who were accustomed to sit in the seclusion of their *terem*, now subscribed to foreign magazines and studied drawings of the latest fashions. (The first regularly published fashion magazine in Russia, *The Monthly Fashion Essay, or Library of Women's Toilette*, began only in 1779.) The mothers hired tutors and governesses to teach their children dancing, elocution, and etiquette. Fathers and mothers of the aristocracy brought their daughters to assemblies, "not so much for amusement as for business," and expected them to know how to greet foreigners in their own languages (German, French, or English), and even to be able to carry on intelligent conversations with them. This form of conduct was unthinkable for women in the sixteenth and seventeenth centuries, but the younger generation took to it rapidly. Even in the second decade of the eighteenth century, foreigners who attended Russian assemblies and celebrations noted that court women "dressed very well, following foreign models," and emulated European modes of makeup and hairstyles. In the fineness of their manners and address, they compared favorably with French and German ladies.[106]

The cut of Russian noblewomen's clothing, for both formal occasions and daily wear, came to resemble French costume of the late seventeenth century. It consisted of an overdress, with skirts and bodice, which was open to reveal the thin linen shift beneath. Russian women were particularly unaccustomed to the rigid corsets, which first appeared in Spain in the sixteenth century and then spread to the rest of Europe. These corsets were both a privilege and a torment for aristocratic ladies. With stays of wood or whalebone, the corset held the figure erect and gave the wearer a proud bearing. The corset was fastened with laces, normally in the back, and because it was difficult to get in and out of a corset alone, wealthy aristocratic ladies had serving maids who could help them dress and undress. Corseting took its toll on women's health, because it was difficult to breath while wearing them, and women became more vulnerable to pulmonary and gastrointestinal ailments. Corsets also interfered with pregnancy. However, the desire to be fashionable prevailed over common sense. Formal dresses absolutely had to have corsets, which were covered with silk and decorated with braid, lace, buttons, and laces.

The corseted bodice contrasted with enormous skirts, which were cut in a circular shape. To make the skirts appear fuller, a framework of hoops was worn underneath them. Contemporaries commented ironically about these skirts: "If this style caught on among ordinary women, too, there would be no way to walk down the street!"[107] Winter skirts were quilted with cotton batting, to substitute for the traditional multilayered clothing that preserved body heat. But the wide skirts imported from France were simply out of place in the context of Russian frosts and snowdrifts.

The aristocratic woman's outer dress—eighteenth-century Russians called it by its French name, *la robe*—represented its wearer's degree of nobility and wealth. Court ladies' walking costumes were so decorated with a large number of stones, gold and silver embroidery, lace, ribbons, and chains that Catherine the Great made a special ruling in order to try to moderate the competition in dress. She ordered that women observe simplicity in the cut and decoration of their garments, and she even directed that they not use, for example, lace wider than four inches.[108] But decrees could not restrain women from making their fashion statements.

In the course of the eighteenth century, the cut and accessories of women's outfits changed several times. In the first half of the eighteenth century, the grand impression of an outfit was achieved through luxuriant trimmings. Vibrantly colored makeup and elaborate hairstyles with long, powdered curls topped by tall, lacy ornaments were extremely fashionable in this period. Women's clothing in the period from 1700 to 1740 reflected the baroque style that dominated in architecture, painting, and sculpture.

In the mid-eighteenth century, the pretentious rococo style came to dominate Russian fashion. Women's walking costumes became more tailored. The narrow waist emphasized the female figure and made it appear petite and fragile. The outfit was completed with complex and extremely tall hairdos. In makeup, beauty spots were the rage.

In the 1770s, styles changed again, and neoclassicism replaced rococo. The complex hairdos and powdered curls disappeared, as did the corsets and hoops. Instead, garments became simpler and more severe, and the cut more eclectic. Fashions reflected the rapid changes in cultural and political life. Thus, the discussions of the "Polish Question" in Russian politics in the 1770s to the 1790s gave rise to the new skirt style of the polonaise, taken from the name of the Polish national dance. The polonaise skirt was worn over a complete dress, open in the front and softly draped. The French Revolution of 1789 followed by the founding of the Napoleonic Empire inspired a loosely cut dress, resembling the ancient Greek chiton, with a high waist and a banded neckline. This "Empire" style lasted until the first decade of the nineteenth century.[109]

While the complex styles favored by fashionable court ladies in St. Petersburg required the skills of master tailors, urban noblewomen's everyday dress became simpler in cut. These dresses were made of flannel, wool, batiste, or heavy, solid-colored silk. In the second half of the eighteenth century, the wardrobes of all Russian noblewomen, whether in the capital or in the provinces, contained a variety of types of everyday garments. In the morning, the lady donned her "morning dress," a gown in a pastel shade, or often white. Later, she put on a "house dress," which had a minimum of frills, ribbon, or other decoration. If she went out during the day, she would wear a "visiting dress" that consisted of a long skirt and a jacket that could be long or short.[110] The favorite fabric patterns consisted of small floral designs or stripes.

Shawls, scarves, and mantles were essential elements in everyday and even formal wear. Russian women wore them not only to accessorize their costumes but also for warmth. The thin fabrics and bare-shouldered styles imported from warmer climates were not suited to the Russian winter.[111] Stockings similarly served the dual purposes of style and practicality. For everyday wear they were made of cotton or wool; for festive wear, of silk. In the first part of the century, stockings were usually colored and sometimes embroidered. Later, in the 1760s and 1770s, fashionable ladies yearned for the white stockings with azure designs or embroidered clocks at the back of the heel that they saw in advertisements.

As in the past, Russian women of the eighteenth century preferred shoes with pointed toes. High-heeled slippers for balls and holiday wear were made of brocade, velvet, or satin. High-heeled leather boots were the normal footwear for everyday, as the Czech visitor Jiri David noted. At the end of the century, high heels became passé, and flat slippers with curled toes in the oriental style took their place.

Hairdos were an important part of Russian aristocratic women's image. In the pre-Petrine period, married women considered it shameful to appear in public bareheaded, and consequently they did not concern themselves with hairstyles. However, coiffures were an essential part of the European outfit, and the new norms forced women to abandon the old rules. The new styles demanded wigs, falls, hairpins, nets, and barrettes, which were usually imported. To keep ladies properly coiffed and provide them with an incomparable look for a special party or ball, dozens of small beauty salons sprang up. "They exhaust themselves with this over-indulgent ornamentation," the thrifty merchant I.T. Pososhkov editorialized. The women who wasted money on hairstyling and other frivolous luxuries seemed to him to be guilty of an unacceptable extravagance that was impoverishing not only them and their families but in the final analysis the whole country.[112]

Hairstyles changed over time: they got higher. If in Peter the Great's time, it was sufficient to curl hair into ringlets and drape them over the back and shoulders, in the 1780s, the hairdo of an aristocratic lady consisted of an extravaganza combining hair, ribbons, feathers, and flowers representing several hours of work by a hairdresser. In keeping with older Russian ideas of beauty, the forehead was left bare, without bangs or sidecurls, and its breadth was enhanced by the high pompadour rising above it.

Hairdos, like dresses, became simpler in the last decade of the eighteenth century. The "natural" look became the mode, and wigs and falls disappeared. The enthusiasm for antiquity and for light, transparent fabrics brought about a new style in cosmetics. "The refined woman ought to avoid such defects as rouged cheeks," the magazine *The Spectator* (*Zritel*) advised its readers; "being thin, pale, and languid—these are her assets."[113] The use of rouge and eyebrow pencil, like traditional Russian costume, was considered in bad taste, marking the wearer as lower class, preserving, as one observer wrote, "the distant past in all its specifics."[114]

Among peasant women, the basic garment remained the shift, as it had been in the previous seven centuries. However, the eighteenth-century shift was constructed differently. The upper portion and sleeves, which were visible, were cut from a finer fabric, and the lower portion, which was covered up, was made from plain linen. The shift was shirred at the neckline and wrists with several lines of cord, so that the sleeves were "gathered fully in pleats around the hands."[115]

Peasant women wore a *sarafan* over the shift. The *sarafan* could take the form of a jumper, or it could be open in the front, in which case a wrap skirt was worn under it. Both the *sarafan* and the skirt were very long, and with its vertical ornamentation or row of buttons it gave the illusion of greater height. The Danish envoy Just Jul, who visited Russia in the early eighteenth century, remarked that to Russians "tallness seems an honorable attribute and one of the conditions of beauty."[116] Everyday *sarafans* were made of homespun and festival garments from heavy silk. They were belted high, just below the bustline. If the wearer did not want her belt to wrinkle her *sarafan*, she wore it underneath instead, directly over the shift. The belt helped to support the breasts, serving the purpose of the modern brassiere.

Over the *sarafan* peasant women wore a short jacket, with or without sleeves, which barely reached to the waist.[117] Russian city women wore a *shugai* (literally an "intimidator," because in the provinces people could not get used to Western styles) and also fur-lined cloth capes. The borders of these capes were also adorned with fur strips at the neck and hem, and they were cut along the lines of Western models rather than traditional Russian ones. The combination of traditional and European styles of clothing was particularly apparent in the new style of coat popular among women of the merchant class. It was a sort of loosely cut round cloak that had slits for the hands and a hood. The upper part was usually made of satin or silk and the bottom of plain wool.

For winter weather, well-to-do peasant and merchant women wore fur coats, as before. Their cut had changed little from the previous centuries, and they came in a variety of styles—waist- or ankle-length, with sleeves or cut as a cloak. Everyday fur coats were made of rabbit or squirrel pelts; for holiday wear, more expensive furs were used, and these were set off with bright turquoise or cranberry silk. The coats were accessorized by hats trimmed with fur around the head and tall peaks that tipped down. A fur-lined cloth muff completed the outfit.[118]

European styles eventually penetrated into the ranks not only of non-noble urban women but also of the peasantry. "In the capital cities and even in the provinces, merchant girls for the most part have already started to dress like German women," a late eighteenth-century observer wrote.[119] The "German" outfit consisted of a skirt, blouse, and kerchief. Before the second half of the eighteenth century, Russian women's costume did not ordinarily include a skirt, and only foreigners or residents of territories under Polish-Lithuanian rule wore them. But from the 1760s on, a skirt and blouse became the everyday outfit of hundreds of thousands of Russian women. Sometimes an apron—also a European borrowing—was added. By the end of the century, the blouses often came with collars made of a different, softer material and with a small tuck. Kerchiefs and scarves became favorite accessories.

Among women of the merchant class, the scarves, shawls, or kerchiefs were worn covering their heads, with the ends tied on top.

Peasant women topped their headscarves with the traditional head-dresses of maidens or matrons. At home or in the fields, peasant women might wear simple caps that covered their hair. But when they went out "among people" for leisure or holidays, they always added the headdresses, which could be tall or flat, covered with fabric or leather, decorated with beads or metallic thread, with or without a veil, depending upon local custom. It was possible to determine whether a woman was from Tambov or Pskov, Tula or Perm, based on the type of headdress she wore. In cold weather, women wore triangular shawls over their headdresses, tying them loosely under their chins or pinning them with a brooch. By tradition unmarried maidens left their hair uncovered and plaited it with ribbons or gold and silver thread. In the northern regions, maidens might braid their hair with pearls.

Stockings entered the Russian wardrobe from Western Europe. Only court ladies wore white and azure stockings; among common urban women, stockings were usually made of dark blue knitted wool.

Peasants and less well-to-do urban women continued to dress in traditional footwear. Shoes of woven bast remained the most distinc-tively Russian type; they were suited to the summer activities of gath-ering mushrooms, herding livestock, and mowing hay. During the frozen winters and slushy autumn and spring months, simple leather shoes were used. As in earlier centuries, these shoes were made from a single piece of rawhide. The feet were wrapped for warmth in strips of cloth, and the shoes were tied on with thongs. As a substitute for boots, women might wear practical overshoes made of bristles, horse-hair, or up to three pounds of wool felt. Of course, felt overshoes did not go with the European-type outfits of fashionable urban women. They preferred to wear expensive imported boots of thin leather that matched their style even if they did not protect from the cold.

In this way, the eighteenth century marked a change in the cos-tume of Russian women—but not all Russian women. The introduc-tion of European fashions separated urban women from peasant women and nobles from non-nobles. Well-to-do urban people be-came quite Westernized. According to visitors from other countries, women, especially, embraced stylish foreign dress.[120] A nobleman from Holstein, Friedrich von Bergholz, wrote, "The Russian woman, who not long ago was crude and uneducated, has so changed for the better that now she lags little behind German and French women in the fineness of her manner and breeding, and sometimes she even has the advantage over them."[121] Thus Bergholz connected the adop-tion of European dress with changes in behavior.

Woodcut, "Please give me the bucket!" Second half of the eighteenth century. The wife, dressed in European clothes, passes the yoke with the water pails to her traditionally clad husband, lest she ruin her fashionable outfit.

But the attitude in the countryside toward Western styles was cynical or even hostile. *Lubki* (woodcuts) reflect popular views and popular tastes; these cartoon-like pictures were the work of unsophisticated folk artists, and they were produced in private factories for lower-class consumption. One common theme in *lubki* was "good" and "evil" women. "Evil" women were always portrayed in European ("German") dress; "good" women were depicted in old Russian garments. In the popular consciousness, pretty girls decked out in European fashion with a tall coiffure were associated with idleness, capriciousness, bad character, and immodesty.[122] The steadfast insistence on preserving the traditional style of dress constituted a statement of opposition to the new ways, a reflection of the determination of the bulk of the Russian people to adhere to their customary life. The gradual intermingling of the Western and the traditional norms of dress, which began in the eighteenth century among urban women, ultimately became irreversible.

Chapter 4

The New Women of the New Epoch: Nineteenth and Early Twentieth Centuries

The Many Roles of Women

Women's roles in Russia in the nineteenth and early twentieth centuries reflected, as before, the general trends of the period. The reign of Catherine the Great concluded the era of female rule, the "Russian matriarchate" of the eighteenth century. The multifaceted reforms that Peter the Great had initiated continued to influence women's place in the social, political, and cultural institutions of the Russian Empire. Between 1800 and 1917, Russia experienced political upheaval: abortive revolutions in 1825 and 1905 presaged the ultimate downfall of the autocracy in 1917; eras of moderate reform under Alexander I and Alexander II alternated with reaction under Nicholas I and Alexander III; a tentative experiment in constitutional government began in the wake of 1905; empire building in the Caucasus and Central Asia contrasted with military defeats in the Crimean War, the Russo-Japanese War, and World War I. Russian society changed dramatically, too: in 1861, the government liberated the peasantry from serfdom; an urban working class arose in response to growing industrialization; the elite intelligentsia sought new ways to define their relationship with the government and the people, developing their own cultural traditions while incorporating those of Western Europe.[1] A new, self-aware women's movement gradually arose in response to these changes. The history of Russian women in this period also constitutes the history of the "Woman Question": the issue of equal rights for women in access to education, in compensation for labor, and in the political arena.

The history of Russia from 1800 to 1914 is filled with outstanding women. Some made their mark in the political realm, others in diverse fields of scholarship, and still others in literature, theater, and the fine arts. Each of these women deserves her own biography; what follows here is just a summary portrait of a few representative figures.

The Empress as Angel of Mercy

The Empress Maria, Emperor Paul's second wife, "left an imprint on posterity through her lucid, beneficial, and broadly humane activities," one of her contemporaries remembered half a century later.[2] Empress Maria (1759–1828) was born Sophia-Dorothea, the daughter of the prince of Württemberg, in Germany. She was brought to Russia in 1776 to marry the future emperor Paul; in converting to Orthodoxy, she adopted the Russian name of Maria Fedorovna. Unlike the ambitious women rulers of the eighteenth century, Maria consciously limited herself to the role of wife. Contemporaries who compared Maria to Catherine the Great noted that "her glory does not glitter with brilliant, heroic actions." The poet G.P. Derzhavin called her "the tsaritsa of a host of bounties" and Alexander Pushkin "the lavisher of goodness and wisdom."

An example of Empress Maria's style is the way in which she gradually took charge of all educational matters in Russia. The head trustee for the Smolnyi Institute, she also donated many thousands of rubles to it. Empress Maria had her own clear sense of the sort of education girls from noble families should receive. "It is not good," she wrote in her diary, *La Philosophie des femmes* (The Philosophy of Women), "for many reasons, that women should acquire too broad a knowledge. Children should be reared with good morals, to lead a household, to supervise servants, and to observe frugality in expenditures." In her opinion, that sufficed for girls' education. The empress prescribed a special structure for educational institutions and a specific curriculum for each social order. For the nobility, the first priority was knowledge of French, dancing, and etiquette. For the urban middle class, the daughters of merchants and *raznochintsy* (intellectuals and professionals), she recommended a practical curriculum, so that they would be able to become schoolteachers and governesses. At the empress's direction, a large number of schools were set up,

Empress Maria Fedorovna, the second wife of Emperor Paul I and patroness of girls' educational institutions. Contemporary engraving.

not only in the twin capitals of St. Petersburg and Moscow but also in the provincial cities of Kazan, Kharkov, Simbirsk, and Poltava. She also established a new state award, named after herself: the "Maria Medal for Unblemished Service to Russia."[3]

In 1797, Maria oversaw the founding of a school for orphan girls, similar to the Smolnyi Institute; it was named the "Mariinskii" in her honor. She donated large sums of money to this institution and to the others under her trusteeship, including bequests totaling 4 million rubles after her death.

With her energy, Maria completely overshadowed her daughter-in-law Elizabeth (1779–1826), the wife of Alexander I, who became empress in 1801. Like Maria, Elizabeth was of German origin; by birth, she was Princess Luisa-Maria of Hesse-Darmstadt. She came to Russia at the age of thirteen as the bride of the future emperor Alexander. The gossip, envy, and perfidy of court life disturbed her. In reaction, she worked out her own style of conduct, characterized by modest restraint and a preference for remaining out of the limelight. She gladly left the foreground to her mother-in-law. But during the panic that accompanied the French invasion in 1812, Elizabeth's serenity and composure provided welcome relief. She organized the Women's Patriotic Society—Russia's first official women's organization—to perform charitable work during the crisis. Later, she initiated the founding of a school for the children of soldiers slain in battle. Like Empress Maria, Elizabeth drew the funds she donated to these institutions not from the state treasury but from her own income; she received a million rubles per year "for her maintenance," of which she donated 800,000 to charity.

Numerous adversities, including the death of several of her children, preyed on Elizabeth's health. The "most modest of Russian empresses," as contemporaries called her, died at age forty-seven, barely half a year after her husband. Her estate, worth millions of rubles, she bequeathed to the Women's Patriotic Society. Thanks to her bequest, the society was able to establish its own schools, to teach needlework and vocational trades; at the end of the century, childcare facilities were founded from this endowment.[4]

The second son of Paul I and Empress Maria, Nicholas I, ascended the throne after the death of Alexander I in 1825. In 1817, he had been married, in accordance with the patterns of the Russian imperial family, to a German princess, Frederika-Luisa-Charlotte of Prussia (1798–1860), who received the Orthodox name of Alexandra. Like other imperial brides, she concerned herself with educational and charitable work. Under her tutelage, a whole system of orphanages and "schools for the daughters of every rank" were founded throughout the country. In the 1840s, St. Petersburg and Moscow even boasted the first business schools for women. In 1845, Empress Alexandra directed the founding of the first Council of Women's Educational Institutions and insisted that it "bring to [her] attention all information concerning questions of training." Alexandra always donated generously to women's education.[5]

Alexandra's son, Alexander II, ascended the throne in 1855, after his father's sudden death. His wife was Princess Maria of Hesse-Darmstadt, who took the Orthodox name of Maria Aleksandrovna (1824–1880).[6] Contemporaries thought that she did not look like an empress. She remained in the shadow of her illustrious and popular husband, the "Tsar-Liberator" who abolished serfdom, and did not try to involve herself in public life or associate herself with her husband's momentous reforms. Instead, she restricted herself to the charitable work traditional for empresses. By her initiative, the first girls' high schools (gymnasiums) were established in 1860, open to the daughters of all social classes. Gradually they spread in every city. At her suggestion (perhaps prompted by clergymen), the first parish schools for girls were set up. Contemporaries credited Empress Maria personally with the founding of the Russian Red Cross, which played a valuable role in the Russo-Turkish War of 1877–78; she provided a huge initial endowment for it. She was well known in Russian society for her patronage of Orthodox associations and for the All-Russian Society for the Blind, which she helped to found.[7]

Unlike his discreet and devout wife, Emperor Alexander II was not known for his fidelity. In 1865, he became enamored of Princess Ekaterina Dolgorukaia, then a student at the Smolnyi Institute. During their affair, Alexander and Ekaterina had three children. After Empress Maria died of consumption in 1880, Alexander entered into a morganatic marriage with Ekaterina, granting her the family name Iurevskaia and the title of "Serene Highness" and making her his uncrowned empress. The emperor dreamed of crowning Ekaterina as his official consort, completing his governmental reforms, and then abdicating the throne to live quietly with his new wife and their children in Nice. But Alexander did not live to fulfill his wish; on March 1, 1881, he was assassinated by the political terrorists Andrei Zheliabov and Sofia Perovskaia. Ekaterina received an enormous bequest of 3.3 million rubles according to the terms of Alexander's will. She used the money to move to France and rear and educate her children. There, far from Russia, the princess and her children survived revolutions and world war.[8]

Alexander II's son, Alexander III, took the throne, and his Danish-born wife became the new empress. Princess Frederika-Dagmar married Alexander III in 1866, taking the Orthodox name of Maria Fedorovna. She was vivacious and ebullient to the point of appearing flighty, but she devoted herself to serving as trustee for asylums and homeless shelters, which provided refuge for the growing numbers of poor and unemployed filling the Russian cities and countryside.

In the late nineteenth century, charitable work became decidedly female in character.[9] Not only women of the imperial family undertook it, but also women from the court, nobility, and wealthy manufacturer and banking families. Women's philanthropic societies, organized by well-to-do ladies, arose in Odessa in 1834 and in Kazan, Voronezh, Ufa, and Kostroma in the 1840s. Princesses Trubetskaia and Shakhovskaia founded the "Fraternal Society" in the 1850s, and the "Ladies' Trusteeship" was formed in the 1870s. By the early twentieth century, philanthropic and charitable associations numbered in the thousands, and female benefactors had donated millions of rubles to them. Most notable among women philanthropists were Grand Duchess Elena, the sister of Nicholas I, Baroness Edith Raden, Baroness Sofia Frederiks, Countess Elena Geiden, and Princess Natalia Shakhovskaia. Grand Duchess Elizabeth, the sister-in-law of Alexander III and the aunt of Nicholas II, founded the Convent of Martha and Mary near Moscow with her endowment; she also became its abbess. The magazine *Messenger of Charity* (*Vestnik blagotvoritelnosti*), founded in 1896, regularly published the names of wealthy women who demonstrated their sympathy for the suffering of others, and reported on the initiatives of organizations providing systematic help to the needy.[10]

Empress Maria Fedorovna's twenty-two-year-old son, Nicholas II, took the throne in October 1894, after the death of his father. His marriage to Princess Alisa-Victoria of Hesse-Darmstadt, called Alix, took place soon after his accession. Alexander III and Empress Maria had opposed the match because Alix's family was impoverished, but Nicholas had fallen in love with her, and his dying father felt obliged to give them his blessing. Empress Maria was angered and saddened by Nicholas's obstinance, and she never reconciled herself to his choice of bride.[11]

Princess Alix, who received the Orthodox name of Alexandra, has become the best known and least respected of Russian imperial

Wealthy patrons gather at a banquet to celebrate the founding of the
Orphans' Institute, St. Petersburg, late nineteenth century.

wives. Her marriage to Nicholas in the wake of his father's death was
widely taken to be an evil omen; "She came to us from the grave," the
popular saying went. Even Alix herself commented in her diary, "The
wedding was like a continuation of the requiem, but in a white dress."
Their coronation on May 18, 1896, ended in disaster, when 1,389
persons were crushed to death on Khodynka Field, where gifts were
being distributed in the tsar's name. The Russo-Japanese War of
1904–5 cost many lives and ended in defeat. Another catastrophe was
"Bloody Sunday": on January 9, 1905, government troops fired upon
peaceful demonstrators in the streets of the capital. The Revolution
of 1905 followed, and ultimately Nicholas was forced to promise a
constitution. But once the government reestablished control, it initiated bloody repressions, and Nicholas and Alexandra bore the blame.
The slaughter of World War I, which began in 1914, concluded their
unfortunate reign. Through these public tragedies, Nicholas and Alexandra bore a private one of their own: their only son and heir,
Aleksei, suffered from incurable hemophilia.[12]

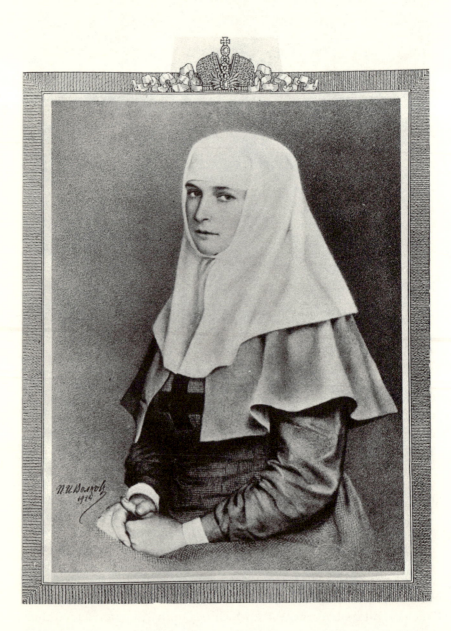

Empress Alexandra, wife of Nicholas II, dressed as a nurse during World War I. Portrait by P.I. Volkov.

The reclusive Alexandra did not reveal the empress's traditional concern for the well-being of her country and its citizens, nor did she support the arts. But she became devoutly Orthodox and observed its precepts religiously, including the three "pious feats" of fasting, prayer, and benefaction. Each year, while the imperial family vacationed in Yalta, Empress Alexandra and her daughters held an auction of their own needlework to raise funds for charity. Alexandra received an income of her own of 36,000 rubles per year, and she donated 22,000 of it as pensions for the indigent. Despite this generosity, she was the object of great popular hostility, especially after the appearance of Grigorii Rasputin at court.[13] Rasputin was an uneducated drifter and self-ordained monk, but his uncanny therapeutic skills with Aleksei made him the tsar's and tsaritsa's closest adviser.[14]

The beginning of World War I intensified popular dislike for the empress. Because of her German origin, she was blamed for Russia's setbacks at the front; there were even rumors of treason. These allegations continued even after the news media carried stories of how Alexandra and her daughters, dressed as nurses, volunteered much time at infirmaries for wounded soldiers.[15]

In 1917, after the overthrow of the monarchy and the Bolshevik seizure of power, Alexandra and her family were exiled to the Urals. In 1918, they were shot. The downfall of the monarchy marked the end of the traditional Russian legal, social, spiritual, and customary order.[16] The philanthropic work that the women of the imperial family carried out to the best of their ability was a manifestation of this vanished order.

Hostesses of Distinction

An important aspect of women's contribution to Russian intellectual and cultural life in the nineteenth century was their patronage of salons. These salons, based in private homes and often hosted by women, sponsored a wide variety of discussion groups, symposia, and other sorts of informal gatherings, where writers, poets, composers, and artists presented their work. Strict censorship throughout most of the nineteenth century inhibited public discussion, not only of governmental issues but also of literature and the fine arts, because the latter addressed political questions in metaphorical language. Consequently, the private salon setting provided an essential forum for the exchange of ideas. Their significance was readily apparent to contemporaries, and leading artists and scholars deeply appreciated how educated hostesses brought together extraordinary personalities, and how these women understood and shared their insights. One participant in the Moscow salon of Avdotia Elagina wrote, "Everything that was intellectual, enlightened, and talented was brought together here. Here young people met and became acquainted with everything that was then outstanding in Russian literature, [art], and scholarship; here they were educated and prepared for their later activities."[17]

Hostesses of salons in the early nineteenth century had to know how to create within their homes a world apart, a circle of contacts determined not by wealth or birth but by intellect and talent. With guests who had already established their reputations, a salon hostess had to be conversant with recent innovations in literature, music, and the fine arts and able to voice her own trenchant opinions. Hostesses invited fashionable writers, musicians, and scholars for evening receptions that often lasted until dawn. Only after the newly produced work had been heard to the end and the last heated argument had been resolved did the guests depart for home.[18]

Literary salons did not bother with the "trite card games" that were the vogue. Instead, people gathered there for "enlightening conversation." The entertainment was not elaborate, but the hostess played a key role. She complimented women guests, "noticing their pretty outfits, and encouraging bashful debutantes." She strove to display "a genuine collaboration with everything lively and gifted, and with every well-intentioned initiative and every heartfelt higher impulse." Without attracting attention to herself, the hostess had to be "an organizational genius, bringing some people together and separating others."[19]

Salon hostesses and participants frequently joined forces. Thus the poets N.M. Iazykov and Karolina Pavlova, the "princess of Russian verse," had a contest, as did Princess Zinaida Volkonskaia, "the tsaritsa of muses and beauty," and the Italian composer Rossini.[20]

Zinaida Volkonskaia came from an old princely family, and she received an aristocratic education at home. She acquired fluency in five European languages, as well as Latin and Greek. Impressionable and intelligent, she yearned to share her wealth of knowledge and sense of wonder with others. She began by staging plays and later turned to literature. She also set up a number of fine arts studios, thanks to which beginning artists had the opportunity to study in Italy. The renowned Russian painters Silvester Shchedrin, Karl Briullov, and Fedor Bruni profited from the training Volkonskaia's studios offered.

Volkonskaia's "Mondays at home" attracted the most notable and talented individuals of her day. "Writers and artists related to her as a patron, and they were accustomed to meeting each other at her brilliant parties, which she knew how to inspire with such talent," Pavel Viazemskii wrote.[21] Volkonskaia's Moscow house, with its fine paintings and marble copies of famous sculptures, attracted poets such as Alexander Pushkin, Vasilii Zhukovskii, and Adam Mickiewicz; musicians such as Fedor Glinka; scholars such as Peter and Ivan Kireevskii and Peter Chaadaev; and political leaders such as Sergei Trubetskoi and Sergei Volkonskii. All of them appreciated the skill their hostess demonstrated in bringing them together.

From 1824 to 1829, Volkonskaia's salon was a hotbed of freethinking. In the autumn of 1826, she organized a reception in honor of the wives of the Decembrists. On December 14, 1825, a group of idealistic young noblemen staged an ill-fated revolution to demand constitutional government and civil rights. Emperor Nicholas I crushed the revolt, and many of its participants were condemned to exile in Siberia. The rebels' wives were told that they could retain their titles and properties, if only they would divorce their treasonous husbands. But they refused and bravely set out to join their husbands in Siberian exile. In daring to honor the Decembrists, Volkonskaia was boldly fulfilling the motto of her salon, "Ridendo dicere verum" ("While laughing, speak the truth"). In the repression that followed the Decembrist uprising, Zinaida Volkonskaia emigrated to Italy.

During the same years, Avdotia Elagina organized her "Sunday salon," patronized by many outstanding writers and poets. Elagina's salon became the meeting place for the Slavophiles—intellectuals who focused on Russian national distinctiveness, in contrast to the "Westernizers," who valued Russia's implementation of West European ideas. Guests at Elagina's home included the writer Ivan Aksakov, the Kireevskii brothers (folklorists), the historian Ivan Beliaev, as well as famous foreign visitors, for example, the German poet Goethe and the naturalist von Humboldt. Elagina's salon was "a prestigious place, where people strove to come in order to gain renown in fashionable circles."[22]

Other, similar salons, headed by "captivating women," appeared in St. Petersburg in the early nineteenth century. One of these was the circle of Sofia Ponomareva. Alexander Pushkin praised her self-assured effortlessness, describing her "like a Grace, kind and educated, like a Muse." Ponomareva was the poetic inspiration for the works of Pushkin's friend Alexander Delvig, the poet Alexander Izmailov, and many others. Individuals who shared progressive views gathered at her salon. There the idea of creating a literary almanac, *The North Star* (*Poliarnaia zvezda*) was born; this journal became the voice of the Decembrists between 1823 and 1825.[23]

Daria Fikelmon, the daughter of the hero of Borodino, field marshal Mikhail Kutuzov, also led a salon that was a "hotbed of free-thinking." Alexandra Rosset-Smirnova, the wife of an Austrian diplomat, had a salon as well, where she received not only high-ranking aristocrats but also progressive nobles who nurtured ideas of establishing a constitutional order in Russia.

The "most sharp-witted and scholarly salon" in St. Petersburg in the 1830s through the 1850s was Ekaterina Karamzina's. She was the widow of the eminent historian, and "the most educated and cultured part of the society of the capital" gathered at her home: the composers Glinka and Dargomyzhskii, the artist Briullov, and the poets Pushkin, Zhukovskii, and Lermontov. She arranged parties where the guests spoke "only in Russian" at a time when educated Russians generally preferred to speak French.[24]

The women who organized these salons invariably had lively minds, broad erudition, fine taste, and charming hospitality. Their role in making these "home societies" work was obvious. Pavel Viazemskii recalled, "Every vital issue of European and Russian political, literary, and societal life had its faithful echo in salons. It wasn't necessary to read newspapers! A worldwide, oral, conversational newspaper was 'published' under the direction and editorship of these kind and generous women. Such unconstrained tolerance, such courteous freedom there was in these multifaceted conversations."[25]

Such idyllic unity of opinion, however, did not characterize all salons. Many of the hostesses, who belonged to the highest ranks of society, were highly critical of the ideas of social change that circulated in salons. For example, the salon of Countess Evdokia Rostopchina pursued the goal of "not allowing our Russia, which is still healthy and young, to be poisoned with alleged enlightenment, where the hidden and pernicious toxin is presented to her in an ill-intentioned and imprudent manner."[26] Rostopchina's salon condemned revolutionary ideas, such as the abolition of the system of legally defined social estates, which the literary critic Vissarion Belinskii advanced in the 1840s. The ideal Rostopchina's guests promoted was that of an enlightened monarch, not that of popular governance. Other hostesses of elite salons of the 1840s and 1850s, such as Princess Evgenia Salias and Baroness Edith Raden, espoused similar views.

Educated noblewomen in the provinces imitated the salon hostesses of the capitals in gathering together the most intellectual elements of society. Alexandra Fuks in Kazan, Elena Vasilchikova in Kiev, and Elizaveta Volkonskaia in Riazan, among many others, enlivened cultural life in the provinces and promoted the development of "interests in literature and enlightenment in local society."[27]

The role and significance of these cultural salons declined after the reforms of the 1860s, but the enlightened elements of the public still gathered for evening discussions in private homes in the capitals.[28] One such meeting place was the home of Elena Shtakenshnaider, the daughter of a court architect and "a personality kind to the highest degree, with a broad literary education and fine artistic flair." The greatest intellects of the day, P.L. Lavrov, M.L. Mikhailov, the Shelgunov brothers, and many literary celebrities gathered in her St. Petersburg living room. Her home was also the site for "public lectures" on chemistry taught to women by N.P. Fedorov.

From the 1870s to the 1890s, salons altered their character. Instead of merely discussing the burning social problems of the day, they became organizations for political action. But because salons were implicated in instances of terrorism, including the assassination of Alexander II, they and all other large gatherings of people were forbidden. The number of salons declined.

Aficionados of literature and the arts, however, continued to gather together individuals with different perspectives and tastes. Women of the middle class—business women, owners of large enterprises, educated millionairesses—became a new type of salon hostess. One of the most prominent was Varvara Morozova, called "Tverskaia" after her residence on Tverskaia Street in Moscow, of the large and wealthy Morozov textile family. "In the morning she taps out accounts in the office, and in the evening, she strikes up wonderful Chopin melodies, discusses the theories of Marx, and engrosses herself in the newest works of philosophers and publicists," a contemporary wrote of her in his memoirs.[29] Varvara Tverskaia gathered the flower of early twentieth-century intellectual society to her home, including Anton Chekhov, Peter Korolenko, Peter Boborykin, and Valerii Briusov.

Varvara Morozova passed her style of entertaining on to her daughter-in-law, Maria Morozova (née Mamontova). Maria Morozova was exceptionally beautiful. She spent her childhood in close company with the Tretiakov family, founders and benefactors of the famous art gallery in Moscow. According to the reminiscences of people who knew her, Maria Morozova was "an active participant in the musical, philosophical, and publishing life of Moscow" even in her youth. Indeed, she became the director of the Musical Society; she was the founder of the Religious–Philosophical Society; and she owned the "Put" ("Path") publishing house. The guests at her salon reflected the developing social and political, and even revolutionary, movements of the turn of the century. Not only literary celebrities and philosophers attended but also political activists from across the spectrum: the Cadet Peter Miliukov, the Octobrist Alexander Guchkov, and Social Democrats (socialists) of various stripes, including Bolsheviks.[30]

In the early twentieth century, women's salons acquired a special significance in the development of new directions in the arts. In St. Petersburg in 1900, the Symbolist circle began to meet at the home of the poet Zinaida Gippius, who was then married to the writer Dmitrii Merezhkovskii. The Symbolists developed a whole new direction in poetry and an entirely new type of artistic conception.[31]

In 1914, Evdoksia Nikitina, a literary scholar and instructor at Moscow University, formed a circle that lasted through the war, the revolutions of 1917, and beyond. For more than half a century "Nikitina's Saturday group" brought together people interested in the arts. Nikitina herself gathered a unique collection of original materials, which was later preserved in the Moscow literary museum.[32]

This second generation of salons, which brought together progressive intellectuals and leaders of the arts, was not restricted to the capitals. Ekaterina Mamontova in the Moscow suburb of Abramtsevo and Elena Polenova in Tarusa, near Serpukhov, formed "workshops" where painters, inspired by traditional Russian crafts, shared their ideas. Another patroness was Princess Maria Tenisheva, who set up a salon at her estate, Talashkino, in Smolensk. Herself an artist, Tenisheva invited Repin, Polenov, Vasnetsov, Serov, Roerich, Vrubel, and Maliutin to discuss the newest concepts and evaluate each other's work. Many of them designed furniture, ceramic ware, and tapestries for the Talashkino workshops. "For a long time she *lived* art," the painter Nikolai Roerich wrote of her. "She was the first to aid the appearance of *World of Art* [*Mir iskusstva*—the major artistic society and publication of the early twentieth century]; she was the first to establish an outstanding museum of the applied arts and ethnography. It is no accident that even abroad the achievements of this princess are valued, a strong presence with a broad sweep."[33]

Many educated Russian women of the nineteenth and early twentieth centuries possessed the essential characteristics to foster the development of intellectual life: exceptional organizational ability, creative inspiration, and a gift for bringing people together, listening to them, and sharing their experiences. These women created the conditions for the essential exchange of ideas and for peaceful, productive intellectual work. Each of these women was an extraordinary individual, who understood the significance and difficulties of creative activity and thus strove to foster it.[34]

Revolutionary Women

The development of a female consciousness in Russia took place in the context of a challenge to traditional conceptions of the proper place of women. The question of women's role in society arose at the end of the eighteenth and the beginning of the nineteenth century. In this period, Russians who could read French became acquainted with the first proponents of women's rights: Jean-Jacques Rousseau, Denis Diderot, Jean Condorcet, and Olympe de Gouges. But reversing the marginalization of women in Russian public and political life was a long process, one that was closely related to the development of broader movements dedicated to political liberation and social transformation. From the first publications especially for women, which appeared in the early nineteenth century, to the foundation of the Women's Patriotic Society in 1812, to the integration of women in political activity, Russian women engaged in an organized struggle for equal rights.

The mothers, wives, and sisters of the Decembrists of 1825 personified the "new female personality" of the early nineteenth century. They received the same upbringing as their sons, husbands, and brothers, based in respect for the humanistic traditions of the eighteenth century. They were wealthy and aristocratic. Along with their male relatives, they lived through Napoleon's invasion in 1812, they experienced the same upsurge of patriotism and national consciousness, and they developed the same love for their homeland. But because these women were busy with familial concerns, they were not suspected of participation in the plot against the monarchy. The aim of the uprising on December 14, 1825, was to overthrow the government and to establish a constitution. The trials and condemnations that followed were unexpectedly and horrifyingly harsh. Any expression of sympathy for "state criminals" was regarded as treasonous. But still the wives of the Decembrists made the ethical rather than the pragmatic choice, in accordance with their own sense of duty and loyalty.

The highest criminal court of Russia convicted 121 Decembrists. Of these, 23 were married, and all of them were sentenced to ten years or more of hard labor, with the loss of noble titles and officer ranks. Their wives were publicly encouraged to repudiate their husbands and retain their titles and wealth for themselves and their children. But eleven of these women refused to betray their husbands, and instead preferred to share their fate. Ekaterina Trubetskaia and Maria Volkonskaia (the daughter-in-law of Zinaida Volkonskaia, the salon hostess), and nine other wives, sisters, and mothers of Decembrists followed their menfolk to Siberia. Gradually other women relatives of participants in the revolt joined them.[35]

What motivated the womenfolk of the first Russian revolutionaries voluntarily to reject their privileges and their former comfortable life, and instead to choose poverty and exile? Was it self-sacrifice, empathy with their menfolk, a sense of justice, or marital duty? The actions of the Decembrists' wives seemed heroic to many people at the time, as well as later. But the women themselves felt otherwise. "What heroines? It is poets who have made heroines of us; we simply followed our husbands."[36]

Princess Ekaterina Trubetskaia felt that her first loyalty was to her husband, and "with a pure and serene conscience," she decided to travel to the city of Chita in Siberia in June 1826. Princess Maria Volkonskaia was the second to arrive at the prison; others followed. The road in Chita where these aristocrats settled was thereafter called "Ladies' Street," and it became the cultural center of Siberia. The authorities' hope of isolating the "state criminals" and consigning their ideas and names to oblivion turned out to be false. Through the medium of their womenfolk, the Decembrists carried on a lively correspondence with the outside world. Several of the Decembrist women—for example, the sister of Mikhail Lunin, Elena Uvarova—undertook to distribute in the capital treatises on political philosophy that had been written in prison.

Maria Volkonskaia, Alexandra Muravieva, and Natalia Fonvizina bestowed their care and attention not only on their husbands and relatives but also upon dozens of other prisoners. They cooked meals for them every day; they sewed and washed clothing; they prepared medicines. Many inmates considered Polina Annenkova-Gebl, Alexandra Entaltseva, and Kamilla Ledantiu-Ivasheva to be their moral support, because they were so able to cheer them up when they were downcast and to soothe them in their grief. The very presence of young, educated ladies restrained the jailers from abusing their charges. The Decembrist women recreated in Siberia aspects of the cultural life of the capital, with a decided feminine slant: they founded public libraries and medical clinics and arranged lectures and concerts.[37]

For the delicately reared noblewomen, the years of Siberian exile were a hard experience. From it they gained not only fortitude but also the impetus to fight injustice. In the 1840s, the Decembrist women living in exile felt it their duty to help all political prisoners. These included the novelist Fedor Dostoevskii, who called them "sufferers blessed in a new path." He gratefully kept the copy of the Gospels—the only book permitted in jail—that these women had given him; they had hidden money between the pages.

This new generation of political prisoners espoused different ideas from the Decembrists; in helping them, the Decembrist women gained new political insights. The Decembrists, so eager to plan the transformation of society and government, had not accepted women as members of their organizations, but the wives of the Decembrists had demonstrated their unswerving devotion to the same ideals and principles.[38] The women revolutionaries of the 1860s felt an unambiguous spiritual kinship with the Decembrist women. Vera Figner, a leading revolutionary from later in the century, asked, "Shall we not recognize them as precursors, as luminaries who illuminated our revolutionary movement from afar?"[39]

But in the mid-nineteenth century, nobody viewed the actions of the Decembrist women as evidence of women's autonomous participation in the struggle for political liberation. Despite all the changes in social consciousness, before the 1850s not even the most progressive publications advanced the idea of women's equality. It was the literary critic and contributor to the progressive journal *The Contemporary* (*Sovremennik*) M.L. Mikhailov who first raised the "Woman Question" in his 1852 article, "Women, Their Upbringing and Significance in the Family and Society." This article comprised the first call for equality for women in society and political life in Russian history, and the "Woman Question" caught on. It dominated literature and journalism, not so much as an issue in its own right but as one manifestation of Russia's more general social problems.[40]

Thoughtful women responded with enthusiasm to the idea of universal education and to the notion that labor was essential for women of all social classes (including the privileged ones) in order to "liberate them from an eternal minority, from a life of dependency," as Alexander Herzen put it. Hundreds of young women fled their parental homes to St. Petersburg, that "laboratory of ideas," in order to study, work, and "not live as drones," but instead to "confirm their independence." They called themselves "New People," or "nihilists," who opposed the old order. They observed a strict simplicity in their dress and lifestyle. In place of the lavish laces and corsets of "missish damsels," they wore black suits or dark dresses with white collars and cuffs. In place of curls and chignons, nihilist women cut their hair short, wore glasses and masculine hats, and smoked cigarettes.

The "New Women" saw their future in educating ordinary people, so they "devoted themselves to mathematics and the natural sciences instead of poetry." The works of Western socialists—Saint-Simon, Owens, Lassalle, and Proudhon—made the rounds, but the textbook for the new mode of living was Nikolai Chernyshevskii's 1862 novel, *What Is to Be Done?* In this book, the author pointed the way to "action and freedom" and how they could be achieved: through the establishment of workers' cooperatives (artels) and communes. The prototype of these forms of "collectivized labor" was the publishing artel that M.V. Trubnikova initiated in the mid-1850s.

Maria Trubnikova (1835–1897) was the daughter of the Decembrist Vladimir Ivashev and Kamilla Ledantiu. She was born in Siberia amid deprivation and hardship, but this background did not crush her. On the contrary, she became the recognized leader not only of the newborn women's movement but also of the drive for democratization in general. She had broad horizons and organizational abilities, and she energetically sought persons with a variety of views. Along with Nadezhda Stasova (1822–1895) and Anna Filosofova (1837–1912), she established the first and only "Women's Publishing Cooperative" to demonstrate how to transform words into deeds. This self-proclaimed "triumvirate" organized not only their publishing outfit but also a "Society of Cheap Apartments," the Vladimirskii women's courses, sewing workshops, and Sunday schools to provide peasants with a rudimentary education.

Many of the organizers of schools, cooperatives, and societies became activists in the movement for women's rights. They felt a strong connection with the revolutionary groups of the day; thus eighteen women entered the Land and Liberty party of the 1860s—the first revolutionary organization after the Decembrists. When underground revolutionary movements began at St. Petersburg University in 1861, women auditors in courses were accepted into the dissident groups on a par with formally enrolled male students. The police kept track of women agitators as they did men; the names of Maria

Bogdanova, Nadezhda Korsini, Nadezhda Suslova, Maria Korkunova, and Anna Engelgardt appeared in their files. Many of the "Women of the 1860s" were arrested. Within the half-decade between 1860 and 1865, the number of women in the revolutionary movement doubled.

By 1870, between 20 and 50 percent of the revolutionary discussion groups were women: student-auditors, high-school pupils, school-teachers, midwives, and nurse-practitioners. The work of spreading the word truly became women's contribution. The To the People movement of the 1860s was begun by women participating in the struggle for liberation. The main goal of this movement, and the Narodniki, or "Populists," who constituted it, was to foment a revolution among the peasantry and thus transform Russian society into one of equality for everyone. This revolutionary propaganda did not elicit the desired response from the peasants, however, and the authorities strongly opposed it. "It could drive us to despair of the revolutionary loneliness in which we lived," Vera Figner later remembered.[41] She and many of her comrades were arrested and condemned in the mass trials of revolutionaries in this period.

Whole families of dissidents were tried together: the three Zasulich sisters, the three Figner sisters, the Liubatovich sisters, the four Paniutina sisters, the four daughters of the merchant Goldenberg. Their defiant speeches before the court later circulated among revolutionaries throughout Russia: "Prosecute us! We have the force of morality, the force of the historical process, the force of ideas behind us! And ideas cannot be speared on bayonets."[42] Under the influence of popular opinion, the sentences handed down in the "Trial of the 50" were mitigated. Several of the women were acquitted; the sentences of others were commuted to jail terms. In the "Trial of the 193," the jury's verdict was stiffer. For the first time in Russian history, five women were convicted of political propaganda and were condemned to hard labor, including Ekaterina Breshko-Breshkovskaia. Breshko-Breshkovskaia devoted more than forty years of her life to revolutionary activity, and she came to be known as the "grandmother of the Russian Revolution."[43]

Out of eighty-four political trials in the 1870s, ninety-five women were convicted.[44] In this period, the political struggle for liberation came to comprise not only propaganda and agitation but also more radical methods. The fervor and impatience of young members of revolutionary circles led them to terrorism. In the trial of Dmitrii Karakozov for his assassination attempt on Alexander II in 1866, thirty-nine women were indicted. Sergei Nechaev's terrorist circle included thirty women. Although their conception of the goals of their struggle were confused, these women terrorists were fanatical in their service to the ideals of the revolution, and they were ready to risk their lives "for the good of society."

On January 24, 1878, the Narodnik Vera Zasulich shot and fatally wounded Fedor Trepov, the governor of St. Petersburg. He had ordered the use of corporal punishment on a political prisoner. Her case was referred to the new, independent judiciary established by Alexander II's reforms. Although the facts of the case were not in question, the jury acquitted Zasulich, regarding her actions as justified. Zasulich's shooting prompted a whole range of terrorist acts, reflecting a determination on the part of revolutionaries to "answer fire with fire"—to respond to decrees and orders issued by central and local authorities and to verdicts by the courts. In the 1880s, eighty-two women were tried in political cases, charged with participation in assassination attempts, harboring conspirators in their apartments, and recruiting new members to revolutionary groups. A significant number of women entered the revolutionary group called the People's Will, which was formed in 1879. Vera Figner, Tatiana Lebedeva, Anna Iakimova, and Sofia Perovskaia (the first woman executed in a political case in Russia), and many other members of the People's Will were distinguished by their selfless devotion to the ideals of "popular happiness," their exacting standards for themselves, their sense of obligation, their integrity, and their conviction about the righteousness of the cause they served. They did not admit any doubt that the methods they chose to advance their struggle were the only correct ones. Their willingness to carry on with their intended goals, no matter what happened, gave these women an enormous reserve of energy and fortitude in the face of the authorities and persecutors. In 1889, Natalia Sigida, Maria Kovalevskaia, Nadezhda Smirnitskaia, and Maria Kaliuzhnaia were convicted of political offenses and were subjected to corporal punishment in the Kariiskii Prison in Siberia. They committed suicide as a sign of protest, and their action ultimately caused a change in policy concerning corporal punishment for women in Russian prisons. The harshness of the sentences, including the condemnation of women terrorists to long periods of incarceration at hard labor or in solitary confinement, not only failed to dampen their revolutionary fervor but on the contrary inflamed it.[45]

The tradition of Russian terrorism survived in the early twentieth century in the militant branch of the Socialist Revolutionary (SR) party, which was founded in 1901. The treasury of this organization was built up partly through voluntary donations from individuals who welcomed terrorism as a method of political struggle and partly through "revolutionary expropriation"—robbery. Among the most notable terrorists of the early twentieth century were Zina Konopliankinova, Tolia Ragoznikova, Tatiana Leontieva, Polina Ivanovskaia, and Maria Spiridonova. Leontieva was the daughter of the vice-governor of Iakutsk; she rejected the position of lady-in-waiting for Empress Alexandra in order to join the terrorists. Ivanovskaia spent the greater part of her life in prison or in exile for her participation in terrorist activity. Spiridonova later became one of the leaders of the SR party.[46]

Alongside the terrorist groups, other political circles arose with a different orientation. These included, first of all, the Marxist Social Democrats, who condemned terror as a method for political struggle. These Social Democratic organizations, which from the beginning included special women's circles (such as those in Ivanovo-Voznesensk, Ekaterinoslav, and Kiev), had as their goal preparation for the coming revolution and the establishment of a dictatorship of the proletariat. Women in these organizations came from the nobility, the urban intelligentsia, and the working class. With the founding of the Russian Social Democratic Workers' party in 1895, women Marxists began to play an active role in agitation in factories and in the distribution of revolutionary literature, including the newspapers *Iskra*, *Sotsial-demokrat*, and *Pravda*. Women Marxists, including Maria Ulianova and Anna Ulianova-Elizarova (who were Lenin's sisters), Nadezhda Krupskaia (who became Lenin's wife), Zinaida Krzhizhanovskaia, and Lia Radchenko became comrades along with men in the revolutionary movement. Many women, such as Maria Sarmentova and Olga Varentsova, came to embrace the ideas of Social Democracy through their participation in workers' strikes and agitation.

By 1914, women composed about 10 percent of the Russian Social Democratic Workers' party. In 1903, the party had split into two factions: the Mensheviks, who espoused the idea of broad party membership and endorsed cooperation with non-Marxist parties to achieve improvements in working conditions and democratization; and the Bolsheviks, who preferred a small, professional party and eschewed pursuit of liberalization, instead directing activities toward the hastening of socialist revolution. But leaders of both factions recognized the contributions women made to the cause of socialism. Both factions actively preached socialist goals among women industrial workers, especially in textile plants, where the percentage of women employees was especially high. Vladimir Ilich Lenin, the leader of the Bolsheviks, wrote, "The experience of all liberation movements demonstrates that the success of every revolution depends upon the extent to which women participate in it."[47] Lenin recommended subordinating the women's movement to the goals first of democratization and then the development of socialism. Bolshevik women shared these goals and actively helped to achieve them.[48]

The liberal democratic movement in Russian politics likewise had a female component. The Union of Liberation, which later came to be called the Constitutional Democrats, or Cadets, included among its members Anna Tyrkova, who belonged to the central committee of the party, Elena Kuskova, Anna Kalmykova, and Liubov Kupriianova, among others. At the same time, many women's organizations were not connected directly with any political party. For example, two newspapers aimed at the female audience, *Women's Affairs* (*Zhenskoe delo*), founded in 1899, and *Women's Messenger* (*Zhenskii vestnik*), founded in 1904, hastened the formation of women's organizations. These included the Russian Society for the Protection of Women, which was founded in 1900 and headed by Princess Elizaveta Oldenburg, as well as the left-wing Union for Women's Equality and the conservative Women's Progressive Party. The group with the largest membership was the Union for Women's Equality, which sought to obtain female suffrage. Feminist and women's suffrage movements were also active in this period; their prominent members included Anna Shabanova, Anna Miliukova, Zinaida Mirovich, and Olga Klirikova. Their energetic organizing led to the First All-Russian Women's Congress in 1908. But by the admission of its leaders, the Russian feminist movement lacked unity in its goals and clarity in its conceptions. This may be explained in part by the feminists' vain attempt to place themselves above class and party distinctions and to keep away from a definite stance in the ongoing social and political struggles in Russia. Still, their efforts to attain equal rights demonstrated that the evolutionary path, the path of gradual advancement toward the goal of the social emancipation of women, could work. There were successes despite government opposition and despite the way the "Woman Question" was consigned to second place, after the seemingly more pressing issues of peace, land, and democratization. When the Duma (parliament) issued a law on workers' insurance in 1912, it granted specific rights to women workers. And in August 1917, the Provisional Government of Alexander Kerensky granted women the right to vote.[49]

Women in the Academy

Women's contributions to scholarship in the nineteenth and early twentieth centuries were part of the larger struggle for access to higher education and positions in teaching and the professions.

In the eighteenth century, Princess Dashkova broke into the world of scholarship by becoming the president of two academies. In the nineteenth century, the ranks of women academics grew. The first Russian woman economist was Maria Vernadskaia (1831–1860), the wife of I.V. Vernadskii, a professor of political economy at Kiev University and Moscow University who encouraged his young wife's scholarly interests. Vernadskaia had received a good education in childhood; she was widely read and fluent in French, German, and English. Her enthusiasm for scholarship did not make her blind to the realities around her; she welcomed her husband's decision to free their serfs, made eleven years before Alexander II's manifesto. She attentively examined the place of women in society and came to the conclusion that only work outside the family could liberate women from servitude and make women free individuals in fact as well as in name. Although she lived only twenty-nine years and had a short career—less than a decade—she accomplished as much as many male scholars did in a lifetime. Within two years, 1858–59, she wrote 120 scholarly articles and a book, *An Attempt at a Popular Account of the Basic Principles of Political Economy*. In these publications, Vernadskaia expressed her own understanding of the need to work and the need for the freedom to do so, and also of the right to private property. With her broad perspective, Vernadskaia welcomed the appearance of joint-stock companies, free trade, and free enterprise, and she recognized the advantages of free competition. Some of her articles presented abstract economic theories in the form of parables; they remain a model of how to present scholarly concepts in an accessible form.

By the late 1850s, the question of women's access to university education was already being widely discussed in Russian society. Admission to universities was, of course, an essential precondition for women contributing to scholarly activity in general. In 1859, St. Petersburg University opened its doors to women, allowing them to audit courses. "Hundreds of ladies and girls" appeared in the auditoriums of Kiev University and Kharkov University and in the lecture halls of the St. Petersburg Public Library and the Rumiantsev Library in Moscow. "Some of them worked, without stopping, from three in the afternoon until nine at night."[50] The most common form of higher education for women in this period was "floating universities," which met in private apartments. There professors and instructors from official programs read lectures for free.[51]

In 1861, I.M. Sechenov, a famous physicist and professor at the Medical–Surgical Academy, organized scientific experiments for the first Russian women medical students, Nadezhda Suslova and Maria Bokova (Obrucheva). But in 1863, the right of women to attend lectures at institutions of higher education was revoked. State authorities regarded these courses as a breeding ground for female Narodniki and feminists. Many of the women who had been auditing courses had to go abroad in order to continue their education. But the difficulty of obtaining passports and visas to travel abroad, and the high cost of the journey, presented obstacles to would-be students. Those women who possessed the financial means and a thirst for knowledge enrolled in universities and technical schools in Paris, Bern, Zurich, Berlin, and Königsberg. Anna Zhaklar, Anna Evreinova, and Iulia Lermontova had received a serious education at home, but they had to leave Russia to continue their studies. Many of these young women went abroad without their parents' permission. Others, such as Elizaveta Dmitrieva and Sofia Kovalevskaia, entered fictitious marriages with sympathetic men in order to pursue an independent path.

Elizaveta Dmitrieva took on a male persona and participated in the Paris Commune. Sofia Kovalevskaia (1850–1891), who became a world-renowned scholar, typifies the aspirations of the women of the 1860s generation. Sofia, the daughter of V.V. Korvin-Krukovskii, a lieutenant-general in the artillery, was fascinated by mathematics even in childhood. Later she entered the private courses in mathematics taught by a professor from St. Petersburg University, where she demonstrated exceptional talent. Sofia decided to go abroad to continue her studies and entered a fictitious marriage with V.O. Kovalevskii, who later became a noted paleontologist. This arrangement gave her the opportunity to study in Heidelberg and Berlin. Famous mathematicians acknowledged her abilities: "not many people can compare with her in diligence, aptitude, zeal, and enthusiasm for scholarship." In 1874, Kovalevskaia was awarded the doctoral degree, in absentia, at Göttingen University, for her work with differential equations. Inspired by this success, Kovalevskaia returned to St. Petersburg. But she was not offered a position at the university there, or even an instructorship in the Higher Courses for Women, but only a slot teaching arithmetic to the lower grades of high school.

For several years she wrote fiction, but in 1883 she left Russia for good to accept an appointment as a tutor at Stockholm University. Within a year, she had become the world's first woman professor of mathematics. The St. Petersburg Academy of Sciences recognized her achievements in 1889, when it voted to make her a corresponding member. However, she never had a chance to pursue her intellectual work in Russia, because she died suddenly soon afterward.[52]

A second Russian woman, Iulia Lermontova (1846–1919), also studied at Göttingen University. Her scholarly accomplishments lay in the area of organic chemistry. She was eventually accepted as an active member of the Russian Chemical Society, and she co-authored publications with Dmitrii Mendeleev, the inventor of the Periodic Table.[53]

Women also entered the field of medicine in significant numbers. By the beginning of World War I, there were about a thousand women pharmacists in Russia, including Anna Makarova, Sofia Doviaglo, and Olga Gabrilovich, whose scholarly articles have had lasting value. Varvara Kashevarova-Rudneva (1844–1899) became Russia's first woman medical doctor, specializing in gynecology. She graduated as valedictorian from the Medical–Surgical Academy in 1868, and she was awarded a doctoral degree in 1876, when she was twenty-eight years old.[54]

In the humanities, not many women became prominent historians, ethnographers, and philosophers. However, there were exceptions. Vera Kharuzina (1866–1931) became the first female professor of ethnography; she wrote on the history of folk beliefs and folklorists. Alexandra Efimenko (1848–1918) became a respected historian and holder of a doctoral degree; her publications included invaluable materials gathered on ethnographical expeditions. Countess Praskovia Uvarova, an archeologist, became the first woman elected to the Russian Academy of Sciences, in 1894. The philosopher Elena Blavatskaia (1831–1891) became a proponent of theosophy, a religious and mystical movement that recognized the sources of divine knowledge in intuition and revelation.[55] The works of these women scholars are cited to this day.

The assiduous research of these talented women bequeathed a legacy of achievements despite conditions particularly restrictive for women. Women who decided to pursue scholarly careers constantly had to justify their choosing their own paths in life, and they were not always successful in doing so. As a contemporary government charter put it, "The increase in the number of women scholars was not desirable"; instead, governmental authorities tried to "set up courses for female persons to prepare them for professions that did not require anything higher than a high-school education, if that," and would serve only to teach them "to be good wives and helpful mothers of families."[56]

Writers and Poets

In the early nineteenth century, when the young Alexander Pushkin was gaining universal acclaim, contemporary women authors encountered significant obstacles. "No, a woman author will never be able to love, nor to become a wife and mother," Vissarion Belinskii, later a zealous proponent of women's rights, once wrote.[57] Such prejudices crushed "more than one talent that promised Russian literature new glory," as Ivan Kireevskii later commented.[58]

The literary works of Elizaveta Kulman, Anna Bunina, Evdokia Rostopchina, Karolina Pavlova, Iulia Zhadovskaia, Nadezhda Durova, Zinaida Volkonskaia, and Elena Gan appeared in the pages of Russian journals, lending immediacy to the hotly debated "Woman Question." Their works were marked by a surprising consistency. All these writers turned their attention to women's elevated humanity and unwillingness to compromise with moral humiliation and familial despotism, and this at the same time as the Compiled Laws of the Russian Empire asserted women's inferiority in society, and a belief in the intellectual inequality of the sexes underlay the entire system of education.

The poetic talent of Anna Bunina was marked by drama and internal tension. The court historian Nikolai Karamzin wrote that "no other woman among us has written so powerfully." A literary critic remarked of Evdokia Rostopchina's poetry that "inspiration emanates not only from her mind but from deep feeling." Iulia Zhadovskaia's poetry was closely connected to the tradition of popular songs; she spoke of the needs and poverty of the people with heartfelt pain.

The literary critic Vissarion Belinskii raved about the book *The Cavalry Maiden*: "Courageous steadfastness and strength, sparkling expressiveness of style, a picturesque story, permeated with secret thoughts." The author of this best-seller of the nineteenth century was Nadezhda Durova (1783–1866), a woman with an extraordinary career. Born into the family of an officer in a hussar regiment, Durova fled her parents' home at the age of nineteen. In the guise of a man, and using the name Alexander Sokolov, she enlisted in an uhlan (light cavalry) regiment. In 1807, she participated in the Russian campaign against Napoleon, and she received the St. George Cross for bravery. When she was released from active duty in 1816, she had achieved the rank of staff captain. Durova made her recollections of military service the basis for her book, which enjoyed stunning success. In the wake of Durova's book, an abundance of similar tales appeared, featuring stalwart heroines who found the courage to transgress societal prejudices in secret adventures.[59]

"Who knows better than I everything that is unpleasant, cruel, and unnatural in the position of women," Durova's contemporary Elena Gan observed.[60] Her semi-autobiographical short story "The Court of the World" expresses the bitterness of misunderstanding and the pain of spiritual loneliness. Alexandra Zrazhevskaia was a writer, translator, publicist, and folklorist. Called a "literary mutineer," Zrazhevskaia first challenged the censors by translating forbidden French novels "with a harmful form of thinking," including the works of Balzac. She also satirically indicted "the three terrible beasts that wage war against women writers: pedantry, philosophizing, and verbosity."[61] Overcoming the intellectual roadblocks put up by the censors, the first women professional writers of children's books, Anna Zontag and Alexandra Ishimova, created absorbing and deeply patriotic stories in the 1820s and 1830s, stories that inculcated in young people not conformity but high ethical norms.

A search for harmony in life and meditations on the possibility of social justice distinguish women's literary production in Russia from the 1860s through the 1880s. The arguments concerning equal rights for women generated by the "Woman Question" not only inspired themes in women's writings but also influenced how they lived their lives. The role of writer for women seemed incompatible with good breeding. "People torment us with mockery, and relatives trip us up," Maria Tsebrikova remembered. Most women writers of this period assumed male aliases: Maria Vilinskaia became Marko Vovchok, Sofia Khvoshchinskaia became Ivan Veseniev, Sofia Soboleva became V. Samoilovich, and Nadezhda Khvoshchinskaia became V. Krestovskii. In order to win the unequal battle for the right to create, women writers needed "either especially favorable circumstances or an enormous strength of character," the contemporary critic Dmitrii Pisarev wrote. They had to possess purposefulness and unusual strength of will. For that reason, it would be unfair to blame them for the tendentiousness that frequently emerged in their literary works or for their didactic and journalistic tone. But these characteristics sometimes alienated readers, who were looking for some reflection of their own experiences or the human condition in general. This was one reason that women writers did not receive the same acclaim as Ivan Turgenev or Leo Tolstoy.

However, many Russian women writers in the second half of the nineteenth century equaled male authors of the "second tier" in their creativity and popularity. For example, the works of the Khvoshchinskaia sisters were richly populated with colorful characters and fine, ironic portraits. Sofia Khvoshchinskaia's favorite theme was the depiction of provincial life, revealing "splendidly portrayed philistinism" as opposed to rural "spirituality" and the "unnatural tastes" of the capital. She was able to publish in the leading liberal journals. Her sister Nadezhda Khvoshchinskaia portrayed the disintegration of the noble family and the problems between fathers and their children. Nadezhda delighted in the courage of the Narodniki of the 1870s and depicted the spiritual bankruptcy of persons who betrayed the ideals of the 1860s.

Many women writers of the early twentieth century continued to focus on the theme of the "ordinary man and woman," whose human worth they defended. This motif of sympathy with the "humiliated and insulted" was particularly evident in the works of Valentina Dmitrieva (1859–1948), a writer of peasant origin. Elizaveta Militsina (1869–1930) also explored this theme; she traveled widely in Russia, and her stories reflect the decay of the Russian countryside, the difficult position of women, and sources of revolt. But for a variety of reasons, the writings of these women prose authors never gained broad understanding and appreciation, and today they are little known.[62]

In the 1880s, Russian poetry was experiencing a decline. Themes of weariness, doom, devastation, and despondency predominated in reaction to the political oppression following the assassination of Alexander II. At the end of the century, however, new movements appeared in Russian poetry: the Symbolists, the Acmeists, the Futurists, and others. These not only reinvigorated Russian artistic life, they influenced cultural life throughout Europe. This became the "Silver Age" of Russian literature—an era of poetic renaissance. Women poets played a prominent role in this diversity of movements: Mirra Lokhvitskaia, Anna Akhmatova, Marina Tsvetaeva, and Zinaida Gippius.[63]

Zinaida Gippius (1869–1945) tended toward the Symbolist movement. She expressed a presentiment of the coming social upheavals and catastrophes.[64] Anna Akhmatova (1889–1966), in contrast, affiliated herself with the Acmeists. Her fame as the writer of lyrical love poetry spread even in her youth. Her poetry proclaimed the high value of everyday experiences, and it was marked by her characteristic intimate and conversational tone. It appealed to an enormous circle of readers, especially to women.[65]

Marina Tsvetaeva (1892–1941) did not affiliate with any particular cultural movement, but her work was perhaps the most characteristic of the era. She came from a family of the intelligentsia; her father was a professor and the founder of the Museum of Fine Arts in Moscow. From childhood, Tsvetaeva had a flair for words; she composed rhymes in Russian, French, and German at age six. Her first collection of poetry, *Evening Album,* was published in 1910, without her family's knowledge. Many famous poets of the day, including Briusov, Gumilev, and Voloshin, expressed their approval of it. They noted Tsvetaeva's originality and "swirling inspiredness." The collections that followed at the rate of one per year ever more clearly outlined the contours of her individual vision. Unlike the Symbolists and Acmeists, Tsvetaeva emphasized her rebellious essence, her unconquerable love of life. She contrasted reckless, daring "Russianness" with the pragmatic and rational West, with its "velvet satiety" and banality. In the 1910s, Tsvetaeva's creative principle of "alone against all others" led to her isolation and loneliness, which determined her later career and productivity. Although she was tragically misunderstood in her own day, the time finally came for her "poetry, like precious wines," as she had foretold.[66]

Many other forgotten women writers of Tsvetaeva's day have recently been rediscovered. They received little acclaim during their lifetimes, and not all of them were first-rate. Several had only modest talent; others, although more talented, were unable to express their gifts fully because of the difficult conditions of their lives. But all of them contributed to the formation of a specifically feminine voice in Russian literature, one that had its own themes and language.[67]

The World of the Arts

A dreamy romanticism and experimentation distinguished the creations of women in the fine arts in the early nineteenth century.

Connoisseurs of Russian ballet in the first third of the nineteenth century identified Avdotia Istomina (1799–1848), a brilliant dancer at the Petersburg Bolshoi Theater, as the ideal. She was the first ballerina to exchange the elaborate stylized stage costume for the classi-cally inspired chiton, which enabled her to dance in a light and airy way. "She flies, like down from the mouth of Aeolus, and beats one leg against another quickly," Alexander Pushkin raved. Istomina pos-sessed many talents as a performer, and she was able to convey the dramatic side of her roles to her audience. She could play all roles—dramatic, tragic, or comedic—with equal finesse. Other ballerinas of the day, for example, Tatiana Smirnova, were also noted for their expressiveness and inspiration in their romantic roles. The ballerina Maria Muravieva (1838–1879) won acclaim for her gentle lyricism and technical style. A critic wrote, "While she dances, diamond sparks rain down from her legs."

The famous opera singer Anna Vorobieva-Petrova (1816–1901) was a contemporary of these marvelous ballerinas. Her career coin-cided with the development of a distinctive national style of singing, one characterized by a broad range, sincerity, and deep emotionality. From 1835 to 1847, Vorobieva-Petrova's enchanting voice and irre-sistible charm as she filled lead roles in operas by Glinka and Dargomyzhskii marked the birth of the Russian national opera.

Ekaterina Semenova (1786–1849) performed a similar function for the theater. This great tragic actress was the daughter of a serf, but thanks to her talent and unusual diligence she became, as Pushkin put it, "the tsaritsa of the Russian stage." Her dramatic style ushered in a new era in the history of the Russian theater and marked the victory of realism. Many leading actresses of the period, including Galina Fedotova, Liubov Nikulina-Kositskaia, Olga Sadovskaia, and especially Maria Ermolova (1823–1928), sought to portray "living truth" on stage. For fifty years, Ermolova performed at Moscow's Malyi Theater. She created over three hundred roles, bringing to them the traits most like her own: nobility, courage, and self-sacrifice. Her performances, suffused with revolutionary enthusiasm, evoked heroic feats. These sentiments harmonized with the values of the era, and Ermolova became the idol of democratic youth.

Both Maria Savina (1854–1915) and Polina Strepetova (1850–1903) made their names in the Aleksandrinskii Theater in St. Peters-burg, but they had different talents and careers. The gentle and refined Savina was acclaimed for her depiction of young heroines who hid a firm will and distinctive character behind a fragile exte-rior. She was considered the embodiment of the ideal Turgenev heroine. Savina, however, also took it upon herself to defend the economic and legal interests of Russian actors, whom she represented in the Council of the Russian Theatrical Society, She also organized a retirement home for aged theatrical performers.

Savina's rival, Polina Strepetova, had a difficult life from the first. She was an orphan, raised by a relative who was a hairdresser, and she received no systematic education. From her early years, she was exposed to the grim side of life. Her origin and upbringing inspired in Strepetova's acting a spirit of protest against injustice that resonated with the revolutionary and democratic impulses in Russian society. A.N. Ostrovskii, Strepetova's favorite playwright, wrote of her, "Such natural talent is a rare, phenomenal occurrence. Her [best] scenes are of women of the lower and middle classes; her enthusiasm is for simple and strong passions."[68] Strepetova superbly conveyed the suffering of Russian women, their inconsolable grief. With her innate candor and emotionality, she opposed the creation of theatrical schools and studios, believing that it was impossible to teach actors to empathize, to depict feelings honestly; this depended upon natural gifts and had to come from inside. With the power of her emotions, Strepetova could make audiences forget the shortcomings of her appearance: she was stoop-shouldered, angular, and unattractive. The authenticity Strepetova brought to her roles shook her audiences, but most theater-goers came not for soul-searching passion but for light entertainment. Furthermore, Strepetova's sharp, direct personality brought her into conflict with the director of the theater, and in 1900 he refused to renew her contract.

Strepetova's talent can be compared only with that of Vera Komissarzhevskaia (1864–1910), who also began her career at the Aleksandrinskii Theater. This petite actress entranced audiences with her shining eyes and expressive voice. In all her roles she captured the drama of the human condition in an unjust world, and the rebelliousness of women striving to find their rightful place in society. Unlike Strepetova, Komissarzhevskaia was a fighter. In 1904, she founded her own theater as an expression of her revolutionary and romantic predilections. During the Revolution of 1905, performances there frequently ended with spontaneous demonstrations.[69]

Among those of Komissarzhevskaia's contemporaries who were painters, several shared her innovative and nonconformist style. Although these artists did not have Komissarzhevskaia's fame or influence, the originality of their work received some recognition from specialists. For example, Herzen, Dostoevsky, and Tolstoy paid attention to the artistic production of Elena Iunge, whose landscapes reflected the realist school of the Itinerants, and of Maria Iakunchikova, a student of the painter Vasilii Polenov.

Iunge and Iakunchikova's works were distinguished by lyricism, restrained use of color, and a harmonious combination of architectural elements and landscape. Elena Polenova (1850–1898) chose different creative themes. She was one of the first to recognize the merit of traditional Russian peasant art: the woodcarvings, embroidery, and ceramics. Her paintings of Russian folktales incorporated the genius of traditional crafts. In addition, Polenova also published picture books for children that presaged the world-famous illustrated fairy tales of I.Ia. Bilibin as well as modern comic books.

The paintings of Natalia Goncharova (1881–1962) revealed a radically new artistic creativity never appreciated in Russia, but which became highly valued in Western Europe. The most important motifs in her work came from the Russian countryside, everyday life in the cities, and the lifestyles of peasants and artisans. From popular woodcuts (lukbi), Goncharova borrowed the simplicity and occasional grotesqueness of her figures. From Russian traditions of iconography, she took stylistic elements and the resolution of color. Goncharova's works sometimes recall the style of children's drawings, sometimes that of signs, placards, or posters. A sharp departure from the accepted styles of the time, they marked the move toward Futurism.

Goncharova also worked in theatrical set design. The famous Russian director Serge Diaghilev recognized her originality and invited her to come to Paris to collaborate with him. In 1913, she designed sets for several ballet and opera performances by Diaghilev's Ballet Russe, and they lived up to all her expectations: they turned out to be colorful and cheerful, with a fairy-tale intricacy.[70]

Another star of Diaghilev's troupe in the early twentieth century was the quintessential ballerina Anna Pavlova (1881–1931). "She had a frank and spontaneous temperament, which raised her past the level of 'artistry' and elevated her to the level of genius," one spectator remembered. From 1899 to 1908 Pavlova danced in the Mariinskii Theater in St. Petersburg, but "she did not make any lasting impression on the public because she did not impress or surprise any of the acknowledged masters of the ballet with her originality." Petite and slender (she weighed under 100 pounds), "her nervous temperament gave her unparalleled quickness of movement, so that she constantly frightened her partners, flinging herself into their arms in an impetuous leap from the staircase or from the back of the stage."

Diaghilev, however, appreciated Pavlova's talent and originality. In 1908 and 1909, she joined his troupe in Paris, where she enjoyed unprecedented success. "It is impossible to describe the feelings that this fragile being, this transparent, weightless creature, evoked. There were moments when you saw a dream, action taking place as though in the air," remembered the dancer Natalia Trukhanova, who performed with Pavlova's own troupe in the 1910s.[71] Pavlova was best known for her performance of *The Dying Swan* with the intricate zig-zag steps of its death agony, set to music by Saint-Saëns. This performance became emblematic of Russian ballet style in the early twentieth century.[72]

The leading star of Russian opera in this period was Antonina Nezhdanova (1873–1950), whose lyric–coloratura soprano was considered one of the best in Europe. With her light, vibrato voice, Nezhdanova created ideal fairy-tale heroines—the Snow Maiden, sorceresses, princesses. Another singer, Nadezhda Plevitskaia (1884–1941), had a more spirited style; she was known for her performances of Russian folk songs. "Everyone, from the monarch to the least tradesman, was captivated by her Russian beauty and the brilliance of her talent."[73] Plevitskaia's strong alto voice brought her fame not only in Russia but also abroad.

Through the international language of music, dance, and art, West Europeans came to appreciate the talent and originality of Russian women artists and performers of the nineteenth and twentieth centuries. Their contributions to the cultural heritage of Russia and the world brought them lasting recognition at home and abroad. These women of the arts revealed themselves to be not only artistically gifted but also independent.

The prominent women of the nineteenth and early twentieth centuries fall into several different types. One type of publicly active woman was the high-society lady, including women of the imperial family, whose charitable work provided essential services in the period when Russia's civic structures were being reconfigured according to West European models. Another type of influential woman was the salon hostess, who fostered the development of literature, philosophy, and the arts in the privacy of her home at a time when public discussion was constrained by government censorship. Female participants in political and revolutionary movements reflect a third type; their efforts, along with those of their male comrades, ultimately led to the transformation of Russian government and society. The women scholars, patronesses, and creative artists similarly strove to be useful to society, to realize their capabilities, and to gain recognition.

Lives in Toil and Leisure

The everyday lives of Russian women of all social orders and classes were filled with joys and sorrows, anxieties and hopes. For many of them, their lives centered around their families and their homes. This was particularly true for peasants, and thus for the majority of Russian women, for even in the early twentieth century, the rural population comprised 87 percent of the people in the Russian Empire.

Daily life remained difficult for peasant women.[74] They performed the same heavy fieldwork as men: mowing, stacking the hay, binding sheaves, and threshing grain. They also kept the vegetable garden, which they planted, weeded, and harvested. They cared for livestock, feeding them, cleaning the barn, shoveling manure, milking the cows, nursing sick animals, and delivering newborns. Peasant women usually got no more than three or four hours of sleep a night during the summer, so they tended to be exhausted from overwork and susceptible to illnesses.

The burdens of agricultural labor forced peasant families to live in multigenerational families, where several women could help one another. All of them worked unceasingly at home, if they were not in the fields. "If you're going to manage a house, you can't sweep with just a feather," the proverb went. Rural women continued to keep house in the traditional manner. Ethnographers who described peasant custom in the nineteenth century noticed that "cleanliness is observed in houses to an extraordinary degree." If the floors were wooden, they were kept to "an amazing whiteness," and neatness in clothing was "an essential rite." Certain household tasks, such as mopping floors and washing clothes, were so labor intensive that all the women worked together on them. Young girls were not allowed to clean, because it was feared that they would use up too much soap, which even in the early twentieth century was very expensive. Linens were usually not washed with soap but instead were soaked in lye or boiled with ashes in a kettle, then beaten with rollers, and finally rinsed for a long time in running water. This work was extremely tiring.[75]

Less labor-intensive duties were strictly divided between the eldest female head of the household, and her daughters, daughters-in-law, and sisters-in-law. They generally got along well, if the male head of the household and his wife treated them alike. The eldest woman, or *bolshukha*, directed everything in the house and did the shopping and cooking. Her eldest daughter-in-law, or all of them in order, helped her. The youngest daughters-in-law had the most unenviable plight:

Russian peasants of the early nineteenth century in everyday clothing and headdresses. From the painting "The Threshing Floor," by A.G. Venetsianov, 1822–1823.

"to do whatever work they are made to and to eat whatever they are given." Young daughters-in-law had to carry water and wood, and on Saturdays they had to heat the bathhouse. Preparing the bathhouse meant carrying between twenty and thirty buckets of water and several armloads of wood, then lighting the stove with its acrid smoke, and finally preparing the birch switches (used for exfoliation and massage) by pouring boiling water over them and soaking them in *kvas* (bread beer) to make them soft. The youngest daughter-in-law also helped the older women in the bath, massaging them with the birch switches, sluicing them with cold water, and serving them tea after they were done bathing.[76]

Minding the fire in the stove and cooking for the entire family required a housewife to be clever, as well as physically strong: the cast-iron pots used for cooking were heavy. In most peasant families, whether rich or poor, the basic diet consisted of rye bread, which was baked once a week, sometimes only by the *bolshukha* and sometimes by every woman in turn. *Bliny* (pancakes) were made from rye or buckwheat flour, and cold kvas was brewed from rye malt. Kasha (porridge), made from any one of a number of grains, was nourishing and easy to prepare. In the nineteenth century, boiled potatoes became a staple in the peasant diet. When potatoes were first introduced in the eighteenth century, rural people were afraid to eat them; at first they mistakenly ate the poisonous greens rather than the tubers, and they became sick and even died. Each housewife had her own recipe for everyday soup, *shchi*, made from cabbage and other vegetables. In well-to-do families, the women made a meat stock and added richness with fat, milk, or sour cream. Poor families ate their *shchi* plain, without meat or milk, "as though for a fast day." The elder women in the family checked up on how well the younger ones kept to the traditional ways of cooking and baking. Innovations were met with suspicion and were often rejected.[77]

During the autumn and winter months, all the women spun thread and wove cloth for home consumption. Each woman had her customary place to sit on a bench by a window. When it got dark, they all sat around the fire. While most housework fell on the married women of the family, spinning, sewing, mending, and darning were properly the work of unmarried maidens. In well-to-do peasant families, where the main goal was the accumulation of wealth, girls were expected to spin even on holidays. Girls invested considerable effort in the productive activities of the family: they wove baskets and nets and even made pottery. Mothers did not allow their daughters to go to parties without taking work along; they were expected to spend their time while visiting with their friends and neighbors spinning, knitting, or winding skeins of yarn.[78]

Despite the difficulties of daily life for peasant women, they made room not only for useful things but also for objects of beauty and not only for daily toil but also for holidays. The holidays could mark church festivals or calendar events, or they could center around work or familial celebrations. *Sviatki*, the carnival period between December 25 and January 6, was celebrated with particular gaiety: riddles, snowball fights, carols, and mummers in costumes and masks. In masquerades, women usually chose to dress up as ladies or gypsies.

The festivities of *Sviatki* rivaled those of *Maslenitsa* (Mardi Gras—the last days before Lent) with its wonderful sledding and sleigh-riding: "Old women and young girls, decked out and sleek-looking, sitting all together in a heap on top of each other, rode out while singing." The favorite *Maslenitsa* contest for young people, including girls, was jumping over a bonfire. An abundance of refreshments completed the celebration of *Maslenitsa*; in every house, the women prepared raised *bliny*. On Trinity Day or Pentecost, at the beginning of summer, girls organized round dances, played catch or mermaid, and told fortunes.

Celebratory customs connected to the beginning or end of planting, harvesting, or taking the livestock to pasture brightened everyday life for peasant women. Despite the burdens of daily life, maidens and young wives were eager to participate in evening strolls, parties, dances, and athletic games, in which reflexes were valued. When playing blind man's bluff, "it was considered a great embarrassment" if a player could not identify her opponents, because the ability to do so demonstrated her sharp hearing and perceptive vision. Later in the evening or in bad weather, peasant women gathered with their friends in someone's home and mixed work with entertainment. On these occasions, married women met separately from those who were only "marriageable." Women who had borne a child out of wedlock were excluded from these parties; they had a bad reputation, and many in the village shunned them.[79]

Traditional customs were preserved in rural communities much more than elsewhere. Russian peasant women of the nineteenth and early twentieth centuries became the primary bearers of Russian traditions of hospitality, mercy, and respect for elders, and they transmitted these to their children. They taught their children to forgive and to ask forgiveness, to offer fraternal assistance to the poor, and to keep their word.[80]

Traditional norms of behavior also influenced customs of other social classes, but the position of women in urban working families was not determined only by peasant precedents. Worker families differed from peasant ones in that a woman's authority was based on how much she contributed to familial economic resources. Women's labor was less valued in factories than men's, and women earned only 42 percent of men's wages for the same work. However, it was difficult for worker families to survive without women's earnings. Just as in rural villages, women's workdays began very early and lasted ten hours or more. The low wage scale forced women to work the maximum amount of time.

Workers lived in "apartments" that were really barracks, in which two families often shared a single cubbyhole divided by a chintz curtain. These dormitories were located far from the factories, so that "the ten-hour workday was increased by as much as three hours of travel each way," one contemporary noted.[81] In the evening, workers had the strength only "to satisfy their hunger, awakened by work and the walk home, and then go to sleep," although "with difficulty one might not only read but also gather one's thoughts." According to information in local council records, in 1915 women workers were significantly less likely than men to attend entertainments such as theaters or movies, and only 2–3 percent of them attended lectures or concerts. In short, urban women workers faced the same responsibilities as rural women did, and they did not enjoy any of the advantages of city life.

Worker families were smaller than peasant ones, and they more often consisted of just parents and children. This change had the positive effect of encouraging the development of solidarity within the family and more egalitarian relationships. The husband and the children turned their earnings over to the wife. She managed the family budget on her own authority, in consultation with her husband. In the cases where daughters-in-law lived in an extended worker family, they did not experience the limitations on their private property characteristic of peasant households, and their time and labor were not exploited by other members of the family. Relationships in worker families were simpler and more congenial than in peasant families, and members showed greater concern for one another. One reason for this was the fact that workers rarely entered into arranged marriages but instead chose their spouses themselves, based on affection.

While the absence of interfering relatives and the fading of familial hierarchies had a positive effect on the relationship between husband and wife, other conditions of worker life were deleterious. The alternation between periods of intense labor and enforced idleness and the crowded and unsanitary living conditions had negative consequences for worker families. One public health worker in the early twentieth century observed that little girls in worker families "due to the living conditions, become acquainted with sexual functions too early." Because "old and young are all mixed together in a heap, and men and women sleep side by side on the floor," girls were accustomed "to seeing the most immodest caresses and they easily fall into a slough of depravity." In urban settings, female drunkenness and prostitution spread, involving even young girls. Frequently factory supervisors forced women workers to provide them with sexual favors under threat of dismissal. The low cultural and educational level of worker families and their material deprivation inhibited child rearing. Women workers often had to bring their infants with them to the factory and rear them there amid the noise and violence.[82]

While in peasant families there was always someone—either aged relatives or teenagers—to look after young children, in worker families children were often left without any supervision at all, or in the hands of babysitters who were only seven to ten years old themselves. Ten-year-old girls frequently held factory jobs, so their lives were significantly more onerous than those of rural girls of the same age. Workers themselves noticed that their daughters, mothers, and sisters "never have a smile on their faces, and are constantly serious."[83]

For all its difficulties, the urban, factory life provided women workers with the independence they enjoyed compared with rural women, and it gave them the opportunity to become active in society. The most energetic working women of the late nineteenth and early twentieth centuries were not content to devote themselves exclusively to their families and homes; instead, they gave priority to other values—revolution and the struggle for new ideals.[84]

But despite all the differences, women of the laboring classes, whether urban workers or rural peasants, had much in common. Women born into worker or peasant families seemed bound forever to their social milieu; they had few opportunities to advance their social status. The chasm between the privileged, wealthy, and educated section of Russian society and those who produced the wealth that paid for their elite culture continued to deepen. The lifestyle of aristocratic Russian ladies bore little resemblance to that of peasant or worker women, and it was structured with completely different priorities.

Aristocratic women, as a rule, lived primarily on their rural estates. Only the most prosperous families could afford to keep their own houses in Moscow, much less in St. Petersburg, so usually nobles rented apartments in the capitals for only a few months out of the year. Right up to the end of the nineteenth century, it was common for only the male head of a noble family to live in the city, while his wife and children remained at his country estate.

Little girls born to aristocratic families began life in the care of a nanny, who until the mid-nineteenth century would have been a serf. Later in life, girls passed into the care of governesses, who were usually French or sometimes German. Children in aristocratic families commonly became proficient in a second language; command of a third language was a mark of better than average education. Girls were educated at home; their curriculum included the rudiments of history, geography, and philology, as well as some instruction in drawing, playing a musical instrument, dancing, and deportment. Girls were taught how to dance and how to carry themselves in order to develop "stateliness, refinement, and grace," so that they would have the poise, carriage, gait, and mannerisms that separated aristocrats from the common people.

It was books that shaped the intellectual milieu of aristocratic young ladies. While in the eighteenth century, a noblewoman who read all the time was a rarity, by Pushkin's time, the "provincial lady, with a pensive sadness in her eyes, with a French book in her hands," became the dominant image. In the early nineteenth century, it was considered dangerous and not entirely proper for women to read French novels. Recognizing that literature influenced young noblewomen's attitudes, "the mother picked out" books for young girls, and they "were not allowed to select for themselves."[85]

Even in households lacking the means to hire governesses or to fill the shelves in home libraries, the education of girls was still considered to be essential. In these circumstances, parents resorted to boarding schools, such as the Smolnyi Institute or the Ekaterinskii Institute, schools that accepted young ladies from less-wealthy noble families. Starting at age ten or twelve, the girls lived at the schools, studying languages and social graces, "and dancing, singing, delicacy, and sighing," as the author A.S. Griboedov put it.

The purpose of education for young noblewomen, whether conducted at home or at school, was to make them attractive brides. Although it was common in the eighteenth century for girls to marry at age fourteen or fifteen, by the early twentieth century this practice had almost entirely vanished. At the same time, aristocratic noblewomen who had not married by age twenty or twenty-two were considered superannuated and doubtless overly fastidious. The lack of a bridegroom by that age was treated as a great tragedy, especially among provincial folk.[86]

For most young ladies, both in the capitals and in the provinces, marriage was the major event of their lives, and they and their families strove to make it successful and advantageous. It is no accident that girls' education continued only until they married. The pursuit of knowledge for its own sake was considered appropriate only for

Religious education class at the Smolnyi Institute school for noble girls in St. Petersburg, late nineteenth century.

the *raznochintsy*, the intellectual and professional middle class. Once a dreamy young lady married, she was rapidly converted into a thrifty housewife managing an estate, or a well-born busybody "with almost laughable pretensions" and "expensive but ugly outfits."[87] Only a small percentage of girls from the wealthiest and most aristocratic families would, through a successful marriage, join the narrow circle of high society women of the capitals and large cities.

One mark of the privileged aristocratic life society ladies led was the right to get up as late as they wanted. In the first half of the nineteenth century, Princess Avdotia Golitsyna bragged that she never went out during daylight and so was nicknamed "*la princesse nocturne*" ("the nocturnal princess"). Urban noblewomen started with a cup of coffee for breakfast and dressed in a daytime outfit at about two or three in the afternoon. They would then go for an outing; fashionably attired ladies in St. Petersburg preferred the road along the Neva and Nevskii Prospect. Dinnertime came at four, and guests might be invited. The meal consisted of Russian cuisine in lavish abundance, with several courses of meat and fish dishes. After dinner, ladies had to pass the time until the evening; some read, others wrote letters. Theatrical performances started at six; ladies attended in order to meet their friends, or sometimes their secret heartthrobs. The day ended with an evening ball. Society women had to be able to carry on a brisk, elegant conversation, peppered with pertinent epigrams, while keeping the steps of the dance. Small talk was the rule during the first dance, a mazurka. Truly aristocratic ladies did not flirt; as Pushkin put it, "There's not a drop of the coquette in her; high society wouldn't stand for it." Only "ladies" of the "demimonde" or "foppish women" conducted themselves boisterously or with affectation, wore faddish clothing, or flaunted their romantic passions.

With their careful upbringing, broad education, and material resources, aristocratic women had unique opportunities to develop their talents and pursue their interests. Not all of them took advantage of their options, but many women yearned for a full and interesting life, especially those who were forced to spend their married years in the countryside looking after household matters on their estates.

The life of provincial noblewomen did not much resemble that of their aristocratic sisters in the major cities. Instead, it was oriented around the family and caring for the children, and it retained more traditional features of the sort characteristic of the peasantry. Only a few of these aristocratic families could afford to replicate the types of houses and clothing found in the capitals. But those who could built vast parks on their estates and European-style mansions with suites of rooms dedicated to specific purposes: entrance halls, living rooms, dining rooms, bedrooms, studies, and nurseries. They filled them with fashionable furniture, "divans and chaises longues, and with them . . . hysterics, migraines, and spasms," one contemporary observed sardonically.[88] The mistresses of these provincial estates tried to move themselves and their families to the city during the winter so that they could enjoy the bustle and social life. But many families did not have the resources to do so. Most provincial noblewomen of modest means "preserved the customs of the good old days," as Pushkin put it. As in the past, they got up early and spent the day going about their tasks, they worried about whether the instructions they had given were being fulfilled, and they kept accounts of income and expenditures. Their practices in the day-to-day management of their estates were rooted in respect for peasant custom and knowledge. They were conservative not only in their way of life but also in their planning of the household economy; they tended to react slowly, and even with hostility, to innovations. Still, the libraries of many rural estates in the late nineteenth and early twentieth centuries contained books offering practical advice on estate management. It is not clear, though, that rural noblewomen read them; they tended to prefer the textbooks used to educate their children and fashionable romantic novels.

The most inveterate proponents of urban life also idealized the traditional order of the rural estates, which they depicted as a "bucolic paradise." To judge by the classics of Russian literature, the life of urban noblewomen was imagined as dominated by society's expectations, while country life placed fewer restrictions on women and left them free to fantasize and follow their whims. Things that were impermissible and reprehensible in the city seemed possible and proper in the country. Rural noblewomen could "spend whole days in their bathrobes" and not do up their hair; they could "have supper at eight o'clock in the evening" when for many city dwellers "it was just time to lunch."[89] Instead of the constant feeling of "being among people," country life was filled with the blissful company of friends and relatives and consequently flourishing domestic happiness and guilt-free pleasure. One such pleasure, and one not reserved solely for romantic girls, was a wistful thoughtfulness, which aided the development of deep feeling. If in the city young people "hurried through life" and "rushed to feel," rural estates were where a Russian woman could learn to love generously, deeply, and selflessly.

Urban contemporaries associated the verdant rural estate and its serene and hospitable mistress with an idyll of family life, "the favorite picture of familial happiness amid rural beauties," as Karamzin wrote. The master of such an estate hoped to find in his wife a friend most of all. It was the mother who was most closely attached to her children; she was wholly responsible for their upbringing and education because schools were frequently located too far away to be of use to them. Many mothers personally taught their children how to read and write and corrected their exercises. In the early and mid-nineteenth century, it was recommended that children learn three pages of poetry per day, translate ten to twelve pages, and spend not less than four hours reading history and geography. This intensive curriculum was to be lightened only during the summer. Some provincial noblewomen were no less well read than the graduates of the leading boarding schools; in addition, in order not to feel cut off from the world, they often subscribed to the newest literature, which was essential for educating their children.[90] The residents of rural estates filled their evening hours with reading, either alone or out loud with others, as was customary at the time. "We read a variety of poetry and prose, and we discussed them, each in his own way, and we were all taken in or we made our critiques, as each of us was able."[91] Mothers often read to their children. The custom of family reading became a feature common to noble households in nineteenth- and early twentieth-century Russia, and many writers, scholars, and professionals recalled it with gratitude.[92]

At rural estates, "sometimes the whole family of neighbors would gather of an evening" at a noblewoman's invitation, and "these unceremonious friends would joke and tease and make fun of everyone and everything," as Pushkin remarked. Rural neighbors would "unceremoniously" drop in "along with their families" in order to pass the time "doing needlework together for their outfits or to decorate their homes."[93] The types of entertainment available to women in the countryside were not so elaborate or diverse as those for the noblewomen of the capitals. During the summer, visits to the neighbors' always included strolls in the gardens or woods. People played cards and parlor games and performed music. Evening get-togethers always featured table-talk, and a meal that was "abundant and tasty."[94] The dishes that rural cooks served to the guests were not noted for their haute cuisine, but every hostess wished to be celebrated among her neighbors for her culinary taste and the *kvas* or berry drinks, *bliny* or sweet *kasha* served in her home.[95]

Hospitality played an even bigger role in the lives of the Russian merchantry. In many ways merchants tried to imitate the aristocracy, but they were less educated and less philosophically inclined. This was particularly true of the women. Wealthy merchants were eager to marry their daughters to a "gentleman," or themselves to marry into noble families. However, noblewomen did not ordinarily associate with merchant circles, and women of the merchant class were rarely accepted among the elite. More often, merchants married the daughters of Cossacks or peasant entrepreneurs. These women had not had the opportunity to gain much of a formal education, although they were expert at preparing baked goods and pickling mushrooms and cucumbers.[96]

The entire mercantile family, like the peasant family, got up at dawn. After tea and a hearty breakfast, the head of the family and his adult sons left for the shop or market. They would return only at eight in the evening. In the case of petty tradesmen, the wife would often work beside her husband at their booth or in the bazaar. But if the family had the means to hire employees, the wife's main responsibilities would be in the home. The heaviest housework was performed by maids, who either worked days or lived in. Merchants' wives "ruled over [them], correcting each one with equal vigilance."[97] The prosperous merchantry might allow themselves an entire staff of servants, who would receive orders from the mistress every morning. Housemaids, nannies, and gardeners were brought in for sewing, mending, laundry, cleaning, and cooking. The wealthiest mercantile families in the capitals had their own dressmakers and, in imitation of noble households, several governesses for the children. In merchant families, the mother usually did not forbid her children to associate with the servants, but she fed them separately.

At the end of the nineteenth century, it became customary for the families who could afford it to spend the summer months outside the city at their dacha (summer house). By the early twentieth century, not only nobles did this but also urban families of middling income, including merchants and tradesmen. Unlike the nobles, the middle-class vacationers spent their time gathering mushrooms and berries and raising vegetables in rented garden plots, where they weeded and watered and harvested their crops. "It was only at six o'clock in the evening that the necessary work was done and everyone could do what they pleased." During the day, these urban women supervised the work of hired girls, thinking that "it would be a good thing for them to learn something from our cook."[98]

While merchants' wives, as a rule, were burdened with a large number of responsibilities regarding the daily life of the household, their daughters spent their days in idleness. Especially in provincial cities, the daughters' lives were monotonous and boring. They spent their time thinking about business receptions, where they had to "make pleasant conversation" with the guests. Only the most farsighted merchants tried to educate their daughters, and then only in the early twentieth century. Before that, in the 1860s, daughters of the mercantile class seem to have attended high school, but they did not enroll in any type of higher education. Only the rare merchant's daughter took an interest in newspapers or magazines, so she might marry into the circle of the intelligentsia or educated nobility. In 1913, only eighty-six out of a thousand urban women in Russia had graduated from the gymnasium.[99]

The most common form of leisure activity for women in tradesman or merchant families was needlework. This consisted most often of embroidery, lace making, knitting, or crocheting. The type of needlework and the degree to which it was essential depended upon the economic circumstances of the family. Girls from poor and middling mercantile families sewed for their own dowries. For girls from rich families, needlework was recreational. Girls gathered together to talk while they sewed, sitting outside in the garden (or at the dacha) in the summer, and in the winter in the living room, if there was one, or the kitchen. The main topic of conversation for bourgeois girls and their mothers was not literature and art, as it was among the nobility, but rather current events in their circle: the worth of this or that bridegroom, dowries, fashions, and happenings in the city. The older generation of women, including those who had families, amused themselves by playing cards or lotto around a big table in the hall. Singing and playing music were less popular among families of tradesmen and merchants; they engaged in them largely for show, in order to demonstrate their "breeding" and "aristocratic tastes." For that reason, it was considered "*bon ton*" to have a piano in the home. But by the early twentieth century, some merchant families became patrons of the arts and developed artistic tastes; in their homes, musical programs became a customary leisure activity.

One of the most popular forms of recreation among the bourgeoisie was entertaining guests. While nobles thought it impolite to drop in on each other without an invitation, via a visiting card, note, or (in the early twentieth century) a telephone call, members of the urban middle class stopped by to visit casually. Refreshments were very important to these get-togethers, and at merchant dinner parties the guests were expected to stay a long time and eat a lot. It was not considered embarrassing for guests to stuff themselves or to drink themselves silly.[100] Fatty meat dishes were served in merchant families not two or three times a week but rather every day, as long as it was not Lent or another fast day. The mistress of the house served tea to her husband and guests herself. It was customary for people to drink the tea from a saucer, so that it would cool quickly, and then to turn the cup upside down on it to indicate that they had finished eating. The head of the family would treat his daughters to an abundance of sweet breads—buns, rolls, coffee cakes, and honey cake—which were purchased or baked for lunch or afternoon tea. Consequently the portliness of bourgeois women became legendary; the proverb went "fat as a merchant's wife." The image of merchants was immortalized in the paintings of Russian artists of the early twentieth century, especially those of B.M. Kustodiev. His works demonstrate both his frank admiration for the healthy, ruddy beauty of these women and his misgivings about their complacent vacuousness.[101]

Thus the daily life of women of the different social strata of Russian society in the nineteenth and early twentieth centuries depended upon many factors: their social origin, their place of residence, their level of education, their circle of acquaintances, and their personal values, as well as the profession and position of their fathers and husbands. The peasantry remained the most conservative and patriarchal, while the other strata of society—the nobility, the merchantry, the lesser bourgeoisie, the intelligentsia, the clergy, the military, and the workers—responded more quickly to social and political changes. The most significant of these were the reforms of the 1860s and 1870s, during which the question of women's status before the law was first debated.

The "Woman Question"

A.G. Goikhbarg, an early twentieth-century jurist and theoretician of family law, asserted, "If the position of a married woman in private law is a true indicator of the culture of a specified country, then it must be concluded that Russia stands incomparably higher than England, France, Sweden, and Norway."[102] This assertion reflected national vanity, not an accurate reading of the status of women before the law. It was true that Russian law even in the period before Alexander II's reforms afforded women of the privileged orders significant economic independence. They had the right to own and dispose of property, to enter into transactions and file lawsuits, and to inherit and bequeath their possessions. They also retained their long-established right to seek a divorce. Family and marital legislation in Russia did not place women in the same dependent and downtrodden position they held in many European countries, in which "women's rights were either substantially curtailed or did not exist at all."[103] The judicial establishment of Russia was called upon "to protect the honor and tranquillity of women by the strictest measures of punishment for insults inflicted on them, freeing them from responsibility for some obligations in which they could become involved because of inexperience and gullibility."[104]

An analysis of the legal position of women, however, one accounting for the stratification of society, challenges these overly optimistic conclusions about their rights in nineteenth- and early twentieth-century Russia. The norms embodied in the Code of Laws of the Russian Empire applied only to a comparatively small percentage of women—those of the nobility and from the clerical and mercantile estates. Most women—that is, peasants—continued to live under customary law. True, peasant communities recognized certain rights for women: if a man behaved in an unseemly manner, the peasant *mir* might even decide to place him under the control of his wife. Even more, a woman who was the head and chief breadwinner of a family had an undisputed advantage in legal status over any of its members. Women in peasant families had fewer inheritance rights, however, and could not receive a passport, which allowed them to travel outside their villages, without permission from their husbands. In case of a divorce, they could not count on payment of alimony. The property that a peasant couple brought into their marriage was considered jointly owned, but at the same time the law established the separation between the property of the husband and the wife, and the right of each to dispose of it "in his own name, independent of each other and not asking mutual authorization documents."

Sex discrimination in the peasant milieu was aggravated by limitations on their social position. Before the Emancipation of 1861, enserfed peasant women could not marry without their owners' permission. Unlike elite women, however, peasants and women factory workers did not have to win the right to work. There was more than enough work for them, although they were paid inadequately for it.[105]

Women of different social statuses understood equal rights in different ways. But there were some unambiguous successes. In the early nineteenth century, jurisprudence began to recognize women's full independence concerning property.[106] Before 1861, this applied only to the privileged orders; serfs were excluded. Full independence in property matters was then understood as abolition of all limitations and reservations concerning the separation between the possessions of spouses in marriage and also the removal of inequality in claims to inherited property. Progressive jurists in the mid-nineteenth century criticized laws that required a father to leave his son, "sometimes an unworthy one, in lavish circumstances with thirteen shares of his property, and his daughter in need with the fourteenth share."[107] In making this argument, they alluded to the medieval Russian juridical tradition, which gave both spouses and children of both sexes equal rights to inherit. The law to equalize inheritance rights was passed by the Duma only in 1912, and then with a limitation: women received equal rights only in the inheritance of movable property; daughters who had brothers could receive no more than one-seventh of an inheritance in land.[108]

From the 1850s onward, the Russian press contained much discussion of the necessity of changing legislation concerning marriage.

Advocates of women's emancipation objected to the prohibition on young women marrying without the permission of their "parents, guardians, or trustees." They also opposed married women's legal dependence upon their husbands. For example, the husband chose where the family would live. Even if the husband depended upon his wife for economic support, and she, "understanding the necessity of increasing her income, wished to change the place of residence," if her husband disagreed, the court usually upheld his decision.[109] Related articles of the code obligated spouses of all social orders to live together. If a wife voluntarily left her husband, the law mandated that she be found and returned to him. The law included no analogous provision regarding absent husbands.[110] These and many other provisions of the law implemented the underlying thesis that "the wife is obliged to submit to her husband as head of the family."[111]

Under the law, only the husband could bestow his social rank on his wife and children. Thus women of lower rank sought to marry noble husbands because it would improve their status. But if a noblewoman married a man of non-noble rank, although she preserved the privileges of her natal rank, her husband and children could not claim them. This system encouraged parents, especially when they had few resources, to press their daughters into the most advantageous union; as a result, many young women found themselves in "the hellish torments of an unhappy marriage."[112]

For unhappily married women, one means of escape could be an "easy and accessible divorce on the basis of a simple agreement between the spouses themselves," as the reformers advocated. Proposals to simplify divorce procedures were often, however, condemned as immoral and licentious. Indeed, many jurists, including those who otherwise endorsed progressive positions, nonetheless called for limiting the legal justifications for divorce, hoping in this way to strengthen "the foundations of the family." Because the Russian Orthodox Church had become increasingly unwilling to authorize the dissolution of marital unions, reformers began to garner increasing support for the idea of civil marriage. Some of this support came from young proponents of the fictitious marriages espoused by the 1860s generation as a means of liberating young women from the tutelage of their parents.[113]

Men rather than women provided the intellectual inspiration for the first women's organizations in Russia, and consequently for challenging women's inequality in society and the political sphere. Some of the same male thinkers—N.G. Chernyshevskii, M.L. Mikhailov,

N.A. Dobroliubov—who developed the concepts of revolutionary democracy were also the first to speak of "the limited circle of activity for Russian women, which is restricted to the bedroom and the kitchen." In his celebrated article "A Woman's Complaint," published in the magazine *Sovremennik*, Chernyshevskii proclaimed, "There is no more terrible position than to remain a housewife one's whole life!" His colleagues argued for "helping women to achieve an independent position" by establishing women's organizations and altering the system of female education so that the curriculum in women's institutions did not differ from that in men's.[114]

Hundreds of people, both men and women, responded to this appeal for the social emancipation of women. Virtually all the journals with a literary or political orientation responded in some way to the tumultuous "Woman Question." Conservative publications tried to protect their readers from the influence of "harmful ideas," while the liberal press argued that women must gain the right to work and the right to higher education as a prelude to full empowerment before the law.

These two demands—to work and to receive education—became the focus for the Russian women's movement that was born in the mid-nineteenth century.[115] Hundreds of women joined in the "battle for equality of rights."[116] They hoped first to obtain the right to attend lectures and take examinations in institutions of higher education and then to teach in the Free (nongovernmental) University of St. Petersburg. They also wanted formal authorization to teach in the Sunday schools—classes that provided basic instruction in reading and arithmetic for factory workers on their day off. The founding, in the 1860s, of the first medical institutes to train midwives reflected a victory in the struggle for both education and the right to work. By the early 1870s, the Petersburg medical courses had educated dozens of midwives. In 1872, V.I. Gere set up the Higher Education Courses for women in Moscow to train them to be teachers. By the late 1870s, similar educational programs had appeared in St. Petersburg, Kazan, and Kharkov.[117]

In the same period, women of the professional middle class joined in a movement to establish "women's artels" specializing in bookbinding, sewing, translating, and publishing. Young women from families of modest means insistently sought employment in craft shops, typographical workshops, and the offices of private manufacturers and railroads. Until the turn of the century, however, the number of women employees remained small. Women employees received lower pay and had no right to merit bonuses, job security, or pensions.[118] Government officials found it easy to justify this legal discrimination against women in the workplace. Count Peter Shuvalov, the head of the Third Section of the Imperial Chancellery, which was charged with maintaining social and political order, posed the question rhetorically: "Can a woman be a good mother and a good housekeeper if she spends half the day in a bureau or office filled with men, where liaisons are inevitably formed and demoralization occurs?"[119]

Count Shuvalov apparently worried about the welfare only of gentle-born women. He did not take into consideration the working conditions of women employed in factories and craft shops, who, by the end of the nineteenth century, made up between 13 and 17 percent of employees in such enterprises. Many enterprises did not adhere to the provisions of the Decree on Manufacturing issued by Alexander II in 1862, which required factories to provide separate living quarters for men and women. Until banned by decree in 1863, the law mandated corporal punishment for women convicted of certain crimes; even the new law allowed the continued use of flogging on women prisoners—a practice that was abolished only in 1893.

Changes were introduced into the legal norms regulating the lower classes only after great effort. In many areas there was no progress at all. In the nineteenth and early twentieth centuries, an important way of improving working conditions for women was to enact laws protecting them from dangerous employment. In 1869, in the period of Alexander II's reforms, a decree was issued to prevent women's employment in the mining industry, but its provisions were advisory rather than mandatory. Only in 1885 were laws issued that forbade night work for women and children in certain types of light manufacturing.[120]

In the late nineteenth century, specially trained medical practitioners oversaw working conditions, including those for women, in factories. These industrial hygienists included "doctrixes"—the women who graduated from the advanced medical courses. In St. Petersburg, these women made up nearly half of medical specialists working in manufacturing enterprises. Concerned about the high rate of post-partum mortality for both mothers and infants among women workers, the industrial hygienists petitioned the government and the Duma. In 1912, a law was issued to protect pregnant women and nursing mothers and to provide them with health and accident insurance. Until that time, pregnant women often worked in factories until the time they delivered, and sometimes even gave birth on the shop floor. They also brought their babies to work with them, keeping them in baskets beside their workplaces. Under the provisions of the 1912 law, women workers in large manufacturing enterprises had the formal right to demand a paid leave for illness or pregnancy. In the case of pregnancy, the woman worker was entitled to two weeks off before the birth and four weeks afterward with a stipend of one-quarter of her wages, provided she had been employed for at least twenty-six weeks out of the year. But women could not always take advantage of these privileges. The insurance stipend was paltry, especially considering that women's wages were much lower than men's. Most illiterate women workers had no knowledge of their rights under the law, and their bosses did not advise them.[121] The injustice of their social and legal position led many women workers to join their menfolk in striking to demand changes in factory rules and the social structure of the country. However, factory owners tended to view their women employees as a "pacific element" in the workforce—one much less likely to sympathize with radical political groups.[122]

Activists from the Russian Social Democratic Party, including both Bolsheviks and Mensheviks, took a great interest in defending the rights of women workers and fighting to extend them. Through socialist publications and through speeches, party activists voiced their concerns and recruited women to their cause.[123] During the Revolution of 1905, when the striking workers of St. Petersburg formed their first city-wide soviet, or council, seven women were chosen as deputies. The soviet organized resistance to the government and voiced its demands in the vocabulary of socialism. It called for political rights for workers, particularly the right to vote, and for the creation of parliamentary institutions. It also demanded economic concessions, including "tangible improvements in the labor and living conditions of women workers," equal wages for men and women, and the creation of factory day-care facilities for infants and young children.[124] The government was forced to concede to many of these demands, although it reneged on many of them after reestablishing control and crushing the soviets.

The nonsocialist political parties drew most of their support from the intelligentsia, nobility, and well-to-do and directed their attention on women's issues toward the ladies of these classes. They devoted little attention to women of the proletariat, much less the peasantry.

Although the self-designated feminists and suffragists (Russian adopted the English word) usually came from privileged circles, they did not neglect the women of the lower classes entirely. The members of the All-Russian Union for Women's Equality, formed in January 1905, argued for the right to vote in direct elections by secret ballot, without restriction on grounds of nationality, religion, or sex. They also demanded that male and female peasants be treated equally in any agrarian reforms that were issued. They organized active support for the creation of medical insurance and safe working conditions for women in manufacturing enterprises, and their support aided in the passage of the 1912 law.[125]

On April 10, 1905, in the midst of the political upheavals of the revolution, the All-Russian Union for Women's Equality organized a meeting, which was attended by over a thousand women.[126] In addition to demanding the right to vote for women, the participants at this meeting formulated other desiderata in regard to equal rights for women. These included, for example, coeducation of men and women in schools, gymnasiums, and universities; the abolition of the death penalty, especially for women; "equal opportunities for women"; and complete equality with men before the law. These demands were later reiterated in the organization's publications.

One right that feminists enunciated and defended as an "obligatory privilege" for a woman was "to control her own body." They understood this to mean "the right of an unmarried woman to have a child" and the right of a married woman "to offer resistance to whoever might force her to do this [bear a child] against her will."[127] Within the context of early twentieth-century debates about sexuality, women's organizations first demanded the legalization of abortion and also the broadening of sex education.[128] (Despite prohibitions, from 1900 to 1914 the number of abortions increased from by two and a half times.) The first congresses of gynecologists in Russia, held in the 1910s, raised the issue of whether female frigidity should be a reason for divorce and discussed the right of women to seek a compatible sexual partner.[129] Feminists, and especially the Society for the Protection of Women, which was founded in 1900, demanded that the government issue legislation against prostitution, which was then legal, in particular inflicting heavy penalties on procuring child prostitutes. Feminists saw these measures not as limiting women's rights but as protecting their health. A congress for the struggle "against the trade in women" met in St. Petersburg in 1910. It condemned the government's system, which had been in place since the 1840s, of licensing and supervising prostitutes through a police and medical apparatus. From the point of view of this congress, this system of legalized prostitution, which devalued women's worth, reduced to naught all the government's pronouncements concerning women's rights.[130]

Not only the All-Russian Union for Women's Equality and the Organization for the Defense of Women but other feminist and suffragist groups as well demanded that the government confirm "freedom and equality before the law, without regard to sex." The Women's Progressive Party, established in 1906, demanded, among other things, the establishment by law of "equality in the family in financial and economic matters, and also the liberalization of divorce." In general this party adopted a liberal stance, calling for a "democratic constitutional monarchy," reforms in the military and an end to the militarization of the country, and changes in labor practices.[131] Feminist organizations could unite behind the platform expressed in the slogan "Peace, Humaneness, and Culture," which they shared with liberals in the Russian political spectrum of the period between 1905 and 1914. However, the members of the liberal political parties—the Cadets and the Octrobrists—were, virtually without exception, male. Participants in the women's movement recognized that "cooperation between the sexes usually means in fact the co-optation" of women into male organizations and parties.[132] For that reason, women's organizations preferred not to affiliate themselves with any political parties but rather to solidify the membership within their own ranks.

The first All-Russian Congress of Women took place in St. Petersburg in 1908. Some of the delegates called for the creation of an "All-Russian Women's Soviet," which would not be affiliated with any political party or any particular social class. This Women's Soviet would focus singlemindedly on the struggle for equality for all women of Russia. However, delegates to the Congress representing political parties, including the Social Democrats, refused to accept this proposal. They believed that the resolution of the "Woman Question" could occur only in the context of a revolutionary transformation of the whole society.[133]

Despite the internal divisions, the ranks of supporters for women's rights continued to grow. After the overthrow of the monarchy in February 1917, the feminist movement became particularly active. As a result of its strength and the long struggle for equality on the part of women from many social classes and a variety of political orientations, Russian women received the right to vote in August 1917. This was before women's suffrage was enacted in the United States or in most European countries.

ЗА У; НАА ЖЕН
ЩИНА ОЛОНЕ
КОЙ ГУБ. КАР-
ГОПОЛЬСКАГО
У ЂЗДА.

Peasant woman from Olonetsk province in holiday dress. Drawing by I.A.
Bilibin, from the series "Peoples of the Russian North."

Crinolines and Sarafans

In the nineteenth and early twentieth centuries, more and more Russian women began to adopt European styles of dress. Fashionable urban women were the first to do so, and the younger generation tended to follow fads, but peasants and women of the lower classes often preferred traditional clothing. As in the preceding centuries, rural women's costume—and sometimes even the dress of urban women—gave clues about their ethnic identity and social class, as well as their wealth, age, origin, and marital status. The symbolic significance of Russian women's costume had not disappeared, but it changed form and was obscured behind European fashions.

Two technological inventions made their mark on Russian women's dress. The first, the invention of the jacquard loom by a French weaver in 1801, permitted the intricate interweaving of threads into complex patterned fabrics. The second invention was the sewing machine in the early nineteenth century; the improved version developed by the American Isaac Singer was distributed worldwide in the second half of the century. Sewing machines were imported into Russia from the United States and Germany, and by the early twentieth century they numbered in the hundreds of thousands. In the countryside, however, clothing was still sewn by hand, with double seams. This clothing, in the author Nikolai Gogol's estimation, "surpassed one's own teeth in durability." In the early nineteenth century, before the manufacture of ready-to-wear clothing became the norm, the lavish outfits of the most fashionable people of the capital were made by hand.

In the early nineteenth century, women's clothing styles were not particularly complicated. Classicism, with its emphasis on simplicity and naturalness, dominated. "In today's outfit," the magazine *Moscow Mercury* (*Moskovskii Merkurii*) wrote in 1803, "the outline of the form is most admired. If the build of a woman's legs from the torso to the shoes is not visible, it says that she does not know how to dress." Fashionable Russian ladies in that period wore dresses made from the thinnest fabrics—muslin, batiste, chiffon, and crepe—with a princess waist, deep décolletage, and short, narrow sleeves. They wore "sometimes only a bodysuit of a flesh color underneath" because "the thinnest slip would remove from a dress of that sort all transparency."[134] The men of the time found such styles to be "not bad": "and rightly, on fashionable women and maidens everything looked so clean, simple, and fresh. Not fearing the horrors of winter, they wore semitransparent dresses, which closely encompassed their supple figures and frankly outlined their charming forms."[135] The predominance in fashion of light-weight white dresses had an effect on make-up styles: fashionable ladies strove for a "noble" paleness—a vogue that continued for decades. The French portrait painter Elizabeth Vigé-Lebrun, who lived in Russia from 1785 to 1801, became the primary propagandist for the new Antique style. She wore the shortest skirts of the day (they reached only to her ankles); her skirts were also the narrowest, clinging to her thighs. Her dresses were accessorized with the lightest scarves or shawls, sometimes edged with ornamentation in the classical mode or sometimes with light down or with fur—what was called "à la russe."[136]

Woman's costume of the mid-nineteenth century, with an Eliseev shawl.
From the collection of the State Historical Museum, Moscow.

Shawls, scarves, and kerchiefs made from a wide variety of fabrics
remained a traditional feature of dress. In the early nineteenth century, they became indispensable to both everyday and holiday dress
for all Russian women. If high-society ladies preferred gossamer
cloaks in keeping with the Antique motif of their outfits, women of
the middle class and in the countryside preferred patterned shawls in
bright colors made from fine wool. At first, all these shawls were
imported from the Far East. But in 1813, the Voronezh landowner
V.A. Eliseev set up the first shawl factory in Russia. He had spent five
years analyzing cashmere shawls in order to determine how they were
manufactured. The quality of the products from Eliseev's factory, and

their rich ornamentation with high color resolution, surpassed any of the imports. Furthermore, the Russian-made shawls, unlike the imported ones, were fully reversible. Despite their high cost, they rapidly became popular, both in Russia and abroad.[137]

Shawls and scarves survived the transition from the Classical style of the beginning of the nineteenth century to the Empire style of the 1810s. Instead of the refined simplicity of the fine Antique shift, the Empire dress was made from heavy and densely woven fabric and crisply decorated. Corsets came back into fashion; they elevated the bust and tightly constricted the waist. The typical dress of the Russian urban woman of Pushkin's day had a bodice closely fitted from the shoulders and a bell-shaped skirt, puffed sleeves, rick-rack, ruches, and flounces, sometimes stuffed with cotton or hair in order to weight the hems and fill out the silhouette. These became the distinguishing characteristics of the styles of the 1830s and 1840s. French lace spun from raw silk was the rage, but as a luxury item it was out of reach for most provincial women.

"A decided predilection for the European" was "a sharp characteristic that distinguishes the educated orders from the uneducated," the literary critic Vissarion Belinskii observed in the 1840s. Following the Paris vogue, Europeanized ladies adopted the hourglass silhouette. Dresses were designed to emphasize the shapeliness of the female figure. The skirts were tightly gathered at the waist and then flared out below, so that the bottom hem reached five feet around. Some styles had trains. In order to hold the skirts out, women wore heavily starched underskirts, sometimes made from crinoline, a stiff fabric woven of horsehair and flax. "Can anyone look without laughing at the monstrous width of these crinolines and the endless train, which is especially ugly when it collects dust from the street?" scoffed one contemporary.[138] Because of this vogue for huge skirts, hosts had to limit the number of ladies they invited for parties, and theaters had to space their seats wide apart in order to accommodate the women in the audience. No censure or ridicule or inconvenience could convince women not to wear the enormous skirts. The peak of popularity for crinolines came in the 1850s and 1860s, when a framework of hoops constructed from steel strips replaced the starched underskirts and stays of whalebone. These new metal hoops were, curiously enough, called "malakhovs," after the lost battle of Malakhov Kurgan in the Crimean War, which took place in this period.

The tightly corseted bodice and wide skirts were set off by sleeves in whimsical forms. In the 1830s the popular sleeve was in the "elephant ear" style; five years later, the puffed "leg of mutton" sleeve was in vogue. In the 1840s, the sleeves were closely fitted to the arms and covered the base of the hand. The size and complexity of sleeves required outdoor coverings that were cut rather loosely, especially on top. Cloaks were popular and practical for urban women of all social classes in the mid-nineteenth century. Lace mantillas, waist-long in front and even longer in back, a style imported from Spain, could dress up even the simplest outfit. Salon hostesses and their guests liked to wear elaborately made light shawls, with drawings of little swans ornamented with hand-sewn downy feathers. Urban women usually wore simple wool cloaks, and in cold weather, ones made of fur or quilted with cotton batting. They resembled traditional Russian styles of outerwear and represented a successful blending of Parisian fashion with the functionality of old Russian costume.

While adhering to Parisian models, Petersburg and especially Moscow fashion plates strove to reveal their own individual flair in their dress. To do so, they accessorized their dresses with bows and ruffles. "If something became the rage, it became the rage in all forms!" Gogol commented sarcastically. "If waists are long, then she [the fashionable lady] will drop it to her knees; if the lapels on dresses are big, hers will be like barn doors."[139] But amid all the tasteless accessorizations of Parisian designs, some were quite artistic, for example, a linen day dress embroidered with straw—the work of a nameless seamstress.

Fashion-conscious women in the provinces copied the styles and color combinations of ladies of the capital more or less dexterously. The wives of local governors usually set the standards. In the 1830s and 1840s, women preferred subdued colors—black, gray, lilac—in shades that were given the most unlikely names: "fainting frog," "toad in love," "dreamy flea," or "spider planning a crime."[140] But while provincial ladies devoted careful attention to their dress when they went out in public, when at home alone they went around in old bathrobes and curlers.

The everyday footwear of provincial women was particularly inelegant. Only in the major cities, and on holidays, did ladies wear satin, twill, or kid-leather shoes and fine, light-colored stockings. Provincial women had to be satisfied with simpler footwear. The most skillful needlewomen sewed themselves blue and white stockings from fine knitted cotton, but they wore them rarely, even to balls. For everyday wear, provincial women put on coarse gray stockings and black shoes made of goatskin, or short boots edged with fur and a red stripe.

M.F. Soboleva, a woman of the merchant class in traditional dress. Portrait by N.D. Mylnikov, 1834.

Even in the capitals women's daily footwear was not particularly elegant: round-toed, low-heeled shoes, decorated with laces or buttons on one side.[141] Elsewhere, the type of footwear women wore varied with their dress but remained traditional in style, cut, and material until the middle of the nineteenth century.

Peasants considered fashionable urban clothing to be for the ruling class and borrowed little from it. In contrast, women of the mercantile class, as well as tradeswomen, tried to combine Parisian fashions with Russian accessories and traditional headcoverings. Women from wealthy merchant circles who attended noble assemblies had a tendency to betray their origins by wearing a tasteless abundance of plumes, laces, and bows and by their predilection for heavy pearls and rings that inhibited the movement of their hands. But it was their hairstyles more than their dress that marked women as from the merchant class: they wore their hair parted severely down the middle and slicked back; married women then added a kerchief shot with gold thread covered by a traditional headdress.[142] Unlike gentle-born ladies, who used cosmetics unobtrusively, merchant women liked to heighten their coloring with rouge, face powder, and mascara.

In the second half of the nineteenth century, styles of dress changed more rapidly. The development of manufacturing and transportation had a direct effect on fashion, as did the growth in the number of newspapers and the acceleration of information exchange in general, which shaped tastes in regard to dress. The trendsetters in fashion gradually came to be the wealthy bourgeoisie rather than the nobility. A well-to-do merchant in the postreform period prided himself that "his wife could not be distinguished from a lady" and tried to provide her and his daughters with outfits in the latest imported styles.

Women's clothing from the 1860s to the 1890s was complex and almost garish in its luxury, especially in the capital cities. No particular style dominated, just as no particular style dominated in architecture in Russia in this period. Instead, it was era of eclecticism. Russian women freely combined elements of costume drawn from a variety of periods and peoples: sleeves of the medieval type, Empire bodice, Greek trim, outer coats à la Pompadour. Jackets with a military flavor, inspired by Hussar, Zouave, or Turkish uniforms, became very popular beginning in the early 1860s.

By the 1860s, giant crinolines were considered not chic but silly. The female silhouette changed sharply, and by the 1870s skirts fit snugly over the thighs. A tunic-style dress became quite popular; often the underskirt and the shorter overskirt were made of contrasting fabrics. Some versions featured a bustle, made of whalebone or cushions, which was worn at the base of the spine to fill out the lavish pleats of the dress.[143] The thrifty wives and daughters of well-to-do officials and merchants sewed their own outfits from velvet, velour, and heavy silk. Similar styles dominated in their interior decorating, with upholstered furniture adorned with fringe and pompoms, elaborate draperies, gilded windowframes, and knick-knacks. Among the old nobility and the intelligentsia, this style was caustically called "overstuffed."

At the same time, a different trend in dress arose among emancipated women of the intelligentsia and the urban lower classes. These women were employed and socially active, and they rejected clothing that interfered with movement, corsets that constricted breathing, and pretentious accessories. The "New Women" and students thought of clothing as a way of expressing their politics. They wore "Garibaldi" shirts, named for the leader of the Italian liberation movement, which were red with a small, turned-down collar.[144] Their stiff jackets, loosely cut shirts with collars, and neckties resembled menswear. In her handbag, a "New Woman" carried a handkerchief, change purse, and wallet, as well as, usually, an enamel or mother-of-pearl cigarette case. The vests, high boots, straight coats, and "Amazon" hats with fur-lined flaps, borrowed from men's dress, marked their wearers as advocates of women's equality.[145]

From the 1860s onward, working women preferred the same sort of simply cut and practical clothing for street wear and for casual visiting. After 1850, the magazine *World Fashion* regularly included patterns intended for a wide range of ordinary women as well as dressmakers. By the end of the nineteenth century, outfits with skirts that softly conformed to the figure and then flared out below, paired with blouses and jackets, were especially popular. This became the uniform of women workers and students. Otherwise women workers wore *sarafans* with matching blouses or calico dresses with fitted bodices and gathered skirts.

When skirt lengths became shorter and stopped covering the ankles in the late 1860s, the change affected the color of stockings and the style of shoes. Women of the urban lower classes—workers and tradeswomen—could not keep up with fashions and still wore round-toed pumps made from rather coarse leather, usually pigskin. Aristocratic and upper-middle-class women chose their footwear carefully, with attention to the weather and occasion. In winter they wore velvet half-boots trimmed with fur, felt overshoes, or high laced boots. In the summer, or at home in the evening, they wore slippers. All chic women's shoes had high heels, which varied in height and style.

It became proper for women to wear white stockings only with white dresses, so for everyday wear they usually chose stockings in a neutral color, such as gray or beige. For holiday outfits, the stockings matched the color of the bottom skirt. Striped or checked stockings were considered particularly chic, and they were worn with dresses and skirts of Scottish wool.

The most common accessories of the fashionable woman of the late nineteenth and early twentieth centuries were gloves and umbrellas.

The gloves were of light-weight, colored chamois, silk, or cotton, and they came is a variety of lengths and styles. Summer gloves were usually of lace or net and sometimes left the fingertips bare. In winter, woolen gloves were a necessity. Umbrellas also had a practical purpose, to protect against the elements in the rainy Russian autumn. In the summer, parasols made a refined shield against the sun. Umbrella handles were made from bone, wood, tortoise shell, and even precious metals.

An elegant appearance required careful attention to hairstyle, which completed an outfit for any occasion. To judge from photographs and portraits from the second half of the nineteenth century, fashionable Russian women wore a startling array of hats: berets, turbans, caps, veils, and especially the chic semitransparent hoods copied from French styles.

To judge from Russian fashion magazines of the 1890s, good taste in dress consisted of knowing how to coordinate the right fabric and the right design. An aristocratic Russian woman might receive her guests in a "dress-up negligée," but her "casualness" had to be carefully planned. Her morning housecoat or kimono, made from a light-weight, light-colored fabric, was appropriate for going down to breakfast or even receiving unexpected guests. However, housecoats and dusters were out of place after midday. The daytime dress for home was usually made of brown or garnet cashmere; this became the uniform for high school pupils. By the end of the nineteenth century, well-dressed urban women had special outfits to entertain guests at home. These outfits were made from less expensive fabric and had less lavish trim than dresses intended for evenings out. Instead, they were supposed to convey a sense of comfort, as though they might be worn every day. Such "boudoir" dresses were cut in a single piece and more loosely than clothes intended for street wear. The hairdos that went with "boudoir" dress lacked flowers or plumes, but tortoiseshell combs and hairpins held in place curls artfully arranged to look tousled.

Fashion magazines recommended that for street wear or visits women supplement their outfits, because it would be in poor taste to go out in just what one would wear at home. Such a supplemental article could be a short cape, a turban, a scarf with matching cap and gloves, or any variety of coat, jacket, or cloak.

Handbags were usually sack shaped, and as a rule only unfashionable Russian women carried them. Sparkly items, whether dress trim, hair ornaments, belts, earrings, brooches, rings, or bracelets, were considered appropriate only with ball gowns. To walk along the street in evening dress, even on the way to the theater or to visit friends, was considered the height of bad taste. Ladies who wore formal outfits and jewelry were supposed to hire carriages. At the beginning of the twentieth century, the wealthiest Russian ladies ordered special *sortie-de-bal* capes made of expensive fabrics or furs to cover their evening gowns while coming and going.

The wives of the upper-middle-class bankers and successful industrialists at the turn of the century furnished their wardrobes from the shops of the best Russian tailors, and their financial resources allowed them to acquire what were then considered the most fashionable accessories and jewelry. Contemporaries, however, could readily distinguish between elegant aristocratic women and bourgeois women who tried to imitate them. Bourgeois tastes were revealed in the choice of fabrics, the overabundance of valuable jewelry, and the too-low décolletages and too-tight bodices of ball gowns. The street wear of the middle class was even more distinctive: merchant women often wore velvet coats, lined with fur or quilting, with wide sleeves and long cape collars, and trimmed with large, figured borders. Russian women of the mercantile class consciously preserved the monumental style of clothing of the 1830s. It permitted them to distinguish themselves from the intelligentsia, which followed European models of costume much more closely.

In general, then, women's clothing styles did not become either simpler or more democratic at the end of the nineteenth century. Fashionable dress was still designed for idle women. The difference between everyday clothing and dress-up outfits worn by the well-to-do and those of people with limited means became especially noticeable in the early 1900s, with the influence of the Decadent and Modern styles. Decadence emphasized slow dying, decline, and fatigue; Modern imitated the "long and flexible shoot of a climbing plant." Both styles left their mark on European and Russian dress styles. The new distinctive silhouette was elongated, winding, and overstated, with an undefined waist and no corset: "everything got long, [the wearer] increased her height with tentacles, which rose high and then fell behind or entwined flexibly."[146]

The most chic silhouette was the "amphora," in which the bodice or tunic was draped in a spiral around the body. The ideal article to drape was the fur stole or the ostrich-feather boa. Ladies who followed the new style ordered dresses that either had high, muffling collars or were low-cut to reveal fine collarbones. The most common fabrics were satin and rustling, matte, watered silk that fell in smooth waves. Typical colors of the Modern style were sea-green, gray-green, ash gray, and black in conjunction with lilac or fiery red. Hairdos were topped with ostrich feathers. Outfits for visiting were topped with hats, sometimes with enormous brims as wide as the shoulders, and sometimes in the form of little turbans with a vertical decoration over the forehead. A sliding step, pale face, mascaraed eyes, and languorous voice were considered cultured. The Modern style enjoyed particular success among the lower and middle bourgeoisie, as well as among the bohemians—the milieu of artists, actors, and poets—where a "refined feebleness" was in vogue.

But not all Russian women adopted the extremes of the Decadent style or tried to make their costume reflect a personal sense of artistic taste. Their clothes often lagged behind the newest fashions, and they had no choice but to avoid extravagance. The cut, color, and trim of their outfits followed the general directions of haute couture, but more conservatively than the models in the magazines. Simple and modest designs won the largest following, for example, the Princess style of dress, and *sarafan*-like skirts with shoulder straps. The latter gained wide popularity among the urban lower class, because it was reminiscent of traditional Russian dress. The clothing of lower-class urban women differed from that of the elite not so much in design as in the choice of fabric and decoration, although some tried to imitate bourgeois lavishness with cheaper materials.

At the same time that lower-class women, who were trying "to be not worse than others," improved upon the models with superfluous bows, lace, fringe, and "pretty little pins" in the shape of angels, hearts, and rhinestones, elite women began to avoid pretention and glitter in their outfits. Clothing became more practical, including items intended for home wear. Robes, housecoats, and kimonos had been inconvenient for women because their hooks or ties in front got in the way of household tasks. Instead, urban women began to adopt simple and loosely cut dresses with aprons over them. Although pajamas made from silk began to appear in the 1910s, they did not become an established type of clothing for home wear at that time but instead remained a symbol of idle wealth characteristic of cinema heroines.

Gradually all elements in the wardrobe of Russian women, whether for morning, afternoon, evening, or even formal wear, became more convenient. This was particularly true of outerwear, where waterproof raincoats rapidly became popular. Practicality also explains the advent of knitted articles, such as sweaters. The enthusiasm for athletic activities such as bicycling, skating, and horseback riding that came into vogue in the 1890s led to new types of clothing that then influenced nonsports wear. Thus everyday outfits came to consist of loosely cut blouses, comparatively short skirts, and, for the first time, pants, cut loosely and reaching just below the knee.

Fashionable footwear in the early twentieth century consisted of high-top laced shoes with light-colored uppers and black, patent-leather toes and heels, or webbed pumps. With evening dresses or ball gowns, women preferred pointed slippers with high heels, which were sometimes decorated with small strands of glitter. It was considered best to match the color of the stockings exactly to that of the shoes.

But most women could not afford to dress stylishly, or even to buy clothing that reflected their individual tastes. Dressmakers and couturiers charged enormous prices for their elegant products. Housemaids, nannies, and governesses could only dream of the fashionable costumes worn by the ladies they served. In addition to noblewomen and ladies of the financier and industrialist class, merchant women could afford chic outfits. Still, contemporaries in the early twentieth century could readily pick out merchant women amid the crowds strolling in parks, theater lobbies, and stores. The expensive dresses imported from Europe or custom made by the best Russian establishments—"Madame Olga's," "N. Lamanova," and "A.T. Ivanova"—lost all elegance on the typically fat and clumsy figures of mercantile wives. Poorly matched accessories and too much jewelry made these women the butt of lampoons.

Unlike middle-class women, women workers did not try to keep up with fashions. Their usual outfit consisted of a gathered skirt and loosely cut blouse, which was worn outside the waistband of the skirt. Many women of the working classes also wore dresses that were designed to be comfortable. When sewing from patterns, they made the bodice wider, the skirt shorter, and the sleeves more fitted and omitted the whalebone stays.[147] This basic outfit was supplemented with an apron and a scarf around the shoulders, knotted at the throat. They preferred inexpensive fabrics such as chintz, calico, corduroy, and polished cotton both for daily wear and for special occasions. The footwear was similarly practical: short boots with rubber uppers, or, less often, heavy loafers with a small heel.

In small factories and workshops, women often dressed not in modern style but rather in traditional peasant clothing: a *sarafan* with a blouse or shift underneath. Even in the early twentieth century, rural women retained their traditional mode of dress with its time-tested design. However, they made these clothes—*sarafans*, overcoats, short coats pleated at the waist, and wrap skirts—from factory-made cloth rather than weaving fabric at home. In the central provinces and the Urals, city fashions had more effect on peasant costume. By the early twentieth century, peasant women began to buy clothes for special occasions ready made from the stores that sprang up not only in the main urban centers but also in provincial towns.[148]

In this way, the distinctiveness of costume by social order, so noticeable at the end of the eighteenth century, began to disappear. In the early nineteenth century, a woman's dress depended unambiguously upon her social order: the type and pattern of the fabric, the design of the outfit, and its ornamentation conveyed a clear and nuanced message about the wearer's position in society. A century later, only peasant modes of dress remained traditional, for all urban women dressed more or less according to modern fashions. And these fashions changed rapidly in response to events in the world of politics, literature, and the arts, as these suggested new images and unusual accessories.

In place of the external signs of social order, dress came to reflect differences in wealth and peculiarities of taste and custom. One author summed up the tendencies in women's costume in his "survey of fashion," published in the magazine *Capital and Country Estate* (*Stolitsa i usadba*) in 1914: "Keenly responsive to the inquiries of the new lifestyle, the dress has become simple and practical. The loose cut, which is comfortable for movement, has definitely won itself a place."[149]

Epilogue

Women in the Soviet Union and After: 1917 to the 1990s

Throughout the many centuries of Russian history, through periods of crisis and periods of peace, women worked, planned, and dreamed. In some eras women's rights expanded, and in others they narrowed. An epoch of stability and cultural flowering under autonomous women rulers of medieval principalities gave way to a period in which women of all social orders saw their rights contract. For a time, women's abilities went largely untapped, but then Russia experienced nearly a century of female rule. In general, then, the history of Russian women moved in a positive direction.

Almost a hundred years ago, the most popular historical publicist of the past century, I.E. Zabelin, posed the question, "Was the female person independent in society in her own right, or was her independence determined only by her affiliation with a male person?"[1] We may respond that the history of the "female person" in Russia from the tenth to the twentieth centuries is one of movement from relatively restricted autonomy for women to increasing recognition of their rights within the family and in society as a whole. But even in the pre-Muscovite period, from the tenth through fifteenth centuries, a plethora of outstanding women rulers, educators, and healers made their mark. During this period, women played a significant role in the family, and their rights under the law to own and manage property and to undertake judicial actions gradually increased. Women's rights did not progress uninterruptedly, however, as the period of seclusion in the *terem* testifies. But the status of women in Russia ought not be be judged solely according to the *terem* of the sixteenth and seventeenth centuries, especially because it affected only a small number of the Muscovite elite.

If the mid-sixteenth century marked a watershed in the history of women, a turn for the worse, the early eighteenth century marked a second watershed, a turn for the better. During Peter the Great's reforms, the restrictive old ways of life, already recognized as anachronistic in the late seventeenth century, were decisively overturned. But within the reforms of the early eighteenth century, much of what was "new" echoed the distant past. The reforms restored women's rights in regard to property and the law, giving these rights a new basis and raising them to new levels. The leading women of the age accomplished much with their intelligence, vision, unfeminine toughness, and overweening ambition. They were individuals of their time, operating according to the values and morals of their society and subject to its conditions.

The nineteenth century was also a watershed, in its own way. Its prime characteristic was the rise of the "Woman Question" and the women's movement, reflecting the development of a consciousness of women's place in society. It was also the period in which an increasing number of women strove to enter into the political, cultural, and academic life of the country. These women had to face misunderstanding on the part of society and the intellectual barriers of prejudice and outdated legal restrictions. Even so they managed to accomplish a great deal.

What, then, happened to Russian women after World War I and the revolutions of 1917?[2]

The decade of 1910–20 was tragic, marked by world war, civil war, revolution, and in their wake famine, devastation, and epidemics. Hundreds of thousands of people died and the lives of millions of people were disrupted. Many of the victims were women.[3] In this decade, too, Russia undertook its great experiment with socialism, which lasted for more than seventy years. The goal of this socialist experiment was to fulfill the long-standing expectations of the Russian people to create a "society of equals," without lies or injustice, and without restrictions on the basis of sex. But the methods used to try to realize these noble ends resulted in something quite different.

Women played a key role in toppling the tsarist government in February 1917. The women workers of St. Petersburg, fearing imminent bread shortages as a result of the ongoing military stalemate, took to the streets to express their displeasure. They were joined by

male workers, and then by the soldiers sent to put down the distur-
bances. A week later, Tsar Nicholas II abdicated. A hastily formed
Provisional Government, made up of deputies from the Duma,
claimed power. A second locus of power formed around the soviets
(councils) of workers, peasants, and soldiers. These soviets sprang up
spontaneously in the course of the February Revolution, building on
the model of their predecessors in 1905, and they acquired the power
to confirm (or refuse to confirm) the decisions of the Provisional
Government. The soviets tended to be much more radical than the
middle-class liberals and intellectuals who dominated the Provisional
Government, and they demanded an end to Russia's participation in
World War I and the redistribution of land and wealth within the
country. But it was the Provisional Government under Alexander
Kerensky that granted women the right to vote. The soviets then
ratified this decision and claimed credit for it.

The Bolsheviks seized power in October 1917 in the name of the
soviets, where they enjoyed extensive support because of their platform of "Bread, Peace, and Land." In their first months in power
(October–December 1917), the new Communist authorities instituted a number of fundamental changes relating to "the measures for
the emancipation of women from servitude." First of all, decrees were
issued to make women's legal standing equal with that of men. While
the Provisional Government granted women only the right to vote,
the Bolsheviks immediately granted women full political empowerment. All workers, without regard to sex, had participated in the
election of deputies to the soviets. The new government set up by the
Bolsheviks included one woman member, Alexandra Kollontai, who
held the rank of people's commissar. The first Soviet constitution,
which was issued in 1918, guaranteed equality of rights for men and
women, and this provision was confirmed in subsequent fundamental
laws. This constitution did place limitations on suffrage, but not on
the basis of gender; people from the "exploiting classes"—landowners, bourgeoisie, clergy, White (tsarist) army officers—were excluded
from the electorate, men as well as women.

On October 29, 1917, only three days after the Bolshevik coup, a
decree was issued to limit the workday to eight hours and to prohibit
women from labor at night and from underground work in the
mines. An edict issued the next day reconfirmed insurance for people
who could not work, including women needing maternity leave. Laws
enacted in December guaranteed all working women a two-month
leave before and after the birth of a child, as well as a monetary grant

equivalent to four months' salary. A new law code issued in September 1918 revoked legal recognition of church marriages and introduced free dissolution of marriages upon the initiative of either spouse. Abortion was legalized in 1920, and hospitals performed them free of charge. New laws stipulated that both parents (even if they were divorced) were responsible for the upbringing and sustenance of their children. Illegitimate children were given a legal status equal to that of children born within marriage.

Marriage was reconceived as a free and equal union between a man and a woman, who thus formed their own family. Informal marriages became very common, and in 1926, the law bestowed upon them recognition equal to marriages that had been properly registered with governmental authorities. The drive on the part of women to choose their marriage partners freely reflected the revolutionary spirit of the period, the weakening of family ties, and a protest against the conservatism of old customs. Although divorce had become easier, most marriages lasted. When a law issued in 1944 required that all marriages, including informal ones, be registered, a high percentage of women recorded that they had been married for ten to twenty years.

Later developments, however, did not carry through the most radical laws issued in the first years after the revolution. The new Soviet authorities thought that "the position of women in Soviet Russia is now ideal from the point of view of the most advanced states" and thus declared the "Woman Question" solved.[4] But the laws concerning women that had been enacted between 1917 and 1924 did not so much defend the interests of women as subordinate them to the goals of "the building of communism" and the "revolutionary education of women of the Party, of the Komsomol [Communist Youth League], and of productive labor."[5] In the autumn of 1919, special sections of the Communist Party were established to work with women, the *Zhenotdely*. The *Zhenotdely* were set up as part of party committees both in the center and at the local level, and they had as their goal "to raise the activity of women in the struggle of the working class for socialism" and then "to put this strength to use."[6] Despite this verbal affirmation, insurmountable obstacles were placed in the way of the formation of any organizations specifically for women.[7]

But Russian women in the 1920s did not feel themselves to be constrained. Many educated women from the intelligentsia, including those who foresaw the drawbacks of the new policies, were inspired by the grand transformation that was taking place and endorsed it sincerely. Women workers felt an even deeper sense of commitment to the building of a new society. Rural society remained more conservative and more skeptical, but peasant women understood the significance of the Decree on Land, for example, which eliminated the main impediments to dissolving extended households and encouraged the formation of nuclear families, in which women had undisputed authority.[8]

Russian women of that period sincerely believed that Bolshevik decrees would bring about their own emancipation, and they were willing to forgo their own happiness so that their children and grandchildren could enjoy the promised bright future. They were not to blame for their belief, but the situation turned out unhappily. The actual position of Russian women, both among the urban population and among the peasantry, became complicated in the late 1920s and early 1930s. The building of the new society demanded an enormous effort, and women were forced to expend their strength, health, and time toward that end. It is not accidental that, as early as 1924–25, the People's Commissariat of Labor rescinded the restrictions on women's labor at night and in dangerous industries. A real liberation of women, one that would allow them to choose whether to enter the workforce or to concentrate solely on their families, remained an unfulfilled dream.

Soviet Russia simply could not manage without the productive capacity of hundreds of thousands of women workers and peasants. More than half of these (53.3 percent) had few skills, yet they were drafted into the building of socialism. However, there were also incentives—for example, housing was provided almost free of charge. But even the housing was problematical: the old owners were forced to share their homes with new residents, and often as many as ten families shared the same communal apartment.

Women workers also received education. For some of them, this was simply learning to read; in 1920, three-fourths of women workers were illiterate. But others learned new professions, including those that previously had been considered typically male, such as electrician or plant manager. *Zhenotdel* activists urged women to continue into higher education via "worker faculties," technical schools, and universities.[9] The magazine *Peasant Woman* (*Krestianka*) was founded in 1922, and it became very popular among women. It was followed in 1923 with the reestablishment of the magazine *Woman Worker* (*Rabotnitsa*), which had been published in the 1910s.

The women's press of the 1920s taught worker and peasant women the right way to organize their households and to look after their children. From 1923 on, the magazines ran columns entitled "Mother and Child" that offered child-care items for sale. In this period, the first public day-care facilities opened; women saw them as the fruits of communism.[10] At first, the day-care workers had to visit homes to convince women to place their children in the nurseries and kindergartens. Most women workers, and peasants even more, were suspicious of communal upbringing, and they clung to their time-honored methods of child rearing. They retained the practice of having children sleep together, in a common bed or on the floor, or with adults, either mother or grandmother. In both urban and rural homes, mothers continued to rock their infants in the traditional hanging cradles and resisted the idea of providing each child with an individual bed. The way of life of most Russian families of the 1920s and 1930s had much in common with that of prerevolutionary workers or, to a slightly lesser degree, peasants. Women's lifestyle bore little resemblance to that of elite women at the beginning of the century.

But for a small number of women from families of the party elite, the early 1930s brought some obvious changes. The revolutionary "socialist experiment" became mired in a rigid, conservative ideology, and the radical, self-denying party leadership of the prerevolutionary period transmuted itself into a conformist, self-indulgent bureaucracy. While the bulk of the population lived in communal dwellings and fed on limited rations, the growing Communist elite enjoyed spacious quarters and rare delicacies. The first two Soviet constitutions, of 1918 and 1924, had required all citizens to work (applying the principle of "whoever does not work shall not eat"); the 1936 Constitution mandated not a *requirement* to work but a *right* to work. But the only persons who could afford not to work were the wives of highly placed and highly paid men, and they became the new leisure class, the women who could spend their time only on familial matters. Urban elite families could also afford servants to do the housework and nannies to look after the children. These servants alleviated the burdens of housekeeping for elite women, but most of these servants were themselves women, usually peasants who had recently migrated from the countryside. The collectivization of agriculture, which took place from 1927 to 1935 amid massive resistance, violence and famine, drove many people, especially women, from their villages.[11]

The new command economy of the 1930s, with its forced collectivization and industrialization, its unrealistic production quotas, and contradictory governmental imperatives, had a deleterious effect on most Russian women. A whole series of new decrees complicated women's already difficult lives. The workweek was lengthened from five to seven days, and women's maternity leave was shortened. A new system of registration and internal passports restricted men's and women's freedom of movement within the country. The government became increasingly controlling and intrusive, ordering mass arrests of ideological deviants, "wreckers" (scapegoats blamed for production failures), and *kulaks* (prosperous peasants). Whole populations were exiled and resettled. A huge network of labor camps, known as the gulag, grew up to house these "enemies of the state," and women inmates worked at the same exhausting and dangerous tasks, such as logging and mining, as men. A decree of the mid-1930s made parents, both mothers and fathers, responsible for crimes committed by their children.

In the 1930s and thereafter, despite the rhetoric of "strengthening the family," political and economic planners undervalued motherhood and child rearing and ignored the physical and psychological welfare of married couples. New laws issued from 1935 to 1944 made divorce more difficult and outlawed abortion, mandating the death penalty or imprisonment in a labor camp for those doctors who terminated pregnancies. Later, the government forbade any discussion of sexuality in the press. Finally, a "tax on childlessness" was established. However sincere these attempts to create solid and highly moral marital unions, they caused personal tragedies for many thousands of women.

Yet despite the new restrictions, purges, collectivization, and industrialization, by the late 1930s life had improved for many ordinary women. They worked on a par with men in factories, collective farms, and governmental and party institutions. New and inexpensive daycare facilities had opened, and Young Pioneer (Scouts) organizations offered summer camps for older children. Health care improved with the building of clinics, hospitals, sanitariums, and spas. The expansion of a network of cafeterias provided women with time-saving options to feed their families, although their cuisine was inferior to home cooking. The number of public laundries also grew, and it became customary at most factories and some collective farms to provide employees with workclothes, essential household goods, bolts of cloth, and sometimes free vacations at spas or resorts.[12]

Rewards of this sort prompted a great enthusiasm for work. The government press further promoted productivity by extolling individuals who showed exceptional initiative. Women were among these ordinary heroes: for example, the textile workers Evdokia and Maria Vinogradova and the tractor driver Praskovia Angelina. The women who worked in government posts were lauded as veritable "mistresses of the country."[13] However, there were no women in prominent positions in the government. Even the "Kremlin women"—the wives of Stalin and his close associates—had no political role; they were powerless to change the system and dependent upon Stalin, who personified that system. Even Alexandra Kollontai, the former people's commissar, was soon excluded from power, although she became the Soviet ambassador to Sweden.[14]

World War II, which Russians call the "Great Patriotic War," required the mobilization of all the country's resources. Because most able-bodied men were mobilized as soldiers to fight the Nazi invaders, women had to take over all the work on the homefront. They did so willingly and selflessly. The length of women's workday reached ten to twelve hours in factories and as much as twenty-two hours in the countryside. Millions of women joined in combat at the front, serving not only as soldiers but also as pilots, snipers, and tank drivers; there were even women in the navy.[15] During the critical years of wartime combat, few people realized how costly the war would be in human terms and how it would affect Russia demographically. But by the time the war ended in 1945, it was clear that many families had disintegrated, and the male population had been much reduced. Millions of women were doomed to unrelieved widowhood, spinsterhood, and childlessness.[16]

Under war conditions, the government could not contemplate measures to improve the condition of women's lives, but after the end of the war, women's concerns reasserted themselves. The restoration of the national economy resulted in a rise in the standard of living. At the same time, women's expectations concerning their lives changed; they were no longer satisfied with the ascetic way of life that had been preached for the preceding decade. But real changes could occur only in the mid-1950s, after the death of Joseph Stalin.

The period of the "thaw" (1954–64) saw the first expression of doubts that the "Woman Question" had in fact been resolved in the Soviet Union, and measures were taken to put its "resolution" back on track. First, in 1956, women were once again banned from work in mines and on fishing boats; women currently employed in such jobs were transferred to other work at the same salary. Many of the Stalin-era decrees concerning the family were abolished. Abortion was once again legalized in 1955. Several years later, restrictions on divorce were eased, and no court hearing was required except in disputed cases.

Measures were devised to strengthen the family, lighten women's burdens, and protect women's health. Material assistance was designated for the neediest single mothers. Women who gave birth to three or more children received a monetary bonus, and the mothers of large families received preferential treatment in housing and household goods. In 1956, women became entitled to 112 days of maternity leave at full pay. In order to accommodate the child-care needs of the numerous widows and single mothers, after-school programs were instituted in 1958. In the early 1960s, decrees were issued to shorten the workday for women who had several children, provide divorcees with a larger alimony, and provide government assistance to the neediest families.[17] One extremely valuable innovation was a provision to allow women paid leave from work for three to seven days to look after their sick children. Working mothers with small children also received job security; they could not be fired from whatever post they held.

The purpose of all these laws and regulations was to "provide for the harmonious combination of motherhood with growing activity in the political and productive spheres for Soviet women." However, this "harmonious combination" in fact meant that women bore the same work obligations as men, as well as all responsibilities at home, which, according to a carefully cultivated ideology of "tradition," fell on women's shoulders. The rapid growth of the number of women in the workforce (from 47 percent of workers in 1960 to 64 percent in 1975, with women forming as much as 73 percent in some professions) reflected not only the rise in the educational level of women but also a disturbing reality concerning household finances: families with children could not manage on one income.

Life in the Soviet Union of the 1960s and 1970s improved noticeably in comparison with the prewar food shortages and the postwar devastation. Electrical appliances, which formerly had been merely the stuff of rumor, became commonplace first in urban and then in rural households. Appliances were also available to rent. Laundries and dry cleaners opened, as well as tailor shops to alter and repair clothing. The variety of pre-prepared foods expanded. All these conveniences had long been available in Western countries, but they were new to Russians. Despite these labor-saving devices, women still worked a "double shift," at home and on the job. Furthermore, the Soviet Union had become "the land of constant shortages," where consumers often could not find even the most basic goods for sale in stores. Soviet women wasted incredible amounts of time shopping for groceries, standing in lines, and laying in stores of food against future shortages. Rural women faced not only these duties but also agricultural labor on the family plot.[18]

Russian women had, however, achieved financial independence. Many of them also were highly educated and held professional positions. By 1970, three out of four physicians were women, and one out of three engineers. Their level of economic and professional responsibility gave women a basis for claiming leadership within the family. But when asked in sociological surveys, women demurred, saying that they and their husbands were "both the heads" of the family. Only in families where the wife did not work outside the home did women respond that the father was the head of the household.[19] In all families, women assumed responsibility for the organization of household activities, oversaw child rearing, and had much influence over the development of their children's career and personal plans. The changes in how families divided household responsibilities altered relations between spouses, but few people were conscious of it.[20]

The two decades of "stagnation" from 1964 to 1985 were marked by a growing but unacknowledged stratification of Soviet society, which was reflected in women's lives. Women in white-collar positions, especially in the large cities, lived very differently from factory workers or peasants on collective farms. The customs and the patterns of daily life diverged, even though the legal status of all women was the same.

In the first years after the war, women began to play a more extensive role in the public and political spheres, participating in professional organizations and party committees as well as the organs of Soviet government. But women's participation occurred primarily at the behest of the authorities, who introduced legal quotas (typically 30–40 percent) for female representation in these organizations. The Soviet state granted equal rights to all citizens, but it confused equality with homogeneity and made no allowance for individual differences. This was especially true in the case of women. Thousands of women received awards for social activism and workplace accomplishments and were lauded in the press. Some of them were truly remarkable, such as Valentina Tereshkova, the first woman cosmonaut. Yet others were completely ordinary; they were selected only in order to fill government quotas for the number of prize-winning women.

Among all the publicly active, and particularly politically active, women of the last decades of the Soviet era, very few made a lasting impression. "Heroines" were selected as models for public emulation because they possessed the right combination of officially approved characteristics, including, first of all, their social origin (working class was best) and ethnicity (Russian). For example, Ekaterina Furtseva, a former textile worker, became minister of culture; she earned the derisive popular nickname of "Catherine III." Only in the arts did talent play an important role in becoming successful, as in the cases of the ballerinas Maia Plisetskaia and Ekaterina Maksimova; the singers Elena Obraztsova, Irina Arkhipova, and Bella Rudenko; and the actresses Iulia Borisova and Tatiana Samoilova.

The economic and political reforms subsumed under the name "perestroika," begun by Mikhail Gorbachev in the mid-1980s, had profound implications for women. The reorganization of the economy resulted in unemployment, and women were often the first to be dismissed from their jobs. Women's life expectancy, which had reached seventy-four years, dropped as a result of the new hardships to levels six to seven years less than in the United States and Western Europe. The lack of economic stability discouraged childbearing; the birthrate, which was already low, dropped still further, and the number of abortions outstripped it, with 196 abortions for every 100 live births. The number of divorces also increased. Although mothers continued to receive the supplemental grants for children enacted in 1981, rapid inflation made them virtually worthless.[21] Women found it easier to give up family and children than to give up their work. This trend was the result not only of the economic complexities of perestroika but also of the high level of education that women had attained.[22]

As soon as the system of quotas for women's participation in government were removed, the number of women dropped precipitously. Although women had previously constituted a third of the deputies in the Supreme Soviet, by the late 1980s only 57 out of 1,063 deputies were women.[23] Rural women, in particular, were effectively excluded from national politics. But the founding of a new political action group, Women of Russia, in 1993 offered a corrective, and the new parliament elected after the crisis of October 1993 included representatives for whom the protection of women's interests was the primary goal. In 1994 the government also turned its attention to stresses on the family. It established standards for minimum income for families of various configurations, and it provided welfare payments for those families whose income fell beneath the poverty line. Although women did not take advantage of the economic opportunities of perestroika at first, younger women, especially later, flocked to new private enterprises and even started their own companies. A quarter of the women in one survey indicated that they were ready to try to start their own businesses.[24]

It is difficult to predict the future of Russian women, but certain developments in the recent past give cause for optimism. Women's active role in society and business, which has developed so markedly in our time, has its roots in the distant past. Contemporary women have the opportunity to draw inspiration from their history and traditions, and with good sense and strength of will, they will forever endure.

Notes

Notes to Introduction

1. For the historiography of women's history, see Linda Frey, Marsha Frey, and Joanne Schneider, eds., *Women in Western European History: A Select Geographical and Topical Bibliography* (London, 1982); Michelle Perrot, *Une histoire des femmes est-elle possible?* (Paris, 1984); Marilyn J. Boxer and Jean H. Quataert, eds., *Connecting Spheres: Women in the Western World, 1500 to the Present* (New York, 1987); S. Jay Kleinberg, ed., *Retrieving Women's History: Changing Perceptions of the Role of Women in Politics and Society* (New York, 1988); S.S. Shashi, ed., *Encyclopedia of World Women* (New Delhi, 1989); and Karen Offen, Ruth Roach Pierson, and Jane Rendall, eds., *Writing Women's History: International Perspectives* (Bloomington, 1991).

2. G. Duby, N.Z. Davis, A. Farge, and M. Perrot, et al., eds, *Histoire des femmes en Occident*, vols. 1–6 (Paris, 1991).

3. C. Claus, *Die Stellung der russischen Frau von der Einführung des Christentums bei den Russen bis zu den Reformen Peters der Grossen* (Munich, 1959); A. Eck, "La Situation juridique de la femme russe au Moyen Age," *Recueils de la Société Jean Bodin pour l'histoire comparative des institutions*, vol. 12 (1962), pp. 404–20; and S. McNally, "From Public Person to Private Prisoner: The Changing Place of Women in Medieval Russia," (Ph.D. dissertation, State University of New York at Binghamton, 1976). For more information on the development of Russian women's studies as a field, see Barbara Alpern Engel, "Engendering Russia's History: Women in Post-Emancipation Russia and the Soviet Union," *Slavic Review*, vol. 51, no. 2 (1992), pp. 309–21; and Barbara Heldt, "Feminism and the Slavic Field," *The Harriman Review*, vol. 7, nos. 10–12 (1994), pp. 11–18.

4. K. Marks [Marx], F. Engels, *Polnoe sobranie sochinenii*, vol. 21 (Moscow, 1968), p. 60; A. Bebel', *Zhenshchina i sotsializm* (Moscow, 1966), p. 256.

5. Among the most successful works on the history of Russian women produced outside Russia are Dorothy Atkinson, Alexander Dallin, and Gail Warshofsky Lapidus, eds., *Women in Russia* (Stanford, 1977); Richard Stites, *The Women's Liberation Movement in Russia* (Princeton, 1978); Eve Levin, *Sex and Society in the World of the Orthodox Slavs, 900–1700* (Ithaca, 1989); Barbara Evans Clements, Barbara Alpern Engel, and Christine Worobec, eds., *Russia's Women: Accommodation, Resistance, Transformation* (Berkeley, 1991); Beatrice Farnsworth and

Lynne Viola, eds., *Russian Peasant Women* (New York, 1992); Laura Engelstein, *The Keys to Happiness: Sex and the Search for Modernity in Fin-de-Siècle Russia* (Ithaca, 1992).

Notes to Chapter 1

1. For a general survey of Russian history in this period, see Janet Martin, *Medieval Russia, 980–1584* (Cambridge, Eng., 1995).
2. N.M. Karamzin, "Izvestie o Marfe-posadnitse," *Vestnik Evropy*, 1803, pt. 9, no. 12, p. 302.
3. "Prestavlenie blazhennoi kniagini Ol'gi, v sviatom kreshchenii Eleny," in *Izbrannye zhitiia russkikh sviatykh, X–XV vv.* (Moscow, 1992), pp. 12–26.
4. For more information on Princess Olga, see N.L. Pushkareva, *Zhenshchiny drevnei Rusi* (Moscow, 1989), pp. 12–22; *Povest' vremennykh let*, ed. V.P. Adrianova-Peretts (Moscow–Leningrad, 1950), pt. 1, pp. 40–45; G.G. Litavrin, "K voprosu ob obstoiatel'stvakh, meste i vremeni kreshcheniia Ol'gi," *Drevneishie gosudarstva na territorii SSSR* (Moscow, 1986), pp. 56–57; John Fennell, "When Was Olga Canonized?" in Boris Gasparov and Olga Raevsky-Hughes, eds., *Christianity and the Eastern Slavs*, vol. 1, [California Slavic Studies, vol. 16] (Berkeley, 1993), pp. 77–82.
5. *Povest' vremennykh let*, p. 80. *Pamiatniki russkogo prava*, vol. 1 (Moscow, 1952), p. 237; vol. 2 (Moscow, 1953), p. 162.
6. On the daughters of Iaroslav the Wise, see *Povest' vremennykh let*, pt. 1, pp. 92, 97; Pushkareva, *Zhenshchiny drevnei Rusi*, p. 22–27; I. Levron, "Anne de Kiev, princesse russe, reine de France," *Miroire de l'histoire*, No. 268 (1972), pp. 118–25; R. Hallu, *Anne de Kiev, reine de France* (Rome, 1973), pp. 240–45; G.V. Glazyrina, "Svidetel'stva drevneskandinavskikh istochnikov o brake Kharol'da Surovogo i Elizavety Iaroslavny," *Vneshniaia politika drevnei Rusi. Iubileinye chteniia* (Moscow, 1988), pp. 14–16.
7. Pushkareva, *Zhenshchiny drevnei Rusi*, pp. 27–32; N.I. Shchabeleva, "Russkie kniagini v Pol'she," *Vneshniaia politika drevnei Rusi. Iubileinye chteniia*, pp. 117–22; S.P. Rozanov, "Evpraksia-Adel'geida Vsevolodovna," *Izvestiia Akademii nauk SSSR. Seriia VII*, no. 8 (1929), pp. 631–39.
8. *Povest' vremennykh let*, pt. 1, pp. 137–39; E. Likhacheva, *Materialy dlia istorii zhenskogo obrazovaniia v Rossii (1086–1796)* (St. Petersburg, 1890); *Polnoe sobranie russkikh letopisei*, vol. 1 (St. Petersburg, 1843), pp. 276, 288.
9. M.A. Bogoiavlenskii, *Drevnerusskoe vrachevanie v XI–XVII vv.* (Moscow, 1960), p. 26; M.N. Ditrikh, *Drevnerusskie zhenshchiny velikokniazheskogo vremeni* (St. Petersburg, 1904), pp. 36–38.
10. *Polnoe sobranie russkikh letopisei*, vol. 2 (St. Petersburg, 1843), pp. 254, 310–11, 318–24, 482–83; K.Ia. Grot, *Iz istorii Ugrii i slavianstva v XII v.* (Warsaw, 1889), pp. 23, 94, 96.
11. V.L. Ianin, *Aktovye pechati drevnei Rusi X–XV vv.*, vol. 1 (Moscow, 1970), pp. 234, 274.
12. Ianin, *Aktovye pechati*, vol. 1, pp. 17–19, 21–23, 33, 71, 83, 130, 156, 163, 173, 183–84, 210.
13. *Polnoe sobranie russkikh letopisei*, vol. 2, p. 313 (under the year 1173); p. 161 (under the year 1180).
14. *Polnoe sobranie russkikh letopisei*, vol. 2, pp. 717, 719, 721, 735, 903–9; H. Grala, "Drugie małżeństwo Romana Mscisławowicza," *Slavia Orientalis*, vol. 31, nos. 3/4 (1982), pp. 111–21.

15. *Polnoe sobranie russkikh letopisei*, vol. 3 (St. Petersburg, 1941), p. 51; N. Serebrianskii, *Drevnerusskie kniazheskie zhitiia* (Moscow, 1915), pp. 110–11; D.S. Likhachev, *Russkie letopisi i ikh kul'turno-istoricheskoe znachenie* (Moscow–Leningrad, 1947), pp. 283–86.

16. For more information on the Mongol rule of Russia, see Charles J. Halperin, *Russia and the Golden Horde* (Bloomington, 1985).

17. See A. Szymczakowa, "Księżniczki ruskie w Polsce XIII w.," *Acta Universitatis Łódziensis. Żeszyty naukowe Universitetu Łódzkiego. Folia historica*, Ser. 1 (1978), no. 29, pp. 29–30.

18. *Polnoe sobranie russkikh letopisei*, vol. 10 (St. Petersburg, 1885), pp. 134, 154; vol. 25 (Moscow–Leningrad, 1949), pt. 1, p. 393.

19. *Polnoe sobranie russkikh letopisei*, vol. 5 (St. Petersburg, 1851), p. 256 (under the year 1407); vol. 8 (St. Petersburg, 1856), p. 36 (under the year 1380) and p. 64 (under the year 1393); S.N. Kaidash, *Sila slabykh* (Moscow, 1990).

20. *Polnoe sobranie russkikh letopisei*, vol. 2, pp. 351, 354; vol. 6 (St. Petersburg, 1853), pp. 42 45; vol. 8, pp. 97–98, 115, 150–52, 184; L.B. Veinberg, "Lichnost' Anny Vasil'evny, velikoi kng. riazanskoi," *Trudy Riazanskoi uchenoi arkhivnoi komissii*, vol. 4, no. 8 (1890), pp. 168–69.

21. N.M. Karamzin, *Marfa-posadnitsa ili pokorenie Novgoroda. Istoricheskaia povest'* (Moscow, 1912); *Polnoe sobranie russkikh letopisei*, vol. 3, pp. 136, 142; vol. 5, pp. 37–38; S.A. Tarakanova-Belkina, *Boiarskoe i monastyrskoe zemlevladenie v novgorodskikh piatinakh v domoskovskoe vremia* (Moscow, 1939).

22. F.I. Uspenskii, "Brak tsaria Ivana III Vasil'evicha s Sof'ei Paleolog," *Istoricheskii vestnik*, vol. 30 (1887); *Polnoe sobranie russkikh letopisei*, vol. 7 (St. Petersburg, 1853), p. 154; A.A. Zimin, *Rossiia na rubezhe XV–XVI stoletii* (Moscow, 1982), pp. 84, 140, 212–13, 230–32.

23. On the forms of marriage in medieval Russia, see Pushkareva, *Zhenshchiny drevnei Rusi*, pp. 70–85; A. Pavlov, *50–aia glava russkoi Kormchei knigi kak istoricheskii i prakticheskii istochnik russkogo brachnogo prava* (St. Petersburg, 1880).

24. On wedding customs in medieval Russia, see *Svadebnye zapisi XV–XVII vv.* (*Drevniaia rossiiskaia vifliofika*, vol. 13) (Moscow, 1790); M. Moroshkin, "Svadebnye obriady drevnei Rusi," *Syn otechestva*, 1848, no. 2, pp. 74–78.

25. On divorce law in medieval Russia, see A. Zagovorskii, *O razvode po russkomu pravu* (Kharkov, 1884).

26. For examples of primary texts concerning the ecclesiastical conception of marriage, see A.I. Ponomarev, ed., *Pamiatniki drevne russkoi tserkovno-uchitel'noi literatury*, no. 2 (St. Petersburg, 1896), no. 4 (St. Petersburg, 1898).

27. On the stereotypes of good and evil women in Old Russian literature, see Pushkareva, *Zhenshchiny drevnei Rusi*, pp. 100–103; L.V. Titova, *Beseda ottsa s synom o "zhenskoi zlobe"* (Novosibirsk, 1977).

28. For more information about the ecclesiastical image of marriage as depicted in literature, see Lyubomira Parpulova Gribble, "Žitie Petra i Fevronii: A Love Story or an Apologia of Marriage?" *Russian Language Journal*, vol. 49, nos. 162–64 (1995), pp. 91–113.

29. For published primary sources relating to sexuality, see A.I. Almazov, *Tainaia ispoved' pravoslavnoi vostochnoi tserkvi*, vols. 1–3 (Odessa, 1894); S.I. Smirnov, *Materialy dlia istorii drevnerusskoi pokaiannoi distsipliny* (Moscow, 1913). For a secondary study, see Eve Levin, *Sex and Society*.

30. For more information on childbirth, see Eve Levin, "Childbirth in Pre-Petrine Russia: Canon Law and Popular Traditions," in *Russia's Women* (Berkeley, 1991), pp. 44–59.

31. Birchbark documents are the best source on women's daily lives. See A.V. Artsikhovskii, M.N. Tikhomirov, V.L. Ianin, et al., eds., *Novgorodskie gramoty na bereste*, 9 vols. (Moscow, 1953–93). See also B.A. Romanov, *Liudi i nravy drevnei Rusi* (Moscow, 1963).

32. For more information on women's monasticism, see Sophia Senyk, *Women's Monasteries in Ukraine and Belorussia to the Period of Suppressions* (Rome, 1983).

33. For more information about women's economic activities, see Eve Levin, "Women and Property in Medieval Novgorod: Dependence and Independence," *Russian History*, vol. 10, pt. 2 (1983), pp. 154–69; and N.L. Pushkareva and Eve Levin, "Women in Medieval Novgorod from the Eleventh to the Fifteenth Century," *Soviet Studies in History*, vol. 23, no. 4 (1985), pp. 71–90.

34. N. Debol'skii, *Grazhdanskaia deesposobnost' po russkomu pravu do kontsa XVII stoletiia* (St. Petersburg, 1903), p. 17; Pushkareva, *Zhenshchiny drevnei Rusi*, pp. 104–7.

35. V.L. Ianin, ed., *Novgorodskie gramoty na bereste, iz raskopok 1962–1976 gg.* (Moscow, 1978), pp. 132–34; V.I. Sergeevich, *Lektsii po istorii russkogo prava* (St. Petersburg, 1890), p. 569.

36. N.L. Pushkareva, "Imushchestvennye prava zhenshchin v russkom gosudarstve X–XV vv.," *Istoricheskie zapiski*, no. 114 (1986), pp. 180–224.

37. On women's inheritance rights, see K. Alekseev, "Ob otnosheniiakh suprugov po imushchestvu v drevnei Rossii i Pol'she," *Chteniia v Obshchestve istorii i drevnostei rossiiskikh pri Moskovskom universitete*, 1868, bk. 2, p. 12; W. Sobocinski, "Historia rządów opiekuńczych," *Czasopismo prawno-historyczne*, vol. 2 (Poznan, 1979), pp. 268–77.

38. On women's use of movable property, see *Polnoe sobranie russkikh letopisei*, vol. 2 (St. Petersburg, 1908), pp. 316–61; S.A. Vysotskii, *Drevnerusskie nadpisi Sofii Kievskoi*, no. 1 (Kiev, 1966), p. 64.

39. Pushkareva, "Imushchestvennye prava zhenshchin"; N.L. Pushkareva [Pushkariova], "Woman and Her Property and Legal Status: Was the XVIth Century a Turning Point?" *La donna nel'economia. XIII–XVIIIss. XXI Settimana d'Instituto "F. Datini"* (Florence, 1990).

40. On women's participation in the judicial process, see V. Demchenko, *Istoricheskoe issledovanie o pokazaniiakh svidetelei kak dokazatel'stvakh po delam sudebnym po russkomu pravu do Petra Velikogo* (Kiev, 1859), pp. 8–18; S. Pakhman, *O sudebnykh dokazatel'stvakh po drevnemu russkomu pravu* (Moscow, 1851), pp. 12–26, 138–50.

41. On women's participation in judicial duels, see Article 36 of the Pskov Judicial Charter, in A.A. Zimin, ed., *Pamiatniki russkogo prava*, no. 2 (Moscow, 1956); N.L. Pushkareva, "Sotsial'no-pravovoe polozhenie zhenshchin v russkom gosudarstve X–XV vv.: voprosy prestupleniia i nakazaniia," *Sovetskoe gosudarstvo i pravo*, 1985, no. 4, pp. 121–26.

42. On women's seals, see V.L. Ianin, *Aktovye pechati*, vol. 1, pp. 234, 274, and others.

43. Pushkareva, *Zhenshchiny drevnei Rusi*, pp. 149–52.

44. On the position of women in medieval Russian criminal law, see M.F. Vladimirskii-Budanov, *Obzor istorii russkogo prava* (Kiev, 1900), pp. 346–47; Pushkareva, *Zhenshchiny drevnei Rusi*, pp. 140–48. For more information on rape law, see Levin, *Sex and Society*, pp. 212–46.

45. A.V. Artsikhovskii, "Russkaia odezhda X–XII vv.," *Doklady i soobshcheniia istoricheskogo fakul'teta MGU*, no. 3 (Moscow, 1945), pp. 3–6.

46. Pushkareva, *Zheshchiny drevnei Rusi*, pp. 242–43; M.G. Rabinovich, "Drevnerusskaia odezhda IX–XIII vv.," *Drevniaia odezhda narodov Vostochnoi Evropy* (Moscow, 1978), p. 44.

47. M.N. Levinson-Nechaeva, "Materialy k istorii russkoi narodnoi odezhdy," *Ocherki po istorii russkoi derevni X–XIII vv.* (Moscow, 1959), p. 13.

48. V.P. Levasheva, "Ob odezhde sel'skogo naseleniia Drevnei Rusi," *Trudy Gosudarstvennogo istoricheskogo muzeia*, no. 40 (Moscow, 1966).

49. S.S. Strekalov, *Russkie istoricheskie odezhdy*, no. 1 (St. Petersburg, 1877), p. 13.

50. A. Nekrasov, *Ocherki iz istorii slavianskogo ornamenta* (St. Petersburg, 1913), p. 77. For more information on women's embroidery designs (albeit based on ethnographical materials of later date), see Mary B. Kelly, "The Ritual Fabrics of Russian Village Women," in Helena Goscilo and Beth Holmgren, eds., *Russia, Women, Culture* (Bloomington, 1996), pp. 152–76.

51. Pushkareva, *Zhenshchiny drevnei Rusi*, pp. 161–62, 243.

52. *Dukhovnye i dogovornye gramoty velikikh i udel'nykh kniazei XIV–XVI vv.* (Moscow–Leningrad, 1950), pp. 312, 350.

53. A.V. Shavinskii, *Ocherki po istorii tekhniki zhivopisi i tekhnologii krasok v Drevnei Rusi* (Moscow–Leningrad, 1935).

54. P. Savvaitov, *Opisanie starinnykh russkikh utvarei, odezh, oruzhiia, ratnykh dospekhov i konskogo pribora* (St. Petersburg, 1896), p. 75.

55. N.I. Gagen-Torn, "Magicheskoe znachenie volos i golovnogo ubora v svadebnykh obriadakh Vostochnoi Evropy," *Sovetskaia etnografiia*, 1983, nos. 5–6, p. 77.

56. M.A. Saburova, "Zhenskii golovnoi ubor u slavian," *Sovetskaia arkheologiia*, 1974, no. 2, pp. 91–92; Saburova, "Sherstianye ubory s bakhromoi," *Sovetskaia etnografiia*, 1976, no. 3, pp. 127–30.

57. G.N. Lukina, "Nazvaniia predmetov ukrasheniia v iazyke pamiatnikov drevnei pis'mennosti," *Voprosy slovoobrazovaniia i leksologii drevnerusskogo iazyka* (Moscow, 1974), pp. 146–48.

58. M.G. Rabinovich, "Odezhda russkikh XIII–XVII vv.," *Drevniaia odezhda narodov Vostochnoi Evropy* (Moscow, 1986), pp. 63–112.

59. N.P. Zhurzhalina, "Drevnerusskie priveski-amulety i ikh datirovka," *Sovetskaia arkheologiia*, 1961, no. 2, pp. 122–23; A.V. Uspenskaia, "Nagrudnye i poiasnye ukrasheniia," *Trudy Gosudarstvennogo Istoricheskogo muzeia*, no. 43, pp. 88–89.

60. L.I. Iakunina, "Novgorodskaia obuv' XII–XIV vv.," *Kratkie soobsheniia Instituta istorii material'noi kul'tury*, no. 17 (1947); I. Vakhros, *Naimenovaniia obuvi v russkom iazyke* (Helsinki, 1959), pp. 25–31.

Notes to Chapter 2

1. For background on this period of Russian history, see Robert O. Crummey, *The Formation of Muscovy, 1304–1613* (New York, 1987), and N.L. Pushkareva, *Zhenshchiny Rossii i Evropy na porogu Novogo vremeni* (Moscow, 1996).

2. For more information on women's participation in behind-the-scenes political activity, see Nancy Shields Kollmann, *Kinship and Politics: The Making of the Muscovite Political System, 1345–1547* (Stanford, 1987); and Robert O. Crummey, *Aristocrats and Servitors: The Boyar Elite in Russia, 1613–1689* (Princeton, 1983).

3. Pushkareva, *Zhenshchiny drevnei Rusi*, pp. 62–70; E. Tseretelli, *Elena*

Ivanovna, velikaia kniaginia litovskaia, russkaia, koroleva pol'skaia (St. Petersburg, 1898); Ia.S. Lur'e, "Elena Ivanovna, koroleva pol'skaia i velikaia kniaginia litovskaia kak pisatel'-publitsist," *Canadian–American Slavic Studies*, vol. 13, no. 3 (1979), pp. 111–20.

4. M.N. Tikhomirov, "Zapiski o regenstve Eleny Glinskoi i boiarskom pravlenii 1533–1547," Istoricheskie zapiski, vol. 46 (1954), pp. 248–88; I.I. Smirnov, *Ocherki politicheskoi istorii russkogo gosudarstva 30–50–kh gg. XVI v.* (Moscow-Leningrad, 1958); and H. Rüss, "Elena Vasyl'evna Glinskaya," *Jahrbücher für Geschichte Osteuropas*, vol. 19 (1976), pp. 481–98.

5. V. Beneshevich, "Agrafena Cheliadnina," *Russkii biograficheskii slovar'* (St. Petersburg, 1905), pp. 132–33.

6. For more information on witchcraft accusations in Muscovy, see Valerie A. Kivelson, "Through the Prism of Witchcraft: Gender and Social Change in Seventeenth-Century Muscovy," in Clements, Engel, and Worobec, eds., *Russia's Women*, pp. 74–94; Russell Zguta, "The Ordeal of Water (Swimming of Witches) in the East Slavic World," *Slavic Review*, vol 36 (1977), pp. 220–30; Zguta, "Witchcraft Trials in Seventeenth-Century Russia," *American Historical Review*, vol. 82 (1977), pp. 1187–207; Zguta, "Witchcraft and Medicine in Pre-Petrine Russia," *Russian Review*, vol. 37 (1978), pp. 438–48.

7. M.N. Tikhomirov, *Rossiia v XVI stoletii* (Moscow, 1962), pp. 105–290; R.G. Skrynnikov, *Ivan Groznyi* (Moscow, 1975), pp. 24–29; S.O. Shmidt, *Stanovlenie rossiiskogo samoderzhavstva* (Moscow, 1973), pp. 78–84, 103–6; *Polnoe sobranie russkikh letopisei*, vol. 13, p. 456; vol. 4, p. 296; vol. 6, p. 30.

8. A.A. Zimin and A.L. Khoroshkevich, *Rossiia vremen Ivana Groznogo* (Moscow, 1982), pp. 100–101; Skrynnikov, *Ivan Groznyi*, pp. 50–52, 148–49; S. Gorskii, *Zheny Ioanna Groznogo* (Moscow, 1912; reprint: Vladikavkaz, 1992).

9. Skrynnikov, *Ivan Groznyi*, p. 51; Shmidt, *Stanovlenie rossiiskogo samoderzhavstva*, pp. 229–39; Shmidt, *Rossiia posle oprichniny* (Leningrad, 1975), pp. 99–108. For a reliable biography of Ivan IV in English, see S.F. Platonov, *Ivan the Terrible*, ed. and trans. Joseph L. Wieczynski (Gulf Breeze, 1986). For more information on Ivan IV's marriages, see Daniel Kaiser, "Symbol and Ritual in the Marriages of Ivan IV," *Russian History*, vol. 14 (1982), pp. 247–62.

10. D.L. Mordovtsev, *Zamechatel'nye istoricheskie zhenshchiny na Rusi*, vol. 1: *Russkie zhenshchiny do Petra* (St. Petersburg, 1874).

11. For more information on how Irina Godunova and other tsaritsas dealt with their political vulnerability as a result of barrenness, see Isolde Thyret, "'Blessed Is the Tsaritsa's Womb': The Myth of Miraculous Birth and Royal Motherhood in Muscovite Russia," *Russian Review*, vol. 53, no. 4 (1994), pp. 479–96.

12. Skrynnikov, *Rossiia posle oprichniny*, pp. 99–101; Skrynnikov, *Boris Godunov* (Moscow, 1978); Skrynnikov, *Rossiia nakanune "Smutnogo vremeni"* (Moscow, 1980), pp. 74–86; S.D. Sheremet'ev, *Tsarevna Feodosiia Fedorovna (1592–1594)* (St. Petersburg, 1902).

13. N. Tikhonravov, "Boiarynia Morozova," *Russkii vestnik*, vol. 59, no. 9 (1865), pp. 5–36; N.S. Danilova, ed., *Povest' o boiaryne Morozovoi* (Moscow, 1991); I.S. Lukash, "Boiarynia Morozova," *Rodina*, 1990, no. 9, pp. 78–87.

14. P.P. Smirnov, E.V. Chistiakova, eds., *Alena Arzamasskaia-Temnikovskaia* (Saransk, 1986).

15. For more information on the *terem* and the image of women in Muscovy, see Nancy Shields Kollmann, "The Seclusion of Elite Muscovite Women," *Russian History*, vol. 10, pt. 2 (1983), pp. 170–87; L.R. Lewitter, "Women, Sainthood, and Marriage in Muscovy," *Journal of Russian Studies*, vol. 37 (1979), pp. 3–11;

Joan D. Grossman, "Feminine Images in Old Russian Literature and Art," *California Slavic Studies*, vol. 11 (1980), pp. 33–70.

16. Lindsey Hughes, "Sophia Alekseyevna and the Moscow Rebellion of 1682," *Slavonic and East European Review*, vol. 63, no. 4 (1985), pp. 518–39; Hughes, *Sophia, Regent of Russia, 1657–1704* (New Haven, 1990); N. Kostomarov, *Russkaia istoriia v zhizneopisaniiakh ee glavneishikh deiatelei* (St. Petersburg, 1886), vol. 2, pp. 475–517; E.F. Shmurlo, "Padenie tsarevny Sof'i," *Zhurnal ministerstva narodnogo prosveshcheniia*, 1896, no. 1, pp. 38–95; A. Ikonnikova, *Tsaritsy i tsarevny iz doma Romanovykh* (Kiev, 1914; repr.: Moscow, 1990).

17. For an English translation, see Carolyn Johnston Pouncy, ed. and trans., *The Domostroi: Rules for Russian Households in the Time of Ivan the Terrible* (Ithaca, 1994).

18. On dwellings in the sixteenth and seventeenth century, see S. Shambinago, "Drevnerusskoe zhilishche po bylinam," *Iubileinyi sbornik v chest' V.F. Millera* (Moscow, 1900); M.A. Il'in, "Arkhitektura," *Ocherki russkoi kul'tury XVI v.*, pt. 2 (Moscow, 1979), pp. 170–208.

19. *Domostroi blagoveshchenskogo popa Sil'vestra* (Moscow, 1849).

20. On children in Muscovite families, see M.G. Rabinovich, *Ocherki etnografii russkogo feodal'nogo goroda* (Moscow, 1978), pp. 193–97.

21. A. Olearii [Olearius], *Opisanie puteshestviia v Moskoviiu i cherez Moskoviiu v Persiiu i obratno* (St. Petersburg, 1906), pp. 201–2. For an English translation of Olearius's travel account, see Adam Olearius, *The Travels of Olearius in Seventeenth-Century Russia*, ed. and trans. Samuel H. Baron (Stanford, 1967).

22. A.K. Leont'ev, "Nravy i obychai," *Ocherki russkoi kul'tury XVI v.*, pt. 1 (Moscow, 1977), pp. 33–76.

23. On *terem* seclusion and the historical debates concerning it, see Pushkareva, *Zheshchiny drevnei Rusi*, pp. 177–209.

24. Levin, *Sex and Society*, pp. 136–59.

25. V.B. Kobrin, "Opyt izucheniia semeinoi genealogii," *Vspomogatel'nye istoricheskie distsipliny*, vol. 14 (1983), pp. 50–60.

26. Rabinovich, *Ocherki etnografii*, pp. 153–60.

27. M.K. Tsaturova, *Russkoe semeinoe pravo XVI–XVII vv.* (Moscow, 1991), pp. 6–20. For an English translation of the Law Code of 1649, see Richard Hellie, ed. and trans., *The Muscovite Law Code (Ulozhenie) of 1649* (Irvine, 1988).

28. *Chteniia v Obshchestve istorii i drevnostei rossiiskikh*, 1881, pt. 2, Appendix 26, p. 81.

29. I.E. Zabelin, *Domashnii byt russkogo naroda v XVI i XVII stoletiiakh*, vols. 1–2 (Moscow, 1862–69), pp. 454–56.

30. G.O. Kotoshikhin, *Rossiia v tsarstvovanie Alekseia Mikhailovicha* (St. Petersburg, 1884).

31. For more information on wedding customs in this period, see Kaiser, "Symbol and Ritual." For an English translation of one set of instructions for weddings, see Pouncy, *The Domostroi*, pp. 204–39.

32. S. Gerberstein [Herberstein], *Zapiski o moskovitskikh delakh* (St. Petersburg, 1908). For an English translation of Herberstein's text, see Sigismund, Freiherr von Herberstein, *Description of Moscow and Muscovy, 1557*, ed. and trans. J.B.C. Grundy (New York, 1969).

33. *Moskovskaia delovaia i bytovaia pis'mennost' XVII v.* (Moscow, 1968), pp. 38–41.

34. For more information on the women of the provincial gentry, see Valerie A. Kivelson, *Autocracy in the Provinces: The Russian Gentry and Political Culture in the Seventeenth Century* (Stanford, 1997).

35. Giles Fletcher, *Of the Rus Commonwealth*, ed. Albert J. Schmidt (Ithaca, 1966), p. 144; Dzh. Fletcher, *O gosudarstve russkom* (St. Petersburg, 1906). For further information on foreign travelers and their reports, see Lloyd E. Berry and Robert O. Crummey, eds., *Rude and Barbarous Kingdom: Russia in the Accounts of Sixteenth-Century English Voyagers* (Madison, 1968).

36. Rabinovich, *Ocherki etnografii*, pp. 126–31. For more information on urban popular culture in this period, see Arthur Voyce, *Moscow and the Roots of Russian Culture* (Norman, 1964), pp. 61–94.

37. For more information on *skomorokhi*, see Russell Zguta, *Russian Minstrels* (Philadelphia, 1978).

38. A.K. Leont'ev, "Byt i nravy," *Ocherki russkoi kul'tury XVII v.*, pt. 1 (Moscow, 1979), pp. 5–29.

39. M.G. Rabinovich, *Ocherki material'noi kul'tury russkogo feodal'nogo goroda* (Moscow, 1988), pp. 213–34.

40. I.E. Zabelin, *Zhenshchina v dopetrovskom obshchestve* (St. Petersburg, 1901).

41. *Gramotki XVII–nachala XVIII vv.* (Moscow, 1969), nos. 44, 247, 249, 252, 255, 258, 268–71, 277–78, 280, 281, 284.

42. Gerbershtein, *Zapiski o moskovitskikh delakh*, pp. 73–74.

43. M.N. Rudnev, "Tserkovnoe sudoproizvodstvo po delam rastorzheniia braka," *Khristianskoe chtenie*, 1902, no. 1, pp. 97–125. For more information on wife beating, see Levin, *Sex and Society*, 237–43.

44. *Kormchaia kniga. Perepechatano s izdaniia 1653 g.*, (n.p., n.d.), chap. 1, nos. 7, 10, 11.

45. Carsten Goehrke, "Die Witwe im Alten Russland," *Forschungen zur osteuropäischen Geschichte*, vol. 38 (1986), pp. 64–96.

46. M.G. Rabinovich, "Russkaia gorodskaia sem'ia v nachale XVIII v.," *Sovetskaia etnografiia*, 1978, no. 5, pp. 96–108; N.I. Balandin and V.P. Gerbiakov, "Perepisnaia landsratskaia kniga Ustiuzhny Zheleznopol'skoi 1713 g.," in *Agrarnaia istoriia Evropeiskogo Severa* (Vologda, 1970), p. 24.

47. Rabinovich, *Ocherki etnografii*, pp. 254–68.

48. D.N. Anuchin, *Sani, lad'ia i koni kak prinadlezhnost' pokhoronnogo obriada* (Moscow, 1890).

49. Fletcher, *Of the Rus Commonwealth*, p. 143; see also Samuel Collins, *The Present State of Russia, in a Letter to a Friend at London* (London, 1671), pp. 21–22.

50. K.V. Chistov, "Russkaia prichet'," *Prichitaniia. Biblioteka poeta. Bol'shaia seriia* (Leningrad, 1960), pp. 13, 92.

51. V.V. Girshberg, "Materialy dlia svoda nadpisei na kamennykh plitakh Moskvy," *Numizmatika i epigrafika*, vol. 1 (1960), pp. 3–77.

52. "Sudebnik 1550 g.," "Stoglav 1551 g.," "Sobornoe ulozhenie 1649 g.," *Rossiiskoe zakonodatel'stvo X–XX vv.* (Moscow, 1986), vol. 2, pp. 97–129, 253–402.

53. Tsaturova, *Russkoe semeinoe pravo*, pp. 36–46.

54. On the legalities of the dowry, see D.I. Azarevich, "Semeinye i imushchestvennye otnosheniia po russkomu pravu," *Zhurnal grazhdanskogo i ugolovnogo prava*, 1883, no. 4.

55. N.P. Zagoskin, *Ocherki organizatsii i proiskhozhdeniia sluzhilogo sosloviia dopetrovskoi Rusi* (Kiev, 1875).

56. I.A. Isaev, "Grazhdanskoe i semeinoe pravo," in V.S. Nersesiants, ed., *Razvitie russkogo prava v XV–pervoi polovine XVII v.*, (Moscow, 1986), pp. 134–37.

57. On inheritance law, see P.P. Tsitovich, *Iskhodnye momenty v istorii russkogo prava nasledovaniia* (St. Petersburg, 1870); I.D. Beliaev, *O nasledstve bez zaveshchaniia* (Moscow, 1858).

58. *Rossiiskoe zakonodatel'stvo X–XX vv.*, vol. 2 (Moscow, 1985).

59. For more on widows' pensions, see Tsaturova, *Russkoe semeinoe pravo*, pp. 65–76.

60. For more information on women's property rights in the Muscovite period, see Sandra Levy, "Women and the Control of Property in Sixteenth-Century Muscovy," *Russian History*, vol. 10, pt. 2 (1983), pp. 201–12; Ann M. Kleimola, "'In Accordance with the Canons of the Holy Apostles': Muscovite Dowries and Women's Property Rights," *Russian Review*, vol. 51, no. 2 (1992), pp. 204–29; and Valerie A. Kivelson, "The Effects of Partible Inheritance: Gentry Families and the State in Muscovy," *Russian Review*, vol. 53, no. 2 (1994), pp. 197–212.

61. On women's rights in civil and criminal law, see A. Bogdanovskii, *Razvitie poniatiia o prestuplenii i nakazanii v russkom prave do Petra Velikogo* (St. Petersburg, 1857); A. Sukhov, "Istoricheskaia kharakteristika drevnerusskogo ugolovnogo prava do XVII stoletiia," *Iuridicheskii vestnik*, 1877, nos. 5–6 (May–June), pp. 37–46.

62. For more information, see Nancy Shields Kollmann, "Women's Honor in Early Modern Russia," in Clements, Engel, and Worobec, eds., *Russia's Women*, pp. 60–73.

63. Petrei de Erlezunda II, *Istoriia o velikom kniazhestve Moskovskom, pro-iskhozhdenii velikikh russkikh liudei, nedavnikh smutakh i o moskovskikh zakonakh, nravakh, pravlenii, vere i obriadakh* (Moscow, 1867), p. 8.

64. Olearii, *Opisanie puteshestviia v Moskoviiu*, p. 210.

65. I.G. Korb, *Dnevnik sekretaria posol'stva ot imperatora Leopol'da I k tsariu Petru I v 1693–1699 gg.* (Moscow, 1868), p. 285.

66. Collins, *The Present State of Russia*, pp. 69–70; Kollinz [Collins], S., *Nyneshnee sostoianie Rossii, izlozhennoe v pis'me k drugu, zhivushchemu v Londone* (Moscow, 1846), p. 21.

67. Scholars have mixed opinions on this etymology. I.I. Sreznevskii identifies two different roots, cf. *Slovar' drevnerusskogo iazyka*, vol. 1 (Moscow, 1989), pp. 119–23. I.E. Zabelin regards the two words as genetically related, cf. *Domashnii byt russkikh tsarits XVI–XVII vv.* (Moscow, 1901), p. 467.

68. G.A. Shleissinger [Schleusinger], "Polnoe opisanie Rossii," *Voprosy istorii*, 1970, no. 1, p. 115.

69. Olearii, *Opisanie puteshestviia v Moskoviiu* p. 211.

70. Collins, *The Present State of Russia*, p. 69; Kollinz, *Nyneshnee sostoianie Rossii*, p. 23.

71. V.F. Gruzdev, *Russkie rukopisnye lechebniki* (Leningrad, 1946), p. 40; Zabelin, *Domashnyi byt russkikh tsarits*, pp. 512–13.

72. Zabelin, *Domashnii byt russkikh tsarits*, p. 467.

73. I. David, "Sovremennoe sostoianie Velikoi Rossii," *Voprosy istorii*, 1968, no. 4, p. 14.

74. Fletcher, *Of the Rus Commonwealth*, p. 153; Dzh. Fletcher, *O gosudarstve russkom* (St. Petersburg, 1906), p. 126.

75. S.M. Soloviev, *Istoriia Rossii s drevneishikh vremen*, vol. 6 (St. Petersburg, n.d.), p. 323.

76. On women's clothing, see N.I. Kostomarov, *Ocherki domashnei zhizni i nravov velikorusskogo naroda v XVI i XVII stoletiiakh* (St. Petersburg, 1906), pp. 52–67; Zabelin, *Domashnii byt russkikh tsarits*, pp. 462–535; Rabinovich, *Ocherki material'noi kul'tury*, pp. 125–213.

77. *Starinnye akty, sluzhashchie preimushchestvenno dopolneniem k opisaniu g. Shui i ego okrestnostei* (Moscow, 1853), pp. 185–88 (no. 103, dating to 1663).

78. *Russkaia demokratichnaia satira XVIII* (Leningrad, 1954), p. 125.

79. Zabelin, *Domashnii byt*, p. 653.

80. On jewelry styles of this period, see P.I. Utkin, *Russkie iuvelirnye ukrasheniia* (Moscow, 1970), pp. 55–80.

81. N.I. Kostomarov, *Domashniaia zhizn' i nravy velikorusskogo naroda* (Moscow, 1993), p. 65.

Notes to Chapter 3

1. For more information on Russia in the eighteenth century, see Evgenii Anisimov, *The Reforms of Peter the Great: Progress through Coercion in Russia* (Armonk, 1993); Paul Dukes, *The Making of Russian Absolutism, 1613–1801*, 2d ed. (London, 1990); and Isabel de Madariaga, *Russia in the Age of Catherine the Great* (New Haven, 1981).

2. V. Korsakova, "Natal'ia Kirillovna Naryshkina," *Russkii biograficheskii slovar'* (St. Petersburg, 1914), pp. 121–35; D.L. Mordovtsev, *Russkie istoricheskie zhenshchiny*, vol. 1, bk. 2 (St. Petersburg, 1874).

3. I.A. Shliapkin, *Tsarevna Natal'ia Alekseevna i teatr ee vremeni* (St. Petersburg, 1898).

4. *Zhitie i slavnye dela Petra Velikogo. Soch. Feodozi, v russkom s grecheskogo perevoda* (St. Petersburg, 1774), pp. 153–54.

5. V.I. Semevskii, *Tsaritsa Praskov'ia* (St. Petersburg, 1883); *Pis'ma i bumagi Petra Velikogo*, vol. 7 (Petrograd, 1918), no. 1.

6. G.V. Esipov, "Osvobozhdenie tsaritsy Evdokii Fedorovny," *Russkii vestnik*, vol. 28 (1860), pp. 182–90; N.G. Ustrialov, *Istoriia tsarstvovaniia Petra Velikogo*, vol. 6, appendix, (St. Petersburg, 1859).

7. K. Arsen'ev, *Tsarstvovanie Ekateriny I* (St. Petersburg, 1856); "Pis'ma k tsaritse Ekaterine Alekseevne," *Russkii arkhiv*, 1889, no. 3, pp. 392–96.

8. For more information on Catherine I, see Philip Longworth, *The Three Empresses: Catherine I, Anne and Elizabeth of Russia* (London, 1972).

9. "Bedstviia i dobrodeteli Natal'i Borisovny Dolgorukoi," *Russkii vestnik*, 1815, bk. 1; S.N. Kaidash, *Sil'nee bedstviia zemnogo. Rasskazy o zhenshchinakh russkoi istorii* (Moscow, 1883), pp. 61–79.

10. For an English translation of Natalia Dolgorukaia's autobiography, see Charles Townsend, ed. and trans., *Memoirs of Princes Natalija Borisovna Dolgorukaja* (Columbus, 1977).

11. M.M. Shcherbatov, "O povrezhdenii nravov v Rossii," *Russkaia starina*, vol. 2 (1870), p. 40.

12. D.A. Korsakov, *Votsarenie imperatritsy Anny Ioannovny* (Kazan, 1880); N.I. Kostomarov, *Russkaia istoriia v zhizneopisaniiakh ee glavneishikh deiatelei*, vol. 3 (St. Petersburg, 1886); V. Stroev, *Bironovshchina i Kabinet ministrov pri Anne Ioannovne* (St. Petersburg, 1909).

13. For more information on Empress Anna, see Longworth, *The Three Empresses*; Mina Curtiss, *A Forgotten Empress: Anna Ivanovna and Her Era, 1730–1740* (New York, 1974); and E.V. Anisimov, "Anna Ivanovna," *Russian Studies in History*, vol. 32, no. 4 (1994), pp. 8–36, reprinted in A. A. Iskenderov, comp., and Donald J. Raleigh, ed., *The Emperors and Empresses of Russia: Rediscovering the Romanovs* (Armonk, 1996), pp. 37–65.

14. "Tsarstvovanie Ioanna VI Antonovicha. Pravlenie v. kng. Anny. Sb. dokumentov," *Russkii arkhiv*, vol. 2, (1867), pp. 162–86.

15. K. Valishevskii, *Doch' Petra Velikogo* (St. Petersburg, 1882); S.V. Eshevskii,

Ocherk tsarstvovaniia Elizavety Petrovny (Moscow, 1870); and E.V. Anisimov, *Rossiia v seredine XVIII v.* (Moscow, 1988).

16. For more information on Elizabeth's motives for humanitarian reform, see Cyril Bryner, "The Issue of Capital Punishment in the Reign of Elizabeth Petrovna," *Russian Review*, vol. 49, no. 4 (1990), pp. 389–416.

17. For more information on Elizabeth, see Longworth, *The Three Empresses*; Tamara Talbot Rice, *Elizabeth, Empress of Russia* (London, 1970); James F. Brennan, *Enlightened Despotism in Russia: The Reign of Elizabeth, 1741–1762* (New York, 1987); V.P. Naumov, "Elizaveta Petrovna," *Russian Studies in History*, vol. 32, no. 4 (1994), pp. 37–72, reprinted in Iskenderov, comp., and Raleigh, ed., *The Emperors and Empresses of Russia*, pp. 66–100.

18. N.D. Chechulin, *Ekaterina II v bor'be za prestol* (Leningrad, 1924); V.A. Bil'basov, *Istoriia Ekaterina II*, 2 vols., (n.p., 1900); *Zapiski imperatritsy Ekateriny II* (St. Petersburg, 1906); "Memuary Ekateriny II," in N.Ia. Eidel'man, *Iz potaennoi istorii Rossii XVIII–XIX vekov* (Moscow, 1993), pp. 154–80.

19. For more information on Catherine II, see John T. Alexander, *Catherine the Great: Life and Legend* (New York, 1989); Marc Raeff, ed., *Catherine the Great, A Profile* (New York, 1972); Isabel de Madariaga, *Catherine the Great: A Short History* (New Haven, 1990); Aleksandr Borisovich Kamenskii, "Catherine the Great," *Soviet Studies in History*, vol. 30, no. 2 (1991), pp. 30–65, reprinted in Iskenderov, comp., and Raleigh, ed., *The Emperors and Empresses of Russia*, pp. 134–76; Brenda Meehan-Waters, "Catherine the Great and the Problem of Female Rule," *Russian Review*, vol. 34, no. 3 (1975), pp. 293–307; Allen McConnell, "Catherine the Great and the Fine Arts," in Ezra Mendelsohn and Marshall S. Shatz, eds., *Imperial Russia, 1700–1917: State, Society, Opposition (Essays in Honor of Marc Raeff)* (DeKalb, 1988), pp. 37–57. For an English translation of Catherine's memoirs, see *Memoirs of Catherine the Great*, trans. Katharine Anthony (New York, 1927).

20. "Sur la princesse Dachkoff," *Oeuvres complete de Diderot*, vol. 17 (Paris, 1876), pp. 487–90; E.R. Dashkova, "Zapiski," in *Zapiski russkikh zhenshchin XVIII–pervoi poloviny XIX v.*, ed. G.I. Moiseeva (Moscow, 1990), pp. 67–281; L.Ia. Lozinskaia, *Vo glave dvukh akademii* (Moscow, 1978). Dashkova's memoirs have been translated into English: Kyril Fitzlyon, ed. and trans., *Memoirs of the Princess Dashkova* (London, 1958).

21. Catherine Wilmot, *The Russian Journals of Martha and Catherine Wilmot*, ed. The Marchioness of Londonderry and H.M. Hyde (London, 1934), p. 201.

22. For more information about Catherine Dashkova, see A. Woronzoff-Dashkoff, "Princess E.R. Dashkova's Moscow Library," *Slavonic and East European Review*, vol. 72, no. 1 (1994), pp. 60–71.

23. N.A. Elizarova, *Teatry Sheremetevykh* (Moscow, 1944).

24. For more information on serf theater, see Priscilla R. Roosevelt, "Emerald Thrones and Living Statues: Theater and Theatricality on the Russian Estate," and Laurence Senelick, "The Erotic Bondage of Serf Theatre," *Russian Review*, vol. 50, no. 1 (1991), pp. 1–34.

25. Collins, *The Present State of Russia*, pp. 8–10, 36, 114; Collins [Kollinz], *Nyneshnee sostoianie Rossii*, p. 3; Ia. Reitenfel's, *Skazaniia sv. gertsogu toskanskomu Koz'me Trebylets o Moskovii* (Moscow, 1905), p. 176; L.N. Semenov, *Ocherki istorii byta i kul'turnoi zhizni Rossii. Pervaia polovina XVIII v.* (Leningrad, 1982), pp. 13–15.

26. M.M. Shcherbatov, *Sochineniia*, vol. 2 (St. Petersburg, 1898), pp. 151–52.

27. On forms of social interaction, see Semenova, *Ocherki*, pp. 161–206; M.G. Rabinovich, "Gorod i gorodskoi obraz zhizni," *Ocherki russkoi kul'tury XVIII v.*, vol. 4 (Moscow, 1990), pp. 252–99.

28. G. Shleissinger, "Polnoe opisanie Rossii," p. 109; I. David, "Sovremennoe sostoianie velikoi Rossii ili Moskovii," *Voprosy istorii*, 1968, no. 4, p. 141.

29. See Semenova, *Ocherki*, pp. 18–19; Rabinovich, "Russkaia gorodskaia sem'ia v nachale XVIII v."

30. Tsaturova, *Russkoe semeinoe pravo*, pp. 6–20.

31. N.A. Minenko, *Russkaia krest'ianskaia sem'ia v Zapadnoi Sibiri (XVIII–pervoi polovine XIX vv.)* (Novosibirsk, 1979), pp. 202–25.

32. M.V. Lomonosov, *Sochineniia* (Moscow–Leningrad, 1961), pp. 467–68.

33. V.A. Aleksandrov, *Sel'skaia obshchina v Rossii XVII–nachala XIX vv.* (Moscow, 1976), pp. 304–95; A.N. Radishchev, *Polnoe sobranie sochinenii*, vol. 1 (Moscow–Leningrad, 1938), p. 373.

34. Lomonosov, *Sochineniia*, p. 468.

35. Tsaturova, *Russkoe semeinoe pravo*, pp. 6–20; Minenko, *Russkaia krest'ianskaia sem'ia*, pp. 209–10.

36. Semenova, *Ocherki*, pp. 62–81.

37. Rabinovich, *Gorod*, p. 294.

38. Minenko, *Russkaia krest'ianskaia sem'ia*, p. 217–19.

39. *Polnoe sobranie zakonov Rossiiskoi imperii* [henceforth *PSZ*], vol. 3, no. 1612; vol. 5, no. 3006; Semenova, *Ocherki*, pp. 22–23.

40. Tsaturova, *Russkoe semeinoe pravo*, pp. 29–32.

41. V.N. Tatishchev, *Istoriia rossiiskaia*, vol. 1 (Moscow–Leningrad, 1962), p. 87.

42. I.N. Boltin, *Primechaniia na istoriiu drevniaia i nyneshniaia g-na Leklerka*, vol. 1 (St. Petersburg, 1788), pp. 472–73.

43. Ibid., pp. 473–74.

44. Semenova, *Ocherki*, p. 85–87.

45. V. Mikhnevich, *Russkaia zhenshchina XVIII stoletiia. Istoricheskie etiudy* (St. Petersburg, 1895), pp. 94–120.

46. For more information on girls' education in eighteenth-century Russia, see Carol Nash, "Students and Rubles: The Society for the Education of Noble Girls as a Charitable Institution," in R.P. Bartlett, A.G. Cross, and Karen Rasmussen, eds., *Russia and the World of the Eighteenth Century*, (Columbus, 1988), pp. 258–27; Isabel de Madariaga, "The Foundation of the Russian Educational System by Catherine the Great," *Slavonic and East European Review*, vol. 57, no. 3 (1979), pp. 369–95; and N.L. Pushkareva, *Chastnaia zhizn' zhenshchiny v doindustrial'noi Rossii (X–nachalo XIX vv.)* (Moscow, 1997).

47. *Pis'ma russkikh pisatelei XVIII v.* (Leningrad, 1980), pp. 45, 360. For more information on images of women in literature of this period, see Joe Andrew, "Radical Sentimentalism or Sentimental Radicalism: A Feminist Approach to Eighteenth-Century Russian Literature," in Catriona Kelly, Michael Makin, and David Shepperd, eds., *Discontinuous Discourses in Modern Russian Literature*, (Hampshire, 1989), pp. 136–56.

48. M.V. Danilov, "Zapiski," *Russkii arkhiv*, 1883, bk. 2, p. 34.

49. V.N. Tatishchev, "Dukhovnaia," in Tatishchev, *Izbrannye proizvedeniia* (Leningrad, 1979), p. 139.

50. A.T. Bolotov, *Zhizn' i prikliucheniia Andreia Bolotova, opisannye im samim* (St. Petersburg, 1871), pp. 554–55; G.P. Derzhavin, *Zapiski* (Moscow, 1860), p. 128.

51. N.I. Shimko, *Novye dannye k biografii Antiokha Dmitrievicha Kantemira* (St. Petersburg, 1891), pp. 53–54.

52. S.S. Shashkov, *Istoricheskie sud'by zhenshchiny, detoubiistvo i prostitutsiia. Istoriia russkoi zhenshchiny* (St. Petersburg, 1872), pp. 811–24; *Russkii byt po vospominaniiam sovremennikov XVIII v.*, pt. 1 (Moscow, 1914), p. 73–146.

53. N. Chechulin, *Russkoe provintsial'noe obshchestvo vo vtoroi polovine XVIII v.* (St. Petersburg, 1889). For more information on Russian aristocratic marriages, as glimpsed through the eyes of English women visitors, see Judith Vowles, "Marriage à la russe," in Jane T. Costlow, Stephanie Sandler, and Judith Vowles, eds., *Sexuality and the Body in Russian Culture* (Stanford, 1993), pp. 53–72.

54. A.N. Radishchev, *Polnoe sobranie sochinenii,* vol. 1 (Moscow–Leningrad, 1938), pp. 36–37.

55. Minenko, *Russkaia krest'ianskaia sem'ia,* pp. 123–39.

56. D.N. Belikov, *Pervye russkie krest'iane-nasel'niki Tomskogo kraia* (Tomsk, 1898), pp. 107–8.

57. Minenko, *Russkaia krest'ianskaia sem'ia,* pp. 123–39.

58. G.N. Potanin, "Iugo-zapadnaia chast' Tomskoi gubernii v etnograficheskom otnoshenii," *Etnograficheskii sbornik,* no. 4 (St. Petersburg, 1864), p. 54.

59. Minenko, *Russkaia krest'ianskaia sem'ia,* p. 138.

60. From a letter found in the Tobolsk branch of the State Archive of Tiumen Oblast, F. 156, d. 72 (1754), f. 23.

61. V.I. Semevskii, "Domashnii byt i prava krest'ian XVIII v.," *Ustoi,* 1882, no. 2, pp. 78–84.

62. N.A. Minenko, "Obshchina i russkaia krest'ianskaia sem'ia v Iugo-Zapadnoi Sibiri (XVII–pervaia polovina XIX v.)," in *Krest'ianskaia obshchina v Sibiri XVII–nachala XX vv.* (Novosibirsk, 1977), p. 116.

63. Rabinovich, *Russkaia gorodskaia sem'ia,* p. 109.

64. "Pis'mo M.V. Lomonosova I.I. Shavalovu," in Lomonosov, *Sochineniia* (Moscow–Leningrad, 1961), p. 471.

65. Bolotov, *Zhizn' i prikliucheniia Andreia Bolotova,* pp. 644–45.

66. G.P. Derzhavin, *Zapiski* (Moscow, 1860), pp. 6–11; S.T. Aksakov, *Semeinaia khronika* (St. Petersburg, 1856); D.I. Fonvizin, *Chistoserdechnoe priznanie v delakh moikh i pomyshleniiakh* (St. Petersburg, 1830).

67. For more information on conceptions of child rearing, see Carol S. Nash, "Educating New Mothers: Women and the Enlightenment in Russia," *History of Education Quarterly,* vol. 21, no. 3 (1981), pp. 301–16.

68. Mikhnevich, *Russkaia zhenshchina,* p. 802; Danilov, "Zapiski," p. 128.

69. G. Sederberg, *Zametki o religii i nravakh russkogo naroda 1709–1718* (Moscow, 1873), p. 22; Reikhtenfel's, *Skazaniia sv. gertsogu toskanskomu,* p. 177.

70. Minenko, *Russkaia krest'ianskaia sem'ia,* p. 134.

71. For more information, see Tsaturova, *Russkoe semeinoe pravo,* pp. 77–89.

72. M.M. Shcherbatov, *O povrezhdenii nravov v Rossii* (St. Petersburg, 1906), p. 66; Zagorovskii, *O razvode po russkomu pravu,* pp. 199–200.

73. *PSZ,* vol. 2, nos. 702, 803.

74. *PSZ,* vol. 5, no. 2789.

75. *PSZ,* vol. 8, no. 5717. For more information on inheritance law in the first third of the eighteenth century, see Lee Farrow, "State Ambitions and Noble Traditions: A New Look at Peter the Great's Law of Single Inheritance," *Russian Review,* vol. 55, no. 3 (1996), pp. 430–47.

76. *Pisanie dokumentov i del, khraniashchikhsia v arkhive Sviateishego pravitel'stvennogo Sinoda,* vol. 9 (St. Petersburg, 1903), no. 519; vol. 21, no. 157; vol. 29, no. 526.

77. *PSZ,* vol. 5, no. 2952.

78. *PSZ,* vol. 13, no. 10111.

79. For more information, see M.K. Tsaturova, *Russkoe semeinoe pravo,* pp. 20–45.

80. "Zapiski V.A. Nashchekina," *Russkii arkhiv,* 1883, bk. 4, p. 287.

81. *PSZ*, vol. 4, no. 1832; vol. 6, no. 3485; vol. 10, no. 7697; vol. 11, no. 8107; vol. 13, nos. 9726, 9950; see also Tsaturova, *Russkoe semeinoe pravo*, p. 71.

82. *PSZ*, vol. 6, no. 3485, chap. 4, art. 8.

83. *PSZ*, vol. 11, no. 8107; vol. 13, no. 10005.

84. *PSZ*, vol. 15, no. 11278.

85. V.A. Aleksandrov, "Semeino-imushchestvennye otnosheniia po obychnomu pravu v russkoi krepostnoi derevne XVIII–nachala XIX vv.," *Istoriia SSSR*, 1979, no. 5, p. 48.

86. For further information, see Semenova, *Ocherki istorii byta i kul'turnoi zhizni Rossii*, p. 45.

87. A.A. Zav'ialov, "K voprosu o brake i brachnom razvode," *Strannik*, 1892, no. 3, p. 453.

88. V.O. Mikhnevich, *Russkaia zhenshchina XVIII stoletiia* (Kiev, 1895; repr.: Moscow, 1990), pp. 224–32.

89. *PSZ*, vol. 5, no. 3013; O.F. Lange, *O pravakh sobstvennosti suprugov po drevnerusskomu pravu* (St. Petersburg, 1886), p. 79.

90. Minenko, *Russkaia krest'ianskaia sem'ia*, p. 170.

91. Ibid., p. 166.

92. A. Efimenko, *Trudovoe nachalo v narodnom obychnom prave*, no. 1 (Moscow, 1884), p. 153; Minenko, *Russkaia krest'ianskaia sem'ia*, pp. 160–62.

93. *PSZ*, vol. 5, no. 3013.

94. Aleksandrov, "Semeino-imushchestvennye otnosheniia," pp. 41–45.

95. Minenko, *Russkaia krest'ianskaia sem'ia*, p. 166.

96. For further information, see K.A. Nevolin, *Istoriia rossiiskikh grazhdanskikh zakonov* (St. Petersburg, 1857), pp. 95–99.

97. M.F. Vladimirskii-Budanov, *Obzor istorii russkogo prava* (Kiev, 1907), p. 655.

98. *PSZ*, vol. 12, no. 8601.

99. Vladimirskii-Budanov, *Obzor*, p. 376.

100. *PSZ*, vol. 3, no. 1135.

101. Semenova, *Ocherki istorii byta*, p. 62.

102. Vladimir-Budanov, *Obzor*, p. 377; *PSZ*, vol. 5, nos. 2856, 2953.

103. *PSZ*, vol. 4, no. 1771.

104. I.G. [J.G.] Korb, *Dnevnik sekretaria posol'stva ot imperatora Leopol'da I k tsariu Petru I v 1698–1699 gg.* (Moscow, 1868), p. 235.

105. B.I. Kurakin, "Zhizn' kniazia Borisa Ivanovicha Kurakina im samim opisannaia," *Arkhiv kniazia F.A. Kurakina* (St. Petersburg, 1899), bk. 1, p. 257.

106. F. Veber, "Byt Moskvy 1716 g.," *Russkii arkhiv*, 1872, no. 7, p. 101; Friedrich Wilhelm von Bergholz, *Dnevnik kammer-iunkera Berkhgoltza, vedennyi im v Rossii v tsarstvovanie Petra Velikogo, s 1721-go po 1725-i god* (Moscow, 1857), p. 80.

107. *Trudoliubivaia pchela*, 1759, no. 9 (September), p. 18.

108. *PSZ*, vol. 21, nos. 15556, 15557, 15569.

109. M.N. Mertsalova, *Istoriia kostiuma* (Moscow, 1972), p. 114.

110. T.T. Korshunova, *Kostium v Rossii XVIII–nachala XX vv. Iz sobraniia Gosudarstvennogo Ermitazha* (Leningrad, 1979), p. 114.

111. R.M. Belogorskaia, and L.V. Efimova, "Odezhda," in *Ocherki istorii russkoi kultury XVIII v.*, pt. 1 (Moscow, 1985), p. 354.

112. I.T. Pososhkov, *Kniga o skudosti i bogatstve* (Moscow, 1951), p. 132.

113. *Zritel'*, August, p. 281.

114. *Ruchnoi dorozhnik dlia upotrebleniia po puti mezhdu imperatorskimi stolitsami* (St. Petersburg, 1801), p. 127.

115. Ibid., p. 110.

116. Iu. Iul' [Just Jul], *Zapiski datskogo poslannika pri Petre Velikom* (Moscow, 1900), p. 83.

117. E. Avdeeva, "Starinnaia russkaia odezhda, izmeneniia v nei i mody nashego vremeni," *Otechestvennye zapiski*, vol. 6 (1853), p. 186.

118. Belogorskaia and Efimova, "Odezhda," p. 367.

119. M.I. Antonovskii, *Opisanie vsekh obitaiushchikh v rossiiskom gosudarstve narodov* (St. Petersburg, 1799), pt. 4, p. 13; K. De Bruni, *Puteshestvie cherez Moskoviiu* (Moscow, 1873), pp. 95–96; I.G. Georgi, *Opisanie stolichnogo goroda Sankt-Peterburga* (St. Petersburg, 1794), p. 605.

120. Georgi, *Opisanie stolichnogo goroda*, p. 70.

121. Bergholz, *Dnevnik kammer-iunkera Berkhgoltza*, p. 70.

122. R.A. Nemtsova, "Dobraia i zlaia zhena po narodnym kartinkam, zakliuchaiushchimsia v izvestnom izdanii senatora Rovinskogo," *Izvestiia Obshchestva arkheologii, istorii, i etnografii pri Kazanskom universitete*, vol. 9, no. 3 (Kazan, 1891).

Notes to Chapter 4

1. For background on the period 1800–1917, see David Saunders, *Russia in the Age of Reaction and Reform, 1801–1881* (London, 1992); and Hans Rogger, *Russia in the Age of Modernisation and Revolution, 1881–1917* (London, 1983).

2. Mikhnevich, *Russkaia zhenshchina XVIII stoletiia*, pp. 318–51.

3. "Maria Fedorovna," *Entsiklopedicheskii slovar' F.A. Brokgauz i A. Efron*, vol. 9 (St. Petersburg, 1901), p. 211.

4. S. Shuazzel'-Guff'e [Choiseul-Gouffier, Sophie de Tisenhaus], *Istoricheskie memuary ob imperatore Aleksandre i ego dvore* (Moscow, 1912), p. 11.

5. P. Lakrua [Lacroix], *Istoriia zhizni i tsarstvovaniia Nikolaia I, imperatora Vserossiiskogo*, vol. 1, no. 1 (Moscow, 1877–88), p. 60; N.K. Shil'der, *Imperator Nikolai I. Ego zhizn' i tsarstvovanie*, vol. 1 (St. Petersburg, 1903), p. 90–91.

6. A.F. Tiutcheva, *Pri dvore dvukh imperatorov* (Moscow, 1928).

7. L. Zakharova, "Aleksandr II," in A.P. Korelin, ed., *Rossiiskie samoderzhtsy* (Moscow, 1992), p. 159–215. For more information on the imperial wives of the first half of the nineteenth century, see Richard Wortman, "The Russian Empress as Mother," in *The Family in Imperial Russia*, ed. David L. Ransel (Urbana, 1978) pp. 60–74.

8. M. Paleolog [Paléologue], *Roman imperatora. Aleksandr II i kniaginia Iur'evskaia* (Moscow, 1924, repr. 1990), pp. 20–21.

9. P.N. Arliian, "Zhenshchina v istorii blagotvoritel'nosti v Rossii," *Vestnik blagotvoritel'nosti*, 1901, no. 9, pp. 40–53. For more information on women's charitable activities, see Adele Lindenmeyr, "Public Life, Private Virtues: Women in Russian Charity, 1762–1914," *Signs*, vol. 18, no. 3 (1993), pp. 562–91; and Brenda Meehan-Waters, "From Contemplative Practice to Charitable Activity: Russian Women's Religious Communities and the Development of Charitable Work," in Kathleen McCarthy, ed., *Lady Bountiful Revisted: Women Philathropy and Power* (New Brunswick, 1990), pp. 142–57.

10. For more information on noblewomen's religious lives and works, see Brenda Meehan, *Holy Women of Russia: The Lives of Five Orthodox Women Offer Spiritual Guidance for Today* (San Francisco, 1993).

11. "Aleksandra Fedorovna," *Istoricheskaia entsiklopedia*, vol. 1 (Moscow, 1961), p. 373.

12. V.I. Gurko, *Tsar' i tsaritsa* (Paris, n.d.); A.N. Bokhanov, "Nikolai II," *Rossiiskie samoderzhtsy* (Moscow, 1993), pp. 307–85. For more information on

Nicholas II and Empress Alexandra, see Marc Ferro, *Nicholas II: The Last of the Tsars* (Oxford, 1991).

13. S.Iu. Vitte [Witte], *Vospominaniia*, vol. 2 (Moscow, 1960), p. 4; Z.N. Gippius, *Zhivye litsa* (Prague, 1925), p. 208.

14. For more information on Rasputin, see Joseph T. Fuhrmann, *Rasputin: A Life* (New York, 1990).

15. Bokhanov, "Nikolai II," pp. 370–85.

16. S.L. Frank, "Po tu storonu 'pravogo' i 'levogo'," *Novyi mir*, 1990, no. 4, p. 213.

17. "Iz vospominanii P.I. Barteneva o khoziaike moskovskogo salona A.P. Elaginoi," *Russkii arkhiv*, vol. 2, 1877, p. 492; Manuscript Division, Russian State Library, Moscow (RO RGB), F. Elag. No. 13.10; M.Sh. Fainshtein, *Pisatel'nitsy pushkinskoi pory* (Leningrad, 1989), p. 63.

18. Iu.M. Lotman, *Roman A.S. Pushkina "Evgenii Onegin." Kommentarii* (Leningrad, 1980), p. 74.

19. *Russkii arkhiv*, vol. 2 (1877), pp. 491–92; A.F. Tiutcheva, *Pri dvore dvukh imperatorov*. p. 70.

20. *Istoricheskii vestnik*, 1897, nos. 3/4, p. 946.

21. P.A. Viazemskii to A.I. Turgenev, February 6, 1833: RO RGB, F. 167 (Viazemskii, P.A.), d. 20.

22. Fainstein, *Pisatel'nitsy pushkinskoi pory*, p. 63.

23. M. Mazaev, *Druzheskoe literaturnoe obshchestva S.D. Ponomarevoi (Iz istorii literaturnykh kruzhkov v Rossii)* (St. Petersburg, 1892).

24. V.A. Sologub, *Vospominaniia* (Paris, 1887), pp. 103–5; Tiutcheva, *Pri dvore dvukh imperatorov*, pp. 69–70; N.I. Panaev, *Literaturnye vospominaniia* (Leningrad, 1928), p. 143.

25. P.A. Viazemskii, *Sochineniia*, vol. 8 (St. Petersburg, 1883), pp. 493–95.

26. Letter of E.P. Rostopchina to V.F. Odoevskii, July 1848: Russian National Library, St. Petersburg (GNB), F. 539 (Odoevskii, V.F.), op. 2, d. 953, f. 9 ob.

27. For more information, see F.A. Litvina, *Literaturnye vechera epokhi padeniia krepostnogo prava* (Candidate's dissertation, Kazan, 1970).

28. *Literaturnye salony i kruzhki. Pervaia polovina XIX v.* (Moscow–Leningrad, 1930), pp. 410–29.

29. Quoted in N.G. Dumova, *Moskovskie metsenaty* (Moscow, 1992), pp. 74–75.

30. Ibid., pp. 100–103; M.K. Morozova, "Moi vospominaniia," Russian State Archive of Literature and Art, Moscow (RGALI), F. 1956, op. 2, ed. khr. 9.

31. A. Volkov, *Ocherki russkoi literatury kontsa XIX i nachala XX v.* (Moscow, 1955). For more information, see Nina Awsienko, "Zinaida Hippius's Literary Salon in St. Petersburg," *Russian Language Journal*, vol. 26 (1978), pp. 83–89.

32. "Nikitinskie subbotniki," *Nauka i zhizn'*, 1962, no. 10, p. 6.

33. N. Rerikh, "Vospominaniia o Talashkine," in *Talashkino. Izdeliia masterskikh kng. M.K. Tenisheva* (St. Petersburg, 1905).

34. For more information on salon hostesses, see Lina Bernstein, "Women on the Verge of a New Language: Russian Salon Hostesses in the First Half of the Nineteenth Century"; Beth Holmgren, "Stepping Out/Going Under: Women in Russia's Twentieth-Century Salons"; and Alison Hilton, "Domestic Crafts and Creative Freedom: Russian Women's Art," in Goscilo and Holmgren, eds., *Russia, Women, Culture*, pp. 209–46; and Munir Sendich, "Moscow Literary Salons: Thursdays at Karolina Pavlova's," *Die Welt der Slaven*, vol. 17, pt. 2 (1973), pp. 341–57.

35. E.A. Pavliuchenko, *Zhenshchiny v russkom osvoboditel'nom dvizhenii* (Moscow, 1988), pp. 10–23. For more information on the Decembrist revolt, see

Anatole G. Mazour, *The First Russian Revolution, 1825* (Stanford, 1937), and Mazour, *Women in Exile: Wives of the Decembrists* (Tallahassee, 1975).

36. M.N. Volkonskaia, *Zapiski* (St. Petersburg, 1904), p. vii.

37. E.A. Pavliuchenko, *V dobrovol'nom izgnanii. O zhenakh i sestrakh dekabristov* (Moscow, 1980).

38. G.A. Tishkin, *Zhenskii vopros v Rossii v 50–60-e gg. XIX v.* (Leningrad, 1984). A translation of chapter 1 of this work was published in *Russian Studies in History*, vol. 33, no. 2 (1994), pp. 6–62.

39. V.N. Figner, "Zheny dekabristov," in *Polnoe sobranie sochinenii v 7-mi tt.*, vol. 5 (Moscow, 1932), p. 372.

40. For more information on the impact of the "Woman Question," see Carolina de Maedg-Soep, *The Emancipation of Women in Russian Literature and Society* (Ghent, 1970); Barbara Alpern Engel, *Mothers and Daughters: Women of the Intelligentsia in Nineteenth-Century Russia* (Cambridge, 1983); Barbara Heldt [Monter], "*Rassvet* (1859–1862) and the Woman Question," *Slavic Review*, vol. 36, no. 1 (1977), pp. 76–85.

41. Figner, *Polnoe sobranie sochinenii*, vol. 1, p. 168.

42. *Revoliutsionnoe narodnichestvo 70-kh godov XIX v.*, vol. 1 (Moscow, 1964), p. 357.

43. For more information on Breshko-Breshkovskaia, see Jane E. Good and David R. Jones, *Babushka: The Life of the Russian Revolutionary Ekaterina K. Breshko-Breshkovskaia (1844–1934)* (Newtonville, 1991).

44. N. Troitskii, *Bezumstvo khrabrykh* (Moscow, 1978), p. 127.

45. For more information on women revolutionaries of the nineteenth century, see Barbara Alpern Engel and Clifford N. Rosenthal, eds. and trans., *Five Sisters: Women Against the Tsar* (Boston, 1975); Engel, "Women as Revolutionaries: The Case of the Russian Populists," in Renate Bridenthal and Claudia Koonz, eds., *Becoming Visible: Women in European History* (Boston, 1977), pp. 346–69; Engel, "From Separatism to Socialism: Women in the Russian Revolutionary Movement of the 1870's," in Marilyn J. Boxer and Jean H. Quataert, eds., *Socialist Women: European Socialist Feminism in the Nineteenth and Early Twentieth Centuries* (New York, 1978), pp. 346–69; Engel, "Women Revolutionaries: The Personal and the Political," in Tova Yedlin, ed., *Women in Eastern Europe and the Soviet Union* (New York, 1980), pp. 31–43; Amy Knight, "The Fritschi: A Study of Female Radicals in the Russian Populist Movement," *Canadian-American Slavic Studies*, vol. 9, no. 1 (1975), pp. 1–17; Cathy Porter, *Fathers and Daughters: Russian Women in Revolution* (London, 1976); Vera Broido, *Apostles into Terrorists: Women and the Revolutionary Movement in the Russia of Alexander II* (New York, 1977); Jay Bergman, *Vera Zasulich: A Biography* (Stanford, 1993); Richard Stites, *The Women's Liberation Movement in Russia* (Princeton, 1978).

46. Stites, *The Women's Liberation Movement in Russia*, pp. 270–73; B. Savinkov, *Vospominaniia* (Moscow, 1990), pp. 85–136. For more information on women SRs, see Amy Knight, "Female Terrorists in the Russian Socialist Revolutionary Party," *Russian Review*, vol. 38, no. 2 (1979), pp. 139–59.

47. V.I. Lenin, *Polnoe sobranie sochinenii*, vol. 37 (Moscow, 1963), pp. 185–86.

48. For more information on women in the revolutionary movements of the early twentieth century, see Beata Fieseler, "The Making of Russian Female Social Democrats, 1890–1917," *International Review of Social History*, vol. 34 (1989), pp. 1–17; Alfred G. Meyer, "Marxism and the Women's Movement," in Atkinson et al., eds., *Women in Russia*, pp. 85–112; Barbara Evans Clements, "Bolshevik Women: The First Generation," in Yedlin, ed., *Women in Eastern Europe and the*

Soviet Union, pp. 65–74; R.H. McNeal, "Women in the Russian Radical Movement," *Journal of Social History*, vol. 5, no. 2 (1971–72), pp. 143–61; Norma C. Noonan, "Two Solutions to the *Zhenskii Vopros* in Russia and the USSR—Kollontai and Krupskaia: A Comparison," *Women and Politics*, vol. 11, no. 3 (1991), pp. 77–99. There are biographies in English of a few prominent women Bolsheviks; see Robert McNeal, *Bride of the Revolution* (Ann Arbor, 1972), on Nadezhda Krupskaia; Barbara Evans Clements, *Bolshevik Feminist: The Life of Aleksandra Kollontai* (Bloomington, 1979); Beatrice Farnsworth, *Aleksandra Kollontai: Socialism, Feminism and the Bolshevik Revolution* (Stanford, 1980); and R.C. Elwood, *Inessa Armand: Revolutionary and Feminist* (Cambridge, 1992).

49. For more information on Russian feminism and suffragism, see Linda Edmondson, *Feminism in Russia, 1900–1917* (Stanford, 1984); and Stites, *The Women's Liberation Movement.*

50. E.F. Iunge, *Vospominaniia* (Moscow, 1914), pp. 215–16.

51. For more information on women's education, see Ruth A. Dudgeon, "The Forgotten Minority: Women Students in Imperial Russia, 1872–1917," *Russian History*, vol. 9, no. 1 (1982), pp. 1–26; Barbara Alpern Engel, "Women Medical Students in Russia, 1872–1882: Reformers or Rebels?" *Journal of Social History*, vol. 12, no. 3 (1979), pp. 394–415; Ann Hibner Koblitz, "Science, Women, and the Russian Intelligentsia: The Generation of the 1860's," *Isis*, vol. 79 (1988), pp. 208–26; Christine Johanson, *Women's Struggle for Higher Education in Russia, 1855–1900* (Kingston, 1987); Engel, *Mothers and Daughters.*

52. P.Ia. Kochina, *Kovalevskaia. 1850–1891* (Moscow, 1981). For more information on Sofia Kovalevskaia, see Ann Hibner Koblitz, *A Convergence of Lives: Sofia Kovalevskaia—Scientist, Writer, Revolutionary* (Boston, 1983); Koblitz, "Career and Home Life in the 1880s: The Choices of Sofia Kovalevskaia," in Pnina Abir-Am and Dorinda Outram, eds., *Uneasy Careers and Intimate Lives: Women in Science* (New Brunswick, 1987), pp. 172–90; and Beatrice Stillman, "Sofya Kovalevskaya: Growing Up in the Sixties," *Russian Language Journal*, vol. 22 (1974), pp. 276–302.

53. Iu.S. Musabekov, *Iu.V. Lermontova* (Moscow, 1967).

54. S.M. Dionisov, *V.A. Kashevarova-Rudneva* (Moscow, 1965); Mary Schaeffer Conroy, "Women Pharmacists in Russia Before World War I," in Linda Edmondson, ed., *Women and Society in Russia and the Soviet Union* (Cambridge, MA, 1992), pp. 48–76; Conroy, "Women Pharmacists in Nineteenth- and Early Twentieth-Century Russia," *Pharmacy in History*, vol. 29, no. 4 (1987), pp. 155–64. For more information on women doctors, see Jeanette E. Tuve, *The First Russian Women Physicians* (Newtonville, 1984).

55. For more on Elena Blavatskaia, see Marion Meade, *Madame Blavatsky: The Woman Behind the Myth* (New York, 1980).

56. *Ustav zhenskikh uchebnykh zavedenii vedomstva uchrezhdenii imperatritsy Marii* (St. Petersburg, 1855), p. 5.

57. V.G. Belinskii, *Polnoe sobranie sochinenii*, vol. 1 (Moscow, 1953), p. 226.

58. I.V. Kireevskii, *Polnoe sobranie sochinenii*, vol. 1 (St. Petersburg, 1864), p. 119.

59. For an English translation of Nadezhda Durova's book, see these two editions: Mary Zirin, trans., *The Cavalry Maiden* (Bloomington, 1988); or Jon Mersereau and David Lapeza, trans., *The Cavalry Maid: The Memoirs of a Woman Soldier of 1812* (Ann Arbor, 1988).

60. Cited in V.V. Uchenova, "Zabven'iu vopreki," in *Dacha na Petergofskoi doroge. Proza russkikh pisatel'nits pervoi poloviny XIX v.* (Moscow, 1987), p. 9.

61. Fainshtein, *Pisatel'nitsy pushkinskoi pory*, p. 13.

62. V.V. Uchenova, "Liki protesta," in *Tol'ko chas. Proza russkikh pisatel'nits kontsa XIX–nachala XX vv.* (Moscow, 1988), p. 13.

63. For more information on women writers of the Silver Age, see Charlotte Rosenthal, "The Silver Age: Highpoint for Women?" in Edmondson, ed., *Women and Society in Russia and the Soviet Union*, pp. 32–47; and Beth Holmgren, "Gendering the Icon: Marketing Women Writers in Fin-de-Siècle Russia," in Goscilo and Holmgren, eds., *Russia, Women, Culture*, pp. 321–46.

64. For a study of Gippius and her work, see Temira Pachmuss, *Zinaida Hippius: An Intellectual Profile* (Carbondale, 1971).

65. On the life and work of Anna Akhmatova, see Amanda Haight, *Anna Akhmatova: A Poetic Pilgrimage* (New York, 1976).

66. For more information on the life and work of Marina Tsvetaeva, see Simon Karlinsky, *Marina Tsvetaeva: The Woman, Her World and Her Poetry* (Cambridge, 1986); Karlinsky, *Marina Cvetaeva: Her Life and Art* (Berkeley, 1966); Lily Feiler, *Marina Tsvetaeva: The Double Beat of Heaven and Hell* (Durham, 1994); Elaine Feinstein, *A Captive Lion: The Life of Marina Tsvetayeva* (New York, 1987); and Jane Taubman, *A Life Through Poetry: Marina Tsvetaeva's Lyric Diary* (Columbus, 1989).

67. For more information on women authors, see Marina Ledkovsky, Charlotte Rosenthal, and Mary Zirin, eds., *Dictionary of Russian Women Writers* (Westport, 1994); Catriona Kelly, *A History of Russian Women's Writing, 1820–1992* (New York, 1994); Toby W. Clyman and Diana Greene, eds., *Women Writers in Russian Literature* (Westport, 1994); Barbara Heldt, *Terrible Perfection: Women and Russian Literature* (Bloomington, 1987); Gitta Hammarberg, "Flirting with Words: Domestic Albums, 1770–1840," in Goscilo and Holmgren, eds., *Russia, Women, Culture*, pp. 297–320; and Diane M. Nemec Ignashev and Sarah Krive, *Women and Writing in Russia and the USSR: A Bibliography of English-Language Sources* (New York, 1992).

68. A.N. Ostrovskii, *Polnoe sobranie sochinenii*, vol. 12 (Moscow, 1952), p. 213.

69. For more information, see Aleksandr Rafailovich Kugel', "V.F. Komissarzhevskaia," *Russian Studies in History*, vol. 31, no. 3 (1992–93), pp. 87–96.

70. For more information on Goncharova's art and other women artists of this period, see Mary Chamot, *Goncharova: Stage Designs and Painting* (London, 1979); and M.N. Yablonskaya, *Women Artists of Russia's New Age, 1900–1935* (New York, 1990). For reactions to Goncharova's work, see Jane A. Sharp, "Redrawing the Margins of Russian Vanguard Art: Natalia Goncharova's Trial for Pornography in 1910," in Jane T. Costlow, Stephanie Sandler, and Judith Vowles, eds., *Sexuality and the Body in Russian Culture*, (Stanford, 1993), pp. 97–123.

71. N.V. Trukhanova, "Anna Pavlova," in *Vstrechi s proshlym*, no. 1 (Moscow, 1983), p. 107.

72. For more information, see Keith Money, *Anna Pavlova: Her Life and Art* (New York, 1982).

73. A.N. Benua [Benois], "Iz moikh vospominanii," in *Sergei Diagilev i russkoe iskusstvo*, vol. 2 (Moscow, 1982), p. 263. For an examination of another opera star of this period, see Louise McReynolds, " 'The Incomparable' Anastasiia Vial'tseva and the Culture of Personality," in Goscilo and Holmgren, eds., *Russia, Women, Culture*, pp. 273–94.

74. For more information on peasant women of the nineteenth and early twentieth centuries, see Farnsworth and Viola, eds., *Russian Peasant Women*; Christine Worobec, *Peasant Russia: Family and Community in the Post-Emancipation Period* (Princeton, 1991); Marjorie Mandelstam Balzer, ed., *Russian Traditional Culture: Religion, Gender, and Customary Law* (Armonk, 1992); David Ransel, ed., *The Family in Imperial Russia* (Urbana, 1976), especially articles by Andrejs Plakans, Peter

Czap, Stephen Dunn, Antonina Martynova, Samuel Ramer, and Nancy Frieden; Barbara Alpern Engel, *Between the Fields and the City: Women, Work, and Family in Russia, 1861–1914* (Cambridge, 1994); and Christine Worobec, "Victims or Actors? Russian Peasant Women and Patriarchy," in Esther Kingston-Mann and Timothy Mixter, eds., *Peasant Economy, Culture and Politics in European Russia, 1800–1921* (Princeton, 1991), pp. 177–206.

75. Minenko, *Russkaia krest'ianskaia sem'ia*, pp. 107–17.

76. For more information on Russian baths in this period, see Nancy Condee, "The Second Fantasy Mother, or All Baths Are Women's Baths," in Goscilo and Holmgren, eds., *Russia, Women, Culture*, pp. 3–30.

77. L.A. Anokhina, M.N. Shmeleva, *Kul'tura i byt kolkhoznikov Kalininskoi oblasti v proshlom i nastoiashchem* (Moscow, 1964).

78. N.A. Minenko, *Zhivaia starina: budni i prazdniki sibirskoi derevni v XVIII–pervoi polovine XIX v.* (Novosibirsk, 1989), pp. 113–26. For more information on peasant women's cloth making and its economic value, see Judith Pallot, "Women's Domestic Industries in Moscow Province, 1880–1900," in Clements et al., eds., *Russia's Women*, pp. 163–84; and Rose L. Glickman, "Peasant Women and Their Work," in Farnsworth and Viola, eds., *Russian Peasant Women*, pp. 54–72.

79. On calendar rituals and celebratory customs, see Linda J. Ivanits, *Russian Folk Belief* (Armonk, 1989), pp. 5–12. For more information on peasant attitudes toward premarital sex, see Barbara Alpern Engel, "Peasant Morality and Pre-Marital Relations in Late Nineteenth Century Russia," *Journal of Social History*, vol. 23, no. 4 (1990), pp. 695–714; and Christine Worobec, "Temptress or Virgin? The Precarious Sexual Position of Women in Postemancipation Ukrainian Peasant Society," *Slavic Review*, vol. 49, no. 2 (1990), pp. 227–38, reprinted in Farnsworth and Viola, eds., *Russian Peasant Women*, pp. 41–53.

80. M.M. Gromyko, *Mir russkoi derevni* (Moscow, 1991), pp. 73–155.

81. I.P. Sidorov, "Ramenskaia fabrika," *Iuridicheskii vestnik*, 1886, no. 1, pp. 149–50.

82. For more information about the social problems of Russian cities in this period as they related to women, see Engelstein, *The Keys to Happiness*; David L. Ransel, *Mothers of Misery: Child Abandonment in Russia* (Princeton, 1988).

83. A.Kh. Sabinin, *Prostitutsiia: sifilis i venericheskie bolezni* (St. Petersburg, 1905), pp. 258–59; O.P. Budina, "Voprosy truda i byt rabochikh. 1912–1914 gg.," in *Etnograficheskoe izuchenie byta rabochikh* (Moscow, 1968), pp. 151–96; V.Iu. Krupianskaia and N.S. Polishchuk, *Kul'tura i byt rabochikh gornozavodskogo Urala. Konets XIX–nachalo X vv.* (Moscow, 1971).

84. For more information on urban working-class women, see Rose L. Glickman, *Russian Factory Women: Workplace and Society, 1880–1914* (Berkeley, 1984); Barbara Alpern Engel, "Women, Work and Family in the Factories of Rural Russia," *Russian History*, vol. 16 (1989), pp. 223–37; Engel, *Between the Fields and the City*; Robert Eugene Johnson, "Family Relations and the Rural–Urban Nexus: Patterns in the Hinterland of Moscow, 1880–1900," in Ransel, ed., *The Family in Imperial Russia*, pp. 263–79.

85. A.E. Labzina, *Vospominaniia* (St. Petersburg, 1914), p. 34.

86. D. Blagovo, *Rasskazy babushki. Iz vospominanii piat' pokolenii* (St. Petersburg, 1855), p. 439. For more information on child rearing in aristocratic families in the nineteenth century, see Jessica Tovrov, "Mother–Child Relationships among the Russian Nobility," and Barbara Alpern Engel, "Mothers and Daughters: Family Patterns and the Female Intelligentsia," in Ransel, ed., *The Family in Imperial Russia*, pp. 15–59.

87. V.V. Kallash, ed., *Dvenadtsatyi god v vospominaniiakh sovremennikov* (Moscow, 1912), p. 275.

88. S. Glinka, "Zapiski," in *Russkii byt po vospominaniam sovremennikov*, pt. 2, no. 1 (Moscow, 1918), p. 215.

89. I.M. Dolgorukii, *Kapishche moego serdtsa* (Moscow, 1890), p. 112.

90. O.E. Glagoleva, *Russkaia provintsial'naia starina* (Tula, 1993), pp. 140–55.

91. I.M. Dolgorukii, "Slavnye bubny," *Chteniia v Obshchestve istorii i drevnostei rossiiskikh*, 1869, bk. 3, pp. 333–34.

92. Glagoleva, *Russkaia provintsial'naia starina*, p. 146.

93. I.P. Sakharov, "Aleksinskii uezd v 1846 g.," Tula Oblast' Archive, F. 790, d. 3, no. 49, p. 18.

94. F.F. Vigel', *Zapiski*, vol. 2 (Moscow, 1892), p. 76.

95. For more information on aristocratic lifestyles in the nineteenth century, see Priscilla Roosevelt, *Life on the Russian Country Estate* (New Haven, 1995); Joyce Toomre, *Classic Russian Cooking: Elena Molokhovets' A Gift to Young Housewives* (Bloomington, 1992); and Darra Goldstein, "Domestic Porkbarreling in Nineteenth-Century Russia, or Who Holds the Keys to the Larder," in Goscilo and Holmgren, eds., *Russia, Women, Culture*, pp. 125–51.

96. N. Vishniakov, *Svedeniia o kupecheskom rode Vishniakovykh* (Moscow, 1905), pt. 3, pp. 91–92.

97. E.A. Avdeeva, "Detstvo v Briusovskom pereulke," in *Nashe nasledie*, 1990, no. 6, p. 110.

98. Ibid., p. 121.

99. L.A. Anokhina and M.N. Shmeleva, *Byt gorodskogo naseleniia srednei polosy RSFSR v proshlom i nastoiashchem* (Moscow, 1977), p. 281.

100. A.V. Nikitenko, *Zapiski i dnevnik 1826–1877 gg.* (St. Petersburg, 1893), vol. 1, p. 128; V.P. Boiko, "K voprosu o sotsial'noi psikhologii krupnoi rossiiskoi burzhuazii vtoroi poloviny XIX v.," in *Iz istorii burzhuazii v Rossii* (Tomsk, 1982), pp. 33–46.

101. A. Lunacharskii, "Vystavka kartin soiuza russkikh khudozhnikov," in M. Etkind, ed., *B.M. Kustodiev* (Leningrad–Moscow, 1960), p. 74.

102. A.G. Goikhbarg, "Zamuzhniaia zhenshchina kak nepravnopravnaia lichnost' v sovremennom grazhdanskom prave," *Pravo*, 1914, no. 51, pp. 3542–44. Under Bolshevik rule, Goikhbarg became one of the architects of early Soviet family law; see Wendy Z. Goldman, *Women, the State and Revolution: Soviet Family Policy and Social Life, 1917–1936* (Cambridge, 1993), pp. 50–57.

103. Stites, *The Women's Liberation Movement*, p. 27.

104. A. Kunitsyn, "O pravakh nasledovaniia lits zhenskogo pola," *Otchet o sostoianii imperatorskogo Khar'kovskogo universiteta* (Kharkov, 1844), pp. 6–7.

105. For more information on women's status in peasant families, see Worobec, *Peasant Russia*, especially pp. 17–75, 175–216; Moshe Lewin, "Customary Law and Russian Rural Society in the Post-Reform Era," Christine Worobec, "Reflections on Customary Law and Post-Reform Peasant Russia," George Yaney, "Some Suggestions Regarding the Study of Russian Peasant Society prior to Collectivization," and Michael Confino, "Russian Customary Law and the Study of Peasant Mentalités," all in *Russian Review*, vol. 44, no. 1 (1985), pp. 1–43; Cathy Frierson, "Razdel: The Peasant Family Divided," *Russian Review*, vol. 46, no. 1 (1987), pp. 35–51 (repr. in *Russian Peasant Women*, ed. Farnsworth and Viola, pp. 73–88); and Rose Glickman, "Women and the Peasant Commune," in Roger Bartlett, ed., *Land Commune and Peasant Community in Russia: Communal Forms in Imperial and Early Soviet Society* (New York, 1990), pp. 321–38.

106. For more information on the projects of N.M. Karamzin and M.M. Speranskii, see V.I. Sinaiskii, *Lichnoe i imushchestvennoe polozhenie zamuzhnei zhenshchiny v grazhdanskom prave* (Iuriev, 1910), pp. 158–88.

107. A.G. Voronov, "Vopros o rodovykh imushchestvakh v deputatskikh nakazakh 1767 goda," *Vestnik prava*, 1905, no. 1, p. 199.

108. *Sobranie uzakonenii i rasporiazhenii pravitel'stva* (St. Petersburg, 1912), sec. 1, no. 107, art. 914.

109. Sinaiskii, *Lichnoe i imushchestvennoe polozhenie*, pp. 288–90.

110. K. Nevolin, *Istoriia rossiiskikh grazhdanskikh zakonov*, vol. 1 (St. Petersburg, 1851), pp. 75, 100.

111. *PSZ*, vol. 33, no. 25947.

112. M.A. Filippov, "Vzgliad na russkie grazhdanskie zakony," *Sovremennik*, 1861, no. 2, sec. 1, p. 528.

113. For more information on the legal status of women, see William G. Wagner, *Marriage, Property, and the Law in Late Imperial Russia* (New York, 1994); and Engelstein, *The Keys to Happiness*.

114. *Sovremennik*, 1857, no. 5, sec. 5, p. 65; L. Bogoslovskaia, " 'Chto delat'?' Chernyshevskogo i zhenskie arteli 60-kh gg. XIX v.," in *Revoliutsionnaia situatsiia v Rossii v 1859–1861 gg.* (Moscow, 1974), pp. 127–28.

115. Tishkin, *Zhenskii vopros*, p. 133.

116. N. Suslova, Letter to F.D. Nefedov, Manuscript Division, Institute of Russian Literature, St. Petersburg (RO IRLI), F. 208, d. 10, f. 3 v.

117. For more information concerning women's access to universities, see Johanson, *Women's Struggle for Higher Education*. For more information on midwives and teachers, see Samuel C. Ramer, "Childbirth and Culture: Midwifery in the Nineteenth-Century Russian Countryside," in Ransel, ed., *The Family in Imperial Russia*, pp. 218–35; Christine Ruane, "The Vestal Virgins of St. Petersburg: School Teachers and the 1897 Marriage Ban," *Russian Review*, vol. 50, no. 2 (1991), pp. 163–82; Ruane, *Gender, Class, and the Professionalization of Russian City Teachers, 1860–1914* (Pittsburgh, 1994).

118. Likhacheva, *Materialy po istorii zhenskogo obrazovaniia*, p. 446.

119. Russian State Historical Archive, Moscow (RGIA), F. 1275, Op. 1, d. 85, ff. 4, 7.

120. For more information, see F.C. Giffin, "The Prohibition of Night Work for Women and Young Persons: The Russian Factory Law of June 3, 1885," *Canadian Slavic Studies*, vol. 2, no. 2 (1968), pp. 208–18.

121. V.Iu. Krupianskaia, O.P. Budina, N.S. Polishchuk, and N.V. Iukhneva, *Kul'tura i byt gorniakov i metallurgov Nizhnego Tagila, 1917–1970* (Moscow, 1974).

122. Stites, *The Women's Liberation Movement*, pp. 166–67.

123. For more information about revolutionary agitation among women workers, see Anne Bobroff, "The Bolsheviks and Working Women, 1905–1920," *Soviet Studies*, vol. 26 (1974), pp. 540–67; and Moira Donald, "Bolshevik Activity amongst the Working Women of Petrograd in 1917," *International Review of Social History*, vol. 27 (1982), pp. 129–60.

124. B.D. Belikov, *Zhenshchina v promyshlennoi inspektsii Zapada. K voprosu o vvedenii zhenskoi fabrichnoi inspektsii v Rossii* (Tver, 1914), p. 51.

125. For more information on the movement for legal rights for women in Russia, see Edmondson, *Feminism in Russia*; Edmondson, "Women's Rights, Civil Rights and the Debate over Citizenship in the 1905 Revolution," and Barbara T. Norton, "Laying the Foundations of Democracy in Russia: E. D. Kuskova's Contribution, February–October 1917," in Edmondson, ed., *Women and Society in*

Russia and the Soviet Union, pp. 77–123; William Wagner, "The Trojan Mare: Women's Rights and Civil Rights in Late Imperial Russia," in Olga Crisp and Linda Edmondson, eds., *Civil Rights in Imperial Russia* (Oxford, 1989), pp. 65–84.

126. A.M. Kharkova, "Vozniknovenie i razvitie zhenskogo dvizheniia Rossii," in *Zhenshchiny strany Sovetov* (Moscow, 1977), pp. 33–34.

127. Rochelle Ruthchild, "The Russian Feminists, 1905–1917" (Ph.D. dissertation, University of Rochester, 1976).

128. *Zhenskoe delo*, August 10, 1910, pp. 10–12; October 25, 1910, pp. 6–7; November 25, 1910, pp. 7–8. For more information on abortion, see Laura Engelstein, "Abortion and the Civic Order: The Legal and Medical Debates," in Clements et al., eds., *Russia's Women*, pp. 185–207.

129. Laura Engelstein, " 'Polovoi vopros' i politicheskii krizis professional'noi intelligentsii posle revoliutsii 1905 g.," in *Reformy ili revoliutsiia. Rossiia 1861–1917* (St. Petersburg, 1992), pp. 172–73; Stites, *The Women's Liberation Movement*, pp. 198–210. For more information on the discussions of female sexuality in the medical community, see Engelstein, *The Keys to Happiness*.

130. For more information on prostitution in late Imperial Russia, see Laurie Bernstein, *Sonia's Daughters: Prostitutes and Their Regulation in Imperial Russia* (Berkeley, 1995); Laura Engelstein, "Gender and the Juridical Subject: Prostitution and Rape in Nineteenth-Century Criminal Codes," *Journal of Modern History*, vol. 60 (1988), pp. 458–95; Barbara Alpern Engel, "St. Petersburg Prostitutes in the Late Nineteenth Century: A Personal and Social Profile," *Russian Review*, vol. 48, no. 1 (1989), pp. 21–44; Richard Stites, "Prostitute and Society in Pre-Revolutionary Russia," *Jahrbücher für Geschichte Osteuropas*, vol. 31, no. 3 (1983), pp. 348–64; Laurie Bernstein, "Yellow Tickets and State-Licensed Brothels: The Tsarist Government and the Regulation of Urban Prostitution," in Susan Gross Solomon and John Hutchinson, eds., *Health and Society in Revolutionary Russia* (Bloomington, 1990), pp. 45–65.

131. "Pervyi vserossiiskii s''ezd po bor'be s torgom zhenshchinami," *Izvestiia Moskovskoi gorodskoi Dumy*, otd. obshchii, 1910, no. 9, p. 9.

132. A. Shabanova, *Ocherk zhenskogo dvizheniia v Rossii* (St. Petersburg, 1911), pp. 326–27.

133. *Pretenzii k zhenskomu dvizheniiu voobshche i k I-omu Vserossiiskomu zhenskomu s''ezdu v chastnosti* (St. Petersburg, 1910), pp. 7–9.

134. V.A. Vereshchagin, *Pamiati proshlogo. Stat'i i zametki* (St. Petersburg, 1914), p. 53.

135. F.F. Vigel', "Zapiski," pt. 2, *Russkii arkhiv*, vol. 3, bk. 10, 1891, pp. 38–39.

136. For more information about women's dress in the early nineteenth century, see Helena Goscilo, "Keeping A-Breast of the Waist-Land: Women's Fashion in Early-Nineteenth-Century Russia," in Goscilo and Holmgren, eds., *Russia, Women, Culture*, pp. 31–63.

137. L.I. Iakunina, "Shali krepostnoi raboty nachala XIX v.," *Trudy Gosudarstvennogo istoricheskogo muzeia*, 1941, no. 13, pp. 232–54.

138. A. Chuzhbinskii, "Beglye zametki," *Severnaia pchela*, 1861, p. 24.

139. N.V. Gogol', *Polnoe sobranie sochinenii*, vol. 8 (Moscow, 1952), p. 178.

140. Vereshchagin, *Pamiati proshlogo*, pp. 61–62.

141. V.I. Kozlinskii, E.M. Berman, and E.D. Kurbatova, *Russkii kostium 1750–1917*, no. 2 (1830–1850) (Moscow 1962), p. 9.

142. P. Vistengof, *Ocherki moskovskoi zhizni* (Moscow, 1842), p. 39; A. Vel'tman, *Prikliucheniia, pocherpnutye iz moria zhiteiskogo* (Moscow, 1895), p. 313.

143. Kozlinskii, et al., *Russkii kostium*, no. 3 (1850–1870) (Moscow, 1963), pp. 8–15.

144. R. Turner Wilcox, *The Dictionary of Costume* (London, 1969), p. 147.

145. Kozinskii, *Russkii kostium, no.* 4 (1870–1890) (Moscow, 1965), p. 21.

146. A. Dziekońska-Kozłowska, *Moda kobieca XX wieku* (Warsaw, 1964).

147. S. Kiselevskaia, "Pozhevskii zavod," *Zapiski istoriko-bytovogo otdela Russkogo muzeia*, no. 2 (Leningrad, 1932).

148. D.L. Kositskaia, N.P. Levinson, and T.A. Lobaneva, *Polozhenie i byt rabochikh metallurgicheskoi promyshlennosti Urala* (*Trudy Gosudarstvennogo istoricheskogo muzeia*, no. 23) (Moscow, 1953).

149. "Damskii mir," *Stolitsa i usad'ba*, 1914, no. 9, p. 8.

Notes to Epilogue

1. Zabelin, *Domashnii byt russkikh tsarits*, p. 9.

2. For a survey of the history of women in Russia in the Soviet period, see Barbara Evans Clements, *Daughters of the Revolution: A History of Women in the U.S.S.R* (Arlington Heights, 1994). For background on Russia in the Soviet period, see Geoffrey Hosking, *The First Socialist Society* (Cambridge, MA, 1990); Martin McCauley, *The Soviet Union Since 1917* (London, 1981); and Vladimir Andrle, *A Social History of Twentieth-Century Russia* (London, 1994).

3. For more information on the roles women played in the Russian Revolution, see Norton, "Laying the Foundations of Democracy in Russia: E.D. Kuskova's Contribution, February–October 1917," and Richard Abraham, "Mariia L. Bochkareva and the Russian Amazons of 1917," in Edmondson, ed., *Women and Society in Russia and the Soviet Union*, pp. 101–44.

4. V.I. Lenin, *Polnoe sobranie sochinenii*, vol. 39 (Moscow, 1969), p. 201.

5. Gail Warshofsky Lapidus, *Women in Soviet Society: Equality, Development, and Social Change* (Berkeley, 1978), pp. 54–94.

6. I.V. Stalin, *Sobranie sochinenii*, vol. 13 (Moscow, 1952), pp. 291–92.

7. For more information on the *Zhenotdel*, see Carol Eubanks Hayden, "The *Zhenotdel* and the Bolshevik Party," and Richard Stites, "*Zhenotdel*: Bolshevism and Russian Women, 1917–1930," *Russian History*, vol. 3, pt. 2 (1976), pp. 150–93; Robert H. McNeal, "The Early Decrees of the *Zhenotdel*," in Yedlin, ed., *Women in Eastern Europe and the Soviet Union*, pp. 75–86; and Barbara Evans Clements, "The Utopianism of the *Zhenotdel*," *Slavic Review*, vol. 51, no. 3 (1992), pp. 485–96.

8. For more information on peasant women after the Russian Revolution, see Farnsworth and Viola, eds., *Russian Peasant Women*, especially the articles by Beatrice Farnsworth, Lynne Viola, and Roberta T. Manning; and Victoria E. Bonnell, "The Peasant Woman in Stalinist Political Art of the 1930s," *American Historical Review*, vol. 98, no. 1 (1993), pp. 55–82.

9. *Sovetskaia vlast' i raskreposhchenie zhenshchiny. Sbornik dekretov i postanovlenii RSFSR* (Moscow, 1921), p. 28.

10. Lenin, *Polnoe sobranie sochinenii*, vol. 39, p. 24.

11. For more information on the process of transforming peasants into urban workers, see David Hoffmann, *Peasant Metropolis: Social Identities in Moscow, 1929–1941* (Ithaca, 1994).

12. For more information on early Soviet-era policies and women's reaction to them, see Goldman, *Women, the State, and Revolution*; Stites, *The Women's Liberation Movement in Russia*, especially pp. 278–438; Barbara Evans Clements, "The Birth of the New Soviet Woman," in Abbott Gleason, Peter Kenez, and Richard Stites, eds., *Bolshevik Culture, Experiment and Order in the Russian Revolution*

(Bloomington, 1985), pp. 220–37; Anne Bobroff-Hajal, *Working Women in Russia under the Hunger Tsars: Political Activism and Daily Life* (Brooklyn, NY, 1994); Mary Buckley, *Women and Ideology in the Soviet Union* (Ann Arbor, 1989); Sheila Fitzpatrick, "Sex and Revolution: An Examination of Literary and Statistical Data on the Mores of Soviet Students in the 1920's," *Journal of Modern History*, vol. 50, no. 2 (1978), pp. 252–78; Victoria E. Bonnell, "The Representation of Women in Early Soviet Political Art," *Russian Review*, vol. 50, no. 3 (1991), pp. 267–88; Bernice Glatzer Rosenthal, "Love on the Tractor: Women in the Russian Revolution and After," in Bridenthal and Koonz, eds., *Becoming Visible*, pp. 370–99; and Diane P. Koenker, "Men Against Women on the Shop Floor in Early Soviet Russia: Gender and Class in the Socialist Workplace," *American Historical Review*, vol. 100, no. 5 (1995), pp. 1438–64.

13. *Vsesoiuznoe soveshchanie zhen khoziaistvennikov i inzhenerno-tekhnicheskikh rabotnikov tiazheloi promyshlennosti* (Moscow, 1936), p. 258.

14. For more information on Alexandra Kollontai, see Clements, *Bolshevik Feminist*; Farnsworth, *Aleksandra Kollontai*; and Cathy Porter, *Alexandra Kollontai: A Biography* (London, 1980).

15. For more information on women's military roles, see Kazimira Janina Cottam, *Soviet Airwomen in Combat in World War II* (Manhattan, KS, 1983); Bruce Myles, *Night Witches: The Untold Story of Soviet Women in Combat* (Novato, 1981); Anne Noggle, *A Dance with Death: Soviet Airwomen in World War II* (College Station, 1994); K. Jean Cottam, "Soviet Women in Combat in World War II: The Ground Forces and the Navy," *International Journal of Women's Studies*, vol. 3, no. 4 (1980), pp. 345–57; Cottam, "Soviet Women in Combat in World War II: The Rear Services, Resistance Behind Enemy Lines and Military Political Workers," *International Journal of Women's Studies*, vol. 5, no. 4 (1982), pp. 363–78; and D'Ann Campbell, "Women in Combat: The World War II Experience in the United States, Great Britain, Germany, and the Soviet Union," *Journal of Military History*, vol. 57, no. 2 (1993), pp. 301–23.

16. V.P. Ostrovskii, V.I. Startsev, B.A. Starkov, and G.M. Smirnov, *Istoriia Otechestva* (Moscow, 1992), p. 62.

17. I.Iu. Radzinskaia, E.M. Shibarina, and Z.A. Iankova, "Zhenshchiny v razvitom sotsialisticheskom obshchestve," in *Zhenshchiny strany Sovetov* (Moscow, 1977), pp. 216–17.

18. L.A. Gordon and E.V. Klopov, *Chelovek posle raboty* (Moscow, 1972), pp. 98–102.

19. Krupianskaia et al., *Kul'tura i byt gorniakov i metallurgov*, p. 168.

20. For more information on the status of women in postwar Soviet society, see Lapidus, *Women in Soviet Society*; Lapidus, ed., *Women, Work, and Family in the Soviet Union* (Armonk, 1982); Susan Bridger, *Women in the Soviet Countryside: Women's Roles in Rural Development in the Soviet Union* (Cambridge, 1987); Jenny Brine, Maureen Perrie, and Andrew Sutton, eds., *Home, School and Leisure in the Soviet Union* (London, 1980); Michael Paul Sacks, *Women's Work in Soviet Russia* (New York, 1976); Sacks, *Work and Equality in the Soviet Union: The Division of Labor by Age, Gender, and Nationality* (New York, 1982); Alistair McAuley, *Women's Wages in the Soviet Union* (London, 1981); Lynne Attwood, *The New Soviet Man and Woman: Sex-Role Socialization in the USSR* (Bloomington, 1990); Igor Kon and James Riordan, *Sex and Russian Society* (Bloomington, 1993); Peter Juliver, "The Soviet Family in Post-Stalin Perspective," in Stephen F. Cohen, Alexander Rabinowitch, and Robert Sharlet, eds., *The Soviet Union Since Stalin*, (Bloomington, 1980), pp. 227–54; Atkinson et al., eds., *Women in Russia*, especially pp.

115–398; Farnsworth and Viola, eds., *Russian Peasant Women*, especially the articles by Norton D. Dodge and Murray Feshbach and by Susan Bridger.

21. *Zhenshchiny v SSSR. Statisticheskie materialy. 1991* (Moscow, 1992), p. 41.

22. T.A. Mashika, *Zaniatost' zhenshchin i materinstvo. Ekonomiko-statisticheskoe issledovanie* (Moscow, 1989), p. 82.

23. V.A. Tishkov, "Zhenshchina v rossiiskoi politike i strukturakh vlasti," in *Zhenshchina i svoboda. Puti vybora v mire traditsii i peremen* (Moscow, 1994), p. 9.

24. V.G. Stel'makh, "Sdelaet li delovaia zhenshchina kar'eru?" in *Zhenshchina i svoboda*, p. 67. For more information on the effects of Gorbachev's reforms on women, see Mary Buckley, ed., *Perestroika and Soviet Women* (Cambridge, 1992); Chanie Rosenberg, *Women and Perestroika* (London, 1989); Vitalina Koval, ed., *Women in Contemporary Russia* (Providence, 1995); Anastasia Posadskaya et al., eds., *Women in Russia: A New Era in Russian Feminism* (London, 1994); Helena Goscilo, *Fruits of Her Plume: Essays on Contemporary Russian Women's Culture* (Armonk, 1993); Sue Bridger, "Young Women and Perestroika," and Mary Buckley, "Glasnost and the Woman Question," in Edmondson, ed., *Women and Society in Russia and the Soviet Union*, pp. 178–226.

Selected Bibliography

Adrianova-Peretts, V.P., ed. *Povest' vremennykh let.* Moscow–Leningrad, 1950.

Alekseev, K. "Ob otnosheniiakh suprugov po imushchestvu v drevnei Rossii i Pol'she." *Chteniia v obshchestve istorii i drevnostei rossiiskikh pri Moskovskom universitete,* 1868, bk. 2, pp. 1–108.

Alexander, John T. *Catherine the Great: Life and Legend.* New York, 1989.

Aleksandrov, V.A. *Sel'skaia obshchina v Rossii XVII–nachala XIX vv.* Moscow, 1976.

Andrew, Joe. "Radical Sentimentalism or Sentimental Radicalism: A Feminist Approach to Eighteenth-Century Russian Literature." In Catriona Kelly, Michael Makin, and David Sheperd, eds., *Discontinuous Discourses in Modern Russian Literature.* (Hampshire, 1989), pp. 136–56.

Andrle, Vladimir. *A Social History of Twentieth-Century Russia.* London, 1994.

Anisimov, Evgenii V. "Anna Ivanovna." *Russian Studies in History,* vol. 32, no. 4 (1994), pp. 8–36.

———. *The Reforms of Peter the Great: Progress through Coercion in Russia.* Armonk, 1993.

———. *Rossiia v seredine XVIII v.* Moscow, 1988.

Anokhina, L.A., and M.N. Shmeleva. *Kul'tura i byt kolkhoznikov Kalininskoi oblasti v proshlom i nastoiashchem.* Moscow, 1964.

Arian, P.N. "Zhenshchina v istorii blagotvoritel'nosti v Rossii." *Vestnik blagotvoritel'nosti,* 1901, no. 9, pp. 40–53.

Arsen'ev, K. *Tsarstvovanie Ekateriny I.* St. Petersburg, 1856.

Atkinson, Dorothy, Alexander Dallin, and Gail Warshofsky Lapidus, eds. *Women in Russia.* Stanford, 1977.

Attwood, Lynne. *The New Soviet Man and Woman: Sex-Role Socialization in the USSR.* Bloomington, 1990.

Awsienko, Nina. "Zinaida Hippius's Literary Salon in St. Petersburg." *Russian Language Journal,* vol. 26 (1978), pp. 83–89.

Azarevich, D.I. "Semeinye i imushchestvennye otnosheniia po russkomu pravu." *Zhurnal grazhdanskogo i ugolovnogo prava,* 1883, no. 4.

Balzer, Marjorie Mandelstam, ed. *Russian Traditional Culture: Religion, Gender, and Customary Law.* Armonk, 1992.

Bartlett, R.P., A.G. Cross, and Karen Rasmussen, eds. *Russia and the World of the Eighteenth Century.* Columbus, 1988.

Belikov, B.D. *Zhenshchina v promyshlennoi inspektsii Zapada. K voprosu o vvedenii zhenskoi fabrichnoi inspektsii v Rossii.* Tver, 1914.

Belikov, D.N. *Pervye russkie krest'iane-nasel'niki Tomskogo kraia.* Tomsk, 1898.

Bergman, Jay. *Vera Zasulich: A Biography.* Stanford, 1993.

Bernstein, Laurie. *Sonia's Daughters: Prostitutes and Their Regulation in Imperial Russia.* Berkeley, 1995.

Berry, Lloyd E., and Robert O. Crummey, eds. *Rude and Barbarous Kingdom: Russia in the Accounts of Sixteenth-Century English Voyagers.* Madison, 1968.

Bil'basov, V.A. *Istoriia Ekateriny II.* 2 vols. N.p., 1900.

Bobroff, Anne, "The Bolsheviks and Working Women, 1905–1920." *Soviet Studies,* vol. 26 (1974), pp. 540–67.

Bobroff-Hajal, Anne. *Working Women in Russia under the Hunger Tsars: Political Activism and Daily Life.* Brooklyn, NY, 1994.

Bonnell, Victoria E. "The Peasant Woman in Stalinist Political Art of the 1930s." *American Historical Review,* vol. 98, no. 1 (1993), pp. 55–82.

———. "The Representation of Women in Early Soviet Political Art." *Russian Review,* vol. 50, no.3 (1991), pp. 267–88.

Boxer, Marilyn J., and Jean H. Quataert, eds. *Connecting Spheres: Women in the Western World, 1500 to the Present.* New York, 1987.

———. *Socialist Women: European Socialist Feminism in the Nineteenth and Early Twentieth Centuries.* New York, 1978.

Brennan, James F. *Enlightened Despotism in Russia: The Reign of Elizabeth, 1741–1762.* New York, 1987.

Bridenthal, Renate, and Claudia Koonz, eds. *Becoming Visible: Women in European History.* Boston, 1977.

Bridger, Susan. *Women in the Soviet Countryside: Women's Roles in Rural Development in the Soviet Union.* Cambridge, 1987.

Brine, Jenny, Maureen Perrie, and Andrew Sutton, eds. *Home, School and Leisure in the Soviet Union.* London, 1980.

Broido, Vera. *Apostles into Terrorists: Women and the Revolutionary Movement in the Russia of Alexander II.* New York, 1977.

Bryner, Cyril. "The Issue of Capital Punishment in the Reign of Elizabeth Petrovna." *Russian Review,* vol. 49, no. 4 (1990), pp. 389–416.

Buckley, Mary. *Women and Ideology in the Soviet Union.* Ann Arbor, 1989.

Buckley, Mary, ed. *Perestroika and Soviet Women.* Cambridge, 1992.

Campbell, D'Ann. "Women in Combat: The World War II Experience in the United States, Great Britain, Germany, and the Soviet Union." *Journal of Military History,* vol. 57, no. 2 (1993), pp. 301–23.

Catherine II, Empress of Russia. *Memoirs of Catherine the Great,* trans. Katharine Anthony. New York, 1927.

Chamot, Mary. *Goncharova: Stage Designs and Painting.* London, 1979.

Chechulin, N.D. *Ekaterina II v bor'be za prestol.* Leningrad, 1924.

———. *Russkoe provintsial'noe obshchestvo vo vtoroi polovine XVIII v.* St. Petersburg, 1889.

Claus, C. *Die Stellung der russischen Frau von der Einführung des Christentums bei den Russen bis zu den Reformen Peters der Grossen.* Munich, 1959.

Clements, Barbara Evans. "The Birth of the New Soviet Woman." In Abbott Gleason, Peter Kenez, and Richard Stites, eds., *Bolshevik Culture, Experiment and Order in the Russian Revolution.* Bloomington, 1985, pp. 220–37.

———. *Bolshevik Feminist: The Life of Aleksandra Kollontai.* Bloomington, 1979.

———. *Daughters of the Revolution: A History of Women in the U.S.S.R.* Arlington Heights, 1994.

————. "The Utopianism of the *Zhenotdel.*" *Slavic Review*, vol. 51, no. 3 (1992), pp. 485–96.

Clements, Barbara Evans, Barbara Alpern Engel, and Christine Worobec, eds. *Russia's Women: Accommodation, Resistance, Transformation.* Berkeley, 1991.

Clyman, Toby W., and Diana Greene, eds. *Women Writers in Russian Literature.* Westport, 1994.

Collins, Samuel. *The Present State of Russia, in a Letter to a Friend at London.* London, 1671.

Confino, Michael. "Russian Customary Law and the Study of Peasant Mentalités." *Russian Review*, vol. 44, no. 1 (1985), pp. 35–43.

Conroy, Mary Schaeffer. "Women Pharmacists in Nineteenth- and Early Twentieth-Century Russia." *Pharmacy in History*, vol. 29, no. 4 (1987), pp. 155–64.

Costlow, Jane T., Stephanie Sandler, and Judith Vowles, eds. *Sexuality and the Body in Russian Culture.* Stanford, 1993.

Cottam, Kazimira Janina [K. Jean]. *Soviet Airwomen in Combat in World War II.* Manhattan, KS, 1983.

————. "Soviet Women in Combat in World War II: The Ground Forces and the Navy." *International Journal of Women's Studies*, vol. 3, no. 4 (1980), pp. 345–57.

————. "Soviet Women in Combat in World War II: The Rear Services, Resistance Behind Enemy Lines and Military Political Workers." *International Journal of Women's Studies*, vol. 5, no. 4 (1982), pp. 363–78.

Crummey, Robert O. *Aristocrats and Servitors: The Boyar Elite in Russia, 1613–1689.* Princeton, 1983.

————. *The Formation of Muscovy.* New York, 1987.

Curtiss, Mina. *A Forgotten Empress: Anna Ivanovna and Her Era, 1730–1740.* New York, 1974.

Danilova, N.S., ed. *Povest' o boiaryne Morozovoi.* Moscow, 1991.

Dashkova, Ekaterina. *Memoirs of the Princess Dashkova*, ed. and trans. Kyril Fitzlyon. London, 1958.

Ditrikh, M.N. *Drevnerusskie zhenshchiny velikokniazheskogo vremeni.* St. Petersburg, 1904.

Dolgorukaia, Natalia. *Memoirs of Princes Natalija Borisovna Dolgorukaja*, ed. and trans. Charles Townsend. Columbus, 1977.

Donald, Moira. "Bolshevik Activity Amongst the Working Women of Petrograd in 1917." *International Review of Social History*, vol. 27 (1982), pp. 129–60.

Duby, G., N.Z. Davis, A. Farge, M. Perrot, et al., eds. *Histoire des femmes en Occident.* 6 vols. Paris, 1991.

Dudgeon, Ruth A. "The Forgotten Minority: Women Students in Imperial Russia, 1872–1917." *Russian History*, vol. 9, no. 1 (1982), pp. 1–26.

Dukes, Paul. *The Making of Russian Absolutism, 1613–1801.* 2d ed. London, 1990.

Durova, Nadezhda. *The Cavalry Maid: The Memoirs of a Woman Soldier of 1812*, trans. Jon Merereau and David Lapeza. Ann Arbor, 1988.

————. *The Cavalry Maiden*, trans. Mary Zirin. Bloomington, 1988.

Eck, A. "La Situation juridique de la femme russe au Moyen Age." *Recueils de la Société Jean Bodin pour l'histoire comparative des institutions*, vol. 12 (1962), pp. 404–20.

Edmondson, Linda. *Feminism in Russia, 1900–1917.* Stanford, 1984.

————, ed. *Women and Society in Russia and the Soviet Union.* Cambridge, MA, 1992.

Elizarova, N.A. *Teatry Sheremetevykh.* Moscow, 1944.

Elwood, R.C. *Inessa Armand: Revolutionary and Feminist.* Cambridge, 1992.
Engel, Barbara Alpern. *Between the Fields and the City: Women, Work, and Family in Russia, 1861–1914.* Cambridge, 1994.
———. "Engendering Russia's History: Women in Post-Emancipation Russia and the Soviet Union." *Slavic Review,* vol. 51, no. 2 (1992), pp. 309–21.
———. *Mothers and Daughters: Women of the Intelligentsia in Nineteenth-Century Russia.* Cambridge, 1983.
———. "Peasant Morality and Pre-Marital Relations in Late Nineteenth Century Russia." *Journal of Social History,* vol. 23, no. 4 (1990), pp. 695–714.
———. "St. Petersburg Prostitutes in the Late Nineteenth Century: A Personal and Social Profile." *Russian Review,* vol. 48, no. 1 (1989), pp. 21–44.
———. "Women Medical Students in Russia, 1872–1882: Reformers or Rebels?" *Journal of Social History,* vol. 12, no. 3 (1979), pp. 394–415.
———. "Women, Work and Family in the Factories of Rural Russia." *Russian History,* vol. 16 (1989), pp. 223–37.
Engel, Barbara Alpern, and Clifford N. Rosenthal, eds. and trans. *Five Sisters: Women Against the Tsar.* Boston, 1975.
Engelstein, Laura. "Gender and the Juridical Subject: Prostitution and Rape in Nineteenth-Century Criminal Codes." *Journal of Modern History,* vol. 60 (1988), pp. 458–95.
———. *The Keys to Happiness: Sex and the Search for Modernity in Fin-de-Siècle Russia.* Ithaca, 1992.
———. " 'Polovoi vopros' i politicheskii krizis professional'noi intelligentsii posle revoliutsii 1905 g." In *Reformy ili revoliutsiia. Rossiia 1861–1917,* pp. 172–73. St. Petersburg, 1992.
Eshevskii, S.V. *Ocherk tsarstvovaniia Elizavety Petrovny.* Moscow, 1870.
Farnsworth, Beatrice. *Aleksandra Kollontai: Socialism, Feminism and the Bolshevik Revolution.* Stanford, 1980.
Farnsworth, Beatrice, and Lynne Viola, eds. *Russian Peasant Women.* New York, 1992.
Farrow, Lee. "State Ambitions and Noble Traditions: A New Look at Peter the Great's Law of Single Inheritance." *Russian Review,* vol. 55, no. 3 (1996), pp. 430–47.
Feiler, Lily. *Marina Tsvetaeva: The Double Beat of Heaven and Hell.* Durham, 1994.
Feinstein, Elaine. *A Captive Lion: The Life of Marina Tsvetayeva.* New York, 1987.
Fennell, John. "When Was Olga Canonized?" In *Christianity and the Eastern Slavs,* vol. 1, ed. Boris Gasparov and Olga Raevsky-Hughes, pp. 77–82. California Slavic Studies, vol. 16. Berkeley, 1993.
Ferro, Marc. *Nicholas II: The Last of the Tsars.* Oxford, 1991.
Fletcher, Giles. *Of the Russe Commonwealth,* ed. Albert J. Schmidt. Ithaca, 1966.
Fieseler, Beata. "The Making of Russian Female Social Democrats, 1890–1917." *International Review of Social History,* vol. 34 (1989), pp. 1–17.
Fitzpatrick, Sheila. "Sex and Revolution: An Examination of Literary and Statistical Data on the Mores of Soviet Students in the 1920's." *Journal of Modern History,* vol. 50, no. 2 (1978), pp. 252–78.
Frey, Linda, Marsha Frey, and Joanne Schneider, eds. *Women in Western European History: A Select Geographical and Topical Bibliography.* London, 1982.
Frierson, Cathy. "Razdel: The Peasant Family Divided." *Russian Review,* vol. 46, no. 1 (1987), pp. 35–51.
Fuhrmann, Joseph T. *Rasputin: A Life.* New York, 1990.
Giffin, F.C. "The Prohibition of Night Work for Women and Young Persons:

The Russian Factory Law of June 3, 1885." *Canadian Slavic Studies*, vol. 2, no. 2 (1968), pp. 208–18.

Glagoleva, O.E. *Russkaia provintsial'naia starina*. Tula, 1993.

Glickman, Rose L. *Russian Factory Women: Workplace and Society, 1880–1914*. Berkeley, 1984.

———. "Women and the Peasant Commune." In *Land Commune and Peasant Community in Russia: Communal Forms in Imperial and Early Soviet Society*, ed. Roger Bartlett, pp. 321–38. New York, 1990.

Goehrke, Carsten. "Die Witwe im Alten Russland." *Forschungen zur osteuropäischen Geschichte*, vol. 38 (1986), pp. 64–96.

Goldman, Wendy Z. *Women, the State and Revolution: Soviet Family Policy and Social Life, 1917–1936*. Cambridge, 1993.

Good, Jane E., and David R. Jones. *Babushka: The Life of the Russian Revolutionary Ekaterina K. Breshko-Breshkovskaia (1844–1934)*. Newtonville, 1991.

Gorskii, S. *Zheny Ioanna Groznogo*. Moscow, 1912; repr. Vladikavkaz, 1992.

Goscilo, Helena. *Fruits of Her Plume: Essays on Contemporary Russian Women's Culture*. Armonk, 1993.

Goscilo, Helena, and Beth Holmgren, eds. *Russia, Women, Culture*. Bloomington, 1996.

Gribble, Lyubomira Parpulova. "Žitie Petra i Fevronii: A Love Story or an Apologia of Marriage?" *Russian Language Journal*, vol. 49, nos. 162–64 (1995), pp. 91–113.

Gromyko, M.M. *Mir russkoi derevni*. Moscow, 1991.

Grossman, Joan D. "Feminine Images in Old Russian Literature and Art." *California Slavic Studies*, vol. 11 (1980), pp. 33–70.

Haight, Amanda. *Anna Akhmatova: A Poetic Pilgrimage*. New York, 1976.

Hallu, Roger. *Anne de Kiev, reine de France*. Rome, 1973.

Hayden, Carol Eubanks. "The *Zhenotdel* and the Bolshevik Party." *Russian History*, vol. 3, pt. 2 (1976), pp. 150–73.

Heldt [Monter], Barbara. "Feminism and the Slavic Field." *The Harriman Review*, vol. 7, nos. 10–12 (1994), pp. 11–18.

———. "*Rassvet* (1859–1862) and the Woman Question." *Slavic Review*, vol. 36, no. 1 (1977), pp. 76–85.

———. *Terrible Perfection: Women and Russian Literature*. Bloomington, 1987.

Hellie, Richard, trans. and ed. *The Muscovite Law Code (Ulozhenie) of 1649*. Irvine, 1988.

Herberstein, Sigismund, Freiherr von. *Description of Moscow and Muscovy, 1557*, trans. and ed. J.B.C. Grundy. New York, 1969.

Hoffmann, David. *Peasant Metropolis: Social Identities in Moscow, 1929–1941*. Ithaca, 1994.

Hosking, Geoffrey. *The First Socialist Society*. Cambridge, MA, 1990.

Hughes, Lindsey. "Sophia Alekseyevna and the Moscow Rebellion of 1682." *Slavonic and East European Review*, vol. 63, no. 4 (1985), pp. 518–39.

———. *Sophia, Regent of Russia, 1657–1704*. New Haven, 1990.

Ignashev, Diane M. Nemec, and Sarah Krive. *Women and Writing in Russia and the USSR: A Bibliography of English-Language Sources*. New York, 1992.

Ikonnikova, A. *Tsaritsy i tsarevny iz doma Romanovykh*. Kiev, 1914; repr. Moscow, 1990.

Isaev, I.A. "Grazhdanskoe i semeinoe pravo." In *Razvitie russkogo prava v XV–pervoi polovine XVII v.*, ed. V.S. Nersesiants, pp. 121–56. Moscow, 1986.

Iskenderov, A.A., comp., and Donald J. Raleigh, ed. *The Emperors and Empresses of Russia: Rediscovering the Romanovs*. Armonk, 1996.

Johanson, Christine. *Women's Struggle for Higher Education in Russia, 1855–1900.* Kingston, 1987.

Juviler, Peter. "The Soviet Family in Post-Stalin Perspective." In *The Soviet Union Since Stalin,* ed. Stephen F. Cohen, Alexander Rabinowitch, and Robert Sharlet, pp. 227–54. Bloomington, 1980.

Kaidash, S.N. *Sil'nee bedstviia zemnogo. Rasskazy o zhenshchinakh russkoi istorii.* Moscow, 1883.

Kaiser, Daniel. "Symbol and Ritual in the Marriages of Ivan IV." *Russian History,* vol. 14 (1982), pp. 247–62.

Kamenskii, Aleksandr Borisovich. "Catherine the Great." *Soviet Studies in History,* vol. 30, no. 2 (1991), pp. 30–65.

Karlinsky, Simon. *Marina Cvetaeva: Her Life and Art.* Berkeley, 1966.

———. *Marina Tsvetaeva: The Woman, Her World and Her Poetry.* Cambridge, 1986.

Kelly, Catriona. *A History of Russian Women's Writing, 1820–1992.* New York, 1994.

Kharkova, A.M.. "Vozniknovenie i razvitie zhenskogo dvizheniia Rossii." In *Zhenshchiny strany Sovetov,* pp. 33–34. Moscow, 1977.

Kivelson, Valerie A. *Autocracy in the Provinces: The Russian Gentry and Political Culture in the Seventeenth Century.* Stanford, 1997.

———. "The Effects of Partible Inheritance: Gentry Families and the State in Muscovy." *Russian Review,* vol. 53, no. 2 (1994), pp. 197–212.

Kleimola, Ann M. " 'In Accordance with the Canons of the Holy Apostles': Muscovite Dowries and Women's Property Rights." *Russian Review,* vol. 51, no. 2 (1992), pp. 204–29.

Kleinberg, S. Jay, ed. *Retrieving Women's History: Changing Perceptions of the Role of Women in Politics and Society.* New York, 1988.

Knight, Amy. "Female Terrorists in the Russian Socialist Revolutionary Party." *Russian Review,* vol. 38, no. 2 (1979), pp. 139–59.

———. "The Fritschi: A Study of Female Radicals in the Russian Populist Movement." *Canadian-American Slavic Studies,* vol. 9, no. 1 (1975), pp. 1–17.

Koblitz, Ann Hibner. "Career and Home Life in the 1880s: The Choices of Sofia Kovalevskaia." In *Uneasy Careers and Intimate Lives: Women in Science,* ed. Pnina Abir-Am and Dorinda Outram, pp. 172–90. New Brunswick, 1987.

———. *A Convergence of Lives: Sofia Kovalevskaia—Scientist, Writer, Revolutionary.* Boston, 1983.

———. "Science, Women, and the Russian Intelligentsia: The Generation of the 1860's." *Isis,* vol. 79 (1988), pp. 208–26.

Kochina, P.Ia. *Kovalevskaia. 1850–1891.* Moscow, 1981.

Koenker, Diane P. "Men Against Women on the Shop Floor in Early Soviet Russia: Gender and Class in the Socialist Workplace." *American Historical Review,* vol. 100, no. 5 (1995), pp. 1438–64.

Kollmann, Nancy Shields. *Kinship and Politics: The Making of the Muscovite Political System, 1345–1547.* Stanford, 1987.

———. "The Seclusion of Elite Muscovite Women." *Russian History,* vol.10, pt. 2 (1983), pp. 170–87.

Kon, Igor, and James Riordan. *Sex and Russian Society.* Bloomington, 1993.

Korsakov, D.A. *Votsarenie imperatritsy Anny Ioannovny.* Kazan, 1880.

Korshunova, T.T. *Kostium v Rossii XVIII–nachala XX vv. Iz sobraniia Gosudarstvennogo Ermitazha.* Leningrad, 1979.

Kostomarov, N.I. *Ocherk domashnei zhizni i nravov velikorusskogo naroda v XVI i XVII stoletiiakh.* St. Petersburg, 1906.

————. *Russkaia istoriia v zhizhneopisaniiakh ee glavneishikh deiatelei.* 3 vols. St. Petersburg, 1886.

Koval, Vitalina, ed. *Women in Contemporary Russia.* Providence, 1995.

Kozlinskii, V.I., E.M. Berman, and E.D. Kurbatova. *Russkii kostium 1750–1917,* no. 2–3. Moscow, 1962–63.

Krupianskaia, V.Iu., O.P. Budina, N.S. Polishchuk, N.V. Iukhneva. *Kul'tura i byt gorniakov i metallurgov Nizhnego Tagila, 1917–1970.* Moscow, 1974.

Krupianskaia, V.Iu., and N.S. Polishchuk. *Kul'tura i byt rabochikh gornozavodskogo Urala. Konets XIX–nachalo XX vv.* Moscow, 1971.

Kugel', Aleksandr Rafailovich. "V.F. Komissarzhevskaia." *Russian Studies in History,* vol. 31, no. 3 (1992–93), pp. 87–96.

Lange, O.F. *O pravakh sobstvennosti suprugov po drevnerusskomu pravu.* St. Petersburg, 1886.

Lapidus, Gail Warshofsky. *Women in Soviet Society: Equality, Development, and Social Change.* Berkeley, 1978.

————, ed. *Women, Work, and Family in the Soviet Union.* Armonk, 1982.

Ledkovsky, Marina, Charlotte Rosenthal, and Mary Zirin, eds. *Dictionary of Russian Women Writers.* Westport, 1994.

Levin, Eve. *Sex and Society in the World of the Orthodox Slavs, 900–1700.* Ithaca, 1989.

————. "Women and Property in Medieval Novgorod: Dependence and Independence." *Russian History,* vol. 10, pt. 2 (1983), pp. 154–69.

Levron, I. "Anne de Kiev, princesse russe, reine de France." *Miroire de l'histoire,* no. 268 (1972), pp. 118–25.

Levy, Sandra. "Women and the Control of Property in Sixteenth-Century Muscovy." *Russian History,* vol. 10, pt. 2 (1983) pp. 201–12.

Lewin, Moshe. "Customary Law and Russian Rural Society in the Post-Reform Era." *Russian Review,* vol. 44, no. 1 (1985), pp. 1–19.

Lewitter, L.R. "Women, Sainthood, and Marriage in Muscovy." *Journal of Russian Studies.* vol. 37 (1979), pp. 3–11.

Likhacheva, E. *Materialy dlia istorii zhenskogo obrazovaniia v Rossii (1086–1796).* St. Petersburg, 1890.

Lindenmeyr, Adele. "Public Life, Private Virtues: Women in Russian Charity, 1762–1914." *Signs,* vol. 18, no. 3 (1993), pp. 562–91.

Longworth, Philip. *The Three Empresses: Catherine I, Anne and Elizabeth of Russia.* London, 1972.

Lozinskaia, L.Ia. *Vo glave dvukh akademii.* Moscow, 1978.

Lukash, I.S. "Boiarynia Morozova." *Rodina,* 1990, no. 9, pp. 78–87.

Lur'e, Ia.S. "Elena Ivanovna, koroleva pol'skaia i velikaia kniaginia litovskaia kak pisatel'-publitsist." *Canadian-American Slavic Studies,* vol. 13, no. 3 (1979), pp. 111–20.

Madariaga, Isabel de. *Catherine the Great: A Short History.* New Haven, 1990.

————. "The Foundation of the Russian Educational System by Catherine the Great." *Slavonic and East European Review,* vol. 57, no. 3 (1979), pp. 369–95.

————. *Russia in the Age of Catherine the Great.* New Haven, 1981.

Maedg-Soep, Carolina de. *The Emancipation of Women in Russian Literature and Society.* Ghent, 1970.

Martin, Janet. *Medieval Russia, 980–1584.* Cambridge, 1995.

Mashika, T.A. *Zaniatost' zhenshchin i materinstvo. Ekonomiko-statisticheskoe issledovanie.* Moscow, 1989.

Mazaev, M. *Druzheskoe literaturnoe obshchestva S.D. Ponomarevoi (Iz istorii literaturnykh kruzhkov v Rossii).* St. Petersburg, 1892.

Mazour, Anatole G. *The First Russian Revolution, 1825.* Stanford, 1937.
———. *Women in Exile: Wives of the Decembrists.* Tallahassee, 1975.
McAuley, Alistair. *Women's Wages in the Soviet Union.* London, 1981.
McCauley, Martin. *The Soviet Union Since 1917.* London, 1981.
McNeal, Robert. *Bride of the Revolution.* Ann Arbor, 1972.
———. "Women in the Russian Radical Movement." *Journal of Social History,* vol. 5, no. 2 (1971–72), pp. 143–61.
Meade, Marion. *Madame Blavatsky: The Woman Behind the Myth.* New York, 1980.
Meehan[-Waters], Brenda. "Catherine the Great and the Problem of Female Rule." *Russian Review,* vol. 34, no. 3 (1975), pp. 293–307.
———. "From Contemplative Practice to Charitable Activity: Russian Women's Religious Communities and the Development of Charitable Work." In *Lady Bountiful Revisited: Women Philanthropy and Power,* ed. Kathleen McCarthy, pp. 142–57. New Brunswick, 1990.
———. *Holy Women of Russia: The Lives of Five Orthodox Women Offer Spiritual Guidance for Today.* San Francisco, 1993.
Mendelsohn, Ezra, and Marshall S. Shatz, eds. *Imperial Russia, 1700–1917: State, Society, Opposition (Essays in Honor of Marc Raeff).* DeKalb, 1988.
Mertsalova, M.N. *Istoriia kostiuma.* Moscow, 1972.
Mikhnevich, V.O. *Russkaia zhenshchina XVIII stoletiia.* Kiev, 1895, repr. Moscow, 1990.
Minenko, N.A. "Obshchina i russkaia krest'ianskaia sem'ia v Iugo-Zapadnoi Sibiri (XVII–pervaia polovina XIX v.)." In *Krest'ianskaia obshchina v Sibiri XVII–nachala XX vv.* Novosibirsk, 1977.
———. *Russkaia krest'ianskaia sem'ia v Zapadnoi Sibiri (XVIII–pervoi polovine XIX vv.).* Novosibirsk, 1979.
———. *Zhivaia starina: budni i prazdniki sibirskoi derevni v XVIII–pervoi polovine XIX v.* Novosibirsk, 1989.
Money, Keith. *Anna Pavlova: Her Life and Art.* New York, 1982.
Mordovtsev, D.L. *Russkie istoricheskie zhenshchiny.* St. Petersburg, 1874.
———. *Zamechatel'nye istoricheskie zhenshchiny na Rusi.* Vol. 1: *Russkie zhenshchiny do Petra.* St. Petersburg, 1874.
Myles, Bruce. *Night Witches: The Untold Story of Soviet Women in Combat.* Novato, 1981.
Ocherki istorii russkoi kul'tury XVIII v. Moscow, 1985.
Nash, Carol S. "Educating New Mothers: Women and the Enlightenment in Russia." *History of Education Quarterly,* vol. 21, no. 3 (1981), pp. 301–16.
Naumov, V.P. "Elizaveta Petrovna." *Russian Studies in History,* vol. 32, no. 4 (1994), pp. 37–72.
Noggle, Anne. *A Dance with Death: Soviet Airwomen in World War II.* College Station, 1994.
Noonan, Norma C. "Two Solutions to the *Zhenskii Vopros* in Russia and the USSR—Kollontai and Krupskaia: A Comparison." *Women and Politics,* vol. 11, no. 3 (1991), pp. 77–99.
Offen, Karen, Ruth Roach Pierson, and Jane Rendall, eds. *Writing Women's History: International Perspectives.* Bloomington, 1991.
Olearius, Adam. *The Travels of Olearius in Seventeenth-Century Russia,* trans. and ed. Samuel H. Baron. Stanford, 1967.
Pachmuss, Temira. *Zinaida Hippius: An Intellectual Profile.* Carbondale, 1971.
Paleolog [Paléologue], M. *Roman imperatora. Aleksandr II i kniaginia Iur'evskaia.* Moscow, 1924, repr. 1990.

Pavliuchenko, E.A. *V dobrovol'nom izgnanii. O zhenakh i sestrakh dekabristov.* Moscow, 1980.

Pavliuchenko, E.A. *Zhenshchiny v russkom osvoboditel'nom dvizhenii.* Moscow, 1988.

Perrot, Michelle. *Une histoire des femmes est-elle possible?* Paris, 1984.

Porter, Cathy. *Alexandra Kollontai: A Biography.* London, 1980.

———. *Fathers and Daughters: Russian Women in Revolution.* London, 1976.

Posadskaya, Anastasia, et al., eds. *Women in Russia: A New Era in Russian Feminism.* London, 1994.

Pouncy, Carolyn Johnston, ed. and trans. *The Domostroi: Rules for Russian Households in the Time of Ivan the Terrible.* Ithaca, 1994.

Pushkareva, N.L. *Chastnaia zhizn' zhenschiny v doindustrial'noi Rossii (X–nachalo XIX vv.).* Moscow, 1997.

———. "Imushchestvennye prava zhenshchin v russkom gosudarstve X–XV vv." *Istoricheskie zapiski,* no. 114 (1986), pp. 180–224.

———. "Sotsial'no-pravovoe polozhenie zhenshchin v russkom gosudarstve X–XV vv.: Voprosy prestupleniia i nakazaniia." *Sovetskoe gosudarstvo i pravo,* 1985, no. 4, pp. 121–26.

——— [Pushkariova]. "Woman and Her Property and Legal Status: Was the XVIth Century a Turning Point?" *La donna nel'economia. XIII–XVIIIss. XXI Settimana d'Instituto "F. Datini".* Florence, 1990.

———. *Zhenshchiny drevnei Rusi.* Moscow, 1989.

———. *Zhenshchiny Rossii i Evropy na porogu Novogo vremeni.* Moscow, 1996.

Pushkareva, N.L., and Eve Levin. "Women in Medieval Novgorod from the Eleventh to the Fifteenth Century." *Soviet Studies in History,* vol. 23, no. 4 (1985), pp. 71–90.

Rabinovich, M.G. "Gorod i gorodskoi obraz zhizni." In *Ocherki russkoi kul'tury XVIII v.,* vol. 4, pp. 252–99. Moscow, 1990.

———. *Ocherki etnografii russkogo feodal'nogo goroda.* Moscow, 1978.

———. *Ocherki material'noi kul'tury russkogo feodal'nogo goroda.* Moscow, 1988.

———. "Russkaia gorodskaia sem'ia v nachale XVIII v." *Sovetskaia etnografiia,* 1978, no. 5, pp. 96–108.

Radzinskaia, I.Iu., E.M. Shibarina, Z.A. Iankova. "Zhenshchiny v razvitom sotsialisticheskom obshchestve." In *Zhenshchiny strany Sovetov,* pp. 216–17. Moscow, 1977.

Raeff, Marc, ed. *Catherine the Great, A Profile.* New York, 1972.

Ransel, David L. *Mothers of Misery: Child Abandonment in Russia.* Princeton, 1988.

———, ed. *The Family in Imperial Russia.* Urbana, 1976.

Rice, Tamara Talbot. *Elizabeth, Empress of Russia.* London, 1970.

Rogger, Hans. *Russia in the Age of Modernisation and Revolution, 1881–1917.* London, 1983.

Romanov, B.A. *Liudi i nravy drevnei Rusi.* Moscow, 1963.

Roosevelt, Priscilla R. "Emerald Thrones and Living Statues: Theater and Theatricality on the Russian Estate." *Russian Review,* vol. 50, no. 1 (1991), pp. 1–23.

———. *Life on the Russian Country Estate.* New Haven, 1995.

Rosenberg, Chanie. *Women and Perestroika.* London, 1989.

Ruane, Christine. *Gender, Class, and the Professionalization of Russian City Teachers, 1860–1914.* Pittsburgh, 1994.

———. "The Vestal Virgins of St. Petersburg: School Teachers and the 1897 Marriage Ban." *Russian Review,* vol. 50, no. 2 (1991), pp. 163–82.

Rudnev, M.N. "Tserkovnoe sudoproizvodstvo po delam rastorzheniia braka." *Khristianskoe chtenie,* 1902, no. 1, pp. 97–125.

Rüss, H. "Elena Vasyl'evna Glinskaya." *Jahrbücher für Geschichte Osteuropas*, vol. 19 (1976), pp. 481–98.

Sacks, Michael Paul. *Women's Work in Soviet Russia*. New York, 1976.

————. *Work and Equality in the Soviet Union: The Division of Labor by Age, Gender, and Nationality*. New York, 1982.

Saunders, David. *Russia in the Age of Reaction and Reform, 1801–1881*. London, 1992.

Sederberg, G. *Zametki o religii i nravakh russkogo naroda 1709–1718*. Moscow, 1873.

Semenov, L.N. *Ocherki istorii byta i kul'turnoi zhizni Rossii. Pervaia polovina XVIII v.* Leningrad, 1982.

Semevskii, V.I. *Tsaritsa Praskov'ia*. St. Petersburg, 1883.

Sendich, Munir. "Moscow Literary Salons: Thursdays at Karolina Pavlova's." *Die Welt der Slaven*, vol. 17, pt. 2 (1973), pp. 341–57.

Senelick, Laurence. "The Erotic Bondage of Serf Theatre." *Russian Review*, vol. 50, no. 1 (1991), pp. 24–34.

Senyk, Sophia. *Women's Monasteries in Ukraine and Belorussia to the Period of Suppressions*. Rome, 1983.

Shabanova, A. *Ocherk zhenskogo dvizheniia v Rossii*. St. Petersburg, 1911.

Shashkov, S.S. *Istoricheskie sud'by zhenshchiny, detoubiistvo i prostitutsiia. Istoriia russkoi zhenshchiny*. St. Petersburg, 1872.

Shliapkin, I.A. *Tsarevna Natal'ia Alekseevna i teatr ee vremeni*. St. Petersburg, 1898.

Shmurlo, E.F. "Padenie tsarevny Sof'i." *Zhurnal Ministerstva narodnogo prosveshcheniia*, 1896, no. 1, pp. 38–95.

Sinaiskii, V.I. *Lichnoe i imushchestvennoe polozhenie zamuzhnei zhenshchiny v grazhdanskom prave*. Iuriev, 1910.

Smirnov, P.P., and E.V. Chistiakova, eds. *Alena Arzamasskaia-Temnikovskaia*. Saransk, 1986.

Stillman, Beatrice. "Sofya Kovalevskaya: Growing Up in the Sixties." *Russian Language Journal*, vol. 22 (1974), pp. 276–302.

Stites, Richard. "Prostitute and Society in Pre-Revolutionary Russia." *Jahrbücher für Geschichte Osteuropas*, vol. 31, no. 3 (1983), pp. 348–64.

————. *The Women's Liberation Movement in Russia*. Princeton, 1978.

————. "*Zhenotdel*: Bolshevism and Russian Women, 1917–1930." *Russian History*, vol. 3, pt. 2 (1976), pp. 174–93.

Stroev, V. *Bironovshchina i Kabinet ministrov pri Anne Ioannovne*. St. Petersburg, 1909.

Taubman, Jane. *A Life Through Poetry: Marina Tsvetaeva's Lyric Diary*. Columbus, 1989.

Thyret, Isolde. " 'Blessed Is the Tsaritsa's Womb': The Myth of Miraculous Birth and Royal Motherhood in Muscovite Russia." *Russian Review*, vol. 53, no. 4 (1994), pp. 479–96.

Tikhomirov, M.N. "Zapiski o regenstve Eleny Glinskoi i boiarskom pravlenii 1533–1547." *Istoricheskie zapiski*, vol. 46 (1954), pp. 248–88.

Tikhonravov, N. "Boiarynia Morozova." *Russkii vestnik*, vol. 59, no. 9 (1865), pp. 5–36.

Tishkin, G.A. *Zhenskii vopros v Rossii v 50–60-e gg. XIX v.* Leningrad, 1984.

Titova, L.V. *Beseda ottsa s synom o "zhenskim zlobe."* Novosibirsk, 1977.

Toomre, Joyce. *Classic Russian Cooking: Elena Molokhovets' A Gift to Young Housewives*. Bloomington, 1992.

Tsaturova, M.K. *Russkoe semeinoe pravo XVI–XVII vv.* Moscow, 1991.

Tseretelli, E. *Elena Ivanovna, velikaia kniaginia litovskaia, russkaia, koroleva pol'skaia.* St. Petersburg, 1898.

Tsitovich, P.P. *Iskhodnye momenty v istorii russkogo prava nasledovaniia.* St. Petersburg, 1870.

Tuve, Jeanette E. *The First Russian Women Physicians.* Newtonville, 1984.

Uspenskii, F.I. "Brak tsaria Ivana III Vasil'evicha s Sof'ei Paleolog." *Istoricheskii vestnik,* vol. 30 (1887), pp. 679–93.

Valishevskii, K. *Doch' Petra Velikogo.* St. Petersburg, 1882.

Volkov, A. *Ocherki russkoi literatury kontsa XIX i nachala XX v.* Moscow, 1955.

Voyce, Arthur. *Moscow and the Roots of Russian Culture.* Norman, 1964.

Wagner, William G. *Marriage, Property, and the Law in Late Imperial Russia.* New York, 1994.

———. "The Trojan Mare: Women's Rights and Civil Rights in Late Imperial Russia." In Olga Crisp and Linda Edmondson, eds., *Civil Rights in Imperial Russia.* Oxford, 1989, pp. 65–84.

Wilcox, R. Turner. *The Dictionary of Costume.* London, 1969.

Wilmot, Catherine. *The Russian Journals of Martha and Catherine Wilmot,* ed. The Marchioness of Londonderry and H.M. Hyde. London, 1934.

Worobec, Christine. *Peasant Russia: Family and Community in the Post-Emancipation Period.* Princeton, 1991.

———. "Reflections on Customary Law and Post-Reform Peasant Russia." *Russian Review,* vol. 44, no. 1, (1985), pp. 21–25.

———. "Temptress of Virgin? The Precarious Sexual Position of Women in Postemancipation Ukrainian Peasant Society." *Slavic Review,* vol. 49, no. 2 (1990), pp. 227–38.

———. "Victims or Actors? Russian Peasant Women and Patriarchy." In Esther Kingston-Mann and Timothy Mixter, eds., *Peasant Economy, Culture and Politics in European Russia, 1800–1921.* Princeton, 1991, pp. 177–206.

Woronzoff-Dashkoff, A. "Princess E.R. Dashkova's Moscow Library." *Slavonic and East European Review,* vol. 72, no. 1 (1994), pp. 60–71.

Yablonskaya, M.N. *Women Artists of Russia's New Age, 1900–1935.* New York, 1990.

Yaney, George. "Some Suggestions Regarding the Study of Russian Peasant Society Prior to Collectivization." *Russian Review,* vol. 44, no. 1 (1985), pp. 27–33.

Yedlin, Tova, ed. *Women in Eastern Europe and the Soviet Union.* New York, 1980.

Zabelin, I.E. *Domashnii byt russkikh tsarits XVI–XVII vv.* Moscow, 1901. repr. Novosibirsk, 1992.

———. *Domashnii byt russkogo naroda v XVI i XVII stoletiiakh.* 2 vols. Moscow, 1862–69.

———. *Zhenshchina v dopetrovskom obshchestve.* St. Petersburg, 1901.

Zagovorskii, A. *O razvode po russkomu pravu.* Kharkov, 1884.

Zguta, Russell. "The Ordeal of Water (Swimming of Witches) in the East Slavic World." *Slavic Review,* vol. 36 (1977), pp. 220–30.

———. *Russian Minstrels.* Philadelphia, 1978.

———. "Witchcraft and Medicine in Pre-Petrine Russia." *Russian Review,* vol. 37 (1978), pp. 438–48.

———. "Witchcraft Trials in Seventeenth-Century Russia." *American Historical Review,* vol. 82 (1977), pp. 1187–207.

Zhenshchina i svoboda. Puti vybora v mire traditsii i peremen. Moscow, 1994.

Zhenshchiny v SSSR. Statisticheskie materialy. 1991. Moscow, 1992.

Index

Abduction, 29, 31

Abortion, 38–39, 127, 178, 239, 258, 261, 263, 265

Academy for the Russian Language, 145, 148

Actresses. *See* Theater

Adrian, Patriarch of Moscow, 123

Adultery, 34, 73, 98–99, 102, 114, 160, 165–66, 169, 191

Agafia of Chernigov, 37

Agafia Sviatoslavna, Queen of Poland, 20

Agrafena, daughter-in-law of Princess Anna of Riazan, 24

Agriculture, 38, 42–43, 98, 143, 157, 166–67, 176, 220, 260, 264

Akhmat, Tatar khan, 24

Akhmatova, Anna, 214–15

Aksakov, Ivan, 197

Aksakov, S.T., 168

Alexandra, Princess of Slutsk, 50

Aleksei, son of Emperor Nicholas II, 193–95

Aleksei, son of Emperor Peter I, 128, 130

Aleksei, Tsar, 80, 83–84, 87, 114, 122, 171

Alexander I, Emperor, 187, 190

Alexander II, Emperor, 187, 191–92, 199, 205–6, 209, 214, 233, 237

Alexander III, Emperor, 187, 192

Alexander, Grand Prince of Lithuania, 63–64

Alexander II, Pope, 13

Alexandra, Empress, wife of Emperor Nicholas I, 190–91

Alexandra, Empress, wife of Emperor Nicholas II, 192–95, 207

Alexius Comnenus, Byzantine Emperor, 16

Alionor, wife of Raoul de Crépy, 13

Alisa-Victoria (Alix), Princess of Hesse-Darmstadt. *See* Alexandra, Empress, wife of Emperor Nicholas II

All-Russian Women's Congress of 1908, 208

Anastasia, daughter of Grand Prince Iaroslav the Wise, 12, 15

Anastasia, daughter of Prince Mikhail of Veria and Belozero, 56

Anastasia Grigorieva, Novgorod boyarina, 25–26

Anastasia Romanova (Zakharina), wife of Tsar Ivan IV, 71–72, 74

Andrei, brother of Grand Prince Vasilii III, 66

Andrei Bogoliubskii, Grand Prince, 18

Andrew II, King of Hungary, 12, 18

Angelina, Praskovia, 262

Anna, daughter of Grand Prince Iaroslav the Wise, 12–14

Anna, daughter of Grand Prince Vsevolod. *See* Ianka

Anna, Empress, 125–26, 130, 132–36, 171, 173

Anna, wife of Prince Fedor Rostislavich of Iaroslavl, 21

Anna, wife of Prince Vasilii Ivanovich of Riazan, 24

Anna Comnena, 16

Anna Leopoldovna, regent, 126–27, 132, 136–37
Anna Koltovskaia, wife of Tsar Ivan IV, 73
Anna Romanovna of Galich, 18–19
Anna Vasilchikova, wife of Tsar Ivan IV, 73
Anna, wife of Grand Prince Vladimir I, 11–12
Annenkova-Gebl, Polina, 202
Apraksina, A.B. (née Golitsyna), Princess, 169
Arabs, 7
Archeology, 5, 17, 30, 43, 54, 211
Argunov, N.I., 152
Aristocracy, 37, 43–44, 47, 49, 51, 54, 56, 63–77, 80–81, 83–87, 89, 92–101, 105, 107–12, 114, 117, 120, 122, 130–31, 134–38, 141–43, 153, 157–58, 163–64, 168–74, 179–83, 185, 192, 197, 201, 225–30, 233, 235, 245, 252–53, 256, 260
Arkhipova, Irina, 265
Artemii, elder of Trinity Monastery, 102
Artisans, 44, 59–60, 85, 100, 218, 236–37
Arzamasskaia (Temnikovskaia), Alena, 82–83, 88
Asia, 3, 20, 99, 116, 243
Austria, 17, 78, 85, 96, 114, 179
Authors. See Writers
Avvakum, archpriest, 80–81

Ballet, 150, 154, 215–16, 218–19, 265
Balsamon, Byzantine author, 16
Balzac, Honoré de, 213
Barrenness, 34, 38–39, 65, 76–77
Bastanov, V.I., 118
Baths, 32, 39–40, 98, 221
Batu, Mongol khan, 19
Beauty, ideals of, 26–27, 37, 54, 60, 65, 73, 78, 112–17, 120, 122, 125, 128, 133, 147, 164, 179–81, 183, 186, 217, 232, 242
Bela III, King of Hungary, 17
Belarus, 61. See also Polotsk
Beliaev, Ivan, 197
Belikov, D., archpriest, 166
Belinskii, Vissarion, 198, 212, 244
Beloozero, 70, 74–75, 79
Belskii family, 69
Belts, 54–55, 59, 117, 167, 183–84, 249

Bergholz, Friedrich von, 185
Berilova, Anna, 150
Bering, Vitus, 131
Bezborodko, Alexander, Count, 144
Bilibin, I.A., 218, 241
Birchbark documents, 30, 37, 41, 43, 45, 47
Biron, Ernst, 135–36
Birth control. See Abortion, Contraception
Blavatskaia, Elena, 211
Bloody Sunday, 193
Blouses. See Dresses
Boborykin, Peter, 199
Bogdanova, Maria, 204–05
Bokova (Obrucheva), Maria, 210
Boleslaw "the Bashful," King of Poland, 20
Bolotnikov, Ivan, 62
Bolotov, Andrei T., 141, 164, 168
Bolsheviks, 195, 207–8, 238, 257–58. See also Social-Democratic Party
Boltin, I.T., 163
Boots. See Footwear
Boretskaia, Marfa ("Posadnitsa"), 25–26, 42, 60
Boretskii, Isaak, mayor of Novgorod, 25
Borisova, Iulia, 265
Bourgeoisie. See Middle Class
Boyar Duma, 65, 69, 77–78, 81, 128
Boyars. See Aristocracy
Breshko-Breshkovskaia, Ekaterina, 205
Briullov, Karl, 196, 198
Briusov, Valerii, 199, 215
Bruni, Fedor, 196
Bunina, Anna, 212
Bulgaria, 61
Buturlin, Princess, 169
Byzantine Empire, 7, 9, 10–11, 14–17, 26, 27, 61

Cadets (Constitutional Democrats), 200, 208, 240
Casimir, King of Poland, 14
Catherine, daughter of Tsar Ivan V, 126–27, 136
Catherine I (née Marta Skavronskaia), Empress, 126–31, 134, 159
Catherine II, "the Great," Empress, 139–48, 151, 153, 161, 163, 174, 177–78, 181, 187–88

Caucasus, 78, 187
Central Asia, 187. *See also* Mongols
Chaadaev, Peter, 197
Charity. *See* Philathropy
Chastity, 29, 31, 35–38, 126, 160–61, 164. *See also* Adultery, Virginity
Child-bearing, 36, 38–40, 105, 113, 168, 237–39, 257, 261, 263, 265. *See also* Children, Pregnancy
Children, 39–40, 45–46, 90–93, 105–11, 171–76, 225–29, 237–39, 260–61; abandonment of, 125, 178; abuse of, 91, 169; care of, 90, 190, 225–26, 229, 231, 237–38, 258, 260–61, 263–64; education of, 29, 91, 125, 168, 213, 225, 229, 231 games of, 90–91, 226, 232; guardianship of, 45–46, 102, 111, 177; illegitimate, 39, 160–61, 223, 239, 258; and inheritance, 45–46, 93, 106–11, 171–73, 175–76, 234; mortality of, 39, 168, 237; orphaned, 42, 107, 157, 190, 217; status of, 39–40, 90–93. 168–69. *See also* Daughters, Family, Infanticide, Regents
Chekhov, Anton, 199
Cheliadnina, Agrafena, 67–68, 90
Cherkasskaia, Princess, 115
Chernigov, 18–19
Chernyshevskii, Nikolai G., 204, 235–36
China, 19, 85
Christianity. *See* Russian Orthodox Church
Christine of Sweden, 16
Chronicles, 5, 7–10, 12–15, 18–20, 25–26, 48, 52, 65, 71–73, 75, 77, 86–88
Civil war, 17–19, 23–27, 62, 75, 77–79, 82–83, 103, 108, 139, 145, 256
Clergy, 32, 34, 36–38, 48, 94–95, 123, 141, 158–59, 162, 169, 191, 233
Cloth, 43, 54–56, 89, 117–20, 182–83, 242, 244, 247, 251–52, 261; production of, 43, 59, 100, 167, 222, 242, 253
Clothing, 53–60, 81, 94–95, 104, 114, 116–20, 125, 175, 178–86, 204, 221, 227–28, 241–53; Eastern influence in styles of 54–55, 182, 243, 247; production of, 43, 59–60, 100, 120, 167, 179, 186, 222, 242–44, 248,

Clothing *(continued)*
252–53; Western influence in styles of, 56, 83, 125, 170, 178–86, 241, 244–45, 247–50, 252. *See also* Belts, Dresses, Embroidery, Footwear, Hats, Headdresses, Needlework, Outerwear, Underwear.
Collectivization, 260–61, 264
Collins, Samuel, 114–115, 155
Commerce, 45, 48, 85, 99, 135, 138, 142–43, 209, 266
Communes *(mir)*, 169, 175–77, 234
Communism. *See* Marxism, Socialism
Concubines, 18, 34, 47, 78–79, 127–28, 151–53, 165
Condorcet, Jean, 201
Constantine Paleologus, 26
Constantine Porphyrogenitus, Byzantine Emperor, 9–11
Constantinople. *See* Byzantine Empire
Contraception, 38
Convents. *See* Monasteries
Cooking. *See* Food
Corsets, 114, 179–81, 204, 244, 248, 250, 252. *See also* Underwear.
Cosmetics, 37, 93, 114–16, 120, 180–81, 183, 242, 247, 251
Cossacks, 79, 82, 230
Courland, 126, 130, 133–34
Crimea, 64, 67, 85, 144. *See also* Tatars
Crimean War, 187, 244
Czechs, 47, 116,˙ 156, 182

Daniil, Metropolitan, 102
Danilov, M.V., 164, 168
Danilova, Maria, 81
Dargomyzhskii, Alexander, 198, 216
Dashkov, Ivan, Prince, 146
Dashkova, Catherine, (née Vorontsova), Princess, 145–50, 209
David, Jiri, 116, 156, 182
Daughters, 46–49, 90–93, 108–9, 172–77; birth of, 39; education of, 90–91, 93, 210, 220–23, 226, 231; inheritance by, 46–49, 93, 108–9, 111, 135, 172–73, 176–77, 234. *See also* Dowry, Family, Household, Marriage
Death, 42, 103–4
Decembrists, 197–98, 201–4
Delvig, Alexander, 197

Denmark, 16, 78, 183, 192
Derzhavin, G.P., 165, 168, 188
Diaghilev, Serge, 218
Diderot, Denis, 142, 147, 201
Divorce, 31, 34–35, 44, 65, 76–77,
    102–3, 127, 169–70, 197, 202, 239;
    laws of, 31, 34–35, 53, 102–3, 106,
    158–59, 161, 174, 233–35, 240, 258,
    261, 263, 265
Dmitrieva, Elizaveta, 210
Dmitrieva, Valentina, 214
Dmitrii, grandson of Grand Prince Ivan
    III, 27
Dmitrii, Prince of Suzdal, 21
Dmitrii, son of Prince Iurii of
    Zvenigorod, 23
Dmitrii Boretskii, son of Marfa
    Boretskaia, 26
Dmitrii Donskoi, Grand Prince, 21–22, 49
Dmitrii of Uglich, son of Tsar Ivan IV,
    74–75
Dobrodeia-Evpraksia (Zoia), 16, 17
Dobroliubov, N.A., 236
Dolgorukaia, Catherine, fiancée of Peter
    II, 131–32
Dolgorukaia, Ekaterina (Iurevskaia), wife
    of Emperor Alexander II, 191–92
Dolgorukaia, Natalia (née Sheremeteva),
    131–33, 150, 165
Dolgorukii, Ivan, 131–32
Domostroi, 88–89, 91, 95, 99–100, 102
Dostoevskii, Fedor, 203, 217
Doviaglo, Sofia, 211
Dowry, 44–49, 106–10, 159, 164,
    171–73, 175, 231–32
Dresses, 54–55, 114, 116–17, 179–84,
    242–45, 247–53
Duma, 208, 234, 237, 257. *See also*
    Boyar Duma.
Durova, Nadezhda, 212–13

Education, abroad, 210–11; of children,
    91, 123, 125–26, 131–33, 143,
    146–47, 150, 158, 163–64, 168, 180,
    188–91, 196, 204, 223, 229–30; of
    women, 12, 15–16, 84, 141, 153,
    163–64, 180, 188–91, 203–5,
    209–12, 226–30, 236, 239, 255–56,
    259, 263, 265. *See also* Schools,
    Universities.
Efimenko, Alexandra, 211

Ekaterinoslav, 207
Elagina, Avdotia, 196–97
Elena, daughter of Grand Prince Ivan III,
    63–64
Elena, daughter of Grand Prince Olgerd
    of Lithuania, 21
Elena, Grand Duchess, sister of Emperor
    Nicholas I, 192
Elena Glinskaia, wife of Grand Prince
    Vasilii III, 63, 65–67, 69, 71, 88
Elena Sheremeteva, daughter-in-law of
    Tsar Ivan IV, 76, 117
Eliseev, V.A., 243
Elizabeth (Elisava), daughter of Grand
    Prince Iaroslav the Wise, 12
Elizabeth I, Empress, 137–42, 156, 173
Elizabeth, Empress, wife of Emperor
    Alexander I, 190
Elizabeth, Grand Duchess, sister-in-law
    of Alexander III, 192
Elizabeth I, Queen of England, 74, 76
Embroidery, 54–55, 69–70, 79, 100,
    116–18, 181, 245
Engelgardt, Anna, 205
Engels, Friedrich, 4
England, 3, 74, 78, 114, 146, 163
Enlightenment, 141–43, 145–47, 154, 165
Entaltseva, Alexandra, 202
Ermolova, Maria, 216
Esip Gorshkov, Novgorod mayor, 26
Ethnography, 5, 102, 211, 213, 220. *See
    also* Peasants.
Euler, Leonhard, 135
Europe, Western alliances with, 8, 10,
    12–14, 16, 20, 22–23, 26, 63–65, 74,
    76, 78, 85, 121, 126, 131, 138–39,
    141; comparisons with, 7, 13, 45–46,
    48, 62–63, 89, 94, 102, 104, 112,
    118, 123, 153, 180, 214–215, 218,
    233, 240, 263, 265; influences from,
    27, 62, 80, 83–84, 99, 103, 119,
    121–30, 135–37, 139, 141–43,
    145–46, 150, 153, 163–65, 170,
    178–85, 197–98, 201, 204, 213, 226,
    228, 241, 244–45, 250, 252; travel
    to, 12–14, 28, 86, 121, 133–34, 147,
    151, 155, 196–97, 210–11, 218;
    travelers from, 5, 33, 79, 85, 89–90,
    95–99, 104–5, 112–17, 119–20, 126,
    133, 135–36, 139, 149–50, 155, 159,
    169, 179–80, 182–83, 185

Evdokia, wife of Grand Prince Dmitrii Donskoi, 21–22, 49, 60
Evdokia Lopukhina, wife of Emperor Peter I, 127–28, 131
Evfimia Gorshkova, Novgorod boyarina, 26
Evfrosinia, St. of Polotsk (Predslava), 15–17, 60
Evfrosinia, St., of Suzdal, 16
Evfrosinia, wife of King Geza II of Hungary, 16–17
Evpraksia (Adelheid), wife of Holy Roman Emperor Henry IV, 14–15
Evpraksia of Riazan, 37
Evreinova, Anna, 210

False Dmitrii. See Otrepiev, Grigorii
Family, 28–29, 88–93, 102–7, 126–28, 220–35, 240, 255–65; relations in, 34–41, 76, 89–93, 95, 100, 102, 104–5, 112–13, 117, 123, 126–28, 132, 155, 162–70, 173, 175–78, 214, 220–24, 229, 234–35, 261, 264; structure of, 42, 92, 167, 171, 220–21, 224, 235, 258–59, 260. See also Marriage, Household, Housework.
February Revolution, 205, 240, 256–57
Fedor, Tsar, son of Tsar Aleksei, 84
Fedor, Tsar, son of Tsar Ivan IV, 61–62, 72, 74, 76, 77
Fedor of Riazan, 37
Fedor Rostislavich, Prince of Iaroslavl, 21
Fedorov, N.P., 199
Fedotova, Galina, 216
Feminism, 201, 203–4, 208–9, 213, 235–39, 248, 256
Feodora Petrovna, wet-nurse of Peter I, 123
Feodosia, daughter of Tsar Ivan V, 126
Feofan Grek, 41
Fevronia, St. of Murom, 37, 100–1
Figner, Vera, 203, 205–6
Fikelmon, Daria, 198
Filosofova, Anna, 204
Finland, 138–39
Fine arts, 6, 148, 196–97, 199–200, 215–19, 251
Fletcher, Giles, 97, 104, 116, 117
Fonvizin, D.I., 168
Fonvizina, Natalia, 202

Food, 42–43, 89, 97–100, 114, 167, 222, 227, 230–32, 260–61, 263, 264; ritual, 29, 32–33, 104
Footwear, 59–60, 119, 179, 182, 185, 245–46, 248, 252
Frederick, "the Great," King of Prussia, 139, 141
Frederick, King of Sweden, 136
Frederick William, King of Prussia, 126
Frederika-Dagmar, Princess of Denmark. See Maria Fedorvona, Empress, wife of Emperor Alexander III
Frederika-Luisa-Charlotte, Princess of Prussia. See Alexandra, Empress, wife of Emperor Nicholas I
Frederiks, Sofia, Baroness, 192
Friedrich-Wilhelm, Duke of Courland, 133
France, 3, 13, 14, 85, 126, 137, 141, 146, 164, 180–81, 190–91, 210, 218–19, 226, 233, 242, 244–46, 249
Fuks, Alexandra, 199
Furtseva, Ekaterina, 265
Funerals, 103–4, 127, 153
Furniture, 89, 228, 247
Furs, 25, 32–33, 55–56, 58, 80, 90, 116, 118, 136, 184, 242, 245, 248, 250

Gabrilovich, Olga, 211
Galich, 18, 19
Gan, Elena, 212–13
Geiden, Elena, Countess, 192
Gentry. See Aristocracy, Pomeste.
Gere, V.I., 236
German Quarter, 85, 127
Germany, 3, 10, 12, 14, 78, 113, 115, 119, 124, 126–27, 133–37, 139, 156, 178–80, 184, 186, 188, 195, 210–11, 226, 262
Geza II, King of Hungary, 16
Gippius, Zinaida, 200, 214
Glinskaia, Anna, Princess, 67–68
Glinskaia, Elena. See Elena Glinskaia, wife of Vasilii III.
Glinskii, Mikhail L., Prince, 65–68
Glinskii, Vasilii, Prince, 65
Glinka, Fedor, 197–98, 216
Godunov, Boris, 74–78, 79.
Godunov, Fedor, 78
Godunova, Irina, 74, 76–78
Godunova, Ksenia, 76, 78–79

Godunova, Maria, 79
Gogol, Nikolai, 242, 245
Goethe, Johann Wolfgang von, 197
Goikhbarg, A.G., 233
Golden Horde. *See* Tatars
Goldenberg sisters, 205
Golitsyn, D.M., Prince, 134
Golitsyn, V.V., Prince, 84–85
Golitsyna, Avdotia, Princess, 227
Golitsyna, M.F., Princess, 128
Golovin family, 76
Golovin, I.F., 162
Goncharova, Natalia, 218
Gorbachev, Mikhail, 265
Gorodislava, sister of St. Evfrosinia of
    Polotsk, 15
Gouges, Olympe de, 201
Government, 16–28, 61–88, 109–12,
    121–38, 142–47, 153–54 171–74,
    237–40, 257–66; reform of, 9, 18,
    23–24, 61–62, 66, 72, 84–85, 88,
    109–10, 112, 121–24, 128–31,
    134–35, 137–38, 142–45, 153–54,
    171–73, 178, 187–88, 197–201, 203,
    208, 233, 238–40, 255–61, 265;
    social policies of, 237–40, 257–59,
    262–63, 266; women's participation
    in, 9, 12, 14, 16–28, 37, 63–79,
    83–88, 95–96, 105, 107, 121–24,
    128–31, 134–47, 153–54, 174,
    255–59, 262, 264–65. *See also* Law
Great Northern War, 121
Greeks, 62, 80. *See also* Byzantine
    Empire
Gremislava Ingvarovna, Queen of Poland,
    20
Griboedov, A.S., 226
Guards Regiments, 130, 137, 141–42,
    146
Guchkov, Alexander, 200
Gumilev, Nikolai, 215
Gustav Vasa, King of Sweden, 67

Hagiography, 5, 19–20, 35, 37, 40, 124
Hair styles, 32, 56–58, 120, 179–83, 185,
    204, 247–48, 251
Hamilton, Mary, 127
Harald Hardrada, 12–13
Hastings, Mary, 74
Hats, 184–85, 204, 248–49, 251. *See
    also* Headdresses

Headdresses, 32, 94, 116, 179, 184–85,
    221, 246–47. *See also* Hats
Health care. *See* Medicine
Henry I, King of France, 13
Henry IV, Holy Roman Emperor, 14
Herberstein, Sigismund von, Baron, 95,
    102
Herzen, Alexander, 203, 217
Historiography of women, 3–6, 88,
    91–92, 105–6, 139, 154, 255, 266
Holy Synod, 128, 161, 170
Honor, 29, 34–35, 41, 45, 52–53, 83, 92,
    105, 113, 233
Households, 28–29, 42–43, 88, 95–100,
    174–75, 220–229; management of,
    21, 33, 42–43, 70, 89–90, 96–100,
    130, 147, 154, 174–75, 188, 220–24,
    226, 228–29, 237, 264; structure of,
    42, 91, 167, 180, 225, 231. *See also*
    Family
Houses, 88–89, 95–96, 228, 224–25,
    259–60
Housework, 42–43, 91, 95–99, 167,
    220–22, 230–31, 236, 260–61,
    263–64. *See also* Children, Food,
    Household, Needlework
Homosexuality, 38
Humboldt, Wilhelm von, 197
Hungary, 12, 14, 16–19, 178
Husbands. *See* Family, Households,
    Marriage, Weddings
Huyssen, Heinrich von, Baron, 133

Iakimova, Anna, 206
Iakunchikova, Maria, 217–18
Ianka, daughter of Grand Prince
    Vsevolod, 14–15
Iaroslav "Osmomysl," Prince of Galich,
    18
Iaroslav "the Wise," Grand Prince, 12–14
Iaroslavl, 21, 40, 66
Iazykov, N.M., 196
Icons, 6, 43, 88, 119, 90, 162, 218
Igor, Grand Prince, husband of Olga, 8
Incest, 31, 92, 158, 161
Industry, 121, 130, 143, 207, 236–38,
    243–44, 247, 252, 261
Infanticide, 38, 127, 178
Ingeborg, sister of Dobrodeia, 16, 17
Ingegerd (Irina), wife of Iaroslav the
    Wise, 12

Inheritance, 22, 25, 44–49, 74, 93, 103,
    106–112, 135, 163, 171–177, 234
Irina, Byzantine noblewoman, 16
Ishimova, Alexandra, 213
Istomin, Karion, 84
Istomina, Avdotia, 215–216
Istvan III, King of Hungary, 17
Italy, 3, 26, 85, 137, 248
Iunge, Elena, 217–218
Iurii, brother of Grand Prince Andrei
    Bogoliubskii, 18
Iurii, brother of Tsar Ivan IV, 65, 68
Iurii, brother of Emperor Peter I, 122
Iurii, brother of Grand Prince Vasilii III,
    66
Iurii, Prince of Zvenigorod, brother of
    Vasilii I, 23
Iushkov, Vasilii, boyar, 126
Ivan VI, Emperor, 136
Ivan III, Grand Prince, 24, 26–27, 64
Ivan, son of Tsar Ivan IV, 61, 72, 74, 76
Ivan IV "the Terrible," Tsar, 61–76, 79,
    88, 98, 117
Ivan V, Tsar, 84, 86, 125, 132
Ivanovskaia, Polina, 207
Ivashev, Vladimir, 204
Izmailov, Alexander, 197

Jewelry, 54, 58–59, 95, 119–120, 179,
    247, 249–251
Judicial procedure, 50–51, 70, 74, 81–82,
    113, 138, 144–145, 177, 205–6, 233
Jul, Just, 183

Kaliuzhnaia, Maria, 206
Kalmykova, Anna, 208
Kantemir, Antiokh, 165
Kantemir, Maria, 165
Kantemir, Matvei, 165
Karakozov, Dmitrii, 205
Karamzin, N.M., 8, 26, 169, 212, 229
Karamzina, Ekaterina, 198
Karl Leopold, Prince of
    Mecklenburg-Schwering, 126
Karl Peter Ulrich, Duke of
    Holstein-Gottorp. See Peter III
Kashevarova-Rudneva, Varvara, 211
Kasimov khanate, 96
Kazan, 64, 67, 96, 138, 190, 192,
    236. See also Tatars
Kerensky, Alexander, 208, 257

Kharuzina, Vera, 211
Kharkov, 190, 236
Kharkov University, 209
Khoriv, legendary prince, 10
Khovanskii, I.A., Prince, 84
Khudiakov, Ivan, 165
Khudiakova, Anna Vasilievna, 165
Khvoshchinskaia, Nadezhda, 213–14
Khvoshchinskaia, Sofia, 213–14
Kiev, 8–10, 12–17, 48, 49, 132, 199, 207
Kiev University, 209
Kievan Rus, 5, 8–17, 25, 116
Kii, legendary prince, 10
Kinship. See Family.
Kireevskii, Ivan, 197, 212
Kireevskii, Peter, 197
Kliment Smoliatich, 38
Klirikova, Olga, 208
Kliuchevskii, Vasilii, 139
Kniazhnin, Ia.B., 148
Kniazhnina, Ekaterina, 150
Kollontai, Alexandra, 257, 262
Kolomenskoe, 65
Kolychev family, 73
Komissarzhevskaia, Vera, 217
Konopliankiova, Zina, 207
Konstantin, son of Grand Princess
    Evdokia, 22
Korb, Johann Georg, 114, 179
Korkunova, Maria, 205
Korolenko, Peter, 199
Korsini, Nadezhda, 205
Korvin-Krukovskii, V.V., 210
Kostroma, 192
Kotoshikhin, Grigorii, 102
Kovaleva (Zhemchugova), Praskovia,
    150–53
Kovalevskaia, Maria, 206
Kovalevskaia, Sofia, 210–11
Kovalevskii, V.O., 210
Krupskaia, Nadezhda, 207
Krzhizhanovskaia, Zinaida, 207
Ksenia, Princess of Iaroslavl, 21
Kulman, Elizaveta, 212
Kupriianova, Liubov, 208
Kuskova, Elena, 208
Kustodiev, B.M., 232
Kutuzov, Mikhail, Field Marshall, 198

Labor. See Housework, Industry, Workers
Land. See Inheritance, Property

Land and Freedom party, 204
Lassalle, Ferdinand, 204
Lavrov, Captain, 173
Lavrov, P.L., 199
Law, 6, 44–47, 63, 105–13, 131, 138,
    142–45, 158–59, 171–79, 233–
    35, 237–40, 256–57, 260, 264;
    civil, 50–51, 111–12, 257, 261;
    criminal, 51–53, 112–13, 127,
    177–78, 261; ecclesiastical, 12,
    30–31, 34–35, 38–39, 51–52,
    102, 161, 170; property, 44–47,
    106–12, 135, 171–77, 233–34;
    protective, 237–38, 257, 259,
    261–63. See also Government,
    Judicial procedure
Law Codes: Compiled Laws of the
    Russian Empire, 5–6, 131, 212, 233,
    235 Law Code (Ulozhenie) of 1649,
    93, 109, 111–13, 156 Russkaia
    Pravda, 5, 44–45
Lebedeva, Tatiana, 206
Ledantiu-Ivasheva, Kamilla, 202, 204
Legislation. See Law
Lenin, Vladimir Ilich, 207–8
Leontieva, Tatiana, 207
Lermontov, Mikhail, 198
Lermontova, Iulia, 210–11
Lestocq, Johann-Hermann, 137
Levitskii, D., 149
Liberation, women's. See Feminism,
    Suffrage, Woman Question
Likhud, Sofronii, 130
Literacy, 13, 15, 28, 259
Literature. See Chronicles, Hagiography,
    Magazines, Newspapers, Novels,
    Poets, Writers
Lithuania, 18, 22, 26, 62–65, 67, 85, 128,
    131, 184
Liubatovich sisters, 205
Livonia, 64, 67
Livonian War, 61, 70, 73
Lokhvitskaia, Mirra, 214
Lomonosov, Mikhail V., 135, 146, 158
Louis XIV, King of France, 85
Luisa-Maria, Princess of
    Hesse-Darmstadt. See Elizabeth,
    Empress, wife of Emperor
    Alexander I
Lunin, Mikhail, 202
Lybed, legendary princess, 10

Magazines, 144–45, 150, 180, 183, 192,
    198, 203, 212, 214, 236, 242,
    248–49, 253, 259–60
Makarov, A.V., 128
Makarova, Anna, 211
Maksimova, Ekaterina, 265
Malevinskii, Arefa, 101
Malfrid, sister of Dobrodeia, 16–17
Maliutin, Sergei, 200
Mamontova, Ekaterina, 200
Manuel, Byzantine Emperor, 17
Marfa, daughter of Tsar Aleksei, 83
Marfa Sobakina, wife of Tsar Ivan IV,
    72–73
Maria, daughter of Prince Temir of
    Kabarda, wife of Tsar Ivan IV, 72
Maria, daughter of Tsar Ivan V, 126
Maria, Princess of Hesse-Darmstadt. See
    Maria Aleksandrovna, Empress,
    wife of Emperor Alexander II
Maria, Princess of Slutsk, 50
Maria Aleksandrovna, Empress, wife of
    Emperor Alexander II, 191
Maria Dobronega, wife of King Casimir
    of Poland, 14
Maria Dolgorukaia, fiancée of Tsar Ivan
    IV, 73
Maria Fedorovna, Empress, wife of
    Emperor Alexander III, 192
Maria Fedorovna, Empress, wife of
    Emperor Paul I, 188–90
Maria Iaroslavna, Princess of Serpukhov,
    wife of Grand Prince Vasilii II,
    23–26, 51
Maria Mikhailovna, wife of Prince
    Vasilko of Rostov, 19–20
Maria Miloslavskaia, wife of Tsar
    Aleksei, 80, 83
Maria Nagaia, wife of Tsar Ivan IV,
    74–75
Marriage, 29–30, 37–39, 93–96, 108–13,
    156–67, 234–35, 258; arranged, 10,
    29–30, 71–72, 93–96, 125–26, 131,
    133, 156–61, 166, 224, 226, 230,
    235; age at, 30, 42, 71, 93, 131,
    156–58, 160, 226; celebration of, 29,
    31–34, 94, 159–62, 170; Christian
    conception of, 29–30, 34–39, 94–96,
    100, 159–60, 166, 170–71;
    companionate, 30, 37, 93, 100–1,
    131–33, 151, 156–57, 164–67, 192,

Marriage *(continued)*
202, 224; consent in, 30, 156–58,
170, 234, 258; civil, 29–30, 94, 235,
258; fictitious, 210, 235; of serfs,
158, 234; sex in, 33, 37–38, 239; of
slaves, 30; violence in, 39, 52–53,
71, 76, 102, 112–13, 117, 166, 172,
177. *See also* Divorce, Family,
Weddings
Marx, Karl, 199
Marxism, 4, 199, 207. *See also*
Bolsheviks, Mensheviks,
Social-Democratic Party, Socialism,
Socialist Revolutionary Party
Matveev, Artamon, 122
Mazovsha, Tatar pretender, 23–24
Medvedev, Silvester, 84
Medicine, 77, 114–16, 137–38, 173, 203,
224, 261, 263, 265; folk, 39, 116;
women's education in, 211, 236;
women's practice of, 15–16, 39, 82,
105, 148, 150, 202–3, 205, 211, 237,
255, 264
Meletis Pigasos, Patriarch of Alexandria,
76
Mendeleev, Dmitrii, 211
Mensheviks, 207, 238. *See also*
Social-Democratic Party
Menshikov, Alexander, Prince, 125, 128,
130–31
Menstruation, 92
Merchants, 72, 138, 156, 184, 230–33,
246–47, 250–52
Merezhkovskii, Dmitrii, 200
Meyerberg, Baron, 96
Mezentseva, Avdotia, Princess, 93
Mezentseva, Marfa, Princess, 93
Michael Romanov, Tsar, 62, 79
Mickiewicz, Adam, 197
Middle class, 72, 138, 142, 156, 184–85,
192, 199, 227, 230–33, 236–38,
246–47, 250–52, 257. *See also*
Artisans, Commerce, Industry,
Merchants
Midwives. *See* Medicine
Mikhail, St., Prince of Chernigov, 19, 20,
37, 44
Mikhail, son of Fedor Rostislavich and
Maria of Iaroslavl, 21
Mikhailov, M.L., 199, 203, 235
Militsina, Elizaveta, 214

Miliukov, Peter, 200
Miliukova, Anna, 208
Miloslavskaia, Anna, 81
Miloslavskaia, Maria. *See* Maria
Miloslavskaia, wife of Tsar Aleksei.
Mir iskusstva, 200
Mirovich, Zinaida, 208
Mniszech, Jerzy, 78
Mniszech, Marina, 78–79
Monasteries, 16, 22–23, 25, 42–43,
48–49, 53, 66, 81, 86, 126; for
women, 15, 35, 46, 51, 65, 70,
73–75, 77–79, 82, 86, 102–3,
127–28, 132, 174, 178, 192
Mongols, 19, 20, 21, 22. *See also*
Tatars
Monks. *See* Monasteries
Mons, Anna, 127
Montesquieu, Charles-Louis de Secondat
de, 146
Morozov, Boris, 80
Morozov, Gleb, 80
Morozov, Ivan, 80, 82
Morozova, Feodosia, 80–83, 88
Morozova, Maria (née Mamontova),
199–200
Morozova, Varvara, 199
Moscow, 18, 21–27, 49, 61, 63–68,
74–79, 85–87, 98, 123, 125–27, 132,
138, 147, 151, 173, 178–79, 190–92,
196–97, 199–200, 209, 215–16, 225,
245. *See also* Muscovy
Moscow University, 150, 209
Mstislav Vladimirovich, Grand Prince,
16–17
Münnich, B., field marshall, 136
Muraviev, M.N., 164
Muravieva, Alexandra, 202
Muravieva, Maria, 216
Muscovy, 5, 21–27, 61–122, 126–27,
171, 174, 256. *See also* Moscow
Mylnikov, N.D., 246
Music, 15, 78, 150, 154, 195, 196–200,
216, 219, 226, 230, 232, 265. *See
also* Ballet, Opera, Theater

Nagaia, Evdokia, Princess, 69
Nagaia, Maria. *See* Maria Nagaia, wife of
Tsar Ivan IV
Nagoi, A.F., 73
Nagoi family, 74

Napoleon Bonaparte, 144, 181–82, 190, 213
Narodniki, 205–6, 209, 214
Naryshkin, Lev, 122–23, 127
Naryshkin, Semen, 123
Naryshkina, Maria, 150
Naryshkina, Natalia. *See* Natalia Naryshkina, wife of Tsar Aleksei
Nastaska, concubine of Prince Iaroslav Osmomysl of Galich, 18
Natalia Naryshkina, wife of Tsar Aleksei, 83–84, 90, 119, 122–25, 127
Natalia, sister of Peter I, 122–26, 178
Nechaev, Sergei, 205
Needlework, 43, 55, 70, 79, 91, 95–96, 100, 126, 167, 190, 195, 230–32
Newspapers, 198, 207–8, 247
Nezhdanova, Antonina, 219
Nepliuev, Ivan, 179
Nicholas I, Emperor, 187, 190, 197
Nicholas II, Emperor, 192–93, 257
Nicholas II, Pope, 13
Nihilists, 203–4
Nikita, first husband of Vasilisa Melentieva, 73
Nikitina, Evdoksia, 200
Nikon, Patriarch of Moscow, 79
Nikulina-Kositskaia, Liubov, 216
Norway, 12–13, 16, 233
Novels, 164, 204, 213–14, 226, 228–29. *See also* Writers
Novikov, N.N., 145, 148
Novodevichii convent, 78, 86–87
Novgorod, 12, 24–26, 45–46, 60, 72, 148
Nuns, 15, 17, 19, 22, 43, 51, 67, 70, 74–75, 77–79, 81–83, 86, 93, 132, 174, 192. *See also* Monasteries

Obraztsova, Elena, 265
October Revolution, 205, 256–57
Octobrists, 200, 240
Oksinia (Ksenia), Princess of Tver, 20
Olav, King of Norway, 12
Old Believers, 62, 79–81, 84–85
Oldenburg, Elizaveta, Princess, 208
Olearius, Adam, 90, 97, 113, 115, 119
Olga, Grand Princess, 8–11, 15, 60, 66
Olga Romanovna, Princess of Volynia, 15
Opera, 151–52, 216, 219
Oprichnina, 61, 70, 72–73, 76, 79, 98
Orlov, Aleksei, Count, 144

Orlov, Grigorii, Count, 141
Ostermann, Johann, 133
Ostrovskii, A.N., 217
Otrepiev, Grigorii (False Dmitrii), 75, 78–79
Otto I, Holy Roman Emperor, 10
Outerwear, 55–56, 117–18, 182, 184, 243–45, 247–53
Owen, Robert, 204

Pakhomov, Nikifor, 175
Pakhomova, Avdotia, 175
Paniutina sisters, 205
Patronage of the arts, 27, 143, 145–46, 151, 195, 196–201, 203, 219, 232
Paul I, Emperor, 148–49, 188–89, 190
Pavlova, Anna, 218–19
Pavlova, Karolina, 196, 212
People's Will, 206
Perovskaia, Sofia, 191, 206
Peasants, 47, 50–51, 53, 82, 98, 100–1, 138–39, 144–45, 154, 156, 160–62, 165–68, 175–77, 179, 183–86, 204–5, 218–24, 228, 230, 233–34, 238–39, 241, 246, 252–53, 259–61, 264–65. *See also* Serfdom
Peter I "the Great," Emperor, 62, 84–87, 90, 121–38, 144–45, 150, 154–59, 162–63, 170–74, 177–79, 183, 187, 256
Peter II, Emperor, 130–34
Peter III, Emperor, 139, 141–42, 146
Peter, St. of Murom, 37, 100–1
Petrejus, Petrus, 113
Philanthropy, 22–23, 47–48, 72, 81, 109, 125, 138, 161, 178, 188–95, 202–3, 223
Philip, son of Anna Iaroslavna, 13
Philosophy, 84, 142–43, 147, 150, 199–200, 202, 209, 211
Physicians. *See* Medicine
Pisarev, Dmitrii, 213
Plevitskaia, Nadezhda, 219
Plisetskaia, Maia, 265
Poets, 84, 150, 164, 168, 170, 195, 197, 200, 202, 212, 214–15, 229, 251. *See also* Writers
Poland, 14, 18, 20, 26, 62, 64, 72, 75, 78–79, 84, 85, 130, 144, 151, 181, 184
Polenov, Vasilii, 200, 217

Polenova, Elena, 200, 218
Poliuzhaia, daughter of Zhiroshka,
    Novgorod burger, 47
Polotsk, 15–17, 70
Polotskii, Simeon, 84, 164
Polovtsy, 7
Pomeste, 93, 103, 107–12, 172–73. *See
    also* Property
Ponomareva, Sofia, 197–98
Pososhkov, Ivan T., 157, 183
Potemkin, G.A., 160
Potemkin, Gregory, Prince, 144
Praskovia, daughter of Tsar Ivan V, 126
Praskovia Saltykova, wife of Tsar Ivan V,
    125–27, 132–33
Predslava, daughter of Prince Sviatoslav
    of Polotsk. *See* Evfrosinia, St., of
    Polotsk
Pregnancy, 38–39, 168, 180, 237–38,
    257, 261, 263
Priests. *See* Clergy, Russian Orthodox
    Church
Princes. *See* Aristocracy, Government
Princesses. *See* Aristocracy, Government
Procreation. *See* Child-bearing, Children,
    Pregnancy
Property, 44–50, 106–12, 148–50,
    171–77, 233–34, 255–56;
    management of, 23, 25, 42–44, 80,
    101, 109–10, 126, 148–50, 154, 175,
    234, 255–56; ownership of, 44–50,
    67, 80, 93, 103, 106–12, 135,
    171–77, 190, 233–34, 240,
    255–56. *See* also Dowry,
    Inheritance, Serfdom, Slaves
Prostitution, 45, 98–99, 114, 225, 239–40
Proudhon, Pierre-Joseph, 204
Provisional Government, 208, 257
Prussia. *See* Germany
Pskov, 8, 46, 60, 185
Pugachev, Emilian, 139, 145
Pushkin, Alexander, 121, 142, 188,
    197–98, 212, 216, 226, 228, 230, 244

Radchenko, Lia, 207
Raden, Edith, Baroness, 192, 198
Radishchev, Alexander N., 145, 158, 165
Ragoznikova, Tolia, 207
Raoul de Crépy, Count, 13–14
Rape, 20, 30, 53
Raskol. See Old Believers

Rasputin, Grigorii, 195
Raynal, Guillaume, 147
Razin, Stepan, 82
Razumovskaia, Maria, 150
Razumovskii, Kiril, 148
Recreation, 34, 90, 93–96, 98–100,
    125–26, 155–56, 163, 170, 179–80,
    195, 196–201, 222–24, 227–31,
    249–52, 261
Regents, 8, 19, 22–24, 28, 65–69, 74,
    84–86, 122–23, 125, 136–37
Reitenfels, Jacob, 155
Remarriage, 31, 42, 44–46, 94, 102–3,
    110–12, 134, 158–59, 172–74
Repin, Ilia, 87, 200
Reproduction. *See* Childbirth, Children
Revolution of 1905, 187, 193, 217,
    238–39
Revolutionaries, 191, 193, 197–209,
    216–17, 219, 225, 236, 238, 248,
    256–57. *See also* Bolsheviks, Land
    and Freedom Party, Mensheviks,
    Narodniki, People's Will,
    Social-Democratic Party, Social
    Revolutionary Party
Riazan, 24, 199
Roerich, Nikolai, 200
Roman Catholic Church, 10, 13–14, 26,
    31, 63–64, 169
Roman Rostislavich, Prince of Smolensk, 16
Romania, 61
Rosset-Smirnova, Alexandra, 198
Rossini, Gioacchino, 196
Rostopchina, Evdokia, Countess, 198, 212
Rostov, 19, 49
Rousseau, Jean-Jacques, 201
Rudenko, Bella, 265
Rus, 7–10
Russian Orthodox Church, 5, 14, 61–64,
    70, 79–82, 103–4, 123, 191, 195;
    attitude toward marriage, 29–31,
    34–39, 94–96, 100, 159–60, 166,
    170, 235; attitude toward women,
    36–43, 70–71, 76–77, 86, 88, 91–92,
    95, 100, 102, 104–5, 114, 117, 162,
    165; attitude toward child-rearing,
    39–41, 90–91; conversion to, 8–10,
    78, 128, 139, 159, 188, 190–92, 195;
    and regulation of marriage, 9, 30–31,
    37–38, 72, 94–95; and regulation of
    sexuality, 14, 31–33, 37–39, 98–99

Russian Revolution. *See* February Revolution, October Revolution
Russo-Japanese War, 187, 193
Russo-Turkish War (1877–78), 191
Russian Academy of Arts, 138
Russian Academy of Sciences, 131, 145, 148–49, 211

Saburov, Ivan, boyar, 65
Sadovskaia, Olga, 216
St. Petersburg, 125–26, 127–28, 134, 138, 141, 146–47, 151–53, 179, 182, 190–91, 193, 197–200, 204, 206, 209–10, 215, 218, 225, 227, 236–40, 245, 256
St. Petersburg University, 204, 209–10, 236
Saints. *See* Hagiography
Saint-Saens, Camille, 219
Saint-Simon, Henri de, 204
Salias, Evgenia, 198
Salons. *See* Patronage of the Arts
Saltykov, F., 163
Samoilova, Tatiana, 265
Sarmentova, Maria, 207
Savina, Maria, 216–17
Scandinavia, 3, 7, 12, 103
Scarves. *See* Outerwear
Schleussinger, Georg, 115, 156
Schools, 15, 70, 135–36, 138, 143, 150, 163–64, 188–91, 204–5, 212, 226, 229, 231, 239, 249. *See also* Education
Scientists, 135, 148, 197, 199, 204, 210, 264–65
Seals, 17, 51, 69
Sechenov, I.M., 210
Seclusion of women. *See* Terem
Semenova, Ekaterina, 216
Senate, 128, 130, 134, 137–38, 173
Serbia, 61
Serfdom, 62–63, 85, 98, 108, 112, 118, 142, 144, 147, 150–53, 158, 168, 175–77, 191, 209, 216, 225, 234. *See also* Peasants
Serov, Alexander, 200
Serpukhov, 23, 200
Sex, 14, 31–33, 37–38, 92, 98–99, 133, 224–25, 239, 261
Shawls. *See* Outerwear
Shchek, legendary prince, 10

Shabanova, Anna, 208
Shafirov, P.P., 131
Shakhovskaia, Natalia, Princess, 192
Shaklovityi, F.L., general, 84
Shchedrin, Silvester, 196
Shcherbatov, M.M., Prince, 133, 135, 155, 169
Shelgunov brothers, 199
Sheremetev, B.P., Field Marshall, 128, 131–32
Sheremetev, N.P., Count, 150–53
Shoes. *See* Footwear
Shtakenshnaider, Elena, 199
Shuiskii family, 67, 76
Shuvalov, Peter, Count, 237
Siberia, 96, 131–33, 138, 145, 159, 161, 165, 175, 197, 202–4, 206
Sigida, Natalia, 206
Sigismund, King of Lithuania, 67
Silvester, Metropolitan of Siberia, 159
Singer, Isaac, 242
Skavronskaia, Marta. *See* Catherine I, Empress
Skavronskii, Samuil, 128
Skirts. *See* Dresses
Skuratov, Maliuta, 72–73, 79
Slaves, 30, 34, 44, 47, 51–53, 92, 99
Slavophiles, 197
Smirnitskaia, Nadezhda, 206
Smirnova, Tatiana, 216
Smith, Adam, 147
Smolensk, 18, 65, 200
Smolnyi Institute, 143, 163, 188, 190, 226–27
Soboleva, M.F., 246
Soboleva, Sofia, 213
Social-Democratic Party, 207, 238, 240. *See also* Bolsheviks, Mensheviks, Socialism
Socialist Revolutionary Party, 206–7. *See also* Socialism.
Socialism, 204–8, 256–60. *See also* Bolsheviks, Marxism, Mensheviks, Revolutionaries, Social-Democratic Party, Socialist Revolutionary Party
Sofia, regent, daughter of Tsar Aleksei, 84–88, 122–25
Sofia, wife of Prince Sviatoslav of Polotsk, 17
Sofia Paleologue, wife of Grand Prince Ivan III, 26–27, 31, 63

Sofia Vitovtovna, wife of Vasilii I, 22–24
Solomonia, wife of Grand Prince Vasilii III, 65
Sophia Frederika Augusta, Princess of Anhalt-Zerbst. *See* Catherine II, Empress
Sophia-Dorothea, Princess of Wurtemberg. *See* Maria Feodorovna, Empress, wife of Paul I
Sources, for the study of women, 5–8, 26, 28, 35–37, 48–50, 52, 71, 79, 83, 87–88, 92, 105–16, 162. *See also* Chronicles, Hagiography, Law Codes
Soviets (councils), 238, 240, 257
Spain, 180, 245
Spiridonova, Maria, 207
Stalin, Josef, 262–63
Staritskaia, Evfrosinia (née Khovanskaia), Princess, 68–71, 74, 79
Staritskii, Andrei, Prince, 68–69, 73
Staritskii, Vladimir, Prince, 69–70, 72
Stasova, Nadezhda, 204
Steppe nomads. *See* Polovtsy, Mongols, Tatars
Stoglav Church Council, 98, 104
Streits, Jacob, 155
Streltsy, 84, 86, 122
Strepetova, Polina, 217
Streshnev, Tikhon, 122, 127
Subjugation of women, 4–5, 21, 32–33, 35–37, 42, 53, 77, 88, 91–93, 95–96, 100, 102, 104–5, 112, 120, 162–63, 165–66, 170–71, 209, 212, 233–37, 240, 255–56, 258
Suffrage, 208, 238–40, 256–57
Sukhodolskii, V.B., 163
Supreme Privy Council, 130, 134
Suslova, Nadezhda, 205, 210
Suvorov, Alexander, Field Marshall, 144
Sviatoslav, Grand Prince, son of Olga, 8, 10
Sviatoslav, Prince of Polotsk, 15, 17
Svidrigailo, Grand Prince of Lithuania, 23
Sweden, 62, 67, 75, 78, 85, 102, 113, 128, 130, 136, 138, 159, 211, 233, 262. *See also* Scandinavia
Switzerland, 210

Tambov, 185
Tatars, 20–25, 27, 64, 67, 72, 85, 91–92, 96. *See also* Mongols

Tatishchev, Vasilii N., 135
Taxation, 8–9, 20, 62, 66, 85, 134, 138, 176–77, 261
Teachers. *See* Education, Schools
Temir of Kabarda, Tatar prince, 72
Temnikov, 82–83
Tenisheva, Maria, 200
Terem, 61, 83, 89, 91–93, 95–98, 105, 117, 121, 123, 125–27, 178, 180, 255
Tereshkova, Valentina, 264–65
Theater, 123–26, 138, 150–55, 168, 196, 216–18, 227–28, 244, 250–52, 265
Time of Troubles, 62, 78–79, 83, 108
Timofeeva, Anna, 150
Tolmacheva, Agrafena, 175
Tolochko, P.P., 57
Tolstoi, P.A., 128
Tolstoy, Leo, 214, 217
Trakhanioty, Iurii and Dmitrii, 27
Treaties, 10–11, 15, 18, 20, 24, 28, 44, 64, 67, 85, 134, 138–39
Trediakovskii, V.K., 164
Trinity-St. Sergius monastery, 69, 79, 86, 126
Telepnev-Obolenskii, I.F., Prince, 65–68
Trepov, Fedor, 206
Tretiakov family, 199
Troepolskaia, Tatiana, 150
Trubetskaia, Ekaterina, 201
Trubetskoi, Sergei, 197
Trubnikova, Maria V., 204
Trukhanova, Natalia, 219
Tsebrikova, Maria, 212
Tsvetaeva, Marina, 214–15
Turgenev, Ivan, 214
Turkey, 85, 135, 144, 173, 191
Tyrkova, Anna, 208

Uglich, 23, 74, 75
Ukraine, 61–62, 80, 85, 122. *See also* Chernigov, Kiev
Uliana, Princess of Volotsk, 55
Ulianova, Maria, 207
Ulianova-Elizarova, Anna, 207
Ulita, wife of Grand Prince Andrei Bogoliubskii, 18
Underwear, 54, 116–17, 180–81, 183–84, 242, 244, 247. *See also* Corsets
United States, 3, 131, 240, 265
Universities, 138, 150, 204–5, 209–10, 236, 239, 259. *See also* Education

Urban II, Pope, 14
Urusova, Evdokia, 80–82, 88
Ushakov, S.F., Prince, 169
Uvarova, Elena, 202
Uvarova, Praskovia, Countess, 211

Varentsova, Olga, 207
Vasilchikova, Elena, 199
Vasilii I, Grand Prince, 22–23
Vasilii II "the Dark," Grand Prince,
    23–24, 42, 70
Vasilii III, Grand Prince, 27, 31, 63–67
Vasilii, son of Prince Iurii of Zvenigorod,
    23
Vasilii Ivanovich, Prince of Riazan, 24
Vasilisa Melentieva, wife of Tsar Ivan IV,
    73
Vasilko, Prince of Rostov, 19–20
Vasnetsov, Victor, 200
Vernadskaia, Maria, 209
Vernadskii, I.V., 209
Veliasheva-Volyntseva, Pelageia, 150
Venetsianov, A.G., 221
Viazemskii, Pavel, 197–98
Vigé-Lebrun, Elizabeth, 242
Vilinskaia, Maria, 213
Vinogradova, Evdokia, 262
Vinogradova, Maria, 262
Virginity, 29, 31, 33, 38, 91–92, 160–61
Vitovt, Grand Prince of Lithuania, 22
Vladimir, city in Suzdalia, 48, 49, 66
Vladimir I, Grand Prince, 11–12
Vladimir, Prince of Serpukhov, 42
Vladimir Monomakh, Grand Prince, 16
Vladimir Vasilkovich, Prince, 46
Volkonskaia, Elizaveta, 199
Volkonskaia, Maria, 202
Volkonskaia, Zinaida, Princess, 196–97,
    202, 212
Volkonskii, Sergei, 197
Volkov, P.I., 195
Volkova, Anna, 150
Voloshin, Maksimilians, 215
Voltaire (François-Marie Arouet), 142,
    146–47
Vorobieva-Petrova, Anna, 216
Voronezh, 192, 243
Vorontsov, Mikhail I., Prince, 137, 146
Vorontsov, Roman, Count, 146
Vorontsova, Anna, 150
Vorotinskii family, 76

Votchina, 107–12, 171–72. See also
    Property
Voting rights. See Suffrage
Vrubel, Mikhail, 200
Vsevolod, Grand Prince, 12, 14, 47
Vsevolozhskii, boyar, 23
War, 10, 61–62, 70, 73, 75, 85, 110, 121,
    124, 128, 130, 135, 138–39, 144,
    153, 173, 187, 193–95, 201, 244,
    256–57, 262; women as victims of,
    19–20, 79, 256, 262; women's
    participation in, 9, 18–19, 26, 67,
    82–83, 190–91, 212–13, 262. See
    also Civil War
Weddings, 29–33, 73, 94–95, 100, 156,
    159–62, 170; church ceremonies of,
    31–33, 94–95, 161–62, 170; pagan
    forms of, 29, 31–33. See also
    Marriage
Westernizers, 197
Wet-nurses, 67, 89–90, 94, 113, 125
Widows, 42, 45, 50, 88, 103, 104, 122,
    125, 158, 167–68, 263 inheritance
    by, 44, 46, 48–49, 74, 105–12, 125,
    172–77
Wills, 42, 44–45, 55–56, 58–59, 65, 74,
    77, 130, 132, 176, 191. See also
    Inheritance
Wilmot, Catherine, 149
Witchcraft, 18, 34, 39, 68, 98
Wives. See Family, Households,
    Marriage, Weddings
Woman Question, 203–8, 212, 233–40,
    256, 258, 262
Women of Russia (political party) 265–66
Women's organizations, 190–92, 201,
    204, 208, 235–36, 239–40,
    265–66. See also Philanthropy,
    Zhenotdely
Workers, 207–8, 223–25, 236–39,
    257–63; conditions for, 192,
    223–25, 233, 237–39, 261–63;
    female, 223–25, 234, 237–39, 248,
    251–53, 256, 259–63, 265;
    organization of, 204, 207–8, 236, 238
World War I, 187, 193–95, 202, 256–57
World War II, 262
Writers, 84, 135, 145, 148, 164–65, 168,
    195, 196–200, 203–4, 212, 230;
    women, 15, 16, 19–20, 78, 81,
    124–25, 131–33, 141–45, 148–50,

Writers *(continued)*
153–54, 165, 188, 196, 200, 209, 211–15. *See also* Chronicles, Hagiography, Newspapers, Novels, Poets

Yalta, 195

Zabelin, I.E., 255
Zakharin, Roman, boyar, 71
Zasulich, Vera, 205–6
Zealots of Piety, 79

Zemskii Sobor, 62
Zhadovskaia, Iulia, 212
Zhaklar, Anna, 210
Zheliabov, Andrei, 191
Zhenotdely, 258–59
Zhukovskii, Vasilii, 197–98
Zontag, Anna, 213
Zrazhevskaia, Alexandra, 213
Zvenigorod, 22–23
Zvenislava, sister of St. Evfrosinia of Polotsk, 15

About the Author

Natalia Pushkareva is a senior research fellow at the Institute of Ethnology and Anthropology, Russian Academy of Sciences, and she serves on the editorial board of the journal *Rodina*. She is the author of *Zhenshchiny drevnei Rusi* (Women of Medieval Russia) (1989), *Zhenshchiny Rossii i Evropy na porogu Novogo vremeni* (Women in Russia and Europe on the Threshold of the Modern Age), and numerous articles.

About the Editor/Translator

Eve Levin is an associate professor of Russian history at Ohio State University and editor of the journal *Russian Review*. She is the author of *Sex and Society in the World of the Orthodox Slavs, 900–1700* (1989).